D0944626

Chosen Fruit

The Personal Life Story of

Dr. Arnold G. Fruchtenbaum,

Founder and President of

Ariel Ministries

Chosen Fruit

The Personal Life Story of

Dr. Arnold G. Fruchtenbaum,

Founder and President of

Ariel Ministries

L. JESSE GRACE

Published by Ariel Ministries
P.O. Box 792507
San Antonio, TX 78279-2507
www.ariel.org

Author's Dedication

This body of work is dedicated to the following:

With my deepest love to:
Yeshua Ha'Mashiach—
God's Only Begotten Son,
Lord and Messiah of the World.

In memory of:
The six million Jews
who perished in the *Shoah*, the Holocaust.

In honor of:
God's Chosen People
in the *Diaspora*—
The Jews, the Apple of God's Eye.

With respect and gratitude to:
Dr. Arnold G. Fruchtenbaum—
God's Chosen Fruit
whose life and teachings reflect
God's Salvation, Mercy, and Favor.

Subject's Dedication

I dedicate this volume of my biography to the memory of

THEO BURGSTAHLER

and to

MANFRED AND HANNA (BURGSTAHLER) KÜNSTLER.

Their role in my life is recorded in this biography.

And to

CHARLES AND EVA CATTELL,

who were willing to play a role as my spiritual "Mom" and "Pop"
at a crucial point in my life. Their role will be revealed in the content
of this biography.

Contents

Foreword

By Dr. Arnold G. Fruchtenbaum

I have been frequently asked to write my autobiography and always had a great desire to do so, as well as record the history of my family and their experiences in the Holocaust, but never had the time to devote to it. As a result, I have prayed for someone to come forward to take on the project and over the years, different people have volunteered, but in the end have failed to follow through for one reason or another.

But God heard the prayer of many people, and two individuals have stepped forward to tackle the project. The first was David S. Turner who produced the family history entitled *When Your Face Was Your Destiny,* published a few years ago. His sources included not only my remembrance of all the stories I had heard, but also of taped interviews of my Israeli relatives who survived the Holocaust and spoke of their experiences and of those who did not survive the war. He also spent a week interviewing my mother and had access to the specific dates, etc., from *Yad Vashem,* the memorial and study center on the Holocaust based in Jerusalem.

The second person was L. Jesse Grace who has produced this present volume. This, too, is not only based on my memories, but also on her travels through various parts of the USA to talk to people who knew me well during my teen years and subsequent periods of my life such as college and seminary. This included Ruth Wardell who led me to the Lord so many years ago and has since passed on to glory. Jesse's zealousness for accuracy and detail meant it took a good number of years to produce this work, but it was well worth waiting for. This work accurately portrays my biography in a way I could never have done on my own, and I am grateful that she took the time to produce it for the public.

Obviously, many individuals played a role in my life—some more than others, and the following is a (not necessarily complete) list of many whom I remember from my days at Shelton College and Cedarville College (now Cedarville University). I have maintained contact with only a few of them, and I do not know who else is still alive and how their lives have developed since I last saw them. However, they have not been forgotten, and if any of them sees this volume, I hope they will make contact with me. Other names not connected with my college days will be listed in subsequent volumes.

Shelton College	**Cedarville College**
Teachers:	**Teacher:**
Dr. Ralph Beich	Dr. Robert Gromacki
Dr. Gary G. Cohen	
Staff:	**Staff:**
Mr. Walter Truesdell	Mrs. A. Chaffee
	"Campus Cop" Slaibough
Students:	**Students:**
Barbara Fornoff	Gary Fisher
Marilyn Greger	Michael Hamilton
Cathy Hubbard	Cathy Hubbard
Keith Irvine	Joseph Hollaway
J. Wesley Johanson	Dale Pritchett
Elizabeth Lynn (Noble) Johanson	Carol (Simonetti) Hamilton
Mary Ann Sleichter	(Mary Ann Sleichter) Miriam Nadler
Karl Kalfaian	Sharon (Tallman) Hollaway
Beverly Lyons	Tim Timmons
Michael (Mick) Nicholls	
Julia Ouzoonian	
Stuart Pastine	
Swee Hwa Quek	
Bonnie Sayre	
Elizabeth Young	

June 25th, 2014

A Most Excellent Bible Exegete

Editorial Note

Some of the most intriguing novels, ostensibly fictitious in character, are based on nuggets of truth. This is the case in Tim LaHaye and Jerry B. Jenkins' *Left Behind* series. Having sold several million copies, the 16-book series is based on solid dispensational teaching. In the first volume, the authors cite their sources of inspiration, one of them being Dr. Arnold Fruchtenbaum's work, *The Footsteps of the Messiah*. This in-depth study of the end times has served as a foundation for sermons and lectures of the most popular pastors and teachers around the globe. A simple Internet search will quickly serve up raving reviews of Dr. Fruchtenbaum's numerous other books and Bible studies. Who is this man? Where did he come from, and how did he develop into one of the finest Bible exegetes of our times?

Clearly called by God to teach, Dr. Fruchtenbaum set out early on to properly equip himself with solid training in order to become a great scholar. He earned a bachelor's degree in Hebrew and Greek from Cedarville University, a master's degree in Theology from Dallas Theological Seminary, and his Ph.D. from New York University with the completion of his dissertation entitled *Israelology: The Missing Link in Systematic Theology*. Additionally, he studied at the Hebrew University of Jerusalem and Jewish Theological Seminary in New York City. Still, many can match Dr. Fruchtenbaum's credentials. What, then, makes him different from others and sought after by men like Dr. Randall Price, who himself is a well-known author and the executive director of the Center for Judaic Studies at Liberty University? Dr. Price explains:

> The teaching ministry of Dr. Fruchtenbaum has impacted me for over 30 years. When I left my training at Dallas Theological Seminary and the Hebrew University in Jerusalem in the early 1980s, I was confused

as to how to put together the academic and cultural information I had received from these two different perspectives. The "Jewish roots" movement offered only limited and often inaccurate theological guidance. When I discovered Dr. Fruchtenbaum's teaching, I found what I needed—someone whose academic training was similar to mine, had processed the biblical, Jewish, and Christian data, and had successfully navigated the conflicting theological perspectives within the messianic movement while maintaining a sound biblical Christology, dispensational hermeneutic, and a balanced view of Messianic Judaism and the local church. Through the years, I have learned from Dr. Fruchtenbaum and used his excellent teaching materials in the courses I have taught in the university and seminary as well as church pastorates. Because Dr. Fruchtenbaum has had the necessary academic preparation and experience within both the Israeli and international messianic communities, he is uniquely qualified and equipped to communicate to this generation.

And communicate he does—through books, at churches, and in Bible schools all over the world. Dr. Joseph Holden explains his institution's choice of adding Dr. Fruchtenbaum to the list of adjunct professors:

> As the president of Veritas Evangelical Seminary [in California], we seek orthodox faculty of uncompromising character who hold a high view of Scripture. I have found Dr. Fruchtenbaum to be a perfect fit for us, offering our students his engaging theological expertise and refreshing Christ-like character. His scholarship and reverence for God's inerrant Word is a particular quality that is often in rare supply these days, but something no Bible-believing institution should be without. Dr. Fruchtenbaum's arsenal is loaded with important key works in Israelology, incisive Old Testament exposition, and insightful theology sourced from independent investigation, all of which offers the perfect environment for learning where doctrine accords with godliness. VES is extremely blessed to have Dr. Fruchtenbaum—he is a rare treasure!

Rev. Chris Heeb of Good News for Israel, the oldest Jewish outreach in North America, explains what distinguishes Dr. Fruchtenbaum from other theologians:

When academics mention the great scholars in Christian history such as Edersheim, Ryrie, Geisler, Kaiser, MacArthur, etc., they should also include Arnold Fruchtenbaum, a pillar in the messianic restoration of systematic theology. I have had the great privilege of having known most of the great modern pioneers of the messianic movement over the past 35 years. Dr. Fruchtenbaum's book, *Israelology: The Missing Link in Systematic Theology*, is the single greatest 'tour de force' on true biblical theology ever written. He has added tremendous insight, clarity, and correction to the anti-biblical Roman Catholic and Reformed Protestant church dogma which through history has been openly anti-Semitic at worst and Replacement Theology at best. When I've come up against a very tough theological issue, I always check the good 'Frucht' tree first for his very thoughtful and thorough perspective.

Dr. Fruchtenbaum's impact stretches beyond the academic world. Mottel Baleston, messianic teacher and outreach minister to the Jewish people, explains:

> During the years I served as leader of a messianic congregation, all our elders made good use of the Bible teaching material written by Dr. Arnold Fruchtenbaum. His sound exposition of what the Scripture says about biblical eldership and the local congregation helped us establish a solid footing. His coming to teach us and his embrace of our Messianic Jewish congregation was a great encouragement.

Bible exegete, teacher, author—how can one adequately summarize the impact of Dr. Fruchtenbaum's work on the world at large? The founder and leader of a messianic congregation in Montreal, Canada, Jacques Gabizon, brings it to the point:

> Dr. Fruchtenbaum has this ability to gather information scattered in the Scriptures and present it in a clear and concise manner; in reading his work, the student of the Bible is blessed and further helped *to rightly dividing the Word of Truth.*

In the biography you hold in your hands, you will find a very intimate portrait of the man, Arnold G. Fruchtenbaum. His story will lead you through some of the most dramatic points of world history and take you on a journey around the globe. It is the story of a Jewish man who, in his teens, came to faith in his Jewish Messiah, embarked on a unique journey of servitude to his God, and impacted not only theologians, scholars, and church leaders, but everyday believers alike. Their journey to spiritual maturity, as well as the outreach to his Jewish people, is what has kept Dr. Fruchtenbaum going for nearly five decades of ministry—to God's glory and for the salvation of Israel.

Christiane Jurik
Director of Publications
Ariel Ministries
November 2014

Author's Notes to the Reader

The purpose of this book is to present a more personal side to Dr. Arnold G. Fruchtenbaum. Known for his foremost Bible scholarship and his in-depth knowledge of the biblical history and geography of the Land of Israel, this indefatigable, itinerant teacher of the Word of God is well respected in many parts of the world today. Most individuals sitting under his teaching have known him only in a church meeting, conference setting, or classroom environment, where his brilliance and no-nonsense style can sometimes be intimidating. The discipline with which he conducts his daily life is truly unsurpassed and his spiritual self-control evident. Being a man of few words and intensely private, Dr. Fruchtenbaum is difficult to get to know personally.

Now that he is in his latter years, having reached his three-score and ten, that is, seventy years, Dr. Fruchtenbaum seems to have outwardly mellowed. The fact that he wanted his biography to be written reflects his readiness for the world to get to know him on a more human level. As such, this book is an attempt to offer the reader a rare glimpse into his personal life. Therefore, all the achievements, progress and happenings at Ariel Ministries and Camp Shoshanah have been kept to a bare minimum in this account. This is not a chronicle of Ariel Ministries, but rather a closer look at a man and his unique life, completely impassioned with and given over to his Jewish Messiah, *Yeshua Ha'Mashiach*. It depicts how God called out this individual to be His servant and how through His grace, the Lord has blessed him to be the chosen fruit among the Jewish people.

The Bible translation employed for the purpose of this biography is the American Standard Version (ASV) of 1901. This is the very same version that Dr. Fruchtenbaum has used since his early days of becoming a believer, which he still uses to teach from at the present time. The ASV of 1901 is known as the version that most closely reflects the original biblical writings. However, some minor updates have been applied to a few terms contained in the quoted verses within this book. This was necessary in order to render the language more comprehensible to the readers in today's contemporary society.

As Dr. Fruchtenbaum has done in recent publications, the various archaic forms of verbs and adverbs in the quoted Bible passages have been modernized. Pronouns such as *thee* and *thou* and related adjectives such as *thine* and so forth have also been modernized, with one exception. The archaic form of *ye* has been retained as the plural form of "you," in order to distinguish it from the singular form of "you." Also, the pronouns, such as *he*, *him*, and *his*, etc. within a sentence referring to the Lord, have been capitalized. The adjective, *thy*, has been retained where it refers to God. Wherever the title *Christ* and the name *Jesus* appear in the quoted verses, the terms *Messiah* and *Yeshua* have been used instead.

In the early part of this book, the terms "Jewish Christian" and "Hebrew Christian" have been used interchangeably, in accordance with their general usage during that time period. These are different terms referring to a Jewish person who believes in Jesus as the Messiah. In more recent decades, the terms Jewish believer, Messianic Jew, or messianic believer have been employed to denote the same definition.

Where references have been made to Dr. Fruchtenbaum's age from the time that he entered the United States until his last year of high school during which there was a discrepancy between his actual age and his legal age on paper, his real age has been used.

In order to achieve a sense of uniformity among the variations of spellings of the first names in the Fruchtenbaum family—be it in Hebrew, Yiddish, or Polish—the spelling of the closest Hebrew transliteration of their names has been followed throughout this book.

Time and space limitations have not permitted the inclusion of all the stories, names, or details of those who have played a part in Dr. Arnold G. Fruchtenbaum's life. On the other hand, some recollections of those interviewed were rather hazy and vague, where the passage of time had caused the fading of certain memories. For those individuals or events that have not been explicitly mentioned or included in this biography, I ask for your understanding.

In the Gospel of John, the apostle wrote: *And there are also many other things which Yeshua did, the which if they should be written every one, I suppose that even the world itself would not contain the books that should be written.* (John 21:25) In a similar sort of way, this is how I view the life of Dr. Arnold G. Fruchtenbaum. Were all the details to be recollected and written, multiple volumes would not suffice to contain them. It is my prayer that his personal life story and his testimony of *Yeshua Ha'Mashiach* through the power of the Holy Spirit will lead many more Jews and Gentiles to God's salvation grace in Jesus the Savior, all to the glory of the LORD Almighty on High.

L. Jesse Grace
April 2014

Prologue

Expulsion, June 1962

It would be truthful to say that his father's strong opposition to Arnold's beliefs led to the eventual rift in their relationship. Six years earlier, in October 1956, at the tender age of thirteen, Arnold had come to the realization that the "Gentile Christian" Jesus was indeed his long-awaited Jewish Messiah, *Yeshua Ha'Mashiach*. Discovering that it was possible to have an intimate relationship with Him, Arnold opened up his heart to receive this Jesus as his personal Savior and Lord. From that point onward, he learned to place his faith and trust in Messiah Jesus to guide, protect, and direct his life.

Even at such a young age, Arnold was fully aware that for him, as a Jewish believer, the road ahead would not be easy. He knew there was a cost in following Jesus, but at the time had no inkling of what shape or form the price would take. Little did he foresee just how difficult his home life proved to be during his high school years. Nor did he imagine that one day he would have to face expulsion from his home and be told to leave the State of California, the day after his graduation.

On that particular Saturday morning in June 1962, Arnold awoke to find himself all alone in his family's second-floor home on Robertson Boulevard in Los Angeles. An uncharacteristic quietness pervaded the entire apartment. Had his parents left unusually early, at the crack of dawn, to catch up with some work at their photo studio located a few miles away? Or had they deliberately made themselves scarce, in order to avoid the awkwardness of witnessing their first-born son's forced departure from home? His three younger siblings were nowhere to be seen. They were probably out playing with their schoolmates somewhere, reveling in their free time, now that summer vacation was in full swing.

Placing the last few items of clothing into his suitcase, Arnold finished packing and turned to leave. There were no "good-byes" to be said, since no one else was around. He gently pulled shut the front door of his parents' home for the last time and slowly descended the back stairwell of the two-story building. Stepping onto the sidewalk toward the car parked by the curb, Arnold was thankful that his ride was already waiting for him. After loading his suitcase into the trunk of the car, he slipped into the passenger's seat as the engine started up.

Deeply saddened to lose his family, Arnold wondered if he would ever see them again. Yet, in an ironic sort of way, he also felt a sense of relief to be leaving. No longer would he have to endure his father's harsh treatment and all the restrictions imposed on him. Nor did he have to hide his Bible and study the Scriptures on the sly any more. At long last, Arnold was free to practice his beliefs, to publicly live out his faith in Messiah Jesus and to engage in open fellowship with other believers.

As the car drove away from the neighborhood, the sun's warm rays beamed brightly across the cloudless azure sky, streaming through the windows. It was a typical, golden southern California morning, promising to be another hot, sunny day. While the car meandered its way through the outlying suburbs of Los Angeles, the sights and sounds that were once familiar to Arnold began to slowly recede into the distance as new vistas opened up before him.

The journey out East would take two weeks with plenty of planned stops along the way. Arnold looked forward to the long stretches of time when he could retreat into his own thoughts to reflect upon his situation. To be expelled from his home was an exceedingly high price to pay for his faith in Jesus the Messiah. However, Arnold's heart had been opened to the truth that *Yeshua Ha'Mashiach* had willingly paid the ultimate price to atone for his sins, freely redeeming him for eternity, by sacrificing His own life, shedding His precious blood and dying an excruciating death on the cross. Like the man in the parable who had found a treasure hidden in the field and, from sheer joy over it, had sold all that he owned in order to buy the field, Jesus had given His absolute all for Arnold through His substitutionary death. Any consequent hardship that Arnold was forced to face because of his belief in *Yeshua* paled in comparison to this magnificent gift of eternal life through the Lord's atoning death and glorious resurrection.

Yet, why did Arnold's father so vehemently oppose his faith to the point of outright rejection of his first-born son? Why had he given Arnold the silence treatment for a whole year? And why did he not only expel his son from the family home, but also demand that he leave California for good?

The antagonism toward Jesus was not uniquely limited to Arnold's father or to his family. It represented the general mindset of the Jewish people, who for centuries had been confronted with a much broader issue in the form of persecution by the Gentiles in the name of Jesus. In their desperate plight, with Jewish traditions and beliefs so deeply entrenched in their collective mind, it was nearly impossible for them to see Jesus in any other light. Sadly, the same was true for Arnold's father.

In order to understand his father's choices and the arising conflicts concerning his first-born son's faith in Messiah Jesus, Arnold would have to go back to the very beginning to trace his Jewish roots and delve into the history of the Fruchtenbaum family. Theirs was a story of suffering and loss; a story of a traditional, ultra-Orthodox Jewish family in Poland, set against the backdrop of the Holocaust and pogroms, where the collision of the Jews and their Gentile persecutors played itself out in the lives of his family members and in his own life, ultimately changing its course.

PART I

~ Survival ~

Our transgressions and our sins are upon us,
and we pine away in them;
how then can we live?

(Ezekiel 33:10b)

The origins of deep-seated barriers erected in the minds of the Jewish people against the Gentiles started as far back as the beginnings of the Christian era. When the mighty Roman legions under the leadership of Titus swept through what is known today as the Land of Israel, they invaded Jerusalem and laid a dreadful siege to the city. After holding out for two years, Jerusalem finally fell in A.D. 70 when it was ravaged by fire, including the burning and tearing down of every stone of the Second Temple. The manner in which the city was destroyed fulfilled the prophecy exactly as Jesus had uttered it forty years earlier:

And when He drew nigh, He saw the city and wept over it, saying, If you had known in this day, even you, the things which belong unto peace! but now they are hid from your eyes. For the days shall come upon you, when your enemies shall cast up a bank about you and compass you round and keep you in on every side and shall dash you to the ground and your children within you; and they shall not leave in you one stone upon another; because you knew not the time of your visitation. (Luke 19:41-44)

And they shall fall by the edge of the sword and shall be led captive into all the nations: and Jerusalem shall be trodden down of the Gentiles, until the times of the Gentiles be fulfilled. (Luke 21:24)

Forced out of the Land from that point onward, the Jews were thrown into a period of history known as the *Diaspora,* an original Greek term for the Dispersion. This worldwide scattering of the Jewish people also marked the beginning of centuries of persecution that continued to modern times. Thus, the words of Moses came true to the very letter, when he said:

And Jehovah will scatter you among the peoples and ye shall be left few in number among the nations, where Jehovah shall lead you away. (Deuteronomy 4:27)

Moses also quoted God as saying to the Jews as a people:

And you will I scatter among the nations and I will draw out the sword after you: and your land shall be a desolation and your cities shall be a waste. (Leviticus 26:33)

No sooner had they settled somewhere in a region of Europe, would the Jews again find themselves under the control and authority of an anti-Semitic persecutor, who wielded his might and power to either kill them or force them out of his domain. Over the centuries, the history of the Jewish people had been one of continual escape from fierce persecution, blatant bigotry and flagrant barbarism. At times, they felt like broken pieces of driftwood, tossed out yonder into the distant open sea, later only to be randomly washed ashore on any land that would accept them. They were in constant search of refuge and safety in a new homeland, agonizing and yearning for a sense of stability and belonging. Yet time and time again, they would be hounded and driven out anew to end up roaming from place to place, often from country to country.

Tragically, starting from about the fourth century, virtually all persecution against the struggling Jews was committed in the name of Jesus Christ, the Church, or the cross. With so much suffering inflicted upon the Jews by the Gentile persecutors in the name of Jesus, a major resistance arose in the minds of the Jewish people against the Gentiles or Christians. To the Jewish mind, the terms were synonymous, one and the same; they were people who worshipped a "god" called Jesus, in whose name the Jews were either killed or persecuted.

How, then, could it ever be possible for the Jews to accept the messianic claims of Jesus? If He were truly their Jewish Messiah, would He not have delivered them from the hands of the conquering Gentiles and set up His Kingdom in the Land? Yet, their experience in history had shown them otherwise: the Jews were persecuted from all sides and scattered from their Land instead. Understandably, a huge chasm of distrust developed in their anguished minds, leading them to distinctively distinguish between "them" and "us"—"them" being the Gentiles or Christians and "us" being the Jews. As long as persecution existed, the Jews continued to maintain an ongoing antagonism toward the name of Jesus and anyone who believed in Him.

A series of catastrophic events over the course of history further fueled the Jews' sense of isolation and bitterness toward the Gentiles. In many parts of Europe, they were periodically massacred—slaughtered or burned en masse— if not expelled, while their properties were seized and other assets confiscated or plundered. The fate of the Jewry in Spain was one of many such instances down through the ages. During the fifteenth to sixteenth centuries at the height of its power, the Spanish Empire was considered indomitable, due to the mighty strength of its Armada. In the same year that Christopher Columbus was due to set sail westward, the Alhambra Decree, also known as the Spanish Edict of Expulsion, was issued on the 30th of March 1492, expelling the entire Jewish community. They were given exactly four months to leave the country.

As one of the largest and most influential communities in Spain, the Jewry, comprising mainly Sephardic Jews, who spoke Ladino, a form of Judeo-Spanish, formed an integral part of its economy. In the chaos of such short notice, Jewish homes and businesses had to be liquidated at absurdly low prices. Scores of Jews never made it out alive, when brigands, hoping to find treasures in their stomachs, knifed many innocent Jews to death. While numbers varied among historians, it was estimated that some 200,000 Jews managed to flee. By the time Spain realized the magnitude of its blunder, it was too late. The economy had already started to falter and eventually collapsed. Those Jews who escaped into neighboring Portugal were subsequently forced to convert to Christianity on the pain of death. Ironically, only a few years later in 1497, Portugal also expelled the Jews, irrespective of their conversion.

A glimmer of hope appeared between the mid-seventeenth and the nineteenth centuries, when the Kingdom of Poland opened up its borders to receive Jewish refugees, who were fleeing from persecution in other parts of Europe. Although periodic pogroms against the Jews occurred in some areas of Poland, over the span of those few hundred years, more and more Jews began to settle in communities or *shtetls*—Yiddish for "little towns"—throughout the territory, eventually numbering nearly three and a half million strong. By the time World War I broke out, Poland had the largest Jewish community around the world in its day.

The Jews living in Poland during that era were free to practice their faith in Judaism. A new religious sect, called the *Chasidim*, literally the "Pious Ones" in Hebrew, soon began to emerge within the Jewish community in Poland. With its origins in the Eastern European regions known today as Ukraine and Belarus, the *Chasidim* continued to grow and expand in influence until it permeated the entire realm of Judaism.

This ultra-Orthodox sect was extremely strict in its practice. The followers were always seen dressed in their traditional black outer garments, wearing large furry hats and sporting long beards and *peiyot*, or rope-like side curls, on each side of the head. They claimed to be descendants of the Pharisees of the New Testament times and theologically, they were. Not only did this sect embrace the *Tanakh*, the entire Old Testament, but it also demanded strict adherence particularly to the traditional teachings and interpretations of the rabbis as the sole means of understanding the *Tanakh.*

When the founder of the movement died, the sect split into several divisions, primarily based on geography. Each division was to be headed up by a *rebbe,* whose control was greater and stronger than that of a rabbi and whose positional authority was passed down dynastically from father to son. One of these divisions, known as the *Ger Chasidim,* [1] exercised its authority in a number of vicinities surrounding the Warsaw area. A *shtiebl*—Yiddish for "little house" or "little room"—of the *Ger Chasidim* could be found in each of the Jewish communities in those localities, where the followers gathered habitually for prayer or for other *Chasidic* Jewish communal rituals.

Heading up a local subdivision of the *Ger Chasidim* was the Fruchtenbaum family, who lived in Pultusk, a predominantly Jewish town, situated on the western bank of the Narew River, about forty-four miles or seventy kilometers north of Warsaw. Numbering around 8,300, the Jewish community constituted more than half of the total population. Arnold's great-grandfather was a leader of this particular subdivision of the *Ger Chasidim* and, like his ancestors, had been put through rigorous training to enable him to take on that role. Tradition dictated that the first-born son of each succeeding generation of the family was to be groomed for this leadership position, and Arnold's father, Chaim Fruchtenbaum, would have been next in line to take over from his grandfather.

All those plans came crashing down to an abrupt halt, when Adolf Hitler launched the German invasion of Poland on the first of September 1939, instigating World War II. The German assault was fierce and swift. Ports were

---

[1] *Ger Chasidim: The Encyclopedia of Hasidism* (edited by Tzvi M. Rabinowicz, 1996, Jason Aronson Inc., London) describes the *Ger Chasidim* as follows: "**GER** (Hebrew, Gur; Polish Gura Kalwaria) The small town near Warsaw was the home of the most influential Hasidic dynasty in Poland. It was founded by R. Yitzhak Meir Alter and continued under his grandson R. Judah Leib and then under R. Abraham Mordecai Alter. At one time, more than 100,000 Jews owed their allegiance to the rebbe of Ger and there was no town in Poland without a *shtiebl* of Ger. The dynasty of Ger is now maintained in Israel by R. Pinhas Menahem Alter, whose brother, R. Abraham Mordecai Alter, came to the Holy Land during World War II. Today, the rebbe's synagogue in Ger, Poland, is a warehouse and the rebbe's apartments are used as a school. The graves of the rebbes have been restored in Ger. Also buried there were Feiga (d.1870), the wife of R. Yitzhak Meir; Yoheved Rebecca (d. 1911), the wife of R. Judah Leib; Yehudit (d. 1922), the wife of R. Abraham Mordecai; and R. Yitzhak (d. 1935), the son of R. Abraham Mordecai."

blockaded, and Polish cities were aggressively bombed from the air. Within a week, on the seventh of September, the Nazis had captured the town of Pultusk. Ten days later, the Soviets pushed across the eastern front. Poland was quickly partitioned under the German-Soviet Non-Aggression Pact, signed before the end of August. A demarcation line was drawn down the middle of the country. The German Nazis occupied the western and central regions including Warsaw, while the Soviet forces took control of the eastern part. Within a matter of two months, the border between the two sides was sealed.

Since Hitler's rise to power in Germany in January 1933, anti-Semitism became the predominant Nazi government policy in all its occupied territories. As one nation fell after another to German Nazi rule in Europe, anti-Semitism that had once lain dormant just beneath the surface, flared up with virulence in many parts of the continent, especially in Poland. The Poles showed no mercy to their Jewish neighbors as the Nazis moved the Jews into slum sections of the cities and erected walls around the ghettos. The possessions of the Jewish people were confiscated, and their businesses were forced to shut down. For the Fruchtenbaum family, there was no exception.

Even before the German Nazis invaded Poland, Arnold's father, Chaim, got his hair cut short and chopped off his side curls, as he had no desire to remain a *Chasid*. This step was also crucial for his survival to go undetected as a Jew. Though he was just a young man around twenty years of age, he possessed an uncanny sixth sense regarding death and was filled with foreboding. Concerned that the Jews were in serious impending danger in the Nazi-controlled territories of Poland, he begged his family members to make their way to the Soviet-occupied side with him, but his pleading fell on deaf ears. No one listened to him.

It seemed that his family either was in denial of the hatred and aggression displayed toward the Jews or simply retreated from the hostilities in quiet acquiescence, hoping that the tumultuous circumstances would eventually subside. They behaved as though they were sleepwalking through a menacing fog, unwilling or unable to grasp the severity of the dangers pressing in on them. Chaim had no recourse but to flee to the Soviet zone on his own. Only when it was too late did his family realize just how right he was. Chaim was not alone in his premonitions about the dangers of the German Nazis. Before the demarcation border was sealed, nearly a quarter of a million Jews in Poland had fled from the Nazi-occupied zone to the Soviet side.

Toward the end of September 1939 during the Jewish feast of *Succoth*, the German Nazis deported the entire Jewish population of Pultusk to the Soviet zone on the other side of the Narew River. A number of Jews were massacred along the way. The Jewish properties and possessions left behind were completely ransacked and pilfered. Many Jewish deportees found temporary refuge in the town of Bialystok. Others, including most of the Fruchtenbaum family, eventually made their way to Vilna, or Vilnius in modern-day Lithuania. These towns were all under Soviet control at that time.

The Jews were on the brink of entering into one of the darkest periods in the history of their people. Persecution increased at an alarming rate as the German Nazis embarked on a deliberate plan of systematic extermination of the Jews. For the most part, the victims were Ashkenazi Jews of Eastern European descent who spoke Yiddish, a fusion of medieval Germanic dialects, Slavic tongues, a smattering of Hebrew, Aramaic, old French and Italian. Those who had early foresight escaped with their lives. The physically stronger among those left behind were rounded up from the ghettos and deported to concentration camps to work at forced labor. The weaker ones were herded onto railcars and transported to extermination camps in various parts of Poland, where they suffered a demise that was more horrific and far crueler than any persecution the Jews had ever encountered in their history.

The Holocaust or *Shoah*, literally "disaster" or "catastrophe" in Hebrew, represented one of the worst atrocities of cataclysmic proportions to be committed in human history up to the present day. With the aim of total annihilation of the Jews, the German Nazis went on a rampage of unbridled savagery in their destruction. An unprecedented number of Jews, approximately six million including nearly one and a half million children, perished in the Holocaust, along with more than five million others who were deemed "unworthy of life" by the Nazis. This was yet another tragic event in the life of the Jewish people that etched its indelible mark upon their collective psyche, further deepening their mistrust and embitterment toward the Gentiles.

The Fruchtenbaum family lost far more than their confiscated belongings. They lost their important standing as respected leaders of the Jewish community in Pultusk. Cultivated over many generations, their family tradition was obliterated practically overnight as they were forced to disperse or go into hiding. The simple joys and pleasures of living, which had been so intrinsically woven into the fabric of their daily life and taken for granted, were precipitously snatched away. Their life together as a big, cohesive Jewish family was forever shattered. Like a damaged oil painting of a tranquil, sunny garden, the once brightly colored flowers were now overridden with dark, ominous paint strokes of hatred, vile destruction and indiscriminate bloodshed.

Chaim had now become a destitute refugee on the run in the Soviet territories, his life in complete disarray, thrown into turmoil by the war. What was going to happen to him? Would he ever reunite with his family? What would happen to the rest of his family who had stayed behind? How could the God of Abraham, Isaac, and Jacob abandon His Chosen People in this fashion and allow the Gentiles to so hatefully vilify, persecute, and chase them like hunted animals? Where was God now? Did He even exist? These were among the many troubling questions pulsating through Chaim's mind as he fled from Poland, his thoughts spinning out of control like a teetering top on the brink of a vicious tornado. He knew that he had to somehow find a way to escape and survive this impending doom. It was only much later after the end of World War II that Chaim would tragically learn of the full, disastrous impact of the Holocaust upon his own family members and discover the lasting effect it would have on his personal destiny.

Out of Siberia

Were it not for the unexpected upheavals, hardships and misfortunes of World War II, Arnold's parents, Chaim and Adele, would never have met. They each, singularly and separately, had been sent to Siberia for different reasons, but shared a common denominator: they were both victims of a war that devastated their respective families.

Chaim's escape to the Soviet side may have kept him from being put to death by the German Nazis, but it did not safeguard him from other calamities. Any hope of a better life was quickly snuffed out, when the Soviets arrested him soon after he crossed the border. Although the Soviet authorities knew that Chaim was a Polish Jew, they detained him nevertheless and accused him, at first, of being a Finnish spy. Later, after moving him to the city of Minsk and further interrogations there, the Soviets charged him for being a German Nazi spy instead and sent him on a prison train to western Siberia.

During the long ride that would take many weeks, German Nazi planes swooped down overhead and bombed the train, damaging portions of it. Surviving the havoc, Chaim finally reached his destination in late 1939 only to be banished to a Siberian prison camp to work at hard labor. Not knowing how long he would be held as a prisoner there, Chaim quickly learned to pick up the Russian language. Nearly two long, grueling years later, his life took yet another unforeseen turn. On the 22nd of June 1941, Germany breached the German-Soviet Non-Aggression Pact and launched a surprise, offensive attack against the Soviet Union, propelling World War II into a new phase.

Needing reinforcements, the Soviets sought political support from the Polish government, which was in exile in Britain at the time. Applying pressure on the Soviets, the Polish government-in-exile consented to providing its political support on the condition that all Polish citizens would be released from the Soviet prison camps. Due to this unexpected turn of events and the fact that he was a Polish citizen, Chaim was freed from imprisonment. However, with the war still raging on and the Germans dominating most of the European part of the Soviet Union at that time, he thought it best to wait out the war in western Siberia. The challenge he then faced was to figure out a way to make a living, as jobs were almost non-existent.

ADELE, AN ONLY CHILD, was born in Balzer (present-day Krasnoarmeysk) and grew up in the Saratov area of the Volga German Autonomous Soviet Socialist Republic (A.S.S.R.) under the communist regime of Joseph Stalin. Toward the end of 1936, when Adele was barely a teenager, the Russian Secret State Police, forerunner of the KGB, came and arrested her father in the middle of the night. Within the following year, they came back for her mother and incarcerated her for being the wife of an "enemy of the state." After that, Adele's imprisoned father was never heard from or seen again, presumably shot dead by the Russian Secret State Police. Her mother was to spend the next nine to ten years in a Soviet prison camp near the city of Akmolinsk (present-day Astana) north of Karaganda in the Kazakh A.S.S.R., known today as Kazakhstan.

With her family destroyed, Adele was sent to an orphanage in the Caucasus region, where she continued her schooling. The next year, she went to live with her father's relatives in the Chechen area. Later, other distant in-law relatives of her father, living in Saratov on the Volga River, took her in. There, she finished her Gymnasium education, equivalent to the ninth and tenth years of school. Just two days after Adele's graduation, Germany sprang its sudden attack on the Soviet Union in Operation Barbarossa on the 22nd of June 1941.

As the conflict intensified between the two countries, the Soviets dissolved the Volga German A.S.S.R. at the end of August 1941. The government claimed that the people of German descent living in that region were harboring German Nazi spies among them. Consequently, all the residents of that territory, regardless of their ethnic origins, were deemed risky to the state and deported en masse to Siberia and the Kazakh A.S.S.R. Adele was among those uprooted. The family with whom she lived in Saratov was permitted to remain, since the husband of that family had enlisted in the Soviet Red Army and was considered a "friend of the state." However, other relatives on her father's side were sent to western Siberia at about the same time as Adele, and initially for the first year, she was able to stay with them in the little village of Baykalovo, south of Tobol'sk in western Siberia.

IN AN INDIRECT WAY, Stalin's bureaucratic government policies of mass transfers of its own population made it possible for Chaim to eke out a living. In that environment, people needed to obtain permission to go anywhere and, thus, had to have passports and other official documents that required photographs. Resorting to his photography skills acquired as a young apprentice back in Poland, Chaim soon entered into business for himself. Managing to obtain a camera, he started taking pictures on the streets of the towns and villages surrounding Tobol'sk, wedged between the Tobol and Irtysh Rivers.

Due to the scarcity of resources, existence in Siberia was by and large at a subsistence level. Most people in the towns and villages did not have much money. There were no stores as such, and having money did not necessarily guarantee that there was food to buy even in the local marketplace. Hence, bartering became common practice in those days. To survive, Chaim bartered his services for food, taking pictures in exchange for eggs, milk, bread, or vegetables from people who raised their own animals or grew their own crops on the collective farms.

One day, while Adele was still living with her relatives in Baykalovo, word spread that a photographer had come to the area to take pictures for the people in the village. Adele had really wanted a photograph of herself at the time of her graduation, but in the ensuing chaos of the outbreak of war with Germany, she did not have the chance. Now that an opportunity had arisen, she eagerly went along with her cousin to seek out the photographer, who happened to be Chaim.

Many months later, Adele was transferred by the state to the town of Tobol'sk, where she was given a job at the local government's finance department to work as a junior bookkeeper, using an abacus. Being on her own, she needed to look for a place to live. An unexpected chance encounter took place that was to change her life. While going from door to door, making inquiries for a room to rent, she bumped into none other than Chaim himself. Having found better accommodations elsewhere, Chaim had just vacated a room in an apartment, so he offered to take Adele to his former landlady to help her secure the room. A whirlwind courtship followed. Within a few months, they decided to get married and together they stayed on in Tobol'sk.

As a young couple, Chaim and Adele lived in the same small room that Adele had been renting, where the kitchen and bathroom facilities were shared with others living under the same roof. Winters in that harsh, bleak Siberian terrain were snowy and bitterly cold, with sub-zero temperatures lasting up to nine months of the year. In the mornings, more often than not, they would awaken, shivering with cold, to find the windows and interior walls covered with frost from the condensation. Massive amounts of snow falling through the night sometimes necessitated having to tunnel their way from the front door to get outside.

For warmth, Chaim and Adele made use of a samovar, a traditional metal container, a type of "self-boiler" used to heat and boil water. It was the most economical way to have a permanent source of instant hot water in the home. This provided something to warm up the body, as the freezing cold would cut right to the bone. Water from the samovar also served as a base for making soup, which was the main staple of the day. Food was very simple, with bread and tea for breakfast and soup for the other meals. Meat was very scarce and consumed only rarely. It was always cooked in soups, so that nothing was wasted and maximum nutrients could be retained.

Procuring food of any kind through the hostile winter months proved very difficult. To survive, the local people resorted to hunting in the forests or ice-fishing on the frozen rivers and streams. At least on one occasion, Chaim brought home porcupine meat, the only food he could find, which he got through bartering. Although it was not exactly the average *kosher* fare for a Jewish family, Chaim and Adele tried to make do with whatever food they could come by. Every now and then, Adele was able to purchase a fish from a vendor in the marketplace, with money she earned from her office job. Those were the times when the soup she cooked tasted extra hearty.

Within the first year of their life together, Chaim and Adele discovered, to their joy, that they were expecting their first child. Adele continued to work through her pregnancy, which proceeded without complications. Close to the time of their baby's birth, the couple went to visit Adele's relatives in the village of Baykalovo, about one hundred to one hundred and fifty kilometers south of Tobol'sk, approximately two to three hours' train ride away. While there, Adele started to go into labor. Cutting short their visit, Chaim succeeded in bartering a ride for them in a horse-drawn wagon, and they hurriedly made their way to a midwife's place.

Being a rather petite woman of around five feet and given that it was going to be Adele's first child, the birth itself did not prove easy for her. After a long and tedious labor, a tiny baby boy was born to Chaim and Adele on the 26th of September 1943 in Baykalovo. They gave Arnold the Russian name of Arichek Genekovich Fruchtenbaum. It was only upon their return to Tobol'sk that Chaim and Adele filed their baby's official birth registration papers there.

Arik, as they liked to call him, turned out to be a fussy baby. He did not sleep through the night and cried incessantly. Having no relatives nearby, it was no small task for Adele to take care of a newborn baby on her own in the midst of a Siberian winter. Thus, she did not return to her office job.

The question of Arik's circumcision on the eighth day after birth never came up. While many Jews were living in the Soviet Union at that time, circumcision was not practiced among them. Neither was it available as a procedure in the hospitals. So, little Arik, though a Jew and a first-born son, was never subjected to circumcision as an infant. Being victims of a cruel war, Chaim and Adele each in their individual way had no desire to observe any religious rites. Chaim had already lost his faith in the ultra-Orthodox Jewish traditions, while Adele, having grown up under Soviet communism, had no belief whatsoever in the existence of God.

At this point in his life, Chaim's only hope was for the war to end, so that he could get out of Siberia. He yearned to make his way back to Poland with his new, little family as soon as it was politically feasible. It thus became a matter of surviving and waiting out the war.

Mass Transport Westward

By late 1944, Chaim had already been in Siberia for about five years, and World War II still had not come to an end as he had hoped. However, Ukraine was finally liberated from the Germans, and the Soviet government initiated the process of mass transport of all Polish citizens westward to Ukraine, eventually to be repatriated to Poland. At long last, Chaim had come one step closer to returning to his roots.

Official lists were issued with the names of Polish citizens who were to be transported to Ukraine to work on the collective farms. Oddly, Chaim's name did not appear on any of the lists in Tobol'sk, even though he was a Polish citizen. His name may have fallen through the cracks, due to his previous imprisonment and his unexpected release. Regardless, Chaim and Adele sold most of their belongings, packed their clothes and prepared themselves for the move. They did not want to pass up this long-awaited opportunity to get out of Siberia with their baby, Arik.

Permission had to be obtained from the Soviet authorities before they could leave Tobol'sk. Government red tape dictated that the address of the new destination had to be reported to the local officials in advance. Having no assigned place to go to in Ukraine, Chaim and Adele decided to give the address of Adele's relatives in Baykalovo as their destination, though they had no intention of going there. When it came time to leave, there happened to be two boats departing from the same port in Tobol'sk, one to Baykalovo and the other to Omsk, the town where those heading to Ukraine would be transferred onto trains. Despite the destination on their paperwork, they took the risk and boarded the boat to Omsk. In the chaos and confusion of people clamoring onto the boats, Chaim and Adele with their baby managed to mingle undetected amid the crowds.

Once the boat reached Omsk about a week later, all the passengers disembarked, but remained at a nearby train station for another week to wait for the train to arrive. No shelters were available, so at night, the people just lay outside in the chilly, open air to sleep under the stars. The rough conditions grew worse when heavy rains cascaded down in torrents one day. Chaim and Adele found their suitcase soaked through, with all the contents inside soggy wet. Prior to leaving Tobol'sk, Chaim had used the proceeds from the sale of their belongings to buy as many rolls of film as he could, in order to be able to take photographs and carry on with his livelihood when he got to Ukraine. Unfortunately, they were all ruined.

After what seemed like an interminable wait, the train finally pulled into the station. Anxious to grab a space, the people pushed and jostled to get onto the train to continue the next leg of their long journey overland to Stalingrad, known today as Volgograd. The squalid and crowded conditions on the train were deplorable. To make matters worse, Chaim and Adele discovered to their utter distress that their luggage had been stolen amid the confusion. By a miraculous stroke of providence, Chaim's camera equipment, which had been packed in another bag, survived the theft. With scarcely any money left, they had no means to buy food for a while. Adele could hardly produce enough milk to feed their baby, who had become very sick and weak by then. Before they left Tobol'sk, little Arik had contracted whooping cough, which he could not shake. Only a year and a few months old at the time, his immune system had not yet built up much resistance. En route, he also caught a cold, which worsened and degenerated into bronchitis during the long train journey to Stalingrad. All these ailments were too overwhelming for the baby's frail body to bear. At one point, he was so hungry that he even stopped crying.

By the time they reached Stalingrad, Adele, who had barely had any liquids or food to consume, was in a much-weakened state. The next leg of the train journey to Kirovograd in Ukraine would take many more days of hard, grueling travel. In her condition, Adele knew that she simply could not go the distance. Sizing up their dire situation, the couple decided that Chaim would go to Kirovograd on his own first. Once there, he would find a way to earn some money, prepare a place and then send for Adele and their baby a little while later.

Scraping together the last remaining bit of their scarce resources, Chaim sent Adele and little Arik on their way to Saratov on the Volga River. Situated about one to two days' boat ride north of Stalingrad, Saratov was much closer and faster to reach than Kirovograd. Adele's hope was that the family in Saratov, with whom she had lived during her last two years of Gymnasium, would take her in temporarily and help her and the baby, while they waited for news from Chaim.

When the boat docked at the port of Saratov and the other passengers disembarked, Adele found herself in a predicament. The town of Saratov was not level with the river, separated by a very steep incline with many steps going up. Already overtaken by sheer exhaustion, Adele could not see how on earth she was going to make it up the steps with the baby carriage. Distraught as to what to do next, Adele was approached by the same Soviet officer, who earlier had helped her on the crowded boat. He had instructed two of his men to clear a little space in a safe corner for her and the baby carriage. Now, he once again ordered two of his soldiers to pick up the carriage and lift it up to the top of the incline steps.

Years later in reflecting upon the scenario, Adele recognized that what the Soviet officer did for her on those two occasions were unique acts of kindness, not normally done for people during that time period in the midst of war. It was clearly evident that the providential hand of God had been extended over her and little Arik. Sadly even to the present day, Adele still could not and would not acknowledge God's care and protection at work in her life in that particular situation.

AFTER A LONG AND TAXING TRAIN RIDE that lasted for many days, Chaim arrived in Kirovograd with no money and no address to go to. Overcome with leaden fatigue, he ended up sleeping in the empty railcars at the train station for the first few nights. Desperate to make some money, but possessing no usable films, Chaim had to first devise a way to get started. Using his Jewish ingenuity, he walked into a big barbershop, doubling also as a hairdressing salon, and started asking people if they wanted to get their pictures taken. With the scarcity of films in those days, people rarely had such an opportunity, so everyone was keen to pay him a deposit. Without their knowledge, Chaim took blank shots with his empty camera. He then went to the black market and bought some rolls of film with the deposit money he had collected. The next day, Chaim went back to the shop to tell the people that something had gone wrong with his camera the previous day and that the photos did not turn out. So, he took their pictures all over again, this time with his camera fully loaded with film. When the photographs were delivered to his customers, they were very pleased with the result, all the while, none the wiser about what had really transpired.

The following day, Chaim saw a photo studio in town and went inside to inquire about a job. It just so happened that a photographer was needed right then and there, so he was hired on the spot. Although his wages were minuscule, Chaim was able to supplement his meager income with his own photography work on the streets of Kirovograd. Seeing that Chaim had no place to stay, Volodya, the young apprentice boy working at the studio, offered to bring Chaim home to his mother, who was taking in boarders. Although the living quarters were very cramped with five people sleeping in the same room, they somehow all got by.

When Chaim was able to save up enough money in the course of about two months, he wired Adele in Saratov and sent funds for her train fare plus a little extra to buy food along the way. By then, while still with only minimal strength, Adele had rested up enough to be able to travel again.

In those days of mass transport of the population, the trains were unpredictable and did not arrive on schedule. Adele could not send a telegram in advance to notify Chaim that she was coming, as she did not know when she could get on a train. Frequently, the trains were so full by the time they pulled up to the station that they continued right through without even stopping. Eventually, Adele ended up in a railcar that had previously been used to transport horses. The stench, the dirt and the cold exacerbated the already overcrowded and unsanitary conditions inside. It was particularly rough on Adele to travel with a frail baby.

At one of the stops along the way, Adele wanted to get something for little Arik to consume. Wanting to save her space and finding it awkward to maneuver the baby carriage on and off the trains, Adele left her son in the care of a fellow passenger and got off quickly to make her purchase. For that short interlude, Adele knew that Arik would be safe by himself. In those days of food shortage, no one was interested in stealing children. Before she could buy anything, all of a sudden, the train started to take off with her baby on board! Mustering all her strength, Adele ran as fast as she could to catch up with the moving train and jumped back on. Apparently, it was not one of the scheduled stops!

When the train eventually pulled into the station and came to a gradual halt at Kirovograd, Adele got off with her baby and all her things intact. She found a consignment area where she could temporarily check in the carriage with her belongings in exchange for a receipt. Armed with only Chaim's address, having no clue where it was, Adele set out to locate the place where he lived. Carrying her baby son in her arms, she began to walk, stopping people along the way to ask for street directions.

After a very long time, Adele finally came to supposedly the right location, but the place looked like a bombed-out barn. Distressed that she might have written down the wrong address and wondering what she was going to do next, she walked a little further behind the building. Stepping into a small courtyard where some laundry was hanging out to dry in front of a little house, she saw several children peering out of a window. Suddenly, a boy flashed her a smile and came running out of the house towards her. It was the young apprentice, Volodya, who worked at the same photo studio as Chaim. He recognized Adele from a picture that Chaim had shown him. Excited, the boy ran off to the studio to fetch him.

With Adele and Arik now in Kirovograd, it came time for Chaim to look for alternative living quarters for them. There was simply not enough space to accommodate all of them in the same room where Chaim was boarding. Decent housing was expensive and hard to come by, but within a week, Chaim had found them a rented room elsewhere. It was situated to one side of a dilapidated kitchen, pot-marked with holes in the ceiling from the bombings and furnished with a stove that did not function. Nevertheless, it was the best that he could provide for them at the time. Although the war had left their life in shambles, at least the little family could stay together again, and that was the most important thing for them.

Unexpected Detour in Ukraine

Even in peaceful times, Chaim and Adele's life would have inevitably been wrought with twists and turns. However during wartime, the disruptiveness of the unpredictable became more magnified for them. Although they desperately wanted to reunite with Chaim's family in Poland, they were obliged to remain in Ukraine for nearly one year, due to their unexpected personal circumstances as a consequence of the war.

Shortly after Adele had arrived with little Arik to join Chaim in Kirovograd, she became critically ill with typhus. In that era of mass transport of the population, disease was rampant. Multitudes of people succumbed to typhus, contracted from their prolonged exposure to contamination from the extreme lack of hygiene. Adele's temperature soared so high that she had to be rushed to a state hospital and kept under watchful care as her life hung in the balance.

At that time, the authorities did not allow the working parent to stay home for any reason. This meant that Chaim could not take care of Arik while Adele was hospitalized. Caught in a bind, he made enquiries at the City Hall concerning his dilemma as to his options. He was advised to leave his baby son at a state-run orphanage or find an individual who could care for him. With no other options available, Chaim was forced to place little Arik temporarily in an orphanage.

Due to the ravages of war, food itself was now in short supply in Ukraine, resulting in a severe, widespread famine. The situation was bleak. With very little food to be found anywhere, there was minimal available for the orphanage. Consequently, a number of children died of starvation, and corpses were removed daily from the premises.

Little Arik's condition had deteriorated to such an extent that his frail body had fast become reduced to only skin and bones. Were it not for his father's resourcefulness in scrounging around for food, the baby surely would have died. After finishing work at the end of each day, Chaim showed up at the orphanage with one or two pieces of bread for his son. Holding Arik and feeding him one small bite at a time, it was apparent to Chaim that his baby son was becoming progressively weaker. When it was time for Chaim to leave and a staff worker came to take the baby back to his crib, little Arik would cling desperately to his father, screaming and crying, not wanting to let go.

It was obvious that the children at the orphanage were not well taken care of by the staff workers and were dying from hunger and neglect. Although the workers did not like to see the children die, as this could lead to an official investigation, they were not above stealing the children's food for themselves or for their families. Seeing little Arik shrink and become skeletal before their very eyes during the few weeks of his stay, the staff workers advised Chaim to take his baby son home. Recognizing how dire the situation was, he knew that if he could not find an alternative solution urgently, Arik would die. In a last-ditch effort to seek out care for him, Chaim found an older woman who did not have to work. He negotiated a barter system with her and entrusted his baby to her care. Although she gave Arik a bit more nourishment than just bread, she did not provide him with the adequate care that a baby needed. With no other suitable options at that point, Chaim was obliged to let this older woman look after his baby son until Adele could return home.

WHILE HOSPITALIZED WITH TYPHUS, Adele also developed complications that affected her legs and she could hardly walk after she got home. Still very weak, she could not even get to the water source outside, let alone carry buckets of water to the room. With Chaim away much of the time, Adele, for the most part, was home alone with her frail baby. Initially as a favor, a neighbor living next door in the same dwelling brought Adele a bucket of water once a day, with which she had to do everything.

During the four weeks of her absence, little Arik had turned into an appalling mess. Not only had he withered away, he was filthy and smelled like a hamper full of damp, dirty laundry. His nose was black and crusted over, and his body was covered with sores. Never before had Adele seen a baby in such bad shape. In addition, Arik had also lost his ability to sit and hold up his head. Adele had to brace him with pillows, in order to prop him up. More distressing was the fact that her baby son did not even recognize who she was any more. Worse yet, he apparently developed a strong dislike for women. He was afraid of Adele and treated her as though she were an enemy, not letting her get close to cuddle or to hold him. Often at night, he would wake up suddenly with a jolt as if terrified by a nightmare and yell, "Tata, tata," crying out for his father at the top of his lungs from his crib.

When Chaim was away during the day, little Arik would allow Adele to feed him, change him, and take care of him, but instead of calling her "mom," he addressed her with the same term used for the workers at the orphanage. As soon as his father came back, little Arik wanted to interact only with him and wanted nothing to do with Adele. It was as if his mother did not exist any more. He would send her off to the far side of the room and insist that she stay there, ignoring her altogether.

Perplexed and somewhat baffled, Adele could not understand why her baby son was reacting so strangely toward her. Months later, the underlying reason surfaced quite unexpectedly. A few of the women who worked at the orphanage came to their home looking for Chaim to get their pictures taken for some documents they needed. Upon entering the room, they chatted amicably with Chaim and Adele and then approached little Arik. Much to their embarrassment and consternation, he deliberately turned his head away from them and categorically refused to look at them or say a single word to them. It became clear in that instant that Arik, even at such a young age, had witnessed the staff workers' treatment of the children, causing him to want nothing to do with them—or his mother.

Only very slowly did little Arik warm up to his mother, eventually calling her "mom" again, which greatly relieved Adele's frustration and her aching heart. While their relationship reached some semblance of normality, her baby son's poor health still continued to be of concern to Adele. Her own health was only just beginning to return little by little. Aside from having survived the life-threatening bout of typhus, she discovered that the long, protracted, high fever had also unexpectedly eradicated malaria from her body for good. Having lived along the banks of the Volga River, Adele used to have an annual recurrence of the disease, which she had to combat with medication. After her typhus fever, however, she never again had another bout of malaria.

LIFE WAS PRECARIOUS during the long period of famine in Ukraine. People on the collective farms, where Chaim rendered his photo services, made use of the barter system. They paid him with what little food they could spare from their own portion, such as beans, onions, carrots and potatoes. Occasionally, they gave him some bacon. The food was worth far more to Chaim and Adele than monetary currency.

The times when Chaim got paid in cash from the workers on the Soviet farms, they could afford to buy some milk for little Arik—five glasses a day to be exact—a little cereal, a loaf of bread, and some honey. At night before going to bed, Adele would drink just one glass of milk, as the rest of the milk was set aside for her son, and eat a small piece of bread with some honey on it. That was the only nourishment she would have all day long. Yet somehow, the family still managed to survive with the little food that they had. It was their saving grace from starvation.

Hunger seemed to be foremost on little Arik's mind a large portion of the time. On one occasion, when he developed a persistent cough, Adele managed to procure some medicine, which was to be administered to him one small teaspoonful at a time at regular intervals. However, after ravenously swallowing a tiny gulp, little Arik was so hungry that he just cried and cried, eager for more of the same, irrespective of what he was consuming. He obviously did not need to be coaxed to take his medicine!

On another occasion, when his parents had finished feeding him and put him to sleep in his crib, little Arik's eyelids were drooping and nearly shut. Chaim and Adele then turned their attention to preparing some potatoes for their own dinner. Just as the potatoes began to boil in the pot, Arik suddenly bolted up and opened his eyes, anticipating more to eat. He refused to go back to sleep until he got himself a hearty helping. Decades later, he would humorously attribute his taste for potato *latkes*, a type of Jewish potato pancake, to that incident.

Arik's reaction to food bemused Chumah, when she came with her husband, Reuben, for a short visit. After Chaim had arrived in Ukraine, he wrote to the last address he had of Yaakov, one of his many siblings,[2] hoping perchance that they might be able to re-establish contact. Through a series of events, the letter somehow reached Yaakov. Another sibling, Chumah, then obtained Chaim's address from Yaakov and applied for a travel permit to come and see his new family.

Chumah had some apples with her. Instead of just accepting one, Arik extended both his arms out and wanted two, grasping one in each hand. Invariably, he ate ravenously, vigilantly clutching tightly onto the food. Whatever Chumah offered, Arik wanted to take two. His earlier experiences of starvation at the orphanage might have triggered an automatic reaction, prompting him to want an extra portion of food whenever he could get it. Perhaps it was the residual fear of having nothing for the next meal that drove him to always want a double portion.

Due to insufficient sunlight and the lack of proper nourishment, little Arik developed rickets and could not walk. During the gray, dreary winter months in Ukraine, the only possible remedy was for Adele to take her baby son to a center where he could be placed under quartz lamps for a short period each day. Though painstakingly slow, Arik did show signs of improvement and eventually learned to walk, just later than the average well-nourished toddler.

As the health of both mother and son was gradually being restored, Chaim's attention turned once again to making plans to continue their journey back to

---

[2] The slightly complicated family relations between Chaim, Chumah, Yaakov, and the other Fruchtenbaum "siblings" are further explained on pages 41 and 42.

his homeland in Poland. The unexpected detour of nearly one year in Ukraine was something that he could not have foreseen. The Allied Forces had gained victory over the Nazis in Europe, and the Third Reich had finally come to an end, with the Germans surrendering on the seventh of May 1945. Several months later, the Japanese capitulated in the Pacific on the second of September 1945, but not before the U.S. atomic bombings of Hiroshima and Nagasaki on the sixth and ninth of August respectively. After so much destruction, World War II was at long last over.

Soon a new year, 1946, was about to dawn. Chaim was anxious to find out what had happened to the rest of his other family members whom he had not seen or heard from since he had fled to the Soviet territories at the beginning of the war. Where were they now? Did they all survive? Would they be scattered abroad, or were they still in Poland? How was he going to find them and would he be reunited with them once again?

Return to Poland

Once World War II had ended, the Soviet government allowed all the Polish people to be mass-transported from Ukraine back to Poland. Since Poland had been taken over by the communists, it posed no ideological issues or threat to the Soviets. To be repatriated, the authorities required proof that the people were already Polish citizens at the time when Poland was partitioned between Germany and the Soviet Union at the outset of the war in September 1939. Foreign spouses of Polish citizens, regardless of their nationality, plus their children were all allowed to enter Poland.

It was February 1946, approximately six and a half years since he had fled from the occupying German Nazis in Poland, when Chaim was finally able to get back to his homeland. Before his arrival in Poland, he could only imagine the extent of the devastation that the war had brought upon his country and upon the Jewish community in particular. Yet, the actual dangers that his little family encountered upon reaching Poland stunned Chaim far beyond his comprehension. Anti-Semitism was rife to an alarming degree in the country. The Jews, who had managed to survive the concentration camps and returning to their hometowns in Poland to look for their loved ones, were shocked at what they found. Instead of being greeted with the traditional bread and salt, expressing welcome, they were brutally killed as the Polish people acted out their ingrained racial hatred. Even though World War II had ended, the Poles still engaged in murdering the surviving Jews, hunting them down and killing them in broad daylight.

When the trains slowed down to a rolling stop at the stations within the Polish borders, ethnic Poles would jump onto the trains, drag the Jews off at random and shoot them in cold blood. Anyone who had features that remotely resembled a Jew was in danger of being pulled off the trains and killed with no rhyme or reason. Such was the depth of anti-Semitism that confronted Chaim as soon as they crossed the border into Poland. His heightened sense of danger immediately kicked in. Wasting no time, he took his little family off the train near one stop, when he feared that some Poles were about to jump onto the train and engage in their arbitrary killing spree. They walked a distance undetected, while Chaim tried to find an alternative means of transportation for them. Later, they were able to board another train that brought them safely to their destination.

Resolving to find his family, through sheer determination, street smarts, and word-of-mouth, Chaim finally got wind of their whereabouts. They were no longer in Pultusk. No one in his family dared to go back to their hometown for fear of being killed. When the family was expelled from Pultusk along with the rest of the Jewish community in the early stages of the German occupation, they were forced to leave behind most of their possessions. Local Poles had a heyday in looting and pilfering their furniture and confiscating their other belongings just as they had done to countless other Jewish homes. At no other time was the prevalence of anti-Semitism more evident than when the Poles refused to help the Jews, but instead supported the torrents of Nazi policies. If the family were to go back to Pultusk now, the local Poles, including perhaps even their former neighbors, would surmise that they had returned to reclaim their possessions and hence be more inclined to kill them, in order to hang onto their ill-gotten gains. Going back to Pultusk would have meant a sure death sentence for the Fruchtenbaum family.

Chaim heard that his family members had gathered in Lodz, a city located several hours by train, south of Warsaw. Upon their arrival, he left his wife and son behind at the train station to wait for him. Since Adele had never met his family, Chaim wanted to find them first before introducing her to them.

Besides, it made more sense for him to scout the city by himself, as he could cover more ground a lot faster on his own. The plan was for him to come back and fetch Adele and little Arik, once he had located his family. Heading to the Jewish neighborhood on the outskirts of Lodz to make enquiries, Chaim was finally able to meet up with his family. He found one brother, Yaakov, and three sisters, Chankah, Genya, and Chumah, who had survived the war. Sadly, Yaakov had lost his wife and their only child, a son. Yehoshua, another brother, had managed to escape to the British Mandate of Palestine sometime during the course of the war, so he was safe. In total, six siblings including Chaim, made it alive through the war, out of a total of ten at that time.

Chaim was shocked to learn that the other four siblings—two brothers, Tzemach and Asher, and two sisters, Chavah and Adah—had perished in the Holocaust along with their mother, Ittah Leah. The husband of Chavah and their two young daughters also perished. From the immediate and extended family, a few had died in the ghetto in Warsaw; some were likely killed in Auschwitz; others were probably shot in the Ponary Forest near Vilna; the rest were most likely murdered in Treblinka or Sobibor. Chaim was inconsolable. Grief and pain gripped him like a vice, shaking and tormenting him to the core as he thought about the horrific torture and enormity of suffering that his deceased siblings and extended family would have had to endure.

Having remained in the Soviet Union for the duration of the war, Chaim only became aware of the disastrous extent of the Holocaust after he had reunited with the surviving members of his family. His mind simply could not fathom the colossal tragedy and the staggering number of Jews murdered in the extermination camps right there in Poland. Of the three and a half million Jews residing in the country prior to World War II, only 70,000 to 80,000 survivors were left by the end of the war. Without the cooperation and support of the local Polish population, it would not have been possible for the German Nazis to murder such an overwhelming majority of the Jewish people in Poland. It was no coincidence that every major death camp was located in Poland and not in Germany. Chaim was disconsolate.

Once the repatriation of the Polish citizens from the Soviet Union got underway after the war, the number of Jews in Poland began to increase to about 150,000 to 200,000. Yet, Chaim realized that their life as a family was never to be the same again, having been torn asunder and fragmented by the loss of innocent lives. This horrific war had also permanently altered the direction of his own life.

Chaim explained to his family that after traveling for so many days, Adele was bedraggled and unkempt, definitely not presentable. Uncertain of how his family would accept her—as Adele was from another country and did not speak Polish—Chaim was reluctant to bring her with him without giving prior notice to his family. Besides, Adele herself felt too embarrassed to come and meet them for the very first time in her filthy condition. Being the loving family that they were, Chaim's siblings chided him, reminding him that they, too, had been in the same situation and knew from experience what it was like to feel dirty and grimy after a long journey. So, they all hurriedly went together to the station to meet Adele and little Arik. The family greeted and welcomed them warmly and brought them home.

As suitable lodging was difficult to find for all the family members to live together under one roof, they each chose to make do with whatever rooms they could rent, in order to live in close proximity to one another. They had no possessions left and became refugees like the rest of the Jews who had returned to Poland. At first, Chaim and his little family stayed temporarily with one of his siblings in their quarters, but moved out shortly afterwards, once they found another room to rent for themselves. To earn a living, Chaim resorted once again to his photography skills, which he employed around the general vicinity of Lodz and the outlying towns.

UP TO THAT POINT, Chaim and Adele had communicated mainly in Russian and sometimes in Yiddish with each other and little Arik. Believing that they could stay and make a new life for themselves in the Lodz area, Adele began to study Polish in earnest. Applying herself, she got quite proficient in speaking the language, which came in handy.

Before leaving Kirovograd, Arik had developed a small red lump on the right side of his neck, which grew larger during their journey to Poland. Once they settled in Lodz, Adele took him to see a Polish doctor, who could not tell what was wrong, so she took him to a Jewish doctor instead. Upon examining the lump, he declared that it had to be lanced and drained. While Adele grasped her son tightly to keep him still, this doctor drew out the puss with a hollow needle-like device. After cleansing and covering the area with a bandage, he instructed Adele to keep it from getting wet when bathing the child and advised them to come back in a few days for a further check-up.

After only a day or so, Arik started crying from painful discomfort. Adele quickly sought out the doctor, who noted that the area had become infected and gave her some ointment to apply. Slowly, the neck healed, leaving a scar. Meanwhile, due to complications, both of little Arik's eyes remained closed for about three months. When they opened again, one eyelid rose only partway, causing the right eye to appear smaller than the left. Undaunted, Adele decided to take her son to an eye doctor, who checked that the right eye itself was fine. As for the eyelid, he recommended that a neurologist take a look at it. So Adele sought out a neurologist, who figured that when the wound on Arik's neck closed up during the healing process, it had pulled and constricted the nerve of the right eyelid. An option was to cut open the scar on the neck to try and release the nerve. Only one specialist surgeon in Warsaw could perform such a procedure. He was scheduled to come to Lodz only twice a year, which meant a long wait before Arik could be examined.

The neurologist suggested that since the child was still so young, the nerve might stretch itself as he grew. The risk of not being able to pinpoint the exact location of the nerve when the scar was opened up and the possibility of inadvertently cutting into the nerve itself were serious considerations. If that happened, the result would be far worse than simply leaving the eyelid as it was. After Chaim and Adele discussed the matter with each other, they decided against pursuing any further procedures and let it go. Arik's eyelid never went back to normal, and to this day, the right eyelid still opens only partway over the eye.

For the first time, little Arik, who was by then around two and a half years of age, enjoyed enough food and regular meals to satisfy his growing appetite. As his health gradually stabilized, Arik settled into a daily rhythm. He started to speak both Yiddish and Polish as he spent time playing with one of his cousins. For a while, it appeared as though life might take on a sense of normalcy for his family, something that they had not experienced up to that point. Unfortunately, any anticipation of a secure life in Poland fell by the wayside as a series of pogroms ignited new waves of persecution against the Jews in various parts of the country.

Pesach Pogrom, 1946

In the spring of 1946, a couple of months after the family's arrival in Poland, it came time to celebrate their first *Pesach*, or Passover Feast, after the end of the war. Jews all over Poland looked forward to this very important occasion, marked by an even greater significance this time. Given that they had just survived a horrific war, they would celebrate not only their historical redemption from Egypt many thousands of years earlier, but also their recent liberation from the occupying German Nazis.

In preparation for both *Pesach* and *Hag Hamatzot*, or the Feast of Unleavened Bread, which was to follow for seven days immediately after the Passover Feast, all the Jewish mothers, including Adele, began to bake bread in accordance with tradition. During this period, only *matzah*, the Jewish unleavened bread, was allowed. Nothing containing yeast or leaven was permitted, as it symbolized sin. Due to the post-war situation, Arik's family did not intend to observe the traditional Jewish rituals of a *Seder* meal at their home on the evening of the Passover Feast. However, they did adhere to the importance of eating only unleavened bread during those eight days as a way of celebrating the Feast.

At about the same time just prior to the *Pesach* celebration, a young Polish Catholic boy had disappeared and was reported missing. This incident ignited a vicious rumor, propagated by the Roman Catholic clergy. The Jews were accused of kidnapping the boy and killing him in a ritual murder, in order to use his blood to make the *matzah*, or unleavened bread, for the Passover Feast. This blood slander spread like wildfire throughout the country, fueling the Poles' already existing hatred of the Jews and instigating virulent pogroms against them. With ruthless savagery, the incited mobs raided and shut down Jewish businesses, ransacked and looted multitudes of Jewish homes and brutally destroyed their synagogues.

On the first night of *Pesach*, as Jewish families sat down to their *Seder*, angry mobs congregated on the streets outside their homes, preparing to attack. Full-scale riots were mounted, organized by the police from the towns and villages and propelled by the Roman Catholic hierarchy. Breaking down the securely locked doors, they forced their way into the Jewish homes and dragged the Jews outside, with the intention of murdering them in cold blood. All the while, Roman Catholic priests stood by, waving and brandishing their big crosses in front of the Jews, simultaneously shouting in Polish the phrase that was all too often heralded in that epoch, "You killed Jesus Christ, so we will kill you."

Terror ran amok among the Jews as chaos and violence escalated. By a stroke of providence, the room where Arik's family lived was "passed over" and spared from the raids and killings. Others were not as fortunate and on that night of Passover 1946, many innocent Jews throughout Poland lost their lives, killed by raging mobs in the name of Jesus. Instead of safety and redemption from the enemies as the Passover Feast was intended to celebrate, tragically, the exact opposite occurred. It was in this horrendous Gentile context of violence and destruction that Arik first heard the Christian name of "Jesus Christ." To the child, this Jesus of the Gentiles was certainly not someone who came to die for him, but rather someone for whom he and his family almost had to die, like the scores of Jews who had been murdered that night and through the past centuries. Based on the traumatic experience of that Passover night, barriers were erected in little Arik's mind—as in so many other Jewish minds—against the Gentiles or Christians, whose world he wanted to have as little to do with as possible.

When the missing Polish boy was later found safe and sound at his grandmother's place, no effort was made by the Gentiles to erase the blood slander against the Jews. The Polish authorities only made excuses, and the Roman Catholic Church responded with indifference at best.

It was hence from the very early years of his life that Arik intuitively felt unsafe as a Jew among the Gentiles or Christians, the two being synonymous in his own mind. He certainly wanted nothing to do with their hateful, murderous Jesus in whose name the Gentile Christian Church was killing innocent Jews. Growing up, Arik's world revolved around "us," the Jews, and "them," the Gentile Christian persecutors.

As a result of such heinous attacks, an atmosphere of panic became widespread in the Jewish communities by the summer of 1946. In the ensuing months, waves of previously returning Holocaust survivors began to flee a second time from Poland. Given the prevailing anti-Semitic attitude, the vast majority of the Jews, fearful of being decimated, simply did not believe that they could be safe in Poland any longer. Multitudes sought to avoid living under a communist regime, which had consolidated its power in post-war Poland. Others wanted to go to the British Mandate of Palestine, which later became the State of Israel. Whatever the reasons, by the fall, over a hundred thousand Jews crossed the Polish borders illegally.

Convinced that settling in Poland would mean a sure death sentence for his family, Chaim also made the decision to leave that very summer. Hardly six months had elapsed since he arrived in Lodz with Adele and little Arik. Now he had to uproot them again. This time, Chaim's siblings did not need much persuasion and listened to him for a change. They, too, started seeking out ways and formulating plans to eventually escape from Poland.

Only God, in His omniscience, could foresee what lay ahead for Chaim and his little family, especially for Arik. The course of his first-born son's life would no longer be to follow the family's dynastic tradition as a leader of a local subdivision of the *Ger Chasidim* in Pultusk. Chaim's own rigorous training and plans for the role had come to naught. The life that he once knew was gone forever. Now that his hopes to build a new life in Lodz were dashed to pieces, he decided to focus all his energies into finding a way to get his family out of Poland. At this juncture, it did not matter to Chaim what country they went to next, as long as it was as far away from Poland as possible and a place where the Jews would be safe from persecution.

Escape from Behind the Iron Curtain

Without the assistance of the Israeli Underground (then known as the Palestinian Underground), Chaim may not have succeeded in escaping with his family. When news of the Polish pogroms spread, it gave rise to a major operation spearheaded by the Underground, an offshoot of an illegal Jewish immigration agency, *Mossad L'Aliyah Bet*, in the British Mandate of Palestine. Persecution of the Jews after the end of the war served as a strong impetus to formulate a rescue plan—a monumental mission of finding, organizing, and bringing out as many of the Jewish remnants as possible from behind the Iron Curtain. The movement was perhaps one of the largest clandestine population transfers in history.

The operation, which became known as the *Brichah*, or the "Escape" in Hebrew, provided surviving Jews in Central and Eastern Europe the possibility of illegal flight. The aim was for the Jews to make their way across the Allied-occupied zones to reach the coastal areas of Italy or France. From there, clandestine ships at various pre-arranged ports would transport them to what later became the State of Israel.

The *Brichah* operatives on the ground scouted for escape routes from Poland, engaging in so-called "black" crossings or illegal border transits at night through dense forest paths. Numerous escape routes were set up, leading to West Germany, Romania and Czechoslovakia (known today as the two separate countries, Czech Republic and Slovakia). These routes were chosen mainly based on geography, but other factors were also taken into account, such as availability of sympathetic and bribable border guards and friendliness of the local population.

Special arrangements through bribes were made with the Polish border police, which granted the *Brichah* a period of thirty days during which the Jewish refugees would be allowed free passage out of Poland through specified exit points. Large houses, known as *kibbutzim* in *Brichah* jargon, were rented in the interior of the country and served as safe houses or assembly points about a kilometer or so from the borders. Designated members of the Underground would await the refugees at those points to lead them across the frontier and hand them over to other *Brichah* guides to continue on their pre-selected escape routes.

As only God could have arranged it, the city of Lodz became the local *Brichah* headquarters in Poland. Hence, it was without much effort that Chaim had heard about the thirty-day window during the summer of 1946 and decided to seize the opportunity. Getting in touch with the Underground, Chaim arranged for his little family of three to get out of Poland. Carrying only whatever they could fit into their backpacks, Chaim, Adele and little Arik joined a group of other fleeing Jews. In order not to attract attention or arouse any suspicion among the local Poles, the group did not take any form of public transportation, but began the long trek of many, many kilometers on foot through the forests.

Their group comprised between thirty to fifty people including a number of children. Five Underground operatives led the way. To protect their convoys, these *Brichah* guides carried arms, which they had bought at the local black market before the journey. After many long days of trekking on foot, they eventually reached the Polish-Czech border.

Because prior "arrangements" had already been made, the group could arrive openly at that specified border crossing. When the *Brichah* guides identified their group as Jews and presented the Polish border police with a list of names, they knew that generally there would be no attempt to match the names to the people. In fact, the guards put their rifles behind their backs, turned the other way and raised their eyes toward the sky, at the same time motioning with their hands for the group to pass by. They looked up at the birds flying overhead, pretending not to see the Jews, thus enabling them to cross over freely into Czechoslovakia.

During the first few hours after crossing the border, the group found themselves in "no man's land." Chaos reigned for a while, due to the huge groundswell of various groups converging simultaneously from other routes. The *Brichah* operatives managed to round up the people one by one in their specific group and organized them once again into a walking party. The group then found out from the *Brichah* guides what it cost for the Jews to make that crossing. It actually took no more than some cartons of American cigarettes. After World War II, they were highly valued in Eastern Europe and used almost like currency for buying, bartering, or trading. At that time, a carton of the Camel brand could purchase and secure the freedom of an entire family of Jews. Consisting of ten packs of cigarettes, one carton could easily fetch up to the equivalent of $150 on the black market. When giving his testimony decades later, Arnold would jokingly say that while cigarettes might be hazardous to one's health and endanger the lives of many, they undoubtedly saved his and that he did one day walk a mile for a camel!

For many weeks under the direction of the *Brichah* guides, the group continued to march on foot through the dense forests toward the Czech-Austrian border. Similar "arrangements" with bribes had also been negotiated in advance with the Czech border police. Trekking by daylight, the group stopped only at certain points where cold food satchels, provided by the Underground, were distributed. Under the age of three at that time, little Arik could walk on his own, but also had to be carried quite a lot. When it got too dark to walk at night, the group slept in their clothes directly on the ground, hidden away under the trees. To evade detection and danger, the children had to be kept still and silent so that their lives would not be imperiled. That was where Arik first learned to be very quiet and guarded, a trait that he carried into adulthood, speaking only when spoken to while in a group.

The day before the group was to make the crossing into Austria, the *Brichah* guides discovered to their dismay that the existing Czech government had collapsed into the hands of the Communist Party. As soon as it gained power, the Party took over control of the border patrol. The Czech police were immediately replaced with Soviet border guards with whom no prior deals had been made for the Jews' safe passage.

Instructing the group to wait in hiding, the *Brichah* guides went up to the border to investigate. They learned that the Soviet guards were under strict orders to allow no one across the Czech border except for Greeks who were returning home from concentration camps. Back with the group, the *Brichah* guides ordered them to burn up and destroy any and everything with their names on it, which would in any way, shape, or form reveal their true identity. That night, birth and marriage certificates, passports, and other identification papers all literally went up in smoke.

The following morning, the group was told to head toward the Czech-Austrian border and pose as Greeks. In fact, no one in the group was Greek, nor did anyone speak a single word of Greek. Then again, the Soviet border police could no more ask them a question in Greek than they could answer. Jews of Soviet background, such as the Fruchtenbaum family, were admonished not to utter a single word in Russian and not to show any sign of comprehension. So, with that simple subterfuge, the group of Jews all posing as Greeks got across into Austria, except for one Underground member. At the last minute, something went wrong, and a *Brichah* guide was shot and killed, the only casualty. Everyone else was safe. Decades later, Arnold would claim that he could apply the verse of Romans 1:16b to himself in a special way in that he was "a Jew first, but also a Greek" for one day!

Once in Austria—now occupied by the Americans, the British, and the French—the group was led on a train to Vienna. Arik's earliest personal recollection went back to the only time that a passenger train was used en route. At one stop, his father got off to barter for some extra food for his family. When the train started to move again and he was still nowhere in sight, his mother gasped with fear, revealing her panic. At the last minute before the train's speed gained too much momentum, his father jumped back on. The risk was worth it, as he had obtained a few eggs, which they ate raw. In Vienna, the American Military Police took over from the Underground and escorted the Jews on open military trucks all the way to West Germany.

Because the Jews had no documents or proof of identity of any kind, they were classified as displaced persons, stateless individuals without citizenship from any country. As an interim solution, they were taken to D.P. Camps, or Displaced Persons' Camps, in West Germany. These were special settlements specifically created for stateless Jews. At that time, the Jews in the British Mandate of Palestine were fighting the British for independence. Thus, the Jewish refugees were deterred from continuing on their journey to their original destination.

Having just risked their lives to escape from behind the Iron Curtain, Arik's family now found themselves classified as stateless refugees without a homeland. Trapped by this totally unexpected turn of events, they could only hope that they would eventually be allowed to enter a country where they, as Jews, could dwell in safety.

D.P. Camps in West Germany

Located mostly in the southern part of West Germany, the Displaced Persons' Camps were set up in the British and American-occupied zones to take in Jewish refugees. As such, the D.P. Camp of Hofgeismar became the home of the Fruchtenbaum family for the next few years starting in August 1946. It was the American MP, or Military Police, not the British, who were in charge of the daily organizing and running of the place.

Being an ally of Great Britain, the United States agreed to honor the policies imposed by the British government to restrict any Jews from opting to emigrate from Europe to the British Mandate of Palestine. Even though the Fruchtenbaum family had physically ended up in the American-occupied zone, the same British restrictions still applied. All the Jewish refugees heading to Palestine were detained at these D.P. Camps.

Only later did it become apparent what impact the *Brichah's* rescue work had on the political front regarding the Jewry's future. By seeking out and bringing to the D.P. Camps hundreds of thousands of refugees, the *Brichah* was putting the pressure on the British government and the world to find a home for the displaced Jews. For the most part, the world had thought that the Jews were gone, the preponderant majority having been exterminated by the end of World War II and the remaining few having been assimilated wherever they happened to be.

Quite unexpectedly, the world was suddenly confronted with the reality of a multitudinous remnant of stateless Jews in need of a homeland. After the end of World War II, it was estimated that some 200,000 Jewish refugees in Europe needed to be resettled. This situation, in parallel with the Jews' fight for independence in the British Mandate of Palestine, eventually led to the birth of the State of Israel on the 14th of May 1948. At such a critical hour in their history, the arrival of the Jewish survivors in Israel infused the newborn country with manpower, vigor, talent, and vitality, which fed the lifeblood of the young nation.

Initially, due to the enormous number of Jews not possessing any proof of citizenship, much confusion dominated for a while in the different occupied zones of West Germany. However, with the help of HIAS, the Hebrew Immigration Aid Society, new identity papers and certificates were gradually issued. Those wanting to go to *Eretz Yisrael*, or the Land of Israel, still known then as the British Mandate of Palestine, had to wait for about two years before their paperwork got successfully processed. They were permitted entry only after the official State of Israel was established in May 1948.

Through the assistance of HIAS, each family was free to apply to any of the countries that had opened their doors to Jewish immigration. Although the general processing time for the required paperwork was quite lengthy and tedious, the waiting time for the United States was by far the longest, due to its stringent stipulations and difficult requirements. Only after the Displaced Persons' Act of July 1948 did the U.S. Immigration Bureau announce the quota of eligible refugees permitted to enter the country. Upon considering his options, Chaim decided to aim for the United States. Little did he realize at the time that it would take nearly five years for the approval to come through.

AFTER A LONG AND UNCOMFORTABLE RIDE on the open military trucks from Vienna, the Fruchtenbaums and the rest of the group finally arrived in the town of Hofgeismar. The D.P. Camp was situated on the site that used to be the army barracks for the German military during the war. Within the compound stood numerous dormitory buildings that had once housed the soldiers, large enough to now hold many thousands of Jewish refugees.

The moment they got off the trucks, Chaim, with his well-developed survivor instinct, immediately went scouting around the compound to seek out the best possible private room in the barracks for his family. He wanted to avoid having to live in a large open room to be shared with several other families. Finding a private room on the upper level of a two-story building, he quickly laid claim to it.

This dormitory consisted of about one hundred rooms in total, with separate communal areas for cooking, laundry and bathroom facilities. Only one room was allocated to each family, irrespective of the number of children it had. Still, with electricity, indoor plumbing and gas radiator heating in the winter months, the conditions were far better than what the Fruchtenbaums had endured in Siberia and Ukraine.

As soon as the family settled in, they were provided with food, water and clothing to get them started. Basic food rations were distributed to each family on a weekly basis. Communal meals, organized by the American MP, were also available in what used to be the army "mess" hall. Since ninety-five percent of the people at the D.P. Camp were Jewish, those refugees who were rabbis made sure that the communal meals were cooked according to *kosher* standards. It was the overall general sentiment that the refugees were certainly not deprived of any basic necessities at this D.P. Camp in Hofgeismar.

Since the environment was predominantly Jewish, those refugees whose professions prior to the war used to be teaching got together and organized a school. The classes were taught in Yiddish, the common language among the Jews of diverse backgrounds. One teacher was assigned to each age group.

During his family's stay at the D.P. Camp in Hofgeismar, Arik was too young to attend school. Later, when he was old enough to do so, he attended a Jewish school at another D.P. Camp, where he learned the Yiddish and Hebrew alphabets and studied Jewish history, geography, and Bible stories from the *Tanakh*.

While a small amount of cash was given to each family, Chaim was able to make some extra money through his photography work. With all the people at the D.P. Camp filing their paperwork to immigrate to various countries, photographs were in high demand. He also went out on the streets of Hofgeismar to take pictures for other people who needed them for their documents. Although the compound was enclosed, the refugees were free to come and go at will, as long as they abided by the curfew and returned before a certain hour at night when the gates would be shut.

35

SOME OF THE HAPPIEST MEMORIES that Arik retained from his childhood took place at the D.P. Camps. Energetic and resourceful, he adapted quickly to each new D.P. Camp environment, finding other Jewish children around his age to play with, mostly little girls. In general, it appeared that more boys than girls had perished at the hands of the German Nazis through the extermination rampage of the Holocaust.

Protected within the enclosed D.P. Camp compound, Arik felt safe to interact with his new playmates and hence was not necessarily a quiet child. During the summer months, he spent most of his time outdoors. Young and carefree, he romped about the grounds of the D.P. Camp, experiencing many pleasurable first-time moments. One day, while he ran around with a couple of his playmates, an American G.I. threw them each a chocolate bar. As Arik bit into his first chocolate ever, the sweet, smooth sensation tantalized his taste buds. Never before had he tasted anything so enticingly yummy. Oh, how he savored every bite!

To entertain the children, the Americans set up a large tent, where Mickey Mouse cartoons were shown from old film reels projected onto a big screen. It was the very first time that Arik was exposed to cartoon movies. Although he did not understand the English spoken by the characters, he enjoyed watching the popular, animated adventures of Mickey Mouse, who soon became a familiar figure to him.

A favorite pastime for Arik during the warmer months was going on motorcycle rides with his father. To relax from his busy photography work, Chaim would borrow a motorcycle from a friend and take his son on long rides through the German countryside, where rows and rows of fields stretched in all directions beyond the horizon. With the wind blowing in their faces and no other vehicles in sight, Arik experienced a sense of elation to have this time alone with his father, sharing in an activity that they both enjoyed, whizzing with unrestrained freedom across the wide, open expanse.

One day, Arik's left foot inattentively slipped and got caught in the spirals of a wheel as the motorcycle sped down a country road. Shocked and terrified from the throbbing pain, he screamed with fear as he was rushed to the hospital where he was immediately put under anesthesia, in order for the doctors to work on his foot. Thankfully, the medical procedures were funded by the D.P. Camp administration. Much to his parents' relief, the accident left no permanent damage and in time, Arik's foot healed completely.

Nonetheless, he did not get on a motorcycle again after that scary mishap, choosing instead to ride a normal bicycle.

Another activity that both father and son engaged in was chess. Even before Arik knew how to read or write, Chaim taught him the rules of the game and how to play. Considering chess as a professional sport, Chaim's all-consuming passion for the game increased in intensity with each passing year. In 1948, he even won the title of Grand Master Champion of the Liberated Jews of Germany, a major chess competition organized for the entrants from the various D.P. Camps around the country. Chaim continued to play chess throughout the rest of his life, but for Arik, chess became more of a hobby, on which he could no longer afford to spend any time after his high school years.

NOT LONG AFTER ARRIVING at the D.P. Camp, Adele suffered a miscarriage. She later became pregnant again and succeeded this time in carrying the baby to full term. She gave birth in the early spring of 1948 to her second son, Edward, a big, healthy baby. The birth itself took place at an external hospital in Hofgeismar designated by the D.P. Camp administration, all expenses paid. The clean, comfortable environment of the German hospital was a radical contrast to the stark furnishings of the midwife's place in Siberia.

No longer suffering from food deprivation, Adele had plenty of breast milk to feed her baby Eddie, as they liked to call him. Some other mothers were not as fortunate and could not produce enough milk to nurse their own babies. Every now and then, a request to use some of her breast milk came to her attention, and she freely gave her milk without charge to those she considered her friends. From others whom she did not know, she received a little bit of money, which helped the family's income.

Once Eddie was weaned off his milk, Adele cooked and mashed vegetables and other ingredients to feed him. Although Arik could eat the regular solid food that his parents ate, he still wanted the same things that his baby brother, four years his junior, was having. This was his way of being part of what his mother was doing daily. So, she would make mashed food for both her sons. Growing up, Arik remembered his mother as being very loving and nurturing, always there for him and his siblings, except for the times when she got sick, resulting from hardships and conditions of deprivation in the past.

The religious rabbis tried to control much of what was going on at the D.P. Camps. For instance, they made sure that the electricity was turned off just before sundown on Friday evenings and not restored until Saturday evening the next day, in order to enforce the people's observance of *Shabbat*, or the Sabbath rest. This meant that all the meals for that period had to be prepared in advance sometime during the day on Friday. Once prepared, the food such as the bread had to be kept in the communal ovens until it was ready to be retrieved the next day for their meals. Having to cook and bake at the same time with all the other people doing the same thing in the already crowded communal cooking area added an extra burden to the family's daily life.

At one of the D.P. Camps where the family stayed when he was a little older, Arik would come into their room before the Friday evenings approached and ask his mother if he should go and fetch candles for the *Shabbat* meal. His parents simply did not care whether or not they had candles for the dinner. Chaim had already lost his faith in Orthodox Judaism, and Adele, a self-proclaimed atheist, was not interested in playing a role in front of the religious Jewish rabbis by lighting candles as prescribed. Independent-minded in her thinking, she resisted conforming to the views of others around her. Chaim was similar in that regard, and Arik picked up on that aspect later on from both his parents. However, if their son wanted candles for the *Shabbat* dinner, then he could have them. The Jewish elders, who organized the school system at the D.P. Camps, also made sure that candles were available free for the taking, and Arik knew exactly where to go to fetch them.

Adele noted that, from early on, Arik was the only one in the family who had a religious bent and a sense of the spiritual in his nature. None of her other children did. Even as a young child, Arik could not help but wonder why his parents did not practice or observe any of the Jewish traditions in their daily life the way some other Jews did at the D.P. Camp. He dared not ask them, as it was an unspoken rule that their religious belief or lack thereof was not a subject they would openly discuss with him. Although Chaim was in no frame of mind to teach his son anything about the religious rituals and their significance, Arik, surrounded by other practicing Jews at such close proximity, nevertheless had the opportunity to learn and absorb the meanings of the various feasts and Jewish traditions.

A couple living in the same building, apparently with no children, took a liking to this young boy and, from time to time, invited him to eat and spend time with them. From this couple, Arik learned the importance of honoring the *Shabbat* by lighting candles at least eighteen minutes before sundown on Friday to mark the beginning of the Sabbath day. For all intents and purposes, the Jewish day began at six o'clock in the evening. Light from the candles symbolized the peace and tranquility of the Sabbath day. It was also meant to enhance the enjoyment of the food on the table. Stumbling around in the dark would take away from the tranquility in the home, and eating in the dark would not bring out the full appreciation of the food. The symbolisms captivated Arik's keen, young mind, enabling him to gain an understanding of the reasons behind the rituals.

Two candles on the *Shabbat* table denoted the dual commandments of God to both remember and to keep the Sabbath, plus an additional candle for each child in the household. A glass of real Jewish fermented wine, the fruit of the vine, also graced the table. It was accompanied by a minimum of two whole loaves of *challah* bread, a kind of braided bread enriched with eggs. The two loaves represented the double portion of manna provided by God for the ancient Israelites in their preparation for observing the *Shabbat* in the desert. In the Jewish tradition, it was the woman's role to light the candles, after which she would wave her hands over them, welcoming in the Sabbath. Covering her eyes with her hands so as not to see the candles before reciting the blessing, she would then remove them from her eyes and look at the candles, thus completing the *mitzvah*, or the ritual, of lighting them.

It was during one of the *Shabbat* meals with this couple that Arik got to taste real Jewish wine for the very first time. As he spent time with them, he grew to respect Judaism and embraced his religious heritage. Sometime later, Arik was saddened not to see them around the building any more. He did not know if the couple had moved away to their new country or had been transferred to another D.P. Camp.

Ulm: Setting the Stage for the Future

Gradually, as more and more Jewish refugees received immigration papers to depart for their new countries, the D.P. Camps correspondingly started to dwindle in size. When Israel became established as an independent nation in May 1948, multitudes of stateless Jews were finally allowed to make their way to *Eretz Yisrael*. With the exodus of so many families, some camps became too small to justify operating on their own. The Allied Forces proceeded to combine the remaining refugees from many different camps into fewer smaller camps, thereby allowing the vacated camps to close down. For the remaining families, the selection of their next D.P. Camp destination was often quite arbitrary. This cycle continued for a number of years until eventually the last of the refugees had gone. As such, in the nearly five years that Arik's family lived in West Germany, they ended up staying in a total of six different D.P. Camps.

After a few years in Hofgeismar, the Fruchtenbaums were transferred to a D.P. Camp in the center of the beautiful city of Ulm, where they remained for about nine months. Of all the D.P. Camps they had stayed in, this one stood out as the nicest. For a refreshing change of pace from their daily routine during the summer months, the family was able to go swimming in the Danube River, the camp being conveniently situated only two blocks away. Adele was sorry to leave that camp.

Although Chaim had turned his back on his faith and no longer believed in God, some part of him sensed that it was his duty to pass onto his first-born son the faith and traditions that he had been taught. He reasoned that it would be up to Arik himself to decide what to do with this faith later on, but it was up to him as the father to teach his son the Scriptures at that time. Reading from his Hebrew Bible, Chaim would translate it into either Yiddish or Polish while instructing Arik. Whenever he had any spare time from his photography work, Chaim also took the opportunity to train him. They would frequently go out for long walks in the countryside or wherever they could be alone. Chaim first began by teaching Arik stories from the *Tanakh*. Having studied the Bible intensively in Hebrew during his own training in Poland before the war, he recounted the stories to Arik from memory, all the while interpreting them orally for him.

While they roamed the countryside together, Arik not only learned the *Tanakh*, but also caught glimpses into his family's history and heritage within the ultra-Orthodox Jewish community. It appeared that his paternal great-grandfather, Baruch Simchah Fruchtenbaum, was a leader of a local subdivision of the *Ger Chasidim* in Pultusk, Poland, a division of the *Chasidim*, an ultra-Orthodox sect of Judaism. Apparently, his great-grandfather, in the role of a *rebbe*, had exerted much influence and authority over the daily aspects of life in their Jewish community.

Arik was awestruck by the rigorous training that his great-grandfather and his father had to undergo, in order to prepare for their leadership role. It seemed that by the time Baruch Simchah was thirteen years old, he had already memorized the *Torah*, or the "Books of the Law," in Hebrew.[3] An astoundingly comprehensive and accurate level of Scripture memory was required. This vast knowledge was to serve as a platform for his lifelong study of the rabbinic teachings and traditions regarding the interpretation of the Scriptures and the Mosaic Law. Hence, his entire understanding of the *Tanakh* was shaped and determined by these rabbinic writings from centuries past. Because his interpretation was purely by rote and totally controlled and predetermined by Jewish tradition, it left him no room to read a text of Scripture and plainly hear what it was actually saying. For this reason, even though Baruch Simchah Fruchtenbaum knew the *Tanakh* in detail, he was never able to see how the prophecies concerning the Messiah were fulfilled in the person of Jesus.

Arik's great-grandparents initially had twelve children, but two had died shortly after birth. Their first-born son, Arik's grandfather, Yitzchak Meir, was born in the year 1897. Unlike the first-born sons of previous generations, Yitzchak Meir was at odds with the strictness of the ultra-Orthodox sect and rebelled against all Jewish religious traditions. Finding the training overly rigorous and not wanting to spend his entire life in the role of a *rebbe* of the Jewish community, he left Pultusk in his late teens to live and study in Warsaw. With a deep passion for music, Yitzchak Meir focused on the violin and mandolin. Aside from his study of music, he spent countless hours playing the violin by an open window in his rented upstairs room. At dusk, waves of exquisite, melodious notes, reverberating from the strings of his instrument, floated through the air, drawing the Jews from the neighborhood to congregate beneath his window to listen. He was a virtuoso, playing beautifully with deep feeling and heartfelt emotion, his expressive music often tinged with an inexplicable melancholy. Each intoxicating note beckoned the hearts of the listeners, stirring in them echoes of nostalgia and longing. The poignancy of the enchanting music resonated in their ears even long after he had finished playing, evoking within them an intense yearning for their Promised Land.

---

[3] The Torah encompasses the five Books of Moses.

Shortly after arriving in Warsaw, Yitzchak Meir met a young woman, a seamstress, who bore him a son, Chaim. In his early teens, Yitzchak Meir had fallen ill with scarlet fever. The lack of proper food intake, resulting from the hard economic times, contributed to the long drawn-out effects of his illness in subsequent years. In addition, he later also developed an angina heart disease. Yitzchak Meir died of a sudden heart attack when his baby boy, Chaim, was barely two years old and he himself only in his early twenties.

It was Yitzchak Meir's wish that his son be raised in the Fruchtenbaum family. This meant that now including Chaim, Arik's great-grandparents had a total of thirteen children, three of whom had already passed away. Thus, Chaim grew up in the same household among the other nine children, who were technically his aunts and uncles, most of them older and one or two younger. He was treated as a sibling rather than a nephew, and his grandfather, Baruch Simchah Fruchtenbaum, became his father figure.

As was customary in that stratum of Jewish society, it fell upon Chaim, as the first-born son of his generation, to be groomed to follow in his grandfather's footsteps. Except for his apprenticeship in photography, Chaim spent all his time in his younger days studying nothing but Scripture, Jewish tradition, and Jewish law. He was destined to prepare for a leadership role in a local subdivision of the *Ger Chasidim* in Pultusk upon the death of his grandfather. Chaim had not even reached his teens, when his grandfather died from a burst appendix on the 21st of September 1931. That year, *Yom Kippur*, the holiest day of the Jewish calendar, happened to land on the same day.

The training undertaken by Chaim was extremely rigorous, particularly in the memorizing of the *Tanakh*. His interpretation of Scripture was likewise prescribed by the rules of the ancient rabbis, who derived their knowledge from the long line of followers of the teachings of the Pharisees from the New Testament times. Therefore, Chaim, too, was never able to see all the passages pertaining to Jesus as the promised Jewish Messiah, *Yeshua Ha'Mashiach*.

As Arik listened to his father recount some of the family's history, he was impressed by the heritage bestowed upon the first-born son of each succeeding generation of the Fruchtenbaum family, their position of religious authority in the Jewish community and the extent of Scripture knowledge acquired. More importantly, hearing his father tell stories from the *Tanakh* instilled in Arik a deep love for the Bible that never left him. The stories challenged his imagination, fed his keen, young mind, and planted in him a strong desire to learn more.

Chaim seized every opportunity to instruct his first-born son with Bible stories, drawing analogies from them as lessons to apply to their daily life. On one such occasion, as they were walking alongside some railroad tracks in town, a freight train transporting carloads of massive logs passed by. Immediately, Chaim pointed out that there was a person in the *Tanakh* who was endowed with unusual physical strength and began recounting the story of Samson in the Old Testament.

All of Arik's early knowledge of Scripture came from his father alone. Gifted with an excellent memory, he remembered conversations verbatim, making Scripture memory a breeze for him. Enthusiastic about what he had learned, he was eager to share his knowledge with the other children at the D.P. Camps. One summer, when he was only about five years old, Arik taught his first few Bible lessons to a small group of young Jewish children gathered around him under a tree. He was simply repeating what his father had taught him, but that was still more than what the other children knew.

Later on, when Arik attended a Jewish school in one of the other D.P. Camps, he found that he was indeed well ahead of his peers. Not possibly able to foresee the potential far-reaching effects of his son's training, Chaim had unknowingly laid the foundation and set the stage for Arik's future lifework. Though Chaim would never take credit for what he had done, Arik's deep-seated passion for God's Word and much of what he later believed owed their origins to those early days, when his father would take him on a walk saying, "Arik, come. I'll tell you a story from the Bible." The teaching and instructions continued even as they were transferred from one D.P. Camp to another over the next few years.

WHILE STILL LIVING AT THE D.P. CAMP IN ULM, a seemingly innocuous incident occurred, which proved to be the hinge of a major turning point in Arik's life some years later. A German Lutheran minister, Theophil Burgstahler, accompanied by his teenage daughter, Hanna, was serving as a missionary to the Jews in Ulm, in addition to the work at his local congregation. Their main function at that time was to provide humanitarian aid by distributing clothing to the newly arrived Jewish refugees. In concert with their practical help, they looked for opportunities to provide a Bible where needed and to evangelize the Jews.

At that time, Theo was associated with the ABMJ, or the American Board of Missions to the Jews (years later renamed Chosen People Ministries), headquartered in New York City. Through the ABMJ Hamilton Branch in Ontario, Canada, Theo received shipments of clothing and food packages to distribute. As the need was very great, he put in a request for additional boxes of clothing. More precious were the New Testaments in Yiddish that were sent to him from the headquarters. Theo and his co-workers cried with tears of gratitude, when many Jews opened up their hearts to their work, and demands for Bibles increased.

When the Fruchtenbaums first arrived at the D.P. Camp in Ulm, it was from Theo and Hanna that they received their clothing. Having initiated contact with the family, Theo and Hanna befriended them during the time that they stayed in Ulm and visited them several times, conversing with Adele, who spoke German. On one occasion, Theo learned that the family had applied to immigrate to the United States. On that particular day, he just happened to have with him an issue of the October 1949 edition of a Messianic Jewish magazine called *The Chosen People*, published by the ABMJ in New York City.

Printed on the bottom of the cover was the address of the ABMJ headquarters in Manhattan, New York. Theo tore off the cover and gave it to Adele, advising her to contact this organization when the family got to New York City. Since she spoke no English at that time, it made more sense to give her only the cover rather than the entire magazine. Theo indicated that the people at the address would be able to help her family. Not quite understanding the exact nature of this organization, Adele simply assumed that it provided assistance to newly arrived Jewish immigrants to the United States. So, she carefully folded up the magazine cover and put it away for safekeeping.

No one could have predicted that, through this magazine cover given without much forethought, the seeds of truth were planted, which would eventually change the direction of Arik's future in a major way. These seeds were sown during a period in his life, when he was being trained and disciplined in the study of the *Tanakh*—at a time when his relationship with his father was at its happiest. Sadly, those same seeds also set the stage that led to the future estrangement between father and son. Only a sovereign and providential God could have foreknown what lay ahead for Arik and how an apparently inconsequential detail in their daily life at the D.P. Camp could one day so dramatically impact the course of his life.

Long Wait for Approval

Over the following few years, while waiting for their immigration papers to come through for the United States, Arik's family was moved from one D.P. Camp to the next, mostly in the American-occupied zone. During their stay at the D.P. Camp in Gabersee near Munich in southern Germany, Adele gave birth in early 1950 to a sweet, little baby girl, Margaret, at an external German hospital in town. After about a year in Gabersee, when the Jewish refugees there decreased rapidly in number, they were relocated several more times to D.P. Camps in Lechfeld, Föhrenwald, and finally, Bremerhaven.

From the outset, Chaim knew that the application process for immigration to the United States would take longer and be more difficult than for other countries. However, he had not anticipated just how involved and tedious the requirements would be, nor could he have foreseen another complication that arose, which was likely to delay their approval even further. During the initial application process to the United States, the American representative filling out the paperwork mistakenly wrote down the year of Arik's birth as 1944 instead of 1943. Once the error was made, it was almost impossible to get it corrected without a lot more time-consuming bureaucracy and paperwork, inevitably leading to an even longer waiting period for their immigration approval. For this pragmatic reason, Chaim and Adele were reluctant to pursue the correction at that time. Thus, the incorrect birth year of 1944 stayed on Arik's documents until it was rectified some fifteen years later. In the interim, he remained one year younger on paper than his actual age.

While Chaim frequently went into town to take photos on the streets, Adele spent most of her time at the camp itself, busy with the care of their three children, particularly the two younger ones. When Chaim was back at the camp, their social life consisted of getting together in the evenings with other refugees for dinner. Adele would cook the family meals at the communal kitchen and bring the food back to their room. Their friends would do likewise, and they would combine their food to eat together around the same table while sharing the latest news.

The main preoccupation of the Jewish refugees centered on the immigration process. News of any sort traveled quickly through the D.P. Camps, mainly by word-of-mouth, especially where HIAS, the Hebrew Immigration Aid Society, was concerned. Because of the sheer numbers of stateless Jews needing new identity papers and certificates, the paperwork was at times very slow in coming through. Often, Chaim and Adele and their friends sat around the table for long hours into the night, speculating about the future, exchanging a repertoire of stories, news, and opinions of any recent events or developments.

While the younger ones went to sleep, Arik would stay up late, unobtrusively listening from a corner of the room to the adults talking in muffled voices. He silently watched their body language and paid careful attention to his father from whom he derived many of his survival skills for later on in life. The adults became so absorbed in their conversation that they lost track of time and forgot that Arik was still awake. The dinner get-togethers only broke up when the flame from the last of the leftover *Shabbat* candles would slowly dim until it disappeared into the puddle of melted wax, leaving a swirl of delicate smoke that filled the room with a burning scent. Perhaps it was from those habitual late nights at the D.P. Camps that Arik became a natural night owl later on.

All kinds of stories were circulating wildly around the D.P. Camps about the strict stipulations and stringent requirements of the American rules. Chaim had heard that if people sneezed, coughed, or showed even the slightest outward sign of deviating from the healthy norm, they might not pass the physical test and their immigration application could risk being rejected by the U.S. authorities. It seemed that the United States wanted to accept only healthy people, with no diseases or illnesses. Moreover, the government was worried about communism and other subversive ideologies. Hence, each application was scrutinized and thoroughly screened, in order to sift out anyone that may have had the remotest communist connections or involvement of any sort. This slowed down the already lengthy approval process even further.

Just before her physical exam, Adele had caught a bad cold. Afraid that she would not pass, Chaim plied her with lots of hot tea laced with honey. His valiant efforts backfired on her urine results, when she was called back and questioned how long she had been a diabetic! Stating that she was not, she was asked to submit another urine sample. Thankfully, the retested results showed that she was indeed not a diabetic. While it was a huge relief that Adele passed her exam, bringing the family one step closer to their goal, there still remained a long wait ahead.

DURING ALL THE WEARISOME YEARS that the Fruchtenbaums spent as stateless Jews, one highlight served to uplift them. Early on, at the D.P. Camp in Hofgeismar, they were thrilled to be reunited temporarily with Chaim's sister, Chumah. When Chaim decided to escape from Poland with his little family in 1946, his surviving siblings did not follow him right away. Although they were all persuaded about the dangers of remaining in the country, some continued to stay on just a little longer in the hopes that perhaps they could make a life for themselves in Lodz. Poland was their homeland where they had their roots, and it was hard for them to leave for good. However in the ensuing years, one by one, each of Chaim's siblings did take necessary measures to flee from the country.

It was while Chumah was en route to Israel, still known as the British Mandate of Palestine, that she and her husband, Reuben, and their little daughter, Ruthie, ended up in Germany for several weeks at the same D.P. Camp in Hofgeismar where Arik's family was staying. Chaim was overjoyed to see Chumah, who shared news of her other siblings back in Poland. For Arik, she was, for all intents and purposes, his auntie, and Ruthie his little cousin. Chumah cooked for the young ones every day, looking after their needs, while Adele got a little break from her routine. With an age gap of just under two years between them, Arik and Ruthie battled with each other over their things with unusual rivalry. Decades later, he could still vividly recall that visit.

Chumah's detour in Germany came to an end all too soon, and after a reluctant farewell, she and her family left to make their way to the British Mandate of Palestine. They were rerouted to southern France to be detained for many months at another D.P. Camp in the city of Marseilles. Eventually in August 1948, they arrived in *Eretz Yisrael*. There, she was able to reunite with Yehoshua, who had escaped years earlier from Poland at the height of World War II. By the end of 1950, most of the rest of the surviving family members, including Chankah and Genya with their own respective families, managed to flee from Poland in one manner or another to Israel. After staying behind in Poland for several more years, Yaakov, the last remaining sibling, and his wife also eventually joined them in 1957.

Among the surviving siblings, Chaim was the only one who opted to immigrate to the United States. Surmising that life in Israel may be more tumultuous and difficult in the initial years, he believed that the U.S. held more promise for a better life. However, with each passing year at the D.P.

Camps, he grew more and more restless and increasingly perplexed at the complicated U.S. bureaucratic process. His patience and perseverance were all the more tried, when he heard about the multitudes of Jewish refugees getting their approval to immigrate to other countries of their choice in far less time. It was discouraging to keep waiting year after year, suspended in limbo, uncertain about their future prospects, not knowing when or if their application to the United States would be approved. HIAS did their best to keep the family informed of the progress of their paperwork as the prolonged waiting continued.

At one stage, after more than four and a half years, Chaim and Adele were so disheartened that they nearly gave up. They seriously considered abandoning their application to the United States, in order to look into requirements for other countries. Chaim's determination to pursue the approval began to slowly wane as the seemingly interminable waiting period dragged on. After nearly five years, just as they were about to redirect their course, their immigration papers to the United States came through.

PART II

~ *Freedom* ~

If ye abide in My word,
then *are ye truly My disciples;*
and ye shall know the truth, and the truth shall make you free.

(John 8:31b-32)

As the ship pulled away from the harbor of Bremerhaven on the 10th of April 1951, the Fruchtenbaum family was at last on the cusp of leaving behind their stateless refugee status to embark on a journey across the Atlantic to begin their new life in America. Close to five years had been spent at the various D.P. Camps. At times, they experienced discouraging moments, and their hopes had faltered. Yet they persevered, hoping upon hope that they would be granted entry to the United States. Now, this long-awaited day had finally arrived. They were on their way to a new homeland, a place where they had heard that the streets were "paved with gold."

Due to the huge number of passengers listed for departure from the same port, the family had to stay for three weeks at the D.P. Camp in Bremerhaven until it was their turn to board their designated ship. The only money that Chaim possessed was the sum of fifty U.S. dollars, exchanged on the black market from earnings he had carefully squirreled away over the years, doing his photography work. Carrying just a few pieces of luggage containing their meager, second-hand clothing, the family finally stepped onto the ship. As the sound of the horn blared forth and the gangplanks were raised, they could sense the relief and excitement of the crowds who, like them, had looked forward for so many years to this promising day.

Their ship, alongside scores of other vessels in those days, was once an old cargo freighter transformed to double as a troopship to carry soldiers across the ocean to fight in the war. Now, it operated as a refugee ship to transport Jewish displaced persons to the United States. As the vessel slowly steered its way up the Weser River toward the open sea, a hush gradually fell over the crowds. Standing there on the deck, lost in their own thoughts, they watched the land recede into the distance, their emotions pierced with a pang of melancholy. Dawning on them was the realization that they were leaving their European mother continent behind for good, probably never to return again. It was sobering and surreal in many ways, as if witnessing their own past fading into oblivion.

Converted to hold several thousand soldiers at one time for ocean crossings during the war, the ship was now packed to full capacity, crowded with refugees, young and old. There were no facilities or quarters to fit a whole family together. The limited number of cabins was reserved only for the aged and mothers with small children. Adele and the two younger children, Eddie and Margaret, were assigned to a small cabin to be shared with an elderly

Russian lady. Chaim and Arik, along with the other men, were relegated to an enormous space on the lower level of the ship, crowded with no partitions, to sleep on hammocks wherever they could find a free spot.

As soon as the ship reached the open sea, Adele fell ill. Succumbing to seasickness, she took to bed in her cabin where she remained for most of the voyage. Arik, too, felt seasick almost immediately, but staying on the lower level of the ship closer to the water seemed to help lessen the swaying motion. Fumes and smells emitting from the large deck vents caused further nausea, when standing downwind on the platform. The Atlantic crossing would take ten days to reach the eastern shores of the United States. The voyage was long and rough, especially for Arik, who was a little over seven and a half years of age at that time. Only toward the end of the ten days did he get used to the motion of the waves. On the other hand, his two younger siblings and his father all felt fine throughout the entire journey.

Everyone on board was required to do basic work of one kind or another on the ship. However, Adele was simply too seasick to be able to do anything, except to lie down. Those who occupied cabins were expected to keep their own quarters swept and cleaned. The women were assigned to help in the kitchen, and the men were given an assortment of clean-up duties on the deck, in the galley, or in the engine room. Mealtimes were organized by shifts. The food was good, but had to be eaten in a hurry to make room for the next shift. Arik tasted his first orange ever, while traveling on the old freighter. The sweet, tangy fruit burst into myriads of juicy morsels, tickling his tongue. It was delicious!

The remainder of the time was theirs to spend either resting or congregating on the deck, exchanging stories of what they had heard about the new land that was an ocean's crossing away. Fleeting moments of fear dissolved into persistent hope in a kind of suspended reality aboard the confines of the old freighter sailing upon the vast open waters. Their dreams of a new life roamed freely in their imaginations, disconnected from their previous earthbound lives and not yet tainted by the hardships they were soon to face. With each rising dawn, they came one day closer to reaching their new homeland, which they had been reassured to be a safe haven for Jewish refugees.

As the ship slowly made its way around the southeastern coast of England, the people caught a glimpse of the White Cliffs of Dover. The only other event that broke the monotony on board was when the ocean liner, the Queen Mary, sailed past with impressive speed in the same direction. It would reach

America in far less time, within only a few days. Equipped with modern engines and expensive state-of-the-art furnishings, the luxury liner was designed to carry wealthy and prominent passengers on their way to vacation or business meetings in America. It certainly projected a marked contrast to the old troopship with destitute refugees on board.

On the tenth day of their long ocean voyage, the passengers could make out a tiny speck of land appearing yonder in the distance. They craned their necks, pressing against the railings to catch a better glimpse of what would be their new homeland. By then, Adele had mostly recovered from her seasickness, so she was able to join the others on the deck. The United States of America was finally within their sight. As the ship approached the Statue of Liberty upon entering Manhattan's harbor, the refugees were filled with relieved exhilaration and eager anticipation, mingled with a tinge of fear and apprehension.

Their hope of a new life of freedom and safety in a democratic country was about to turn into reality. At the same time, they knew that they would have to face the unknown in a world where everything, including the language, was strange and unfamiliar to them. After having escaped with their lives, they were destitute, with nothing but their meager belongings and the clothes on their backs. They would have to start from scratch and build a new life. Their emotions swung the entire pendulum, oscillating from unshakable hope to utter despair. Was this really a country where their dreams could come true? Later, they would learn from experience that the streets of America were not "paved with gold" as they had heard before arriving. However, opportunities did abound, if they were willing to work hard at realizing their own dreams.

It was thus on the 20th of April 1951 that Arik's family finally reached their new homeland. Stepping off the gangplank onto American soil for the very first time, they were ready to build a new life in a free country where they were no longer in danger of being killed or persecuted because of their Jewish background. There was just one last step left for the stateless Jewish refugees to take before they could be considered legal residents of the United States of America—the processing of their paperwork through the Special Immigration Quarters at the entry port.[4]

---

[4] Decades later, having heard that the names of the refugees entering the United States through Ellis Island would be commemorated on the Wall of Honor at that site, Eddie Fruchtenbaum sent off a generous, monetary donation to the Ellis Island Foundation to

HIAS workers were on hand to help with the registration, as no one among the refugees could speak or read any English. Many forms with personal details had to be filled out. The wait for their turn took more than twenty-four hours, which was very exhausting for the children. Meanwhile, food and water were provided for the families in the waiting area. When it came time to process the Fruchtenbaum family for entry, they experienced just how foreign the country and the language were and realized how much of an adjustment they would have to make in their new life in America. It felt as though they had been catapulted into an alien world, where even filling out a basic form appeared to be an insurmountable challenge to them.

As the registration continued, the question arose regarding the Americanizing of their names. Chaim's name, being very unfamiliar to the Americans, thus became Henry. As far as Arik's name was concerned, HIAS consulted with his parents, who gave their consent for his name to be changed to Arnold. Unfortunately, in the chaos of rushing through the processing of so many refugees at one time, HIAS made an error. Arnold's middle name somehow got dropped off his new registration documents in the United States. This came to his parents' attention only after they had settled in their new country. It would take a number of years before circumstances enabled them to rectify the errors on his paperwork.

AFTER A TAXING AND SEEMINGLY interminable immigration procedure at the port, the refugees were gathered together and taken to their temporary accommodations in a hotel on 34th Street in Manhattan. Each family was assigned to one room, and a miniscule allowance was given to help them get started. Free meals could be eaten at a soup kitchen, but it was located too far from the hotel to be worthwhile for Arnold's family. The cost alone of the roundtrip bus fares three times a day for the five of them would practically

---

have his family's names recorded for posterity. When his mother, Adele, discovered what Eddie had done, she pointed out that they had not entered America through Ellis Island. At that time, Ellis Island was in the last years of the closing-down process and was no longer open for immigration purposes. Instead, the Fruchtenbaum family had entered through another immigration processing center at the harbor in Manhattan. By the time Eddie found out the actual facts of the situation, it was too late. The money had already been donated and could not be retracted, resulting in a financially costly faux-pas for him. Thus to this day, five Fruchtenbaum names appear on the commemorative walls of Ellis Island.

wipe out the meager allowance they were given. So, Henry—as Chaim would be called from then on—with his enterprising spirit, went out and bought bread and other items that they could eat together in their hotel room.

The IRO, or International Refugee Organization, offered a lot of assistance and support to help families find housing and jobs, so that they could settle into their new life as quickly as possible. The organization gave Henry an address located on another side of town, where he could go and take a look at an apartment for rent. No other information was provided. Since he spoke no English and had no clue about directions, he soon got lost. He had to retrace his steps and start all over again to find his way to a different part of the city called Spanish Harlem.

Although Henry did not like the arrangement of the shared set-up with another family, his choices were limited to the type of places he could afford at that time. The upstairs of the apartment was already occupied by a couple who moved out almost immediately after the Fruchtenbaum family moved in. Apparently, they had found a more suitable place elsewhere for themselves. A lady took the space upstairs, which included the bedroom and bathroom, while Arnold's family occupied the living room and dining area downstairs. However, the bathroom upstairs and the kitchen facilities downstairs had to be shared between the two parties.

For the first few months of their new life in America, the Fruchtenbaums experienced many daunting challenges and changes. Everything was so foreign to them, so different from the way things were done in Europe. It was very hard for them at first, as they could not speak the language and had to depend upon others to help them with even the most mundane things. Thankfully, the IRO continued to provide practical assistance to help them integrate into their new culture and surroundings.

As soon as they moved into their place in Spanish Harlem, Henry and Adele took up the opportunity to attend night classes to study English, which were offered free of charge. Although they both made strides in their basic spoken English, it was Adele who worked at mastering the language. She was determined to become fluent in English and to feel comfortable communicating in it the way she did in Russian, Yiddish, Polish, and German.

It was difficult for Henry to find a job at first, especially in photography, because of his lack of knowledge of English. Unlike in Europe, there was no work for him on the streets of New York City. People here were not in need of photographs for documents the way the Europeans were. He felt frustrated and discouraged during his interviews, when the prospective employers would point to his inability to comprehend instructions in English on how to get the job done. They claimed that it would take too long for them to explain everything to him. Although he eventually obtained a basic understanding of the spoken language, Henry continued to struggle to communicate well in it. He never quite grasped the written language. After countless attempts, he finally found a job at a printing company, running a machine that cut labels for soft drink bottles and also for tags used by clothing manufacturers.

To help the children grasp some of the new language, Adele bought second-hand comic books from the corner store, particularly those featuring Mickey Mouse. It was quite straightforward for her to follow along with Mickey's adventures through the comic books and match the words to the pictures, in order to teach them to her children. Arnold was already familiar with the characters from having watched the cartoon movies of Mickey Mouse at the D.P. Camps. Little by little, they all began to assimilate some of the language.

Living in a predominantly Hispanic neighborhood during those first few months in America, Arnold came face-to-face with many new situations that he had never experienced before. Having spent nearly five years in the safety of the D.P. Camps in West Germany among Jews who spoke Yiddish, he had not been exposed to any other social environment. Here in Spanish Harlem, the majority of the neighborhood children spoke Spanish to one another on the streets. At first, without realizing the difference, Arnold began to pick up phrases in Spanish, thinking that it was the language of his new country!

Henry was discovering that there existed unspoken but distinctive boundaries, which separated his family from the other ethnic communities around them. Arnold personally experienced this reality quite early on. As a young boy with a keen mind in a new country, he was curious about many different things. Before coming to America and living in Spanish Harlem, he had never come across a Hispanic person, nor had he ever heard the Spanish language spoken. Whenever Arnold stepped across the street, the other children chased after him, bullied him, called him all kinds of names and punched him here and there. Bewildered as to why he was often beaten up by the other children, Arnold kept wondering what he had done wrong. All he did was walk to the other side of the street! He could not understand why there was so much open hostility against him.

When Henry noticed what was happening, he started looking for alternative housing. He wanted his children to be around English-speaking neighbors.

The shared living arrangement was not ideal for his family either, so he decided that as soon as he found a steady job and could afford to rent a place just for his family, he would move.

Henry and Adele quickly learned to network among the other Jewish refugees. Congregating regularly on Sunday afternoons at a park on the Lower East Side, they exchanged news and other useful information regarding apartments or possible job openings. Meeting with the other Jewish immigrants was also a way for the family to socialize and help one another to get acquainted with the different customs of their new country. Although the initial period was hard on them, the freedom that they, as Jews, found in America was worth all the long years of waiting for their immigration approval to come through.

Adjusting to Life in Brooklyn

Life for Arnold's family during the first few years in America was not easy, and adjustments had to be made in all areas, both as a family and as individuals. At the D.P. Camps back in West Germany, Arnold used to see his father very often during the daytime. Here in New York City, he got to see him only in the evenings, and even then, his father had to leave frequently to attend night classes to study English. While at first Henry continued to teach his son the Bible at night, those times grew more and more sporadic as the months went by. Eventually, the lessons stopped altogether, and Arnold had even less contact with his father, except at the dinner table. Gone were the carefree and happy days when father and son went on motorcycle rides through the fields outside the D.P. Camps, or when they took long walks in the countryside. Henry's main concern was how to provide sufficiently for his wife and three young children. The stresses of striving to earn a living to make ends meet contributed to his general unavailability to his family. However, Arnold's love for the Bible never waned. He continued to exhibit a deep spiritual interest in the Scriptures, retaining all that his father had taught and instilled in him in the past.

After about three months of living in the shared set-up in Spanish Harlem, Henry found a place in Brooklyn just for the family. It was a two-bedroom apartment on the third floor of a building located on Fulton Street in Brownsville. The couple that owned the building also operated a small supermarket on the ground floor, while living above it on the second floor. Inexperienced in the housing market, Henry discovered over time that their monthly rent was higher than average. Some time later, he realized that they were living in a predominantly African-American neighborhood, his family and their landlords being the only white people on the block.

Here on Fulton Street, Arnold was fascinated to see other children whose skin was so brown and who looked so different from the children he had known back at the D.P. Camps in Europe. Unfortunately, he again learned the hard way that the other neighborhood children simply did not accept him. What he did not realize was that in this area of Brooklyn, there were territorial divisions controlled by a number of gangs. Crossing the street to the other side meant an actual breach of an invisible boundary. In the eyes of the street gangs, Arnold was treading into a completely different neighborhood, which was off limits to him, being a Jewish boy.

It was in the midst of this difficult situation on Fulton Street that Arnold started school in September 1951. He attended the first grade at PS-156, a nearby public school in Brownsville. With the ongoing conflicts in the neighborhood, it was an unsettling experience for Arnold to begin his early education as the only Jewish boy among the African-American children. He struggled in school initially due to his lack of English, but within a few months, he began to pick up the language and understood enough to be able to communicate.

Still, on the playground during recesses, he refrained from talking and inter-acting with the other children. Although Arnold's lack of communication caused his teacher some concern, she thought that perhaps he was just too shy to try out his new language. Apparently, she had no idea that the real reason behind Arnold's reticence was because his schoolmates did not want to play with a Jewish boy.

In addition to the mixture of strong accents when he ventured to speak in English, Arnold had trouble with spelling. The teacher talked to Adele about helping her son learn the correct spelling of words. This perplexed Adele, as she barely knew any English herself, apart from the alphabet and a few basic conversational phrases. However, the teacher assured her that she did not need to know the language in order to help Arnold learn how to spell. She simply needed to hold a sheet of paper with the correct spelling of the words in front of her and just match those words to the ones Arnold wrote out. That way, she could check his spelling. So, Adele carefully followed these instructions, which appeared to work. Arnold was soon spelling correctly, and his vocabulary began to grow.

Adele employed the same methodology for her two younger children to help them with their spelling once they started school. Margaret turned out to be quite a reader from a very young age even before she entered school. At first, Adele thought that Margaret might have been remembering the words orally from the Mickey Mouse comic books, but she was actually picking up the individual written words. Obviously, Margaret did not have any trouble in school with spelling.

By helping her children learn to spell correctly, Adele found that her own English was improving and expanding along the way. Wanting to make sure that the children adapted quickly to their new life in America, Henry and Adele decided that as soon as they themselves could converse in the new language, they would speak to their children exclusively in English at home.

In the public school system, Arnold was initially placed in a lower grade than the one he would have been in had he possessed fluency in English. Hence, at the age of seven going on eight, he was older than the other children in the first grade. Once he got past the first few months of struggle, he rapidly acquired more skills in correctly spelling words in English. Stimulated by his new knowledge, he demonstrated tremendous progress. One month before the school year ended, Arnold's English improved enough to be bumped up to the second grade. He completed the last month of the second grade before the summer vacation started, in essence having skipped most of the second grade except for the tail end. He stayed at the same school through the fourth grade.

On the streets, the perpetual abuse and bullying from the other children in the neighborhood showed no signs of abating. Arnold became aware that even in his new home country, one's skin color or one's ethnic background made a considerable difference whether a person was accepted or excluded. He observed that it influenced what happened to a person in social settings and how one was treated. At such an early age, he had already begun to experience firsthand the antagonism and animosity displayed toward him for being a Jew. The attitude of racism and prejudice against his people, prevalent even among young school-age children, came as a real eye-opener for Arnold.

Noting that the situation on Fulton Street was not conducive for his children and preferring to live among other Jewish people, Henry moved the family to another part of Brownsville in Brooklyn to a place on Herzl Street. At that time, this area was quite densely populated with Jews. In the neighborhood of Herzl Street, Arnold found himself surrounded by other Jewish families as he had been at the D.P. Camps in West Germany, so he felt more at ease there.

The Jewish children from the neighborhood were a nice, friendly, secular bunch. They often included Arnold in many of the street games they played outside, one being stickball, a game adapted from the rules of baseball. A broom handle or a similar kind of stick substituted as the bat, and a high-bouncing ball, such as a tennis ball, was used instead of a hard ball. Manhole covers counted as the bases, and walls of buildings or street curbs served as foul lines. The children were very resourceful. Arnold made one good friend, a young Jewish boy named Stanley Klein,[5] who lived in the same neighborhood. The two had many fun times together.

At home, Arnold was an obedient child. Being the oldest, he sometimes got stuck with the task of babysitting his two younger siblings while his parents were out. An age gap of over four years between him and Eddie and over six years between him and Margaret meant that they were too young to be his playmates. So, he ended up watching them instead, while they played with each other.

His younger siblings were not always the easiest to look after. One incident proved the pitfalls of being the older brother. Arnold had been babysitting as usual that particular evening. When his parents returned home, they discovered that the valve of the gas radiator had been opened. Much to their fright and panic, the gas had been leaking out, permeating all the rooms. It would have taken only one match to be lit to set the whole apartment aflame. Henry and Adele automatically assumed that Arnold had played with the valve and sternly reprimanded him for his irresponsibility in endangering the lives of everyone in the household. When Arnold claimed innocence and

---

[5] The name has been altered slightly to protect the privacy of the individual.

denied having touched the valve, they did not believe him. His father gave him a long, hard spanking for it.

The beating really hurt, but the physical pain did not match the emotional distress that Arnold felt at being accused of something he honestly had not done. Maybe, it was his little brother who had played with the valve, but if Eddie had done so, he never admitted it. The truth of the matter was that Arnold had certainly done nothing wrong. He felt ostracized and was sorely disappointed that he was not believed.

Ever since the Bible lessons from his father had stopped altogether, Arnold rarely got to have much contact with him. He noticed that his father's moods were often erratic, and his temper flared up from time to time. At the D.P. Camps, Henry was more even-keeled, but here in America, he seemed to have changed rather drastically with his wild mood swings. Arnold seldom got into trouble, but every now and then, he did get spanked on his bottom by his father and at least once or twice, had to suffer through a belting session.

IN THE EARLY YEARS of their new life in Brooklyn, Henry's lack of a good grasp of the English language led to some amusing incidents that could have happened only to recently arrived immigrants. Being by nature somewhat impulsive, combined with his limited English vocabulary and comprehension at the time, he had a tendency to make hasty decisions that did not bring about the desired results. One such instance had to do with their family name. Investigating all possible avenues to come up with ways for his family to integrate more into the mainstream of American society, Henry even went so far as to change their last name. Their family name, Fruchtenbaum, was very unusual and difficult for most people in America to pronounce. So Henry went to the immigration office to inquire about altering the name. Without consulting anyone, his impulsiveness propelled him to file the paperwork to have the family name officially changed from Fruchtenbaum to Fruit.

Only after it was all said and done, did Adele find out about it. When she asked her husband why he had chosen the name, Fruit, he replied that the way the lady at the office pronounced the word, it had sounded so nice that he decided to adopt it. By the time Henry acquired enough English to understand the meanings and connotations of the word, Fruit, he promptly went and got the name reverted back to Fruchtenbaum. However, for about two years, Arnold went by the name of Arnold Fruit, which from time to time elicited teasing bouts from the other children at his school.

Although Henry had a steady job at the label printing company, he found the work of operating the machinery to be very tedious and uninspiring. Nonetheless, he persevered with it, because he needed to support the family. Consequently, his camera lay idle for several years. This long interlude often caused him much inner anguish and self-doubt. In Siberia, Ukraine, and West Germany, he had learned the ropes quickly. He knew how to pull the strings and could easily figure out how things got done, but here in America, he appeared to have fallen into a rut of tedium and ennui. Unable to attain a good grasp of the language, he felt stuck. Boredom seeped in and his self-confidence eroded. Frequent bouts of moroseness and anxiety plunged him harmfully into a dark pit of insecurity and occasional despair.

In contrast to her husband, Adele mastered a fair amount of the basics of English within the first year of their new life in America. She even landed herself a job as an assistant to a professional photographer, who did freelance work for the schools nearby. All those years of assisting Henry in the past had taught her the essentials, and she could now put those skills into good use in Brooklyn. She was thus able to contribute to the family's income through her work, in an effort to help defray some of their living expenses.

The family lived on Herzl Street for about two years, during which the nature of the neighborhood began to change. Many of the Jewish families moved away, and the neighborhood gradually evolved into a predominantly African-American community. The environment became less safe, and conflicts arose once again between Arnold and the other children on the street. This situation precipitated a decision by Henry to move the family out of Brownsville, coinciding with his growing desire to live in a Jewish neighborhood. After some searching, he found a promising place for the family to rent. Located on Blake Avenue in another part of Brooklyn called New Lots, the place consisted of a storefront with an apartment in the back. The opportunity had finally come up for Henry to resume his profession. The storefront opened up the possibility of turning it into a photo studio and film shop. This gave him the impetus to launch his own photography service. At long last, he attained the breakthrough he had wanted in his attempts to get back into his profession. Still speaking halting English, the area suited his work just fine, since he could fall back on his Yiddish there.

To say that New Lots was a Jewish community would have been an understatement. It was so Jewish that the Gentiles called the section Little Israel. This area of Brooklyn also comprised many other separate, ethnically distinct communities, including African-Americans, Italians, Puerto Ricans, Irish, and other white Gentiles all located in the general vicinity nearby. The New Lots community was ninety-nine percent Jewish, with Yiddish widely spoken in the area, especially among the newly arrived immigrants. The Jews even had their own newspaper in Yiddish. Henry felt right at home there, and Arnold once again started to play stickball on the streets with the other Jewish youngsters. Most of the neighborhood children attended the same public school at PS-64 as did Arnold, who by then was in the fifth grade. One time, he was even asked to be in a school play, but because of his heavy accent, he was given the role of Santa's helper, a non-speaking part. Unfortunately, after his family moved to New Lots, he lost contact with his friend, Stanley Klein.

With the photo studio and film shop set up, Henry began in earnest to seek out freelance photography jobs. Three blocks from the storefront was a Roman Catholic church, where he obtained quite a lot of business, taking pictures of children dressed for their first communion. He also sought out work from the Jewish community. A photographer was needed whenever the Jewish families celebrated special occasions, such as weddings and *Bar Mitzvahs*, which they wanted to remember. These traditions were celebrated more for social reasons than for religious beliefs. Most of the Jewish immigrants who came to America were agnostic. Due to the atrocities they suffered during World War II, the majority had lost their faith.

Because the studio and shop did not generate sufficient income, Henry had to continue working at his regular job at the label printing company. To assist her husband at the store, Adele left her job and started taking care of the day-to-day inquiries and administrative functions of the business. Someone had to look after the store when Henry went off-site to carry out his photography shoots, so she filled that role. Her English was much better than Henry's, especially when speaking over the phone, so she handled most of the interfacing with the customers. Having their mother at the storefront also presented an advantage for the children. She was always there when they returned home from school. With the apartment right in the back of the store, they could come to her whenever they needed her for anything.

Since the family's move to Blake Avenue, Arnold was expected to help out at the storefront after school and during weekends. Henry taught him how to function in the darkroom, developing films and making prints. Strict and demanding, he gave very precise instructions, which Arnold was required to follow explicitly. Insisting that there was only one chance to get it right, Henry admonished his son not to make any mistakes. If a roll of film got ruined in the darkroom, the photos could not be replaced. Over time, Arnold learned the tricks of the trade and mastered the techniques of developing good black-and-white photos.

Henry sometimes took Arnold along to his photography shoots at Jewish celebrations and occasionally to assignments at churches. While Arnold was exposed to the Jewish rituals and observed them with interest, he did not comprehend the significance behind them. His father had no interest in explaining the Jewish traditions to him and was not familiar with any of the church rituals, so Arnold simply assisted where he was needed, refraining from asking questions.

When Eddie became old enough, Henry sometimes took him along separately. However, Eddie showed no interest in photography and was too young at the time to work at the storefront. It was Arnold who later took up photography and pursued it as a hobby in a variety of ways in his adulthood.

WHILE LIVING ON BLAKE AVENUE, Adele discovered that she was pregnant again. This would be her first baby to be born in the United States. When the labor pains started and she was preparing to go to the hospital, Arnold informed her that he wanted her to bring home a little African-American baby and that he would like to have another little sister. Apparently, he held no grudges against the African-American children in general, even after having been bullied and beaten up by them. Thus in early 1958, Adele gave birth to a little baby boy, whom they named Arthur.

With the addition of another child to the family, making ends meet became even more of a priority for Henry. As a result, he had even less time for the family, although he still made all the decisions. For the most part, Adele's attitude toward her husband was that of a typical, submissive Eastern European wife who went along with most of his decrees. She never openly argued or opposed him in front of the children. However, being somewhat independently minded, she did challenge him every now and then, by asking him questions about the reasons for his choices.

It was not in Adele's nature to go against her husband in how he disciplined the children. From time to time, Henry would spank them. In general, he was very strict, especially with the boys, instigating many restrictions to which they had to adhere. If they did not obey to the letter, he would discipline them by making the boys get their hair cut much shorter than the length they wanted. It was a way for him to convey to them that since they did not do exactly as he had stipulated, they would have to live with the consequences. Except for one or two occasions, Adele never laid a hand on her children even when they misbehaved. She was always available for them, there to love and nurture them. Arnold recalled her wonderful Eastern European cooking as well as her Jewish dishes, especially her *matzah* ball soup, *gefilte* fish, and a type of Russian-Jewish hamburger. She somehow managed to juggle taking care of the children while still working at the storefront.

Over time, Arnold noticed that the stress of coming to America had taken its toll on his father in more ways than one. Henry frequently displayed a rollercoaster stream of emotions, and his temper became more short-fused and erratic. He flared up in anger much of the time and was often verbally abusive to the children. Berating and belittling them, he constantly put them down. Gradually, the changes in him that were at first imperceptible magnified to the point where Arnold could hardly recognize him as the father he knew back at the D.P. Camps.

Encountering *Yeshua Ha'Mashiach*

In the autumn of 1956, while the Fruchtenbaums were living on Blake Avenue and Arnold had entered the seventh grade, they received an unexpected visit from a very tall Gentile lady, who arrived at the door unannounced. Arnold's parents politely invited her in. Introducing herself as Ruth Wardell, she talked with them for quite some time. During their conversation, she mentioned that she was from the ABMJ, American Board of Missions to the Jews, headquartered on 72nd Street in Manhattan. A new branch had just been opened about a mile from the Fruchtenbaums' residence. A Jewish Christian meeting would be held there, to which Ruth Wardell invited the entire family to attend, including the children. She went on to reveal that she had obtained their name from a card that was given to her by the ABMJ headquarters.

Adele realized that this lady was from the same organization that she had visited several years previously in 1951, soon after the family's arrival in New York City. Once they had settled in their apartment in Brooklyn, she had dug out *The Chosen People* magazine cover that Theo Burgstahler had given to her at the D.P. Camp in Ulm, which she had kept in her purse since October 1949. Figuring that the ABMJ provided assistance to new Jewish immigrants, she mustered up enough courage to take the subway to Manhattan. Once she found her way to the address on the magazine cover, she asked to speak to Dr. Joseph Cohn whose name was printed on the cover. Dr. Cohn happened to be out of the office at the time, so Dr. Daniel Fuchs, who later headed the ABMJ, received her. Unfortunately, they were not able to understand each other. Adele could barely speak any English then, and Dr. Fuchs was unfamiliar with any of her other languages. So, he wrote down her name and address on a three-by-five card, assuring her that she would be contacted as soon as it was feasible. At that time, the ABMJ did not have any workers in the area where the Fruchtenbaums lived, so the card was filed away in the interim. He fully expected a follow-up visit within a few weeks, but that did not happen. It took more than five years before someone got in touch with the family in the form of a cold call by their missionary worker, Ruth Wardell.

Although the ABMJ already had several branches in other parts of New York City, it was not until after mid-1956 that the Mission started up the East New York Branch in a densely Jewish-populated area of Brooklyn. The facilities—offered free of charge for the Mission's use—consisted of two rooms in the church house across the street from the main building of the East End Baptist Church. Meetings were held in the smaller of the two rooms, while the larger one functioned as the fellowship hall where refreshments were served or where the children engaged in their arts and crafts. With no crosses on the walls, the rooms were conducive for the Mission's purpose to reach out to the Jews. Gentiles were discouraged to attend, lest they became distractions or stumbling blocks to the Jews, who wanted nothing to do with the Christians, their hateful "god" Jesus and their crosses.

Three full-time ABMJ workers served at the new station. Kenneth Anderson oversaw the general operations, Eleanor Bullock focused on the women's ministries, and Ruth Wardell led the children's and youth programs. Searching through the ABMJ files collected over the years, the contact addresses of Jewish families within a certain radius of the new branch were pulled out. Soon, workers were dispatched to do visitations, making one-on-one contact with the Jewish people in the community. They extended invitations by going from door to door or by giving out tracts to passers-by on the streets. In that era, cold-call visits were a viable means of outreach. If the workers had to phone up in advance, their proposed visit would more than likely be declined. It was Dr. Daniel Fuchs, who gave Ruth the three-by-five card with the contacts of the Fruchtenbaum family. Updating the details, she visited the next day.

Sitting in the same room, listening to the Gentile lady talk with his parents, Arnold heard the expression, "Jewish Christian," for the very first time. It was used interchangeably with the words, "Hebrew Christian," which apparently was another way of saying the same thing. Arnold could not help but think what a total contradiction in terms that expression was. A person had to be either a Jew or a Christian, but never both simultaneously. In Arnold's mind, anyone who considered himself both a Jew and a Christian at the same time was bound to be some sort of a "schizophrenic"—two opposing personalities inhabiting the same body!

At that time, it was not clear to Arnold whether or not his parents understood the true nature of the organization or much of what the lady was sharing with them. Their English was still not proficient, and Ruth did not speak any of the other languages they knew. However, they did not object, when she extended her invitation to the whole family. She was disarmingly friendly, and as she got up to leave, she made arrangements to pick them up and bring them to the Mission station the following week.

Arnold's curiosity was piqued, and he went along to his first meeting. His two younger siblings, Eddie and Margaret, came with him that evening and so did his mother. Upon arrival, Eddie and Margaret were led to the fellowship hall, where they spent their evening engaging in all kinds of creative arts and crafts. In the meeting room, about twenty-five Jewish people were in attendance. Arnold sat in one of the back rows while his mother sat somewhere nearby to one side, so she could not directly see his face during the presentation.

As the meeting commenced, a gentleman, who introduced himself as Kenneth Anderson, began to present the Messiah in the person of Jesus as depicted in the Old Testament. The more Arnold listened, the more agitated he became. It did not bother him that there were Jews at the meeting discussing Jesus. He had expected as much. After all, many Jews had lost their faith in the God of Abraham, Isaac, and Jacob as a consequence of the Holocaust. When they immigrated to America, perhaps they had so wanted to integrate into the mainstream of the society that some of them even went so far as to adopt the Gentile beliefs in Jesus. However, what really angered

Arnold was that the person leading the meeting had the audacity to use the Jewish Bible, the *Tanakh*, to talk about their Gentile "god" Jesus!

All his life, Arnold had been brought up with the sharp distinction between "us," the Jews, and "them," the Gentiles or Christians. He was taught that the Jews had their own Bible, the *Tanakh* and the Gentiles or Christians had theirs, the New Testament. The Christians believed in their "god" Jesus, who was found in the New Testament, but Jesus was not supposed to be in the *Tanakh*. Nevertheless, here were these Jewish people who kept using the Jewish Bible to talk about this Jesus. What a lot of nerve the organizers had, firstly to invite the Jewish individuals to their Christian meeting and then to claim that their hateful Gentile "god" Jesus was the Jewish Messiah by trying to prove it through the *Tanakh*! It was preposterous!

At the end of the presentation when Arnold regrouped with Ruth Wardell, he had a lot of pointed and probing questions. She was taken aback by this young boy's good grasp of the Hebrew Scriptures and his in-depth, searching questions. Seeing his agitation written so plainly across his face, she could tell that Arnold was in no mood for any discussion and wisely decided not to reason with him. Instead, she simply offered him a challenge. She gave him a New Testament and asked him to take it home to read and see for himself whether or not Jesus fulfilled all the things that were prophesied about Him and did all the things that the Jews expected their Messiah to do. Arnold accepted the Gentile Bible, not because he was open-minded to Miss Wardell's challenge, but because he was inwardly determined to prove, once and for all, that she and the rest of the "schizophrenics" were wrong.

After the family was dropped off at their home, Arnold began to read the New Testament and continued over the following weeks. Adele was not aware that he had been given a New Testament, so he was able to read through it without his parents noticing. What Arnold thought he would be reading compared to what was actually in the text could not have been more divergent. He had been taught that the New Testament was a very Gentile book, full of idolatry, containing descriptions of big church edifices and stained glass windows, with black-robed priests waving incense, bowing down before statues and inciting their people to go kill the Jews in the name of their "god" Jesus. That was the kind of persecution the Jews in Europe had experienced firsthand from those who claimed to be Christians, so Arnold assumed that the instructions to kill the Jews must have come from their Bible. Completely contrary to his preconceived notions, Arnold discovered to his utter amazement that the New Testament was a very Jewish book. The opening line of the Gospel of Matthew immediately caught his attention. It read: *The book of the generation of Messiah Yeshua, the son of David, the son of Abraham.* (Matthew 1:1) It could not get any more Jewish than that! With references to Pharisees, Levites, rabbis, Jewish theological debates, Temple sacrifices, and so on, everything in the book reflected the Jewish way of thinking in its day. It even recounted the various Jewish theological issues that led to the controversies between Jesus and the Pharisees. The theological contents were all quite familiar to Arnold, and the thoroughly Jewish nature of the New Testament intrigued him and captivated his attention.

By the time he finished his reading, the defenses in Arnold's mind had gradually dissolved. He became convinced that this Jesus had to be the Messiah of Israel. If not, then there would be no such thing as a Messiah, something that the Reform Jews had alleged all along. If not, then the Orthodox Jews, including himself, would have been living in a dream world, hoping for something that was never going to happen.

At this point, Arnold had reached what the Jewish missions called "stage one." Jews arriving at this point would be thoroughly convinced that Jesus is their long-awaited Messiah. Yet, they would never take the next step—"stage two," of receiving Him, owning Him, accepting Him on a personal level, and allowing Him to change their lives—due to their fear of what the consequences could entail. They might be kicked out of their homes, rejected by their friends, expelled from the synagogues, divorced by their spouse, or lose their jobs, and be ostracized by the Jewish community at large. In short, they could be thrown out into a strange and unfamiliar Gentile world, about which the Jews had been sufficiently warned in the past. To break through such mental barriers erected in their minds against the Gentiles or Christians would take a monumental effort. Every Jewish person about to enter "stage two" would be confronted with the inevitability of some sort of sacrifice, a troubling prospect often leading to a struggle in that person's heart in making this type of decision—never an easy one for a Jew.

SEVERAL WEEKS ELAPSED after Arnold's first meeting at the ABMJ's branch, before another opportunity came up for him to attend a second time. Meanwhile, he had just celebrated his thirteenth birthday. Although the meetings were held on a weekly basis, Arnold could attend only when a ride was available. The Mission station was located too far for him to walk, and he had no money to take a bus. As arranged, Ruth Wardell came to pick them up. Standing on the street, Arnold felt somewhat reluctant within and hesitated to go. However, not having any good excuses to stay behind, he piled into the car along with Eddie, Margaret, and his mother. Arnold's mind continued to race through all the warnings that he had been taught about the Gentiles or Christians and the consequences of following their "god" Jesus. Now, those same thoughts engulfed him with fear and trepidation as he rode to the meeting.

During their last meeting, Ruth had realized just how poorly prepared she had been to handle Arnold's serious, in-depth seeking. When she got home that night, she immediately pulled out her Isaac Leeser[6] translation of the Hebrew Bible and went to work to collate her answers to his questions. This version had the Hebrew on one side and the English on the other side. It was the most accepted English translation of the Hebrew Bible for the Jewish people. She wanted to be fully prepared for her next meeting with this remarkable, young boy.

Painstakingly, she pored over every messianic prophecy in the Old Testament, comparing the various other Bible translations to the Isaac Leeser translation, and perused the New Testament to highlight the points where Jesus had fulfilled all those prophecies about Himself. While she did her study preparations, Ruth prayed that God would speak to Arnold's heart and also prayed for her ability to communicate the truth, so that he would one day come to faith in *Yeshua Ha'Mashiach*.

Arnold could hardly concentrate and focus his mind on the message being presented at that second meeting. He was not so angry any more and looked forward to sitting down with Miss Wardell to go through his questions. It was astounding to Ruth how someone his age could know so much of the Old Testament Scriptures, Jewish history and traditions, and rabbinic theology and interpretations. According to what she knew of Jewish traditions, Arnold would have been considered very religious and certainly on his way to becoming a *yeshiva bocher*, a rabbinical student in Talmudic studies, and later

---

[6] Isaac Leeser (1806–1868), a devout Jew born in Germany, immigrated to the United States at age seventeen where he became a well-known rabbi. His translation of the *Tanakh* (based on the Masoretic Text) from Hebrew into English in 1853 is commonly known as *The Leeser Bible*. It became the standard Bible for the English-speaking American Jewry.

even a rabbi. At that point, she had no idea about Arnold's religious heritage as the first-born son of his family nor about the Orthodox Jewish teachings he had received from his father. Although Henry no longer believed the teachings to be true, he had conveyed them to his son as truth.

Arnold and Miss Wardell carefully examined the Scriptures to see if Jesus fit the descriptions and expectations concerning the Messiah. First, Ruth brought out the Isaac Leeser translation. She let Arnold verify that the Old Testament was indeed what the Jews considered to be their Bible, the *Tanakh*. Then, she turned to the Old Testament, particularly to Isaiah chapter 53, and together they went from the Old Testament to the New Testament and back again. They went back and forth many times together to study and compare the Scriptures concerning all the teachings about the Messiah. Prophecy after prophecy was revealed to Arnold from the Old Testament:

✿ that the Messiah would come from the seed of the woman (Genesis 3:15);

✿ that He would come from the lineage of Abraham (Genesis 12:3; 18:18);

✿ that He would be from the tribe of Judah (Genesis 49:10);

✿ that He would come from the seed of Isaac (Genesis 17:19; 21:12; 26:2-4)

✿ that He would come from the seed of Jacob (Numbers 24:17, 19);

✿ that He would come from the seed of David (Psalm 132:11, Isaiah 11:10; Jeremiah 23:5 and 33:15);

✿ that He was to be born of a virgin (Isaiah 7:14);

✿ that He was to be born in Bethlehem (Micah 5:2);

✿ that He would be the first-born son (Exodus 13:2);

✿ that He would be God Himself (Isaiah 9:6-7);

✿ that He was to be a prophet like unto Moses (Deuteronomy 18:15);

✿ that He would be rejected by His own people and suffer for their sins (Isaiah 52:13—53:12);

✿ that He would be crucified and His hands and feet would be pierced (Psalm 22:16);

✿ that He would be resurrected (Psalm 16:1-11);

✿ that He would bring salvation to the Gentiles (Isaiah 49:6);

✿ and that the New Covenant would be written in the people's hearts (Jeremiah 31:33).

By the time they were through going back and forth between the Old Testament and the New Testament, Arnold could see from the *Brit*

Chadashah—literally the "New Covenant" Scriptures in Hebrew, or the New Testament—that every single prophecy concerning the Jewish Messiah foretold in the *Tanakh*, the Old Testament, was fulfilled in the person of Jesus. Arnold also understood why Jesus was the only One who could serve as the sacrificial Lamb as a ransom to take away the sins of the world and how in putting his faith in the finished work of Jesus on the cross and accepting this payment for himself, he could be saved from perdition and have eternal life through salvation in Jesus.

Everything meshed together so nicely that something clicked in Arnold's mind and heart. The *Ruach Ha'Kodesh*, or the "Spirit of God" in Hebrew, had broken through the barriers erected in his mind and softened his heart toward the person of *Yeshua*. When Ruth asked him if he believed that Jesus was the Messiah, or the Promised One, and if he accepted as truth all that was written about Jesus, Arnold acknowledged that indeed he did believe. God's Holy Spirit had opened his eyes to the truth, and he was "born again." He had at last encountered his Jewish Messiah, *Yeshua Ha'Mashiach*!

In accordance with the verse in Romans 10:9, . . . *if you shall confess with your mouth Yeshua as Lord and shall believe in your heart that God raised Him from the dead, you shall be saved*, Arnold bowed his head, accepted Jesus as his Messiah, and opened up his heart to receive Him as his personal Savior and Lord. Years later when giving his testimony, Arnold with his characteristic sense of humor would jokingly say that he himself joined the ranks of the "schizophrenics" that day, when he came to faith in Messiah Jesus!

God had worked through many people and circumstances to bring Arnold to that point of readiness in his spiritual journey to receive Jesus into his heart. So much had transpired in the interim. Perhaps, if his father had not been so disciplined with him in teaching him so much of the *Tanakh*, Arnold may not have known enough of the Bible to be able to discern the truth about Jesus. God's perfect timing was reflected in the years of delay before an ABMJ worker visited his family. God knew that a boy of thirteen, well grounded in the Hebrew Scriptures and searching for the truth about the Messiah, would be far more receptive to the Gospel message than would an untrained seven year-old immigrant, who had just arrived in America and spoke no English.

In His providence, God had arranged for the ABMJ's East New York Branch to be opened at just the right time and in just the right geographical location, about a mile from the Fruchtenbaums' home. God's hand upon the situation was even more evident, when it turned out that Arnold was the only Jew who was saved at that Mission station. Because it was located in such a deeply entrenched Jewish area, the Mission station had difficulty in developing. It closed down and discontinued about a year and a half after Arnold had come to salvation.

Who would have thought that a simple magazine cover given to his mother by a German Lutheran minister at a D.P. Camp would play such a significant role in Arnold's own life some seven years later? Yet, it was this very magazine cover and the subsequent contact made with the ABMJ headquarters, which became the pivotal hinge that permanently altered the course of his life. Arnold had come to a living faith in Jesus the Messiah. Only an omniscient and omnipotent God could have brought about such a marvelous outcome from a simple piece of paper!

For Ruth Wardell, that moment when Arnold received Jesus into his heart was so very precious. Being a missionary worker of the ABMJ, she understood what a struggle it was for Jews to enter "stage two" and come to personally accept Jesus as their Messiah, due to the serious consequences involved for them. Arnold had done something that he said he would never do. Yet, he decided to choose the truth over the consequences. For Arnold, the joy of encountering *Yeshua Ha'Mashiach* and the spiritual freedom found in Him far outweighed and overshadowed any subsequent opposition that he may end up having to face.

Decades later, Ruth took her old Isaac Leeser English translation of the Hebrew Bible and got the binding repaired and the covers fixed up. It was the very Bible that she had used to show Arnold the Scriptures about Jesus the Messiah on the night that he was saved. When she gave the Bible to Arnold as a gift, his eyes lit up, realizing just how special that moment was, when he came to the Lord.

Not only was Arnold's salvation itself a wonderful gift from God, the timing was truly amazing. At the age of thirteen, instead of going through his rite of passage according to Jewish tradition in a coming-of-age ceremony, a *Bar Mitzvah*, or "son of the commandment" in Hebrew, Arnold was "born again" as a believing Messianic Jew with faith in *Yeshua Ha'Mashiach*.

RIGHT AFTER RECEIVING THE LORD JESUS, Arnold did not feel any different. Being only thirteen years old at the time, he was not under any huge burden of guilt of big obvious sins. He did not have any major, unhappy problems in his life up to that point, so he did not feel any special sense of relief that often accompanied the committing of one's life to the Lord. All he knew was that the Bible spoke the truth about the Messiah, and this personal conviction in his heart led him to accept Jesus as his Savior. Arnold had always believed what he had been taught in Judaism about God and the *Tanakh*. He knew a lot about God and about all the rituals that were performed to please and honor Him, including the formal prescribed prayers in Judaism, memorized for use in those rituals. However, he did not know that he could have a personal relationship with God, that he could come to know Him personally through His Son, Jesus, and that he could commune with the Lord and grow in His grace. Once Arnold was saved, the transformation within him was not immediately apparent, but as time went on, he experienced many inner changes and growth in his walk with the Lord. He could testify to the truth: *If therefore the Son shall make you free, ye shall be free indeed.* (John 8:36) It was Arnold's early training in the Hebrew Scriptures that served as a firm foundation upon which a strong testimony of the Gospel witness was later built, after he came to faith in *Yeshua*.

At the meeting that evening, all the verses presented were taken from the Old Testament. Arnold could not ascertain if his mother had made a connection between those verses and the person of Jesus, as her English was still not very proficient. After attending a couple more meetings with Arnold, she stopped going altogether. Since then, Adele had never talked with her son about the nature of those meetings or ever had a conversation with him about the Mission station. Whenever Arnold broached the subject later on, she would simply shut him down. Even to this present day, she would still refuse to talk about that experience or what had occurred during that time period.

While Arnold's two younger siblings, Eddie and Margaret, went along with him to the Mission station whenever he got a ride, they did not connect with anything spiritual there. They simply enjoyed the creative arts and crafts activities. Margaret was an excellent reader, and whenever she was asked to read a passage of Scripture, she read it beautifully. However, unlike Arnold, neither sibling had any spiritual inclination or interest in seeking the Messiah, even though they both had been exposed to the Gospel message.

A short while after Arnold had accepted Jesus as the Messiah and received Him into his heart, he made his beliefs known to his parents. He did not get the negative reaction from them that he had anticipated. In particular, his father's response was neither negative nor positive. It appeared that his parents did not take him seriously at first, figuring that it was a kind of childish fad, a phase that Arnold was going through at the beginning of his teenage years. So, they simply ignored it and did not give it much thought.

The situation only came to a head a number of weeks later, when Arnold asked his parents for permission to be baptized. The answer he got from his father was a resounding NO, period. Jews did not believe in Jesus, and Jews most certainly did not get baptized! What was Arnold thinking? There was no room for any discussion on the matter. Henry's decision was final and resolute. There were no two ways about it.

Henry exercised his Jewish patriarchal rule, and his wife went along with his decree. Children from Eastern European homes were expected to be obedient to their parents in all regards, especially those brought up in the Orthodox Jewish traditions. Arnold was expected to uphold that upbringing even in America. So, he obeyed and submitted to his father's authority on the issue, knowing that he could not bring up the subject again in his presence.

Other than the heated run-in with his parents regarding his baptism, Arnold did not receive much overt opposition from them during the first year after he became a believer. His father allowed him to attend the weekly meetings and to participate in the various activities at the Mission station whenever he could get a ride. Arnold was very grateful to get to participate in all the programs. Yet every now and then, he could detect a sense of antagonism coming from his father toward his beliefs. It was imperceptible at first, but little by little he began to feel the cracks that were gradually emerging in their relationship. Henry's differential treatment of Arnold compared to his siblings was subtle at first, but it became more pronounced as time went on.

Messianic Youth Fellowship

Although Arnold already possessed an impressive knowledge of the Scriptures, he still faithfully attended Ruth Wardell's weekly evening classes at the East New York Branch whenever he could get a ride. He did not want to miss anything, diligently studying and eagerly drinking in the Word of God. Through the ABMJ, he also came into contact with a small group of Jewish believers in his age bracket from across Long Island and New Jersey. Spending time with them gave him a real sense of joy and belonging. The little group became like a family to him, and Ruth Wardell his spiritual mom.

Happy in his newfound faith, Arnold was constantly on the lookout for ways to witness to others, propelled by his great love for Jesus the Messiah. Once a month, the Mission organized evangelistic outings for the teenagers in different localities away from the ABMJ headquarters to give them an opportunity for direct outreach and witnessing. This often involved holding open-air meetings on Saturday afternoons to hand out tracts and present to people the wonderful news of salvation in Messiah Jesus. On other occasions, they joined big youth rallies to share the Gospel message. In addition, they participated in a Sunday morning worship service at a different church each month, where they would give their testimonies to the congregation.

In that era and even to the present day, the Gentile Christians had very little contact with Jewish believers and had even less knowledge about the difficulties that most Jewish believers encountered in their families for coming to faith in Jesus. A few of the Jewish teenagers had parents who were already believers, but most were from very secular families. Being a Messianic Jew was indeed highly unusual in those days. At one of the congregations, the teenagers were asked where each was from. When it came to his turn, Arnold called out that he was born in Siberia, a totally unexpected answer. It surprised the people how a Jewish boy so young, coming from such a far-off place as Siberia, could end up becoming a messianic believer in New York City! The congregation was greatly blessed as they listened to all the various testimonies.

While Arnold was thriving in his faith among his fellow believers, things at home were slowly beginning to unravel for him. His father's erratic temper flared up more frequently than before, constantly nit-picking on this, that, or the other. Even though Arnold continued to help out at the storefront and in the darkroom every day after school and on weekends, it never seemed quite enough to please his father. Only when Henry was completely absorbed in a game of chess did his anger temporarily abate. Playing chess appeared to be consuming him more and more. On the odd occasion, he even played a game or two of chess with Dr. Daniel Fuchs of the ABMJ.

Although Henry did not openly oppose Arnold's beliefs, there were increasing signs of disapproval. Arnold noticed that his father was withdrawing his affections and excluding him from the few things that the family did together. For instance, once they settled in Brooklyn and tried to adopt some of the American ways, the family began to celebrate each child's birthday with a cake. A month or so prior to his conversion, Arnold had his thirteenth birthday and he got a cake, as usual. However, the following year on his fourteenth birthday, the family carried on as if it were any other day. There was not the slightest hint that the family even remembered that it was Arnold's birthday. It seemed as though the whole family contracted amnesia and had completely forgotten about it. Yet, when it came time for his siblings' birthdays, the family continued to celebrate each one with a cake as they had done before.

Submitting to the situation, Arnold did not allow these circumstances to take away his joy in Messiah Jesus. He was thankful that his father did not prohibit him from actively participating in the youth events. Arnold experienced real acceptance and support from the other Jewish believers in his group. They loved one another and often prayed together. Identifying themselves as the M.Y.F., or the Messianic Youth Fellowship, they wanted as a group to accomplish tremendous exploits for the Lord.

Aside from the monthly outreaches, the group also held its own weekend retreats during the school year in October, February, and May, usually at the Liebenzell Mission Retreat Center in Schooley's Mountain, New Jersey. Leaving New York City toward the end of Friday afternoon, they would spend two nights at the Mission House and then get back late Sunday afternoon. Depending upon the size of the group, Ruth Wardell and one other ABMJ worker would drive them and serve as their chaperones for the weekend. The retreats gave the teenagers an opportunity to come together and fellowship with one another in a relaxed atmosphere, which they all enjoyed.

On one such occasion at the end of October 1957, when Miss Wardell drove a carload of teenagers on her own to the retreat center, she stopped en route to pick up Arnold. As they were about to leave, his mother handed Ruth a box, which she put into the back of the station wagon, and the group continued on its way.

The next morning after a hearty breakfast, they listened to a missionary lady talk about her experiences in China and all the marvelous things that God had done for her there. In the afternoon, they came up with a bubble-blowing contest and then went into town to go window-shopping. By the time the group got back, they were all pretty hungry and enjoyed a tasty dinner of cold cuts, potato and tomato salads, pickles, homemade bread and butter, plus cake for dessert. Afterwards, they again all piled into Ruth's station wagon and went to watch an auctioneer in action.

On and off all day, the teenagers teased Miss Wardell about the box that Arnold's mother had given her, eager to know what was inside. Ruth said it was a surprise and that they had to wait until that evening to find out. Once they got back from the auction, she brought out the box, containing a surprise birthday cake for Arnold! As his actual birthday had already taken place about a month earlier, no one would have guessed, and they all enjoyed the cake together.

The others in the group could not have known what was going on inside Arnold's home with regard to his father's angry flare-ups and constant put-downs. They certainly would not have imagined the differential treatment that he had received on his recent birthday compared to the celebrations his siblings got on theirs. Although Adele had gone along with Henry and completely ignored Arnold's birthday at the time, she apparently did not agree with her husband's decision. She had a tender spot for her son and did not want him to feel excluded from the family. Since she could not do anything for him at home, the weekend retreat was just the right opportunity for her to give him a surprise to acknowledge his special day. The gesture was so unexpected, and it warmed Arnold's heart to be able to share the cake.

The next day being Sunday, the group organized its own worship service. The same missionary lady of the previous day presented them with a short sermon. After a delicious lunch, they played a game called Bible baseball, essentially a Bible quiz, which not surprisingly, Arnold won. All too soon, it was time to head back to New York City. The group politely thanked the host of the Mission House for the wonderful time they had together, hoping and praying that they could come back again for the next retreat in February the following year.

In those days, the teenagers were all well behaved, so Ruth Wardell could manage them by herself when the numbers were not too large. Even so, sometimes she would sit on the stairs at night after the group supposedly had gone to bed, just to ensure that the boys stayed downstairs and the girls stayed upstairs without visiting one another's rooms. Although there was not that much for the teenagers to do at the retreat center, it took very little to keep them occupied. The group might draw pictures together, or often Arnold would make up Bible games or quizzes for the others to play. They all got a lot of enjoyment out of those simple activities.

These weekend retreats provided Arnold with a much-needed break away from his home. There in the beautiful surroundings, he could enjoy fellowship with the other teenage Jewish believers and just have a good time. It was a place for him to learn more about the American ways in table etiquette, general manners and culture, and where he could grow more spiritually. Arnold looked forward so much to these events.

The youth group even had its own monthly newsletter called *Teens for the Messiah* in which the members took an active interest, volunteering to write all the contents themselves. Within a year, Arnold was contributing feature articles on various biblical topics, under the guidance of Miss Wardell at the Mission station. He also put his hobby in photography to good use and took some great shots of the group at the retreats, a few of which were included in the newsletters.

When he first became a believer, Arnold was given a Scofield Reference Bible, which he studied daily with vigor and discipline. As a result, he continued to learn and to grow in the faith. Because of his great love and passion for the Word of God, he wanted to share his knowledge of the truth with others. Writing on topics that were close to his heart was one of the many ways that he witnessed to the truth of Jesus the Messiah and God's love for His Chosen People.

Having discovered that he could be in a personal relationship with God through communing with Him in prayer, Arnold began to bring his specific requests before God. A little over a year after he received Jesus into his heart, he wrote an article on how God answered his prayers.

Prayer is a wonderful thing. You would be surprised to see the things that could be done by it. Do not expect God to answer all your prayers. He may answer only some of them— those that He knows should be granted you. Now, you may ask me how I know that God answers prayer. Well, once God answered one of my prayers, which I will never forget. For one year now, I have kept this a secret. Only one other person in the world knows about it, Miss Ruth Wardell. But now, I am ready to share this with everyone else.

It happened on Christmas Eve, in 1956. I was reading the Bible and I came across the part that tells about the star, which shone over Bethlehem the night Jesus was born. After I finished reading, I hoped very much to see the star. So, I prayed to God that if it would be His will, He would let me see that same star... I prayed all night with no results. Finally, still looking at the sky, I fell asleep and dreamed a most wonderful dream, in which I saw a very beautiful star. When I awoke, I knew in my heart that God had answered my prayer, as I pray He may answer yours, through Messiah Jesus, our Lord.[7]

A couple of months later, Arnold wrote yet another article, sharing how marvelously God had arranged for him to go on the next retreat.

For months now, since I came home from the October 1957 retreat, I couldn't wait until the 21st of February, the date set for the next one. I was dying for that weekend to get here and counted the days off, one by one. But then—kaplunk—on that Sunday before that special weekend, the biggest snow storm in years hit the city and I began to get worried that the trip would be cancelled. So, I did the only thing that could possibly help. I prayed.

On Wednesday, my father told me that no matter what happened I would not be able to go. So, again, I prayed. Then, on Wednesday night, I called Miss Wardell and asked her if the trip was cancelled. She said it had not been. To make sure, she told me that she would call me up on Thursday. My father was afraid that the roads would be too icy. So, again, I prayed and asked God that if it would be His will, He would somehow provide a way for me to go.

Just as she had promised, Miss Wardell called me up and said that the trip was still on. My father still had not changed his mind, even though Miss Wardell said that the roads were perfect. So, at nine o'clock, when I went to bed, again, I prayed. I don't know how God worked it between nine and ten-thirty, but at ten-thirty, my father said to me that if the weather man predicted fair weather, then I should call Miss Wardell and tell her to pick me up. So, I went to sleep with new hope. The next day, as soon as I woke up, I got hold of "The New York Times" and looked at the weather report. A half hour later, I called

---

[7] Excerpts: *Teens for the Messiah*, January 1958

Miss Wardell and said to her, "Pick me up." You can guess
what the paper said. Isn't God wonderful?[8]

In May 1958, the youth group went on their spring retreat, the last one before
their school year ended in late June. It was during this weekend retreat that
Arnold preached his first sermon at the worship service on Sunday morning.
He had only a couple of weeks to prepare for it. Yet, he took control of the
podium and showed no signs of nervousness, speaking authoritatively from
the Book of Job on the theme of suffering. He showed how God allowed
people to suffer, and while the reasons may not be made known to them in
this life, they would know in the next life why certain things happened to
them here on earth. His message was for people to let God be God.

Looking back many decades later, Ruth Wardell still recalled how impressed
she was when this teenage boy, with a little *yarmulke*—Yiddish for
"skullcap"—on his head, stood in front of the group and expounded on the
Book of Job as if he were a seminary graduate. The staff workers at the
Liebenzell Mission House were equally astounded at the scope of Arnold's
knowledge and how masterfully he treated the subject without using any
notes. Right then and there, Ruth knew in her heart that here was a potential
missionary to the Jews—one who would someday make a profound impact
upon the Jewish community.

AS SOON AS ARNOLD RETURNED from the retreat in May 1958, the
Fruchtenbaum family left New York to move to California. Henry had been
researching and planning this move for quite some time. The area around
Blake Avenue where they resided was becoming more African-American
again, like the previous areas where they had lived. He noticed that when the
Jewish immigrants first arrived in New York City, they would live in a
community where many of their people congregated. However, once they
earned enough money, they would move out of the neighborhood to settle
somewhere else across the country.

Because Henry still did not have a good grasp of English, his photography
business largely depended upon operating within the Jewish community,
where he could communicate in Yiddish. As New York City became more of

---

[8] Excerpts: *Teens for the Messiah*, March 1958

a transient place, he found that this caused instability for his business and he was losing customers. To maintain his business among the Jews and keep up with the fluctuating nature of the Jewish community, he would have had to move the family constantly around New York City, which was not ideal. He had taken a trip to Florida and also to California to assess which place would be more suitable for his photography business. After some consideration, he chose to go to California, specifically to the Los Angeles area. He felt that the Jewish community there was more stable, without such a sharp division between the various ethnic communities as there was in New York City.

Prior to World War II, most Jews lived in East Los Angeles. After the war, they mostly lived in West Los Angeles in areas such as Hollywood, Beverly Hills and Santa Monica. East Los Angeles then evolved into a more transitory base for newly arrived Mexican immigrants. Although the Jews living in California were secular for the most part, there still resided a small minority of devout Orthodox Jews, who practiced their religious rituals. They were more settled and tended to stay together in one location, as they needed a minimum of ten men to form a *minyan* in order to hold a prayer service in a synagogue and required *kosher* butcheries, *kosher* bakeries and other *kosher* food stores.

One of the reasons Henry did not openly oppose Arnold's beliefs during the first year of his faith in Jesus as the promised Jewish Messiah may have been because he knew that he would soon be moving his family away from New York City. Perhaps he figured that once his son was geographically separated from the ABMJ workers of New York, his youthful enthusiasm for his newfound faith would dissipate. Even though he himself no longer taught Arnold the *Tanakh*, Henry had still wanted his first-born to be taught the Bible. The ABMJ workers appeared to support the Jews without any anti-Semitism, so if anyone could teach the Bible straight to Arnold, they would be the ones to do so. In addition, Henry saw no harm in the organized, well-chaperoned activities for the youth. Hence, he let it carry on for the time being, knowing that he would move the family far away to the West Coast, which he believed would eliminate the problem once and for all.

With no opportunity to meet the members of his Messianic Youth Fellowship again before he left, Arnold wrote a letter to say "good-bye."

I write this to say "good-bye" to all of you—I am moving to Los Angeles and although I don't want to move, I know it is the will of God that I do so. *"We know that all*

things work together for good to them that love God."
(Romans 8:28a) … When I reach California, I will start
high school in September. During these four years, I will
be saving money to go to a Bible school. During the summer
months, do not let anyone turn you away from Jesus. Don't
forget to read at least one chapter from the Bible every
day. Continue, or start giving out, as many tracts as
possible. I pray the Lord will bless you all.[9]

At the time he wrote the letter, Arnold did not realize that the public school system in Los Angeles allocated three years each to junior high and senior high. He would thus have one more year of junior high left to complete before entering high school. Regardless, he was already making plans to save money to go to a Bible college afterwards. His zeal for the Lord was not going to be so easily dimmed or wiped out.

By the time the youth group received the September issue of the newsletter, the East New York Branch had already closed down. Ruth Wardell was transferred back to the branch in Levittown on Long Island, Eleanor Bullock to another branch in Brooklyn, and Kenneth Anderson accepted a pastorate outside of the ABMJ. Without doubt, God's purpose for that Mission station to be opened at that particular time and place was for Arnold to come to a saving knowledge of God's grace for His people through Jesus the Messiah. Ruth Wardell had taught and discipled him into the milk of the Word and helped him socially to make friends in the youth group. Arnold himself would soon come to realize just how crucial that time period in Brooklyn was for him in preparation for his years out in California.

---

[9] Excerpts: *Teens for the Messiah*, September 1958

Moving to California

Henry had gone ahead of the family to Los Angeles to look for a place for them to live. As soon as he found a small house on Westmount Drive in West Hollywood, Adele and the four children flew out to join him in May 1958. Since the new home needed about a month or so of repair work to make it livable, the children got farmed out separately to stay with different relatives. Adele remained in the house to do all the fixing, painting, and cleaning.

Two sisters of Arnold's great-grandfather had left Europe prior to World War II to immigrate to the United States. Their families were now living in California. Having these relatives in Los Angeles was a bonus, but it was not Henry's main reason for deciding to move the family to the same state. It had more to do with the future of his photography business and the likelihood of earning a steadier income in Los Angeles.

Since the school term was still in session when the family arrived, Arnold finished the remaining part of his eighth grade at Bancroft Junior High School in Los Angeles while staying with his relatives. To get to and from school, he took the school bus every morning and afternoon. Because of his strong Brooklyn accent in English, mingled with his other foreign accents, Arnold was put in a speech impediment class for about a month, in conjunction with his normal curriculum.

By the time the school term ended, the small house was finally ready, and the family moved in. Arnold shared a room with Eddie. Margaret, being the only girl, had her own room, and baby Arthur stayed in his parents' room. Living in Los Angeles was a big change from New York City. The pace of life in California seemed to be more laid back, and the weather was certainly very pleasant. Initially, Henry found a job as a photographer working for someone else, but he aimed to set up his own store once the family's life became a bit more settled.

That first summer away from New York was very trying for Arnold. He longed to participate in the M.Y.F. activities and especially missed the annual two-week camp for Jewish teenagers, organized by the ABMJ over the summer vacation period. Called Camp *Sar Shalom*, literally "Prince of Peace" in Hebrew, it was held in mid-July at a Mennonite campsite in Honey Brook, Pennsylvania, which the ABMJ rented for that period. Jewish teenagers from all over New York, New Jersey, Pennsylvania, and along the East Coast as far as Washington, D.C., were encouraged to attend. Designed as an outreach ministry, it was offered free of charge, especially welcoming non-believing Jewish youth in the hopes that they would come to know Jesus as their Messiah.

Arnold's first experience of Camp *Sar Shalom* was in the previous summer of 1957 while he was still living in Brooklyn. At that time, he was able to get permission from his father to attend. The ABMJ provided the transportation from Brooklyn to Honey Brook. It was there that Arnold first met Burl Haynie, a Gentile ABMJ worker who had only recently transferred from the branch in Los Angeles to the ABMJ in New York City. He was at Camp *Sar Shalom* to teach the Word of God alongside the other counselors and workers.

By the time Arnold met him, Burl was already in his mid-forties. With a wonderful smile on his face and a big infectious laugh, he spoke slowly with a strong Texan accent. The teenagers there all thought that Mr. Haynie was quite a novelty because of his deep, western drawl, very different from the typical "Brooklynese" spoken at a rapid pace on the streets of New York City, which they considered to be regular English. Arnold was a newly saved believer and did not particularly relate on a personal level with Burl Haynie at that time. However, Mr. Haynie was a willing teacher, and Arnold an eager pupil, so a type of teacher-disciple relationship began to develop.

Finding the Bible classes stimulating, Arnold learned an enormous amount during the two weeks. The morning classes were divided into different age groups. The afternoons were for recreational activities or naps. The evening Bible classes after dinner were combined for all ages. Arnold soaked up all the teachings like a sponge. Having had such a blessed time at the camp, he wished that he could be there again. Alas, with his family's move, the closest he could get to Camp *Sar Shalom* that summer of 1958 was to reminisce about it in his daydreams.

When the new school year started in September, Arnold entered the ninth grade at Bancroft Junior High School, his last year of junior high. He enjoyed classes such as literature and history, but strongly disliked mathematics, his worst subject, doing minimal work to get by.

BEFORE LEAVING NEW YORK CITY, Arnold had obtained the contact details of the ABMJ in Los Angeles. Once he arrived, he got in touch to start attending meetings as he had done in New York City. Initially, he was able to get to some of those gatherings while staying with his relatives, who had no idea what the meetings were about. However, as soon as the family moved into their rented house and Arnold asked if he could go to a meeting, his father reprimanded him immediately. Henry was downright furious and gave his son a stern lecture, categorically forbidding him to attend any kind of meeting or activity, be it Messianic Jewish or Gentile Christian. His open animosity may have been provoked by the fact that they had relatives living in the same city, and he did not want them to know about his son's outlandish messianic beliefs. Regardless of the reasons, Arnold's relationship with his father seemed to have taken a dramatic turn for the worse.

The radical change in Henry's behavior appeared to coincide with the family's move from the East Coast to the West Coast. Even though it was quite uncomfortable to be around him in New York City, he still maintained some semblance of tolerance toward Arnold's beliefs and had not stood in the way of his son's involvement with the Mission station there, even allowing Eddie and Margaret to tag along. At that time, Henry was certainly not openly antagonistic toward Arnold's convictions. However, once in California, his attitude seemed to have veered in the opposite direction to one of extreme intolerance. Eddie and Margaret had not gone very regularly to the Mission station in New York City, but when they did go, they really enjoyed the arts and crafts. Once in Los Angeles, they dropped out of the picture altogether. They simply were not interested. On the other hand, Arnold's continuing strong commitment to his messianic beliefs became a major irritation to his father.

While living in New York City, Henry had already started yelling at the other children for small infractions, but more so at Arnold for any and every little thing depending upon the state of his moods. Here in California, his anger intensified and escalated into loud shouting. He even began yelling at his wife, which he had not done before. Adele never responded in kind and simply talked to him quietly.

Life at home grew increasingly difficult for Arnold due to his faith in Jesus the Messiah. His father applied pressure on him in both overt and subtle ways. Privileges were taken away one by one, and Arnold began to feel the isolation in a real way toward the end of his ninth grade. Not only was he forbidden to attend gatherings of any kind, Jewish or otherwise, he was also not allowed to read the Bible. It was during this time that Arnold personally experienced the truth of Jesus' words, as recorded in the Gospel of Matthew:

Think not that I came to send peace on the earth: I came not to send peace, but a sword. For I came to set a man at variance against his father and the daughter against her mother and the daughter-in-law against her mother-in-law: and a man's foes shall be *those of his own household. He that loves father or mother more than Me is not worthy of Me; and he who loves son or daughter more than Me is not worthy of Me. And he that does not take his cross and follow after Me is not worthy of Me. He that finds his life shall lose it; and he that loses his life for My sake shall find it.* (Matthew 10:34-39)

The only bright spot in Arnold's life that first year in California was his ongoing link to the M.Y.F. in New York City. Through his contributions to the newsletter as its editor and his correspondence with Ruth Wardell, Arnold felt connected to them. Ruth wrote him long, encouraging letters, and Arnold would share his inner thoughts with her in return. Burl Haynie took it upon himself to mentor him long-distance through his regular monthly phone calls. Knowing the pressures that Arnold was undergoing at home with regard to his messianic beliefs, Burl wanted to ensure that he did not turn away from his faith. Many Jews who believed in Messiah Jesus would eventually give up on following Him, due to the tremendous pressures exerted upon them by their families and friends to forsake their convictions. Arnold, however, remained steadfast and faithful.

In addition to Camp *Sar Shalom* taking place every summer, Burl Haynie was planning the launch of a new Memory Camp in the summer of 1959 on behalf of the ABMJ at another campsite in the Adirondack Mountains in upstate New York. Being a keen learner of the Word of God, Arnold yearned to take part. As an incentive, the teenagers were offered a paid trip if they could have the one hundred and twenty assigned Bible verses memorized before the start. Over a prior ten-week period, they were expected to learn twelve verses by heart each week. A local ABMJ worker would check on the accuracy of the recited verses and then send the results to the ABMJ headquarters.

Upon receiving all the materials, Arnold diligently set to work, aiming to qualify for a paid trip. The first one hundred and twenty verses dealt with the "Principles of God's Triune Nature." In one of his letters to Ruth Wardell, he wrote:

> This Saturday, I will be half finished with my verses for
> camp and God willing, I will no doubt see you soon. I find
> them very easy. [10]

His heart's desire was granted, when Burl Haynie sent him the roundtrip Greyhound bus tickets. By the grace of God, Arnold somehow got permission to attend. Perhaps, he just happened to ask during one of his father's rare moments of a better mood. Maybe Henry felt that he could not refuse the generous offer of a paid trip from the ABMJ workers, who had done so much for Arnold and his younger siblings while they lived in Brooklyn. It was possible that he may not have really understood the concept of the Memory Camp, and upstate New York was far away from the relatives in California. Whatever the reasons, the tickets were already in-hand. Arnold was elated to have a chance to escape from his home life for a short interlude to get some much-needed respite from his father's constant harassment about his faith.

Included with the bus tickets was also some cash that Burl Haynie had sent to buy food along the way. En route, Arnold enjoyed the scenery during the daytime and slept in his adjustable, reclining seat at night. After three to four days on the bus, he met up with his teacher in New York City and had a brief visit with Ruth Wardell. From there, Burl gave him a ride, a ten-hour drive partially on unpaved roads in those days, to upstate New York near Lake Champlain for their very first Memory Camp in the densely forested Adirondack Mountains.

Lonely Years in High School

Returning home to California on the Greyhound bus, Arnold had plenty of time to relish his memories of the marvelous time he experienced at the Memory Camp. After more than a year, it was great to see some members of

---

[10] Excerpt: *Teens for the Messiah*, March 1959

his M.Y.F. once again, but he was disappointed not to see them all. Approximately twenty teenagers from the various ABMJ branches along the East Coast attended. However, only three aside from Arnold himself came from his local youth group in New York City. How he wished that more of his fellow M.Y.F. members could have joined him!

Arnold was very enthused to be given this tremendous opportunity to learn so much from the Word of God and to be among other Jewish believers. The two weeks at camp flew by all too quickly. After he got back home, he wrote Ruth Wardell an impassioned letter, pleading with her to encourage the others to attend the Memory Camp the following year:

```
I sure was disappointed not to see more of our own
teenagers at the camp. Get the teenagers to learn the
verses. Do anything. Tell them they won't be able to go on
retreats for a whole year. I just got to fellowship with
them next year. Camp was just wonderful, and I loved every
minute of it. I sure do miss the retreats. I sure would
like to go on one up to the Liebenzell Mission.[11]
```

By the time the Greyhound bus wound its way toward the outskirts of Los Angeles, three to four days had already transpired. Arnold did not mind the long ride, as it gave him a few extra days on his own before he arrived home. He was glad to have had the break to get away from the mounting tension between father and son. Sometimes, his father was so overbearing it was crushing. What mood would he be in now?

Shortly, the family would be moving to another house, this time in a different part of Los Angeles called Beverlywood, located further south from the West Hollywood area where they were currently living. Henry had found a storefront to rent for his own photography business on Fairfax Avenue in a predominantly Jewish area and wanted the family to live closer to it. Their rented house on Beverlywood Street was located just a few miles from Fairfax Avenue, which would considerably ease his daily commute to and from his workplace.

The move happened to coincide with Arnold's need to change schools in the upcoming academic year, having just completed the ninth grade in June.

---

[11] Excerpt: *Teens for the Messiah*, September 1959

When the new school term started in September 1959, Arnold entered his first year of senior high in the tenth grade. Due to the location of his house on Beverlywood Street, the nearest public school in their allocated zone was Hamilton High School, situated conveniently about five blocks' walking distance from his home. As the third largest high school in the Los Angeles area, the student body numbered some three thousand, about eighty percent Jewish, the majority being very secular. Each class comprised thirty to forty students. While most of the teachers of Arnold's classes were Jewish, the overall split between Jewish and Gentile teachers in the entire high school was about half and half. The remaining twenty percent Gentile students consisted of Caucasians, African-Americans, Hispanics mostly from Mexico, and a few Asians. During classes and school games, the various groups mingled together, but once the day was over, they stayed within their own ethnic groups for their social life. The Jewish students hardly ever socialized with the Gentiles.

From the outset, Arnold felt like an outsider. He sorely missed engaging with the members of the M.Y.F. back in New York City and felt very much alone as the only messianic believer in his entire school. In a letter to Ruth Wardell at the beginning of the school year, he poured out his heart about how much he missed those wonderful weekend retreats:

> As I am writing this letter, you and Mr. Haynie and the teens are having a good retreat, which I miss so much. Oh, what I would do to have fellowship with you all again. I still don't have any fellowship here in L.A. I have just read about our teenage group in the "Chosen People" magazine. I am glad that our group is really getting places, but it breaks me up inside seeing that I cannot share with you.[12]

It was equally lonely for Arnold at home even with his siblings around. Though the house on Beverlywood Street was a bit bigger than the previous one, he still shared a room with Eddie. However, due to their age gap, there was scarcely any interaction between them. Besides, his siblings did not care about spiritual matters. Previously, it was not possible for Arnold to do much

---

[12] Excerpt: *Teens for Messiah*, October 1959

Bible study on his own, since his father had forbidden him to do so. Thus, his Scofield Reference Bible remained unopened. Now, at least he had an ASV Bible received at the Memory Camp, which because of its size he could keep hidden to sneak in a study here and there, when Eddie was not around.

Arnold's sense of isolation grew more acute, after his father forbade him to attend any meetings or to have anything to do with messianic groups, where he could find true fellowship. Even if there were a radio in his room, he would not have been allowed to listen to any Christian programs. In another letter to Ruth, he reminisced about the retreats and how they got started in Brooklyn:

> Our teenage group has really grown large and now there are
> about 20 members. All of them must really enjoy fellowship
> with each other. The thing I miss so much. I usually spend
> the weekends thinking about the group. As I think back, I
> see the amazing way that God has formed this group. God
> did it with a joke…I kiddingly said, "Why not go to
> Liebenzell Mission?"… And boom we had it… I do so much
> miss the fellowship with you all. [13]

Life at home was a matter of surviving his father's ongoing harassment with his harsh lectures and unpredictable temper flares. At the dinner table, Henry would sometimes single out what he disliked about Arnold's beliefs or pick on other things. There was no escaping the atmosphere of conflict and uneasiness that prevailed in their relationship. Arnold often found himself in an unenviable position of having to endure listening to a litany of allegations hurled at him in one of his father's spirited harangues. The emotional lacerations from these verbal whip lashings would take a very long time to heal.

One day, much to Arnold's surprise, Henry blurted out that he had renounced his faith in Judaism and no longer believed in the existence of God. In other words, he had become an atheist. What a revelation! Apparently, he had already given up his beliefs when he reached Siberia, after having been accused of being a German Nazi spy and sent to a Siberian prison camp. When he met Adele in Tobol'sk, he had already lost his faith, while she had always been a self-professed atheist. Arnold could not have known any of

---

[13] Excerpt: *Teens for the Messiah*, November 1959

this previously, based on the disciplined way in which Henry had trained him. Now, he realized that his father had never once stated outright that he believed any of the things he was teaching his first-born. It was no wonder that Arnold had not seen his father practicing any of the traditional Jewish religious beliefs and rituals in their home. Henry's desire to live in a stable Jewish community was more for the sake of making a living in photography than for any other reason. His bread-and-butter for years was taking photos of Jewish ceremonies such as weddings and *Bar Mitzvahs*, for which he had to be in contact as much as possible with the Jewish community. Raised in the *Chasidic* ultra-Orthodox sect of Judaism, he was very familiar with the traditions and rituals in different synagogues and knew what was important to photograph as a souvenir. He was also well versed in what was required for the Conservative and Reform congregations, enabling him to sign contracts with various synagogues to function as their official photographer for all the events within an agreed period of time.

Here in America, it was enough to be identified with a Jewish community to be considered Jewish. One did not have to practice Judaism nor adhere to any of the religious traditions. Hence, multitudes of very secular American Jews with no faith in Judaism still considered themselves Jewish and were accepted as such. For them, feasts such as Passover or the Feast of Tabernacles were celebrated largely as secular social holidays the way secular Americans celebrated Christmas and Easter for social reasons without having any belief in Jesus. Most secular Jews had no idea about the true significance of those feasts.

Every now and then, Arnold's family would have a meal at home with a few more items than usual and call it a celebration for either Passover or the Feast of Tabernacles. They did not follow the prescribed rituals for the traditional religious celebrations. Like most other secular Jews, neither his mother nor his siblings had any concept of what those feasts meant in Judaism. For them, it was just something they did as part of a social custom among the Jewish people.

Although the Jewish community in Los Angeles was more stable and less transient than the one in New York City, Yiddish was not as widely spoken as Henry had hoped. English was the norm for most Jews in their homes and businesses. Only the old rabbis in the synagogues and the older generation who practiced Orthodox Judaism could converse in Yiddish. Henry still had difficulties in English and struggled in particular with the written language. He could not yet manage to fill out any legal documents and did not understand the bureaucratic procedures in the United States. He had to rely on his wife to do the bulk of the paperwork for the business. Adele also worked alongside him at their photography store to handle all the non-Yiddish speaking customers. His frustrations sometimes got the better of him, and he would sink into deep bouts of insecurity. At those times, his anger would explode over even the most trivial of matters, directed mainly at Arnold.

MOST DIFFICULT FOR ARNOLD to overcome in California was the lack of fellowship. Being the only Messianic Jew in his entire high school made him an outcast among the Jewish students. Almost all the Gentiles in his school were non-believers and not interested in anything Christian, so to them, Arnold was indeed an oddity. He did not participate in any extracurricular activities after school, had no friends and became a loner. Toward the end of the first semester of that school year, he wrote to Ruth Wardell about his lack of fellowship:

> Well, as for my fellowship there is nothing. I am always waiting for a letter from New York, for from there do I get my fellowship. I can hardly wait for the day to come when I will be in New York so I can get fellowship. This is one of the things that drive me to memorizing the verses. I read in our paper of the many get-togethers and I sure miss going on them. I am praying that if it is the Lord's will, I may be able to come to N.Y. earlier this summer, for my school ends June 18th. Maybe then we can go on a retreat to the Liebenzell Mission.[14]

It would be a long wait before the summer months came around. The only thing that kept Arnold going was his anticipation of reuniting with the M.Y.F. and actively engaging in the summer camps. In the meantime, he exchanged many letters with Ruth and faithfully wrote the feature articles and editorials for the newsletter every month. Aside from memorizing the required verses for the upcoming Memory Camp, Arnold had little else to do over the weekends.

---

[14] Excerpt: *Teens for the Messiah*, December 1959

Eventually toward the latter part of the school year, Arnold became friends with a very secular Jewish boy by the name of Larry Levy.[15] They hung around with several other boys in Larry's circle of friends and did a few things together. Among the movies they saw that year, his favorite was *The Magnificent Seven* starring Yul Brynner and Steve McQueen. Arnold really enjoyed the music and the action-packed cowboy heroism on the big screen. To fit in, he adjusted to the teenage fashion of the West Coast in those days, with leather jackets and greased hair slicked back.

The friendship with Larry Levy was short-lived. As soon as Larry found out that Arnold was serious about his faith in Jesus, he cut off all contact. His reaction was typical of any Jewish person, whether secular or Orthodox, toward the issue of Jesus against whom they had a mental barrier. So, Arnold was back to square one in terms of friendships. He knew that it was the price he had to pay for his convictions and belief in Jesus the Messiah.

In the midst of his sense of isolation, he discovered that there were three or four believers out of the twenty percent Gentile students at his high school. These believers actively participated in a YFC, or Youth for Christ, ministry program on campus, not sponsored by the school, but functioning separately like a club. Arnold was able to have some contact with these believers through his participation in the club at school, but never at a church. This was a bright spot of encouragement for him. At least, he was not the only believer at his high school, although he still remained the only Jewish believer there.

One day, a couple of the girls among the believers asked him if he would teach them the Bible. The Youth for Christ ministry program placed a heavy emphasis on evangelism, but did very little in the way of discipleship. A Presbyterian church across the street from the school let them use one of the rooms for their study. Arnold gladly prepared the lessons, and the group met once a week right after school. His parents had no way of knowing about this activity, as they worked all day long at the photography store a few miles away, and Arnold always arrived home before they did.

In one of his letters to Ruth Wardell that year, Arnold shared the new development with her:

---

[15] The name has been altered slightly to protect the privacy of the individual.

This is a little concerning the Bible club I started. We
call it "Youth Bible Study." I have three people started
in it. The first meeting, we all gave our testimonies. The
next four meetings, I taught them Eschatology, and last
Friday, I gave a lesson on Matthew 13.[16]

Still, Arnold longed for more fellowship than the minimal contact he had with
the believers during their weekly Bible study together. He often felt nostalgic
for the fun times he had on the special weekend retreats at the Liebenzell
Mission in New Jersey. The weekend of the big snowstorm in New York City
stood out clearly in his memory. He had prayed that if it would be the Lord's
will, God would somehow make it possible for him to attend the weekend
retreat and God did! For that weekend, Arnold had wanted very much to play
a song on his violin for the group. He had started taking private lessons before
the beginning of the eighth grade back in Brooklyn. His violin had a crack in
it, so he saved up enough money to get it fixed and even got the strings
replaced with new ones. For months, he had been practicing that song and
was thrilled to be able to finally play it at the retreat.

His private violin lessons lasted less than a year and ended when he left
Brooklyn. After coming to California, he took the music classes offered at
Bancroft Junior High School. At Hamilton High, he continued his music
classes and played in the high school orchestra as part of the second violin
section. He never advanced far enough to play in the first violin section,
consisting of more skilled players. He could read music well, but found it
difficult to hit the right notes on his strings. By sitting in the second violin
section, whenever he made a mistake, the first violin section could cover up
for him, given that they were excellent violinists and sat up front in the
orchestra closer to the audience.

From what Arnold had been told, his violin was a family heirloom that had
once belonged to his paternal grandfather, Yitzchak Meir, the virtuoso who
died at a young age. Apparently, the two sisters of his great-grandfather had
brought the violin over with them from Poland to America prior to World
War II. Their families were living in Los Angeles at the time Henry made his
first visit to California to scope out the area. The story was that they gave the
violin to him for keeps, as it had supposedly belonged to his father. Henry, in

---

[16] Excerpt: *Teens for the Messiah*, December 1959

turn, had brought the violin back with him to New York City and handed it down to Arnold who was the next generation.

There was no way of verifying the authenticity of the story, as Arnold had also heard several other conflicting versions of that same tale. Regardless of the various stories, one thing was for certain. Unlike his grandfather, Arnold was no violin virtuoso and definitely not endowed with any exceptional musical talent. When he played the song on his violin at the retreat, Ruth Wardell and the staff at the Liebenzell Mission were not astounded the way they were when he preached his first sermon.

FOR THE MOST PART, Arnold wiled away his free time waiting for a letter from Ruth, finding solace in reading about the youth group activities back in New York City, or practicing the violin. He also prayed at length about his future and what he was to do with his life after Bible college. During one of those lonely times while studying the Bible, a verse in the Gospel of Luke jumped right out at him: *...and that repentance and remission of sins should be preached in His name unto all the nations, beginning from Jerusalem.* (Luke 24:47) Instantly, Arnold knew with absolute conviction that he was to engage in some form of Jewish ministry. He understood that he was to reach the Jews as a priority to teach them about Jesus, their promised Jewish Messiah.

Countless secular Jews read both the Old and New Testaments, but for historical and geographical reasons only, not for any spiritual insight. Out of ten Jews who read the New Testament, at most, one or two would see Jesus as the Messiah. The rest would either be too spiritually blinded to see the truth or would deliberately choose not to believe for fear of the inevitable consequences likely to come from their families and friends.

Once Arnold realized his calling, he lost all interest in high school. He took the minimum number of classes to get by and did just enough to maintain a B to C grade average. Math continued to be his worst subject, which he usually passed with a C or a D. He could not wait to get out of school and go to a Bible college, away from the ongoing troubles he encountered at home with regard to his faith. Only much later was he to recognize the uniqueness of his particular situation in having discovered his calling so early on in life. Meanwhile, counting the days one by one, he eagerly anticipated going back to New York for part of the summer. He had all his one hundred and twenty verses memorized and once again qualified for a paid trip to the second Memory Camp in 1960.

After what seemed like an interminable wait, the school year finally ended. However, much to Arnold's dismay, his father overruled him with other plans for the summer. Henry decided that Arnold could convert the garage of their house into a bedroom for his own use, no longer needing to share a room with Eddie. Arnold could finally be by himself. Eddie would soon be starting his first year of junior high in the seventh grade. The youngest brother, Arthur, was now old enough to be sharing a room with Eddie. Being the oldest of the siblings, it made sense for Arnold to have his own room. Converting the garage was a good solution, but the work had to be done that summer. Regrettably, this meant that he would not be able to attend the Memory Camp. However, once he had his own space, Arnold could more easily study the Bible undetected, out of sight of his parents. So in the end, it would be worth the sacrifice of missing out on the Memory Camp for one summer.

The relationship between father and son had become so strained that there was no longer any normal conversation between them. Their interaction was reduced to Henry giving Arnold short and succinct orders, such as to clean his room, to do this chore, or to run that errand. If he wanted anything lengthier to be conveyed, he communicated through his wife.

Although from all outward appearances Arnold seemed to have complied with Henry's prohibitions, he had not given up his faith nor turned his back on following Jesus. With his father's strong opposition to all activities relating to his beliefs, it would not have been wise for Arnold to go to New York that summer anyway. The likely aftermath of Henry's explosive reaction upon his return from the Memory Camp would have been unbearable. Given that he had two more years of high school left to complete, it was best for Arnold to stay low for a while and not give any further cause for more conflict and friction.

In one of Burl Haynie's regular monthly phone calls, he informed Arnold that he could come out to California for two weeks over the summer and provide him with one-on-one discipleship. While Arnold wished that it could have been the other way around with him going to New York instead, he was glad to receive the special, private tutelage from his mentor. His parents never knew about these calls, as Burl phoned in the late afternoons when Arnold was home alone from school, before his parents came back from work. Mr. Haynie took Arnold under his wings as a disciple, teaching and mentoring him even from a distance.

By the time Burl Haynie came to California, the garage conversion was already in progress. Because his parents were still working at the photography store during the day, Arnold was able to meet with his teacher outside the home. He had a most rewarding time studying the one hundred and twenty verses pertaining to the topic of "Messiah's Person and Nature." On some days, they met for one or two hours; on others, they met for five hours. Mr. Haynie also taught Arnold some basic American social skills on how to better relate to people. Being Eastern European and having grown up in a Jewish neighborhood in the heart of Brooklyn, Arnold would sometimes rub people the wrong way by the straightforward, almost intrusive questions he used to ask. His mentor coached him about the different cultural sensitivities of the people here in the United States.

All too soon, the two weeks came to an end, and it was time for Burl to return to New York to run the second Memory Camp. Once again, Arnold found himself without fellowship with other believers. Nevertheless, he somehow made it through. Letters of encouragement from Ruth Wardell and the prospect of having a room all to himself in the garage helped to propel Arnold past his sense of loneliness and isolation.

In September 1960, Arnold entered the eleventh grade. He had moved into the converted garage toward the end of the summer and was truly thankful to be able to stay out of sight of his parents as much as possible. His mother came into his room every now and then to clean it, but his father never set foot in his room. Removing Arnold from the main area of the house may have been a measure that Henry took to make his son feel isolated from the rest of the family as a means of pressuring him into abandoning his faith in Jesus. Notwithstanding, Arnold was glad that he could hide his Bible away securely in the garage and study it when his parents were not in the house. Since he loved studying the Word so much, he did not need to discipline himself to do it. He stayed on course, not once veering off track.

Memory Camp in the Adirondacks

Two years had passed since the last time Arnold was on a Greyhound bus heading out East to New York. Now, in the summer of 1961, his father once again granted him permission to attend the Memory Camp. In his heart, Arnold knew that it was God's answer to his prayers, for he had longed to get away from his home life for part of the summer. Since he again qualified for a paid trip, the tickets were sent to him. This time, Arnold would be taking the bus to Dallas, Texas, where Burl Haynie had made prior arrangements for his son, Harold, and his wife to pick him up on their way from Odessa, west of Dallas, to New York City.

As the Greyhound bus pulled out of the Los Angeles terminal, Arnold began to feel a surge of excitement. A kaleidoscope of highlights filled his mind as he remembered all his experiences at the first Memory Camp two summers earlier in 1959. He could still recall how satisfying it felt to recite the one hundred and twenty verses accurately by heart, twice through without stopping. His diligent work had paid off, winning him an unexpected prize, a *Strong's Exhaustive Concordance of the Bible*!

Burl Haynie was there at the camp on his own, teaching the classes as well as supervising the overall activities. Each day, from Monday through Friday, the lessons focused on the detailed exposition of twelve verses at a time, thus covering all one hundred and twenty verses in the two weeks. The course was based on a five-year model called Miracle Camps, produced by another ministry, focusing on a different biblical topic for each year. Burl had taken the basic material and revised it to create a study with a Jewish orientation to make it relevant to the Messianic Jewish teenagers. As the group studied the Word of God together, Arnold avidly soaked in all that his mentor had to teach.

At the beginning of that first Memory Camp, each teenager was given a Bible, the 1901 American Standard Version, which Burl used for his teaching. He highly recommended it as the translation closest to the original text. Because he taught only from that version, it was later affectionately dubbed "The Haynie Bible." Arnold was very happy to get it then, as he could take it home and hide it from his parents, sneaking in some studies on his own while they were away at work.

Burl kept the teenagers busy and out of trouble by working them really hard. After breakfast and a short devotional, morning classes began at nine o'clock sharp and lasted until noon. After lunch, the afternoons were open for activities such as berry-picking, mountain climbing, walking, or swimming in the little lake on the other side of the camp property. Before dinner, a quiet devotional period was scheduled, but the teenagers were too wound up to buckle down for that, having just spent an active afternoon outdoors. In the evenings after dinner, the group assembled together again for a time of general study and worship. Then, it was off to bed. Arnold loved every minute of the camp life.

Situated in the heartland of the Adirondacks, the campsite was off the beaten track in a small clearing amid endless acres of forests. On the campgrounds stood two old army barracks, not in any particularly adequate condition. One functioned as the boys' dormitory. A small, old bathhouse close by was used as their shower. The other slightly newer structure with an interior shower stall served as the girls' dormitory. Another simple wooden building, comprising a kitchen and dining hall, doubled as the classroom where the group studied the Bible each day.

With only limited running spring water, the camp facilities were extremely basic and the living conditions very rough. However, the meals were good and plentiful, cooked by the hired kitchen help. While the weather was hot during the daytime, the temperatures could sometimes drop quite low at night even during the summer. Those were the nights when the teenagers were very thankful for the used army blankets and sheets that came with the old surplus army cots on which they slept. They did not complain about the very rustic camp environment and had all they needed for the two weeks.

It was at the initial Memory Camp in 1959, where Arnold first met Rose Burnham, an elderly, but sprightly and energetic lady whom everyone affectionately called Aunt Rose. Arnold learned that prior to returning home to the Adirondacks due to poor health, she had been a missionary to the Navajo people out West, more precisely the Four Corners area where Utah, Colorado, Arizona, and New Mexico meet. One winter, the ministry ran out of food, and she lived off the corn reserved for the chickens. She attributed her poor health to this hard winter. While working at the local Essex County tax office in New York as a property title searcher, Rose was the first to see which tracts of land had taxes owing. In those days of big lumber business, companies would purchase the land with a mere down payment, log off all the trees, and default on the property taxes. The county tax office would then confiscate the land and offer it up publicly to the highest bidder. Simply by paying off the taxes, Rose was able to gain ownership of the property even before it went to auction. Thus, she was able to acquire many thousands of acres of land in the Adirondack Mountains including the 265 acres, which she had set aside as a summer Bible campsite. She called it Camp Heathcote in honor of her mother, whose maiden name was Heathcote.

Arnold had heard through Burl Haynie that even though Rose Burnham was a Gentile herself, she had a heart for Jewish missions. With this God-given burden in mind, she contacted the ABMJ headquarters in New York City and offered them the property for the purpose of using it as a summer Bible camp for Jewish students. At that time, the ministry did not want to be saddled with the year-round upkeep of the property just for a short summer camp once a year, so they declined her offer. However, the ABMJ chose to rent the campsite for two weeks each summer, in order for Burl to run the five-year Memory Camp program.

That was how Arnold had come to be acquainted with this idyllic spot nestled in the heart of the Adirondacks. He had been mesmerized by the magnificent beauty and tranquility of the surrounding luscious forests, especially the area around Trout Pond, the lovely little lake on the camp property. In contrast to the hectic pace of city life, the campsite offered an oasis of peace in which to study the Holy Scriptures. While he deeply appreciated the private one-on-one study time with Burl Haynie the previous summer out in California, Arnold's experience of being in the inspiring, spiritual environment of the camp remained unmatched. As he traveled eastward, he could not wait to spend more time there again.

Once he got dropped off in New York City, Arnold went to see Ruth Wardell briefly, before meeting up with his teacher. Another Jewish lad, a couple of years younger than Arnold, would be joining their drive up to the beautiful Adirondacks. Arnold had initially met Robert Futoran, whom everyone called Bob, two years earlier at the first Memory Camp in 1959. Bob had been actively involved with the other teens in the work of the ABMJ in Washington, D.C., where he lived. His background was very different from Arnold's, born in the United States to a Jewish father and a Gentile mother, both believers. Arnold and Bob did not necessarily "connect" with each other during that first Memory Camp. Now under the supervision of Mr. Haynie, the two lads would be doing rough manual labor on the grounds together for two weeks prior to the start of the Camp. The aim was to make the property more and more presentable each year. Tall, with imposing physical strength, Burl Haynie had a strong work ethic and believed in rewarding a job well done. He liked to put in a good day's worth of work during the daytime and kept the two boys fully occupied in the evenings with in-depth Bible studies under his private tutelage. The daily discipline that he instilled in the lads stayed with them even long after they left school.

Upon arrival, they immediately set off to work, felling trees along the little sandy beach in front of Trout Pond and sawing off the low hanging branches to provide an unobstructed view to the lake. The other major job involved hooking up the water pipes to the little spring located up the hill to equip the campsite with some limited running water for the kitchen. A line also had to be connected to the lake to pump out water, which was then treated with chlorine to be used for the showers. To protect and keep the property private after clearing a path to the lake, they erected a gate across it near the main road to prevent the local public from using it. A hillbilly family living down the road in a rented rundown shack completely disregarded the caution signs at the entrance. The man had built his own dugout canoe and parked it on the beachfront of the lake. Burl Haynie did not like it at all, but had to go away for a couple of days.

Bob, on his initiative, decided to take matters into his own hands and drilled two holes into the canoe to sink it. To make things worse as a joke, Bob inadvertently told the owner of the canoe what he had done. The man got very angry and complained to Burl Haynie upon his return, demanding payment for the damage. The teacher was not happy and summoned his two pupils into his makeshift office in the main wooden structure to question them about the relevant details of the situation.

Arnold had learned about the incident only after the fact, so he was not at all involved. However, in order that Bob would not have to take all the punishment alone, he stepped in and used the term "we" when explaining their intention. Hence, Mr. Haynie thought that both boys had done the deed. As a result, they both got punished with a withdrawal of certain privileges for a number of days. Bob really appreciated Arnold's gesture in coming alongside him. From that moment onward, the two became fast friends. Working together, they got to know each other's family situation. Arnold shared with Bob what he was going through at home. They soon became like brothers.

To build a wooden staircase from the top of the hill to the lake first required the wood to be preserved with a layer of creosote on the outside. Using a brush to spread the solution on the logs, the two lads applied it at a hefty pace to get as much done as possible. Since the day was so hot, they both took off their shirts, seeing that they were on private property and no one else was around. As they swooshed the brushes around the logs, they inevitably splattered some of the formula onto their bare skin.

In the evening, they both felt increasingly uncomfortable with a burning sensation, which got worse as the night wore on. Burl also felt the same way as the boys. Finally, they took a look at the label of the can and discovered the warning regarding the magnified sensitivity to the sun if any solution got onto the skin. By now, their sensation felt even more acute than serious sunburn. For the first time, the two pupils saw their teacher close to tears, as his condition was far worse than theirs.

Needing to get immediate medical attention, the lads piled into Burl's truck. Being in such a remote area in the mountains, they had no clue where they could find a hospital emergency room or a doctor. By that time, it was already very late, between eleven o'clock and midnight. As they drove around the nearest town to seek help, they could not even find the police station. Deliberately breaking every single traffic rule they could think of, they wanted to attract the attention of patrolling policemen, to get directions to a medical center. Ironically, not a single policeman turned up that night. They desperately drove around until they finally found someone who gave them the private address of a doctor.

Waking him up in the middle of the night, they sought his help. Coming to the door in his pajamas, the doctor took one look at them and advised them to go to an all-night drugstore and buy themselves a jar of Noxzema Cream. That's exactly what they did. Containing camphor, menthol and eucalyptus among other ingredients, the smooth, light cream produced a cooling sensation over the affected areas of their skin. The burning sensation almost immediately began to subside. It took a long time before the burns completely healed, but that Noxzema Cream really worked. They could not believe the drama they had to go through for that simple remedy. It was most certainly an unforgettable night!

WHILE BURL HAYNIE WAS VERY SERIOUS about Bible study, it was not in a dull way. He imparted to an unpolished New York teenager like Arnold a discipline of study and a joy of learning that evoked a real desire to want to learn more. He was a real, big, and gentle man in all senses of the word, despite his burly stature with his ten-gallon cowboy hat and leather boots. Apparently, Burl's gentle side was not always so. Prior to his conversion in 1950, he was said to have been quite a tough man, not someone to be trifled with. In his capacity as a sheriff in Texas, he often went into local bars by himself to break up brawls and fights among the thugs. Married with two children, he and his wife lived a pretty wild life. However, after he was saved, he gave up that life including his wild side. His wife simply could not cope with the changes and opted out through a divorce. Burl remained single ever since and continued to teach the Bible through various avenues, always focusing on the Jewish people.

The topic of the one hundred and twenty verses for the third Memory Camp was "God's Redemptive Work." Arnold once again recited all one hundred and twenty verses accurately by heart. The more he studied, the stronger his love and passion for the Word became. He eagerly set his mind on gaining the necessary skills on how to truly study the Bible, thus acquiring even more in-depth knowledge. Burl Haynie taught him how to systematically go about digging deeply into the Word for himself. The teacher made the pupil memorize "The Golden Rule of Interpretation." Each time they sat down to study the Bible, Mr. Haynie would insist that he recite the quote by Dr. David L. Cooper, under whose ministry he had studied at the Biblical Research Society while working with the ABMJ in Los Angeles:

> **When the plain sense of Scripture makes common sense, seek no other sense. Therefore, take every word at its primary, ordinary, usual, literal meaning unless the facts of the immediate context, studied in the light of related passages and axiomatic and fundamental truths, indicate clearly otherwise.**

Arnold learned how to apply that Golden Rule in all his biblical studies, looking closely at the context of the passages, considering the broad spectrum as well as examining the details. In a sense, it was akin to an investigator reviewing the evidences of a case, not missing any clues, yet not jumping to any conclusions out of context. The studies at the Memory Camp delved into some fairly deep doctrinal questions, which explored certain issues that even churches dared not risk venturing into.

Although Burl had a high interest in prophecy, he never went to the extremes of sensationalism and "newspaper exegesis" that were prevalent in popular prophecy conferences. In those early days when Arnold was prone to speculating at times, his teacher would frequently tell him, "Do not speculate." In the course of time, Arnold learned his lesson well and avoided such tendencies. He let Scripture be the final authority over events. Coupled with his excellent memory, Arnold was shaped by the foundation his mentor had laid for him in those formative years. It was from this doctrinally solid base that he was discipled into the meat of the Word, learning how to truly study the Word for himself and growing into maturity in the faith later on.

Burl also taught Arnold how to apply Scripture to his daily life, even in areas that may have seemed theoretical at first. For instance, he lived with the constant expectation of the Rapture of the Church and once even told Arnold that he expected to be alive at the time of this event. In keeping with the verse in Second Timothy 4:8, Burl Haynie really did look forward to the Lord's "appearing."

Aside from the intensive Bible classes in the mornings, Arnold and Bob also had plenty of time to take in some fun-filled activities in the afternoons. Like the majority of boys in their teens, they began developing an interest in girls and talked on and off about what they were like. They spotted a few new girls who had joined their evening study and worship times. Although the Memory Camp curriculum was closed to the public, the children of kitchen staff or friends were free to attend the general evening sessions, irrespective of whether they were Jewish or Gentile believers. Arnold noticed that one of them was the same girl whom he had seen two years earlier on the other side of the camp property. Whenever he had an opportunity, he would linger at the lovely lake to soak in its peacefulness. He vividly recalled a particular walk he took late one afternoon. Heading down the path toward Trout Pond, he was surprised to see a girl coming in his direction. He had not expected to see anyone else there, as the only people on the property at that time were the teenagers attending the Memory Camp. As they walked past each other near a birch tree in total silence, Arnold felt that there was something nice and different about the girl. However, she seemed to give him a strange look as she walked by.

The girl appeared to be Gentile, a few years younger than him, no more than twelve or thirteen years of age at that time. Arnold wondered who she was and what she was doing on that private property. There was something special about her, but Arnold could not pinpoint what it was. In the intervening two years while daydreaming during one of his very lonely times at home, he had even written an essay about their chance meeting near the birch tree. Arnold wondered then whether he would ever see her again. It was interesting that for the first time in his life, he thought about someone whose name he did not even know.

Now that she was right there, Arnold's heart skipped a beat. He was ecstatic to see her again! This time, both he and Bob ventured to strike up a conversation with her and the other two girls, who turned out to be her younger sisters. Quite quickly Arnold realized that this girl could not see out of one eye. That was the reason she appeared to have given him a strange look, when she had glanced at him that day on the path to the lake. It was not easy to find time to chat during the evening sessions. They could talk only in little snippets here and there, either just before the sessions started or right after the evening ended. Always in a group, they never had an opportunity to sit down and have a long conversation together.

Slowly, Arnold began to piece together bits of information about her personal situation. The girl was Gentile, and her name was Mary Ann. There were four children in the family—an older brother and three sisters with Mary Ann being the oldest of the girls. Her father, Reverend L. Joseph Morrow, was currently shepherding a congregation in Kenmore, a suburb of Buffalo, a city on the far western side of New York State. Her family's ties to the campsite dated back many years. In the 1950s, when her father was the minister of Essex Community Church, he also itinerantly served the nearby towns of Wadhams and Whallonsburg, close to the eastern state line. At that time, Rose Burnham had invited him to lead a summer Bible camp for the local children on the property of Camp Heathcote—located about twenty miles from Essex—which he did for several years. Wishing for him to continue doing so every year even after his move to Kenmore, Rose Burnham sold him a house including lake access rights for one U.S. dollar. Thus, Mary Ann and her family were in the area each summer while the Memory Camp was in session. That was how Arnold and Mary Ann found themselves crossing paths with each other for the very first time two years earlier near Trout Pond.

Mary Ann's father shared Rose Burnham's love for the Jewry as well as her vision for the camp to be used to teach them the Bible. Both Rose and Rev. Morrow desired, dreamed, and prayed that God would set apart the campsite to meet the spiritual needs of the local children as well as the Jewish people.

Burl Haynie also had a vision for the property to continue to be used as a Bible camp for the Jews. He would often spend hours in prayer in his room on his knees. Sometimes, he would walk outside around the grounds, alternately praying silently and out loud. He prayed constantly for the fulfillment of his vision. Arnold was beginning to see how the threads of different people's lives were coming together to form a common vision for the campsite. Surely, God was at work.

That summer, Arnold again acquired a huge amount of Bible knowledge from Mr. Haynie's in-depth teachings. He loved the intensity of the two weeks, which were packed with classes, activities, and fellowship. Knowing that it would be another year before he could enjoy this kind of fellowship again, he soaked it all in. After the third Memory Camp ended, Arnold and Bob stayed behind for another two weeks to clean up the campsite, while engaging in more in-depth evening studies with their teacher and mentor.

Silent Year Leading to Expulsion

While Arnold was away at the third Memory Camp during the summer of 1961, his family made yet another move. His parents had saved up enough money from their photography business for a down payment to purchase a large two-story corner building on Robertson Boulevard, two blocks away from Hamilton High School. It consisted of two storefronts on the ground floor and two apartments on the upper level. Henry's intention was to set up his own photography store in the larger of the two storefronts, while continuing to rent out the smaller unit to the artist who was already a tenant. The family would initially live in one of the two upstairs apartments while renting out the other.

During the first year of living there, Henry and Adele continued to maintain their business in the rented photography store on Fairfax Avenue. They were obliged to honor the contract of the lease to the existing tenant in the bigger storefront, which had not yet expired at the time the ownership of the building changed hands. Upon the end of the tenant's lease, Henry would not be renewing it, as he planned to move his own photography business into that storefront. In the interim, he and Adele still had to leave the house each day and drive several miles to get to their workplace on Fairfax Avenue.

The new building was located in a predominantly Jewish neighborhood. An Orthodox synagogue stood conveniently right across the street. As the building was even closer to Arnold's high school than their Beverlywood Street house was, he could remain in the same school for his twelfth grade. The area on the opposite end of Hamilton High was gradually beginning to evolve into more of an African-American neighborhood, but on this side of the campus, the area remained largely Jewish for quite a number of years. However, Yiddish was less and less spoken as the demographics slowly changed.

As soon as the Greyhound bus drove into the terminal at the station in Los Angeles, Arnold got off and found his way directly to the family's new home address. When he arrived, he could see that the family had already settled into their second-floor apartment during his absence of over seven weeks—two weeks each before, during and after the Memory Camp plus several days of traveling on both ends. After having had his own room in the garage and staying out of his parents' sight as much as possible, he now discovered that once again he would be sharing a room with Eddie.

Arnold was not sure what kind of mood his father would be in on that particular day. He felt quite tentative about their interaction, as things had been terribly strained and contentious between them lately. Henry was prone to sudden outbursts of anger, just because he felt frustrated about his life in general. More likely than not, his father would be picking on him about something or another, unleashing an angry tirade of accusations against him, spilling out words laced with acrimony.

Though Arnold hoped to avoid being embroiled in yet another heated one-way feud with his father, a clash seemed almost inevitable. The self-doubt and insecurity that Henry had felt when he first arrived in New York City were now replaced with a severe sense of harshness and obstinacy. He ruled the household with an iron fist, petulantly laying down his commands and decrees, demanding to be obeyed to the letter without question. Sometimes, he exerted himself so forcefully that it caused havoc in the family's daily life, negatively impacting them all.

Contrary to what Arnold had anticipated when he walked into the apartment, his father did not even cast a passing glance in his direction. He did not utter a single word. At the dinner table that evening, the general conversation revolved around the activities of the other siblings only. Henry completely ignored him, saying absolutely nothing to him, acting as if his son did not even exist. So, Arnold in turn said nothing back, seeing that his father had stopped speaking to him altogether.

In the Eastern European home environment, especially among Orthodox Jews, the children were expected to be respectful to their parents in all regards and to speak only when spoken to. It would have been up to Henry to initiate a conversation. Sadly, Arnold was soon to discover that he would be subjected to his father's inexorable policy of total silence for his entire last year of high school. Not a single word passed between father and son that whole year.

This extreme type of silence treatment was not unknown in the Orthodox Jewish culture in which Henry was raised. In particular, the *Chasidim* believed that the pain of silence dealt with the feelings of pride and indifference on the part of the child. It was a restrictive method by which a parent disciplined the child to gain wisdom through the pain of silence and to return to the way the parent wanted the child to behave. Henry used this drastic measure to show Arnold how vehemently opposed he was to his son's beliefs. It was his way of trying to force his first-born to renounce his faith in Jesus.

Arnold was now living through one of the more dire consequences of his faith. He was experiencing a severe rejection similar to the manner in which some Jewish believers got treated by their families for their faith. While still living, they would see their own graves in a cemetery with the dates of their birth and death marked on the tombstone. The date of death corresponded to the day when that person became a believer in Jesus as the Messiah. For that Jewish family, such a child was as good as dead to them. Arnold felt that this was also how his father was treating him, the reproach painful to bear.

While living in the same apartment and eating at the same table, it was as though Arnold were not even physically present. What little allowance he used to get ceased with Henry's decision to stop speaking to him. The other siblings did not care about what was going on with their older brother, whom they considered to be rather strange. Adele, being the submissive Eastern European wife that she was, simply went along with her husband and turned a blind eye to the situation. She went about her daily life, relating to her son in her usual manner, as if nothing were amiss.

Although initially the silence treatment was extremely awkward and hurtful, Arnold in an ironic sort of way felt freed up. His father was no longer telling him what to do or what not to do. There were no more hassles, no more lectures, no more pressures, no more rules, no more yelling, and no more confrontations. In short, Henry no longer interfered in his son's life, and Arnold finally had the freedom to do what he wanted with regard to his faith. In a strange sort of way, the silence had annulled and lifted all the restrictions previously imposed upon him.

Arnold could at last freely practice his beliefs, attend messianic meetings, have fellowship with other believers, and participate in any group activities he chose. Whenever he could get a ride, he would go to gatherings and engage with other believers. He even started attending regular Sunday morning worship services at Concordia Lutheran Church located about a mile from his home. Pastor H. O. Egertson loved the Jewish people and welcomed Arnold warmly. Since it was not too far away, he walked to and from the church. Arnold also began to actively give his testimony in various churches that he came into contact with through the local ABMJ office in Los Angeles. In many ways, the silent year became a spiritually productive period for Arnold as he looked to God for strength.

Knowing that his father was fueling the fires of animosity deep within himself, Arnold continued to maintain an attitude of respect toward him. Thus, he did not openly study the Bible inside the home. While his parents were away working on Fairfax Avenue, Arnold was alone for about three hours each day after school. As soon as classes were over, he would walk straight home and study the Bible on the sly until he heard his parents drive up to the building around five-thirty. He would then quickly hide his Bible study materials away in a safe place and turn his attention to doing his regular homework for school.

Because Eddie participated in many extracurricular activities at his junior high school and got home only around six o'clock in the evening, Arnold had the room all to himself. He knew in his heart that he was called to Jewish ministry and planned to go to a Bible college in preparation. However, he also wanted to have as much Bible knowledge as possible before he entered college. Deeply passionate about the Word, he set forth to undertake an intensive period of systematic Bible study on his own during his last year of high school. He also focused on the writings of Dr. David L. Cooper, who had discipled Burl Haynie, Arnold's own teacher and mentor. Those few afternoon hours that he spent immersed in the Word soon became the highlight of his day.

Because Arnold's home was only two blocks away from his high school, he could actually hear the loud cheering of the students whenever their football team scored a touchdown or their soccer team scored a goal on the fields. There were many other after-school extracurricular sports activities such as softball, volleyball and basketball, but Arnold did not participate in any of them, not even as a spectator. He was a loner and had no interest left in high school. He could not wait to get out of there as soon as possible. So, while his schoolmates were enjoying themselves and having fun at the games, Arnold spent time alone in his room studying the Bible on the sly.

During his senior year, Arnold carried on teaching the Bible once a week for about nine months to the few believing Gentile schoolmates in the Youth Bible Study Club, which had now increased to about four or five people. He focused on the study of Dispensations, the Covenants and various other topics. Later, Arnold took on a part-time job as a janitor for Concordia Lutheran Church, where he attended the weekly Sunday morning worship services. He worked on Wednesdays for a couple of hours after school, cleaning up a room used for their midweek meetings. On Saturdays, he worked all day cleaning and setting up for the main worship service on Sundays. He wanted to save up some money to put toward his Bible college education the following year.

Seeing that Henry had bound himself by his iron will and refused to speak to him, Arnold knew that he could not count on his father to teach him the usual things that he, as a teenager, needed to learn. So, he found a Gentile believer in his class, who was willing to teach him how to drive. This believer was the son of Chinese immigrant parents who owned a laundry shop in the vicinity. His classmate would frequently take his car out with Arnold after school, so that he could practice the driving skills that he had been taught. Thus, Arnold was able to obtain his driver's license by the time he graduated from high school.

WHEN ARNOLD'S PAPERWORK WAS FIRST PROCESSED at the D.P. Camps for immigration to the United States, his birth year was recorded in error as 1944 instead of 1943. Upon entering the United States, his middle name mistakenly got dropped off his new registration documents. Hence, all those years, Arnold's legal age on paper was always one year younger than his real age, and he had no middle name. There was no way to rectify those errors without the proof of a certified copy of his birth certificate. With Arnold having been born in Siberia, it was no easy task for his parents to get a hold of a copy of the necessary birth certificate to prove his real birth year and his middle name. However, those were the legal requirements in the United States if corrections were to be made.

Their one tiny thread of connection to Siberia was through Arnold's maternal grandmother, Emma Suppes. She had been incarcerated between nine to ten years in a Soviet prison camp near the vicinity of Akmolinsk, north of Karaganda in the Kazakh A.S.S.R., starting when her daughter was barely a teenager. Upon her release, she was employed as a cashier at the head office of a chain of restaurants in the city of Karaganda.

Not knowing what had happened to her daughter, Emma wrote a card to the family in Saratov with whom Adele had lived during the last two years of her Gymnasium. It just so happened that her card arrived right during the time when Adele and little Arik were temporarily staying with this family, while waiting for Chaim to send funds to enable them to travel down to Kirovograd to join him in Ukraine. What exquisite timing!

Adele eagerly wrote back to the address in Karaganda, and thus the two started corresponding once every three months. Just prior to the family's departure from Kirovograd to be repatriated to Poland, Adele wrote to her mother one last time. In the turmoil of the journey to Poland, followed by the ensuing upheaval of escaping once again, only to be detained at the various D.P. Camps in West Germany for so many years, Adele was not able to write to her mother. The tense and unsettling political situation in Europe during that time period prohibited all mail and other means of communication between the West and East.

It was only several years after the family had settled in the United States that Adele attempted to make contact with her mother again. She wrote a card to the last address she had of her in Karaganda in the hopes of tracking her down, but by then, Emma had already moved to another town. Nevertheless, someone at the head office of the chain of restaurants just happened to know where she had moved to, so the card was forwarded to her. Thus, mother and daughter joyfully reconnected once again after so many years of disrupted communication. From then onward, they kept in regular contact through their letters. Now, Adele requested her to please try and obtain an authentic copy of Arnold's birth certificate from the authorities in Tobol'sk, where his birth was registered. Emma managed to procure the necessary document and sent it to California by the time Arnold entered his senior year of high school.

Only then was the family able to provide the evidence required to revert his birth year from 1944 back to 1943. This meant that on the 26th of September 1961, Arnold legally turned eighteen years old, matching his real age.

As for his middle name, it was finally added to his full name on his American legal papers. In the Russian culture, a child's middle name was automatically the father's first name plus an ending of "ovich," meaning "son of" for a male child, or an ending of "tovna," meaning "daughter of" for a female child. Henry's first name, which in Hebrew was Chaim, went through several translations. In Polish, it was Heniah or Henyek, and in Russian, it was Geniak or Genek. Thus, Arnold's middle name became Genekovich, meaning "son of Genek." Officially, Arnold's full legal name in the United States finally became Arnold Genekovich Fruchtenbaum. Since he was the only one among his siblings to be born in Siberia, he was thus the only one who had a Russian middle name.

Approximately two months before Arnold finished high school, his father relayed a message to him. Typically, the family communication in an Orthodox Jewish home was very hierarchical. In the days when the silence treatment had not yet been imposed, Arnold would first speak to his mother to ask permission about something. Then, she would speak to his father about it, who in turn would give an answer to him through his mother again. It was the same principle at work this time. One night while Arnold was reading in bed, Adele slipped into her son's room and delivered the news: Henry had issued an ultimatum that Arnold was to get out of the home as soon as he graduated from high school. Not only was he expected to leave their home, but he was also told to depart from California for good. Not prone to showing any emotions, Adele conveyed the message in a matter-of-fact, straightforward manner, going along with whatever her husband decreed. She merely suggested that Arnold might consider going back to New York City.

The ultimatum triggered a new crisis in Arnold's spiritual life. Since he had become a believer, he had experienced many problems at home, including the silence treatment. Now, it had come to this. Never before could he have imagined that he would actually be put out of his parents' home! His father's main concern was protecting his photography business and being able to continue making a steady living in the Jewish community. Henry was afraid that if word got around that his first-born son had become a "Christian," he would no longer be able to maintain his contracts with the various synagogues, which in turn might permanently ruin his business.

Since Arnold's birth year had just recently been rectified, he was now over eighteen and hence lawfully an adult. Henry could expel his son from their home without being legally liable. Had the birth year remained in error on Arnold's documents in the United States, his father would not have been able to throw him out at this time, as Arnold would have legally been only seventeen and thus underage. In essence, Henry had disowned his first-born and banned him from returning. This place would no longer be Arnold's home, and he was not welcomed here any more. Once he left, he would not be able to carry on a relationship with his family, nor see them again in this home. The price that Arnold had to pay for his faith in Jesus was very high and very real indeed.

At that time, Arnold could only turn to the Lord and pray for His guidance and reassurance. He felt that God was directing him to return to New York City, where he had first encountered his Messiah Jesus. While reading through the Apostle Paul's letter to the Philippians in the Bible, Arnold found comfort and solace in God's promise in the verse that said: *And my God shall supply every need of yours according to His riches in glory in Messiah Yeshua.* (Philippians 4:19) Fully convinced that God's Word was true, Arnold knew that he would indeed have to depend entirely upon the Lord for all his needs, as he had only $120 in his pocket upon his high school graduation.

BY JUNE 1962, ARNOLD HAD COMPLETED all his high school requirements, and graduation day finally arrived. Ever since he had discovered his calling, he had lost all interest in his classes and wanted solely to study the Bible. Hence, he had passed with only very average grades, doing just enough to get by. He was very much looking forward to attending a Bible college, although at that point, he had no idea how it was going to be funded.

The graduation ceremony was scheduled for that Friday, but Arnold did not bother to attend. He simply went to the high school administration office in the afternoon and picked up his diploma. What was the point of attending the ceremony? No one in his family would be there to help him celebrate this milestone anyway. Even if they did come, how awkward would it be with his father not speaking to him? In fact, his parents had never attended any of his events at school: not his elementary school graduation, not his junior high school graduation, not even the time when he had played the role of Santa's little helper in a school play.

Arnold did not have any real friends in high school, and most of the Gentile believers to whom he had taught the Bible once a week were not even in his graduating class. Coming to this special occasion would be his classmates' families and friends, surrounding, hugging, chatting, and congratulating them and then going out together to a nice place for lunch to celebrate. Amid all that joviality, Arnold would be alone by himself. It was best not to go. Besides, Arnold had very little time left. Graduation day was his last day to be allowed in his parents' home. The next day, bright and early, he would have to leave. He needed to get his packing done and make sure he cleaned up his room before he left on Saturday morning.

It had been a difficult year, yet in many ways, it was a fruitful year. Cocooned in his own little world of silence at home, without any more of his father's harsh interference, Arnold was able to get an enormous amount of Bible study done. On his own in the enclave of safety in his room, those three hours in the afternoons became so precious. He learned to grow in his faith and to rely upon the Lord. It would have been nearly impossible for him to get through those tough years in California, had he not experienced the most wonderful year and a half in Brooklyn after his conversion, sharing fellowship with the other teenage Jewish believers through the Messianic Youth Fellowship of the ABMJ network. That period in New York City was like a small hiatus, sheltering him from the storms of life that were about to engulf him in California. By the grace of God, Arnold somehow managed to make it through to his high school graduation and attained his diploma. Now, he was looking forward to seeing his fellow believers again back in New York this summer and to experiencing God's guidance and provision for his future.

PART III

~ *Provision* ~

And my God shall supply every need of yours
according to His riches in glory in Messiah Yeshua.

(Philippians 4:19)

It was a glorious Saturday morning in June 1962, fresh and sunny, with clear blue skies and not a cloud in sight. Unlike the beautiful weather outside, Arnold's heart was awash with sadness at the prospect of never seeing his family again. Because of the large age gap, Arnold's younger siblings had no affinity with him. Having no spiritual interest, they did not get involved at all in their older brother's life. Even though his siblings knew that Arnold would be leaving their home on Robertson Boulevard for good, they did not approach him about his departure, nor did they even bother to say "good-bye." Arnold had to accept that his family simply did not share his messianic beliefs and could only pray for an open door to their hearts so that one day the unsurpassable message of salvation in Jesus the Messiah would break through their barriers.

Though Arnold had traveled from Los Angeles to New York City a couple of times in the past, this journey would be like no other. A sense of finality surrounded this trip, as he would not be returning to California. While the car headed eastward leaving Los Angeles behind, Arnold's sadness gradually subsided into a gathering sense of melancholy. As he watched each familiar sight slip by the window and disappear behind him to become part of his past, his thoughts reverted to the events leading up to his departure.

Ever since Henry had issued the ultimatum a couple of months earlier to expel him, Arnold's life seemed to have taken on a surreal dimension as his mind tried to grapple with the facts and reality of his situation. That his own father had completely rejected and disowned him—first through his silence treatment and then by demanding that he leave California—was all too difficult to digest. After all, Arnold was the first-born son. How was it possible for a father to turn his back on his own child for nothing else other than his differing spiritual beliefs? In Henry's eyes, his son's belief in this Jesus of the Gentiles as the Messiah was an absolute betrayal of their Jewish beliefs, in many ways tantamount to spiritual treason. It did not matter that as a result of the Holocaust, he himself had abandoned his own faith and practice of the ultra-Orthodox Jewish traditions. That his first-born son would veer so far from the generations of Jewish community traditions and follow the Gentile "god" Jesus, was unthinkable. Furthermore, the potential adverse effects on his photography business in the Jewish community of Los Angeles could cost him his livelihood, and he feared being financially ruined. Hence, Henry simply had to put an end to his son's messianic beliefs by whatever means possible.

The mounting tension and strain in the relationship with his father had created havoc in Arnold's life. Having to suffer a perpetual rollercoaster of charged emotions, aimed at forcing him to give up his faith, took its toll. The frequent confrontations with acrid verbal explosions, pummeling down on him, left invisible emotional lacerations on his heart. In light of his father's unpredictable moods, it was amazing that Arnold even got to attend the third Memory Camp at all. Perhaps, Henry did not quite understand the exact nature of the Memory Camp, thinking it was a Bible camp, where the teenagers were taught the *Tanakh*. Or perhaps, he simply wanted Arnold out of the house to avoid the awkwardness of having him around while the family was moving to Robertson Boulevard. Undertaking such a major move during his absence was possibly another step in making Arnold realize that he was being excluded from the mainstream of his family's life and activities, due to his faith. Regardless, it was apparent that Henry was prepared to take whatever measures necessary to stamp out Arnold's beliefs and prevent them from spreading to his other children.

The harassment that Arnold endured through his high school years was painfully difficult to bear and grew worse with time. Yet, he never imagined that a day would come, when his father would categorically refuse to speak to him and go so far as to completely disown him and expel him from their home.

It was thus that Arnold found himself packing his entire worldly possessions into one suitcase, the day after his graduation, with only $120 in his pocket, money earned and saved from his part-time work. As the car drove across the California state line into Arizona, the full physical reality of his situation came to the fore. Arnold had to accept the fact that there would be no turning back. In his heart, he knew that he had lost his family and that he would never be allowed back in his home again.

Yet for Arnold, renouncing his faith was out of the question. He had encountered the Messiah. Life, as he knew it, would never be the same again. Even though he had to suffer the painful consequences of his beliefs and total estrangement from his family, he chose to stand firm in his faith, no matter what the cost. Despite his unfavorable circumstances, Arnold felt a deep sense of inexpressible joy within his heart as he centered his life in Messiah Jesus. No one and nothing could take that faith away from him, not even the trauma of being expelled from his home, for what could ever be worth more than his salvation?

In a way, Arnold felt relieved that he could start afresh, no longer subjected to his father's iron rule, nor having to endure his strong opposition. He was finally free to openly live out his faith in Messiah Jesus and endeavored to follow the example of the Apostle Paul who said: *forgetting the things which are behind and stretching forward to the things which are before, I press on toward the goal unto the prize of the high calling of God in Messiah Yeshua.* (Philippians 3:13b-14)

Instead of the three or four days that a Greyhound bus normally took to get to the East Coast, this ride from an acquaintance would take about two weeks to reach Washington, D.C. From there, Arnold planned to catch a Greyhound bus to New York City, where he would meet up with his mentor, Burl Haynie. The man giving Arnold a ride had organized many stops along the way to visit people he knew. A Messianic Jewish couple, having heard Arnold's testimony during his senior year in high school, had introduced him to this man, a World War II veteran, about twenty years his senior. He was a Gentile believer, a Pentecostal adherent of an extremist segment. As they drove eastward, they made various stops in Kentucky and Tennessee, where this man had contacts in some Pentecostal churches. It seemed that his goal was to expose his passenger to those churches in an attempt to persuade him to change over to their genre of worship in expressing their beliefs. Arnold was not at all impressed by their "charismania." He had studied the Bible enough not to be easily swayed to switch to their form of worship. However, these strangers whom he met were kind enough to open up their homes to accommodate the travelers with beds or with meals. Thus, Arnold experienced firsthand God's provision in supplying his needs during the two weeks of travel across the country.

As the car meandered its way toward the East, Arnold had ample time to marvel at God's protective hand over his life since birth. That he did not perish in his early years reflected something of the miraculous, as God spared his life time after time. Against all odds, he and his parents had escaped starvation and survived the grueling years of the Holocaust and subsequent pogroms. By God's grace, he had come to America with his family, and in God's providence, he had come to believe in *Yeshua Ha'Mashiach.* He thanked God for bringing into his life Ruth Wardell and Burl Haynie, who both in their individual way nurtured his spiritual growth and helped him to get through the tough years at home.

Soon, Arnold was about to embark on four years of intensive study of God's Word to learn more about his Messiah Jesus. His heart yearned to share the truth with his fellow Jews about the magnificent news of God's eternal plan for His Chosen People through His Son, Jesus. The only way to explain and make any sense of the Jewry's plight in world history was to see God's wonderful future purpose for His Chosen People from the standpoint of Scripture. All of God's promises of blessing to them through the Abrahamic Covenant would be fulfilled during the Millennial Kingdom yet to come. Arnold longed for the Jewish people to come to know their Messiah *Yeshua*.

BY THE TIME ARNOLD ARRIVED IN NEW YORK CITY, he had spent only $17 out of the $120 he had in his own pocket. Burl Haynie drove him to Levittown on Long Island where he stayed at Ruth Wardell's home for several weeks. Knowing that Arnold may occasionally find himself in a situation at college where he might need some type of formal attire, Ruth bought him a suit. In mid-July, she and Arnold drove to Camp *Sar Shalom* in Honey Brook, Pennsylvania, where he had attended for the first time in 1957, when he was still living in Brooklyn. Now, five years later, he was back, this time as a volunteer worker for two weeks, getting free room and board while helping out with the Jewish teenagers.

When Camp *Sar Shalom* was over, Arnold rode back to New York City and met up again with Mr. Haynie who drove him to the campsite in the Adirondack Mountains. His friend, Bob Futoran, had already come up from Washington, D.C., a couple of weeks earlier. The two lads would spend the next two weeks helping their teacher prepare the grounds for the fourth Memory Camp. Aside from hooking up the water supply as they had previously done, one of their main jobs was to install a septic tank, for which they had to dig a trench. For the rest of the time, they engaged in general maintenance work.

It was great for Arnold and Bob to reconnect again after one year. Bob was sorry to hear that his friend had been put out of his home because of his faith. Their background and experiences in life were so different. Bob had grown up in a genteel, middle class environment composed of educated people from a diversity of international backgrounds integrated into one community in Washington, D.C., with very supportive parents. In contrast, Arnold had grown up in an immigrant family in a predominantly Jewish community in Brooklyn, New York, next to other distinct ethnic groups, where the children often had to compete on swagger. It was difficult for youngsters to survive in the rough neighborhoods of New York City without a certain sense of projected arrogance.

Bob's parents first met Arnold during the previous summer of 1961, when they had come up to help Mr. Haynie with the chaperoning of the other first and second year Memory Camp teenagers in their afternoon activities. As the five-year curriculum progressed, there was a new class of students each summer. Other teachers taught those classes, while Mr. Haynie continued with the original group. At that time, Bob's parents did not take too well to Arnold. They thought that he was a bit rough around the edges with a vague sense of arrogance about him. Dressed in his casual West Coast fashion, Arnold came across to Bob's conservative parents as a bit of a hoodlum, especially with his strong accent and strange tone to his clipped speech. Despite their initial misgivings, Bob's parents did not object to their son's friendship with him.

Their initial impression of Arnold was not too far-fetched. When he returned to the third Memory Camp in the summer of 1961 after a two-year absence, some members of his Messianic Youth Fellowship were a bit surprised to see the outward changes in him. For most thus far, their world consisted only of New York City. California appeared to be some far away, exotic place that they had never visited before. So, when Arnold came back to the East Coast attired in his California mode in a leather jacket complete with his greased hair slicked back, they took note.

This summer of 1962, however, Arnold had cleaned up. He was no longer dressed in his West Coast fashion, and his hairstyle returned to the more conservative East Coast cut. Perhaps, it was the loneliness of the years in California that drove him to take on some of the worldly airs, but now that he had returned to the East Coast for good, he left all the modish trends behind. He was still interested in girls, of course, and looked forward to seeing Mary Ann Morrow again, but she was not there. He later heard that her father had died that summer, so her family could not come to their summer home in the Adirondacks.

The topic of study for the fourth Memory Camp was "The Life of Christ and His Appearances." Arnold's group had dwindled in size from around twenty to less than ten students. As usual, Arnold had accurately recited all one hundred and twenty verses related to the topic. He found the discussions on some of the deep theological questions very stimulating and drank it all in.

Most churches did not come close to exploring some of the controversial issues that they examined together. He looked forward to more in-depth study when he got to college.

During his senior year in high school, Arnold had looked into different Bible colleges to see which ones offered the type of courses in his areas of interest, which were Hebrew and Greek. The first option, King's College in Briarcliff Manor, New York, did not offer Hebrew. The second option, Philadelphia College of the Bible (now Philadelphia Biblical University) in Langhorne, Pennsylvania, did not have the two majors that he required. The only college that offered both Hebrew and Hellenistic Studies as a combined double major was Shelton College in Ringwood, New Jersey. So, Arnold applied there and was accepted. It was his intention to enroll for the fall semester 1962, if he could find a way to pay for the tuition and fees.

EVER SINCE HE GOT SAVED AT THE AGE OF THIRTEEN, Arnold yearned to be baptized by *tvilah*, Hebrew for "total immersion." At the time, his parents had flatly refused him permission, and the subject was shut down. In their Jewish minds, baptism was the crucial step from which a Jew had no return. Even if a Jew professed to believe in Jesus, he was not considered truly serious, nor was the decision permanent, until baptism. There was always hope that the person would eventually grow out of the phase or could be persuaded to renounce Jesus before that step.

In Arnold's case, his parents had expected his messianic beliefs to fall by the wayside once his childish interests had faded. Much to their dismay, their first-born continued to hold fast to his faith in Messiah Jesus. While he was living with his parents, Arnold knew that he could not bring up the subject of baptism ever again. However, now that he was on his own, he could make his personal decisions and be responsible for them. He definitely wanted to take the step of obedience and be baptized. The most conducive time and place to have this ceremony was right after the ABMJ's Annual Summer's End Conference, which was held in the latter part of August every year. All the ABMJ staff workers would gather at the New York headquarters on 72nd Street for a few days of meetings. Arnold wanted Dr. Daniel Fuchs, who by then was the head of the organization, to officiate the ceremony and to baptize him.

His baptism took place at the baptistry on the ground floor of the ABMJ headquarters building. Another member of the M.Y.F., a girl, was baptized on the same day. It was a lovely ceremony, one that Arnold had waited for so many years to become a reality in his life. Surrounded by Ruth Wardell, Burl Haynie, and many others from his youth group, it was a moving time for the ones being baptized as they each gave their individual testimony and acknowledged the work of Messiah *Yeshua* in their life. It was a momentous occasion for Arnold as he was totally immersed in the water. He knew in his heart that this was a special day that he would remember for the rest of his life.

After the ceremony, Arnold stayed a few more days with Mr. Haynie in his little efficiency, a rented one-room studio in the house of an elderly Swedish lady. Another tiny room off to the side functioned as his office. An extra bed was put in the room for Arnold to sleep at night. He had nowhere else to go and needed a place to stay until early September, when the college campus would be open for the new students. The already limited space became even more cramped with an extra bed, but the teacher and his pupil somehow managed to make do.

While Arnold was at the fourth Memory Camp, he had hatched what he figured to be a brilliant plan as a solution to his dilemma of how to pay for his college tuition. By deferring his enrollment at Shelton College, he would take a year off to work and earn as much money as possible with a full-time job in New York City and possibly a second part-time job, saving up every penny to start his studies the following year. God seemed unimpressed with Arnold's intention and gave him no peace about it. Burl Haynie was not impressed either. He simply commented to Arnold that if it were God's will for him to study at Shelton College, then God would provide for all of his needs. Next, he taught his pupil a saying by J. Hudson Taylor, the foremost missionary to China in the nineteenth century: "God's work done in God's time will never lack God's support." Burl himself lived by faith according to that saying as reflected in how he conducted his daily life. So before Arnold left the campsite that summer, he made the decision to proceed directly to college that fall semester and let God deal with the tuition and fees. It was a matter of learning to trust the Lord to provide the necessary funds to get him through. He had avidly read about J. Hudson Taylor's marvelous faith-based ministry in China, and was equally impressed with George Müller's life of faith in Bristol, England. In the early 1900s, this stalwart believer had cared for tens of thousands of orphans without ever telling others about his needs. In both circumstances, God had always come through with His provision.

By the end of the summer, Arnold had spent most of his remaining $103, leaving him a paltry sum of $20 from the original $120 he had at the beginning of the summer. The total cost of tuition and fees plus other expenses amounted to approximately $2,000 per year at Shelton College, equivalent to about $20,000 in present-day currency terms. That was one hundred times more than the meager $20 he had left in his pocket, which was not going to get him too far. All his worldly possessions were contained in his one and only suitcase. He would have to depend solely upon the Lord to provide for him in his new life at college in the fall. Facing an unknown future, Arnold again found encouragement and reassurance in God's Word: *And my God shall supply every need of yours according to His riches in glory in Messiah Yeshua.* (Philippians 4:19) Trusting God, Arnold purposed in his heart that he would look only to Messiah Jesus and no one else to provide for all his personal needs.

Despite the many hardships he encountered, Arnold would come to experience a deep, inexpressible joy as he witnessed firsthand the wonderful ways through which God answered his prayers. He could not have known it then, but God had chosen him to be His servant, saved through Messiah Jesus, to bear spiritual fruit. As his life unfolded in the decades to follow, Arnold proved indeed to be God's chosen fruit from the very beginning.

God's Provision Begins

In September 1962, Arnold walked into the business office of Shelton College, having just registered for his courses and walked out with a bill of $750 to be paid by the end of the first semester. As a private Christian liberal arts college, Shelton did not receive any big endowments the way many secular colleges did in the United States and hence offered very little in the way of scholarships. Not being a state university, neither did it qualify for grants from the government to assist deserving individuals. The college operated largely upon the tuition paid by the students.

Walking down the corridor with the bill in his hand, Arnold prayed silently to God in his heart, "Lord, You would not let me work a year first, so You are going to have to provide this money by the time payment is due." Shelton College had an interesting payment policy. The student was allowed to start the semester without any payment until the end. This meant that Arnold had four months to settle his bill. Otherwise, he would not be permitted to continue his studies the next semester.

The college tuition, including a shared room in the dormitory and meals at the college cafeteria, was not Arnold's only financial obligation. He still needed to pay for his textbooks, clothes and incidentals for each new semester. Adding these other expenses, Arnold needed a total of about $1,000, equivalent to $10,000 in current-day terms, to get through the first semester. For him, this was an enormous sum.

Thinking back to God's provision beginning from the time he left Los Angeles, it was evident that God's hand had been upon him every step along the way to Shelton College. If God could move the hearts of strangers to supply his needs, then surely God would not abandon him now. Arnold knew from experience how faithful God had been to him and wanted to trust Him fully without reserve to provide for his every need. Hence, he decided that it would be his personal policy going forward never to make his own needs publicly known, not even to his close personal friends, as that would violate the faith principle. He would not even ask his friends to pray for him, because he wanted to make sure that no one would give him money out of any kind of sympathy, but rather only from the prompting of the Lord. Just as J. Hudson Taylor and George Müller had done in their lives, Arnold always prayed privately, asking God for the things he needed and then watched God provide for him time and time again. It was a policy he kept to the present day.

About ten days prior to the start of the semester, Arnold was allowed to come on campus to settle in his dorm room to begin working at the college library. For thirty-five to fifty cents an hour, he worked about twenty hours per week during the semester when classes were in session. He processed new books and magazines, cataloging each one for circulation. Another task was to mend, bind and repair old books that had been worn out or damaged from a lot of usage and handling. He was very grateful for this part-time work that the college had granted him to help defray some of his costs. The business office applied his earnings directly to the tuition that he owed for the semester, so no cash passed his hands. While not earning much, every penny counted toward paying off his bill. Arnold was able to keep this part-time job during his entire time at Shelton—a true blessing from the Lord.

God's provision came in a myriad of miraculous ways. Whenever Arnold needed something, the money was always there. During the four months of the first semester, he would often find cash in a plain envelope placed in his mailbox on the college campus. Sometimes, he would find checks sent from people living a third of the way across the country as far as Indiana— benefactors whom Arnold had never met nor heard of before. At other times, checks were sent to the business office at the college in the strictest of confidence to be applied directly to his tuition, on the stipulation that their identity remained anonymous. Arnold had no idea how these supporters had come to hear about a short Jewish lad of five feet four inches, studying on a Christian college campus in New Jersey.

It was possible that some of the people who sent him money had heard his testimony in the past, when he spoke at various churches. They might have been people who had learned about him through word-of-mouth from others who somehow knew his story. Or, they may have been connected in some way to the ABMJ offices or the Concordia Lutheran Church and had read about him through their networks. Regardless, Arnold was living by faith, and God proved faithful in supplying all his needs through the glorious riches in Messiah Jesus.

At the end of the first semester when payment was due, Arnold walked into the business office to discover that the bill of $750 had already been paid up in full! In fact, instead of Arnold owing the college money, it was the college that actually now owed him money for the semester! The business office hence applied the surplus money to his tuition bill for the second semester of that academic year. One of his Gentile roommates, who worked part-time at the business office and had thus heard about Arnold's situation, came up to him in the cafeteria that evening and said, "Boy, you really are Jewish, aren't you?!"

ALTHOUGH SHELTON COLLEGE WAS LOCATED IN RINGWOOD, New Jersey, just south of the New York state line, Arnold took time on weekends to join the Messianic Youth Fellowship in Brooklyn. Together with Ruth Wardell, he went with three or four teenagers a couple of times per month to give their testimonies in the nearby areas. On any given Sunday, they would go to a different church to minister during the evening meetings. Every once in a while, they went to churches that were located in other parts of New Jersey, a couple of hours' drive away.

Most of the time, Arnold would arrange to meet Miss Wardell and a few of the teenagers somewhere in New York City to get a ride to the church where they would be speaking that evening. He never missed a meeting. Usually, one of the other members of the group spoke first. Arnold would be the last one to give his testimony about what the Lord had done for him in his life. He was a good speaker and took command of the podium, although he spoke with a strong accent in a clipped rhythm, which was not always easy to understand or follow. With so few Jewish believers at that time, he was somewhat of a novelty, so people paid attention and took note of his message.

On one occasion, the group was to minister at a church located quite far in southern New Jersey. Arnold happened to be in another part of the state that afternoon at a prior engagement. Ruth thought that surely for this one time only, he would miss this particular meeting as an exception to his excellent attendance record. However, shortly after the meeting started, much to the group's surprise, in walked Arnold. He had hitchhiked all the way across the state just to get to the meeting! He wanted to always honor the Lord and remain faithful to Him.

When the evening ended, Ruth drove Arnold for over an hour and a half back north to New York City, where she dropped him off at a train station. It was past eleven-thirty at night, and the public buses had already stopped running. The trains ran quite sporadically at that time of the night, so Arnold had to wait for over an hour before he could catch a train up to Ringwood, New Jersey. With no public transportation so late at night in Ringwood, Arnold walked the three miles from the train station to his college campus. By the time he got back to his dorm, it was two or three o'clock in the morning. So, he just rolled into bed in his street clothes, in order to get up bright and early the next morning for his classes. Being a night owl, Arnold normally struggled to get up in the morning, so he wanted to squeeze in as much sleep as he could in the few hours that he had left. Most others would not have gone to such lengths to attend those meetings, but Arnold was truly faithful to his commitments.

For Christmas that year, his friend, Bob, invited Arnold to stay with his family in Washington, D.C., over the holidays. Bob's parents noticed the change in Arnold and, after getting to know him a bit, decided that he was a decent lad, that there was hope for him yet, and started to take a liking to him. They treated him like one of their children. Bob was the oldest child in the family and had five brothers and one sister. Hence, he viewed Arnold as one of his brothers. During the school year, he sometimes came up to see Arnold over a weekend, and at other times Arnold went down to visit Bob. Thus, their friendship continued to grow.

When the second semester of his freshman year ended, Arnold again walked into the business office of Shelton College to settle his bill. To his great relief and joy, he discovered that God had once again arranged for the entire bill to be paid up! As was the case the previous semester, there was even some extra money left over in his account, which could be credited to the fall semester of his second year of college. Arnold was both amazed and grateful at the way God had come through so wonderfully for him in supplying all his needs.

DURING THE SUMMER OF 1963, Arnold went to New York City to work at the printing and mailing department headed by Burl Haynie at the ABMJ on 72nd Street in Manhattan. Arnold did odd jobs, filing, sorting, collating, stapling and so on, to mail out tracts and magazines to the donors. For his accommodation, Arnold stayed at the ABMJ building on Throop Avenue in Williamsburg, Brooklyn, the base for the large youth and teenage ministry in the area. The ground floor consisted mainly of office space. A large gym that doubled as an activities hall occupied most of the second floor alongside several rooms. The third floor apartment was rented out to a tenant family. The ABMJ placed a bed for Arnold in one of the rooms on the second floor, which also comprised a bathroom plus kitchen facilities.

By mid-July, it was time to take a break from his work at the ABMJ print shop to go up to the Adirondacks. As in the previous year, Arnold would be working on the campgrounds for two weeks in preparation for the fifth Memory Camp, the last segment of the five-year cycle. His friend, Bob, arrived in time to join him and Mr. Haynie on their drive up to the campsite.

Burl Haynie was a very demanding boss, both at the ABMJ print shop and at the campsite. Due to his physique and his background as a police officer, he was a naturally imposing man. In many ways, he was a strict taskmaster, working the boys very hard on the campgrounds, making sure that the lads put in a full day's labor. Pretty soon, Arnold and Bob came up with a nickname for him and began affectionately referring to him as "Bullwhip Haynie." All in the spirit of fun, the two pooled together their resources at the end of the summer and bought him a whip as a gift. Burl proudly displayed it on the wall of his office in the print shop for the next several years.

Arnold learned many important lessons from his mentor regarding a strong work ethic. According to Mr. Haynie, it was not a matter of whether or not one wanted to do the work, but a matter of doing what needed to get done. It included putting in a full day's work, the discipline of always being on time, and daily setting aside time to study the Word of God. The teacher truly cared about his students and took a personal interest in their spiritual formation. Arnold also learned from him that it was possible to exercise both self-discipline and self-control.

The topic of the fifth Memory Camp covered "The Prophetic." It was of special interest to Arnold, and the classes delved into some deep discussions on what the Scriptures revealed about the future. The group had further dwindled in size and in the end, only three of the teenagers in the original group, namely, Arnold, Bob, and one other student, Rachel, successfully completed the five-year program. As Burl Haynie believed in rewarding the students for their hard work, the final prize for going through the entire five-year cycle and accurately reciting all the verses was a multi-volume set of the *International Bible Encyclopedia*. Arnold was absolutely thrilled to get this prize, as it would serve as excellent reference material for his biblical studies in college.

MUCH TO ARNOLD'S DELIGHT, the nice girl, Mary Ann, her older brother, and her two younger sisters were at the campsite that summer. Their mother, Olive Morrow, had taken on the job of cooking for the Memory Camp. The three girls worked in the kitchen, helping their mother cook the meals and clean up afterwards. Both Arnold and Bob found the girls attractive. The middle sister, Beth, was quite tomboyish, but the youngest one, Kathy, was very cute. Mary Ann was bubbly and lots of fun to be around. There was a lot of interaction between Arnold and Mary Ann that summer, although still mostly in a group setting. Sometimes after lunch, when the lads were helping the girls clean up, they would engage in typical, fun-loving teenage behavior, pulling the girls' braids, or chasing them around the tables, throwing wet dishtowels at one another. During the evening sessions, Arnold and Mary Ann passed notes to each other, writing little messages alongside Scripture verses or music lyrics. When they felt really daring, they would sometimes sit together in the back row and sneak in a little handholding every now and then.

It was apparent that Arnold was extremely fond of Mary Ann. Toward the end of the time at camp, he had written on the cover of her notebook, "Miriam Hannah Tomorrowbaum," a very interesting combination of their last names—Mary Ann's being Morrow and Arnold's being Fruchtenbaum—plus the implication for the future in the word, Tomorrow. Neither one discussed what that name meant. However, his entry was a seed that was planted, marking the beginning of a friendship that developed as they kept up a writing relationship and got to know each other better through their letters.

In the autumn of that year, Arnold entered his second year of college, and Mary Ann started her last year of high school. For both Thanksgiving and Christmas of 1963, Arnold went to visit Mary Ann at her home, which was by then in Williamstown, New Jersey. As they talked and spent time together, their friendship grew more deeply. When it was time for him to return to his college after Christmas, no specific plans were made for when they would next see each other. Arnold would no longer be going up to the Adirondacks, as he had finished his five-year cycle of the Memory Camp. However, they continued to correspond.

It was only after the first year in college that Arnold realized how much more of the Bible he had learned from Mr. Haynie just in the short few weeks during one summer than he did in a whole year of classes at Shelton. Those five summers had made a deep impact on his knowledge of the Scriptures and on his spiritual growth. In many ways, it appeared that God had brought about the five years of Memory Camp uniquely for Arnold's training, helping to lay the foundation for his future life's work. The following year, the entire Memory Camp cycle was discontinued. The ABMJ never again had a program of that nature in its ministry. Burl Haynie's teachings molded and shaped Arnold in such a way that the influence remained strong even long into the latter years of his life.

First Two Years at Shelton College

As the only Messianic Jewish student on the Shelton College campus, Arnold found himself in a very unique and unusual position. Much to his disappointment, he soon came to realize that the undercurrents of anti-Semitism were prevalent among many of the Gentile Christian students as well as some of the faculty members. Most of his professors were Gentile believers, whose prevailing position was a form of Replacement Theology known as Covenant Theology. They wrongly believed that the Church had replaced Israel and that all the promised blessings to Israel were now transferred to the Church. This, then, became a source of conflict in the classroom between those professors and Arnold, who, as a Jewish believer, held to a Dispensationalist viewpoint that there were two distinct peoples of God, namely, Israel and the Church, as clearly taught in the New Testament. Sadly, only a couple of the professors at Shelton College adhered to this theology, one of whom was Dr. Ralph Beich, Arnold's Hebrew and Greek professor.

From time to time, Arnold experienced harassments on campus, because he was Jewish. One day, he found a swastika painted on the door of his dormitory room. His three Gentile roommates were not anti-Semitic in their attitude. The four of them got along just fine, so it could not have been one of them who had done it. Sometimes, when he was walking across the campus, Arnold would be subjected to abusive name-calling. At other times, while he was waiting for a ride on the far side of the campus, his tormentors would occasionally use scare tactics on him by lighting a fire in front of a building close by. They were part of a white supremacist crowd and were not nice people to begin with.

During Arnold's second year at Shelton, one other Messianic Jewish student enrolled in his first year. Unable to cope with the harassments he received on campus because of his Jewish background, he transferred out of Shelton upon the completion of just one semester. However, Arnold carried on, strengthened in his resolve to obtain his degree in the majors he selected. In his classes, he experienced huge frustrations, as he was centrist while Shelton College's position was far right-winged, very conservative, being founded upon a Presbyterian background. A pathetic lack of solid Scripture knowledge prevailed among the student body. Some even believed that all peoples of African descent were cursed from the time of Cain. There was one Jamaican Christian student there on campus, and Arnold ended up being his protector from the harassments he was subjected to from the racist crowd.

Although the college president was not overtly anti-Semitic, the undercurrents would surface every now and again. While Arnold never complained about his situation, it was an unspoken expectation that because he was different from the other students, he would be treated differently. It was the first time in Arnold's life as a believer that he had experienced anti-Semitism firsthand in a Gentile Christian context. For the most part, the faculty treated him with respect, but that was not the case with a sizable minority of the students.

REMAINING ACTIVE IN THE M.Y.F., Arnold continued to go with a group of three to four teenagers a couple of times per month to different churches on Sundays to speak and to give his testimony. He had a lot of contact with Ruth Wardell and stayed at her place on numerous occasions over the weekends. He also contributed regularly to the newsletter in his role as editor. Instead of the name, *Teens for the Messiah*, it was now called *Ha-Adouth—The Witness* and published quarterly instead of bi-monthly. In one of the issues, Arnold wrote an article entitled, "The Hebrew-Christian in a Christian College," describing his experiences.

> The path of the Hebrew-Christian college student tends to be narrower than those of other Christians and those of other Jews. He seems to be an odd stone in the mainstream of society, conspicuous to the Jews by his Christianity and to the Christians by his Jewishness. He, more than his fellow Christians and fellow Jews, becomes the center of attention... Unique? Enigma? At any rate, he is a deviant from the norm—sometimes to his advantage and sometimes not.
>
> What does the Hebrew-Christian college student have to face that is peculiar to him alone? The Hebrew-Christian in a Christian college is faced with a predominance of Gentile Christian environment. Sometimes, he finds another Hebrew-Christian to share the burden, but more often than not, he stands alone. Whether or not he faces any anti-Semitism is usually dependent on the type of Christian college he chooses. Anti-Semitism is a strong element of Shelton College... Christian colleges, which take a Dispensational doctrinal position are usually lacking in anti-Semitism, since such elements would be inconsistent with Dispensationalism. But, we wish only to deal with a pro-Semitic type of Christian college.

It does not take long before everyone knows that the student is Jewish. He soon receives various epithets of his Jewishness, he is kidded, always reminded that all Jews are rich and of course all his friendly tormentors have good Jewish friends back home or somewhere in the distant past. All these things are spoken to him in fun and harm is never intended by them. It is their way of making conversation and the Hebrew-Christian learns to take it, although now and then it gets on his nerves.

A very unique position of the Hebrew-Christian in a Christian college is that of being expected to be an accomplished Bible scholar. He is expected to have a perfect understanding of Hebrew, know the Scriptures inside out and be able to expound deep biblical truths, which are unavailable to non-Jews. So, as a result, rarely does a day pass without questions being put to him by other students. Such questions, usually asked out of simple curiosity, sometimes prove amusing, such as "What exactly is circumcision?" The amusement comes that after twenty years the young man realizes that he is circumcised!

Faculty members are also a source of numerous questions, especially in Bible classes. Teachers with certain ideas usually turn to Hebrew-Christian students for support. If an instructor believes that only unleavened bread should be used for Communion, he asks the Hebrew-Christian if the Jews would ever use leaven for the Passover. The Hebrew-Christian of course answers in the negative, but he feels like adding, "We don't use Welch's grape juice either." But he refrains, for this he also learns to live with. He is soon forced to study Scripture more thoroughly, in order to be able to answer these questions when they come to him, for more is expected of him..[17]

Academically, Arnold excelled in his Bible classes, always getting A's for his grades. However, his grade point average in the first couple of years fell

---

[17] Excerpts: *Ha-Adouth—The Witness*, April-June 1966

slightly short of the perfect 4.0 mark, due to the math classes he was obliged to take. Being a liberal arts college offering a well-rounded education, Shelton required basic courses in all fields to be taken in addition to those in one's major. Arnold never liked mathematics and struggled with it all through his junior and senior high school years. Now that he was required to take the more complex math classes in college, he had to suffer through them yet again, barely scraping by with a C.

For exercise, Arnold worked out in the gym playing basketball with a few other students, running up and down the court, shooting hoops. Not tall enough, Arnold did not qualify to be on the college basketball team, but he liked the competitiveness of the sport and the workout that the basket shooting gave him. In college, Arnold was extremely competitive and played hard to win every time. He once played a game of ping-pong with someone and lost. For the next time, Arnold practiced and practiced and practiced, to make sure that he would win the game, even though it was not a formal competition. He enjoyed winning. Yet, he was not a sore loser, very graciously accepting defeat when he lost. Nevertheless, Arnold's goal for every game was to win, even if he played with a friend just for fun.

His competitiveness and keenness to win held Arnold in good stead when he entered a chess competition in college. Having learned how to play chess at the D.P. Camps even before he knew how to read or write, Arnold was very skilled at the game for someone his age. Requiring a good memory, strategies and mental prowess, chess was the right kind of game for Arnold. Although he had not played through his high school years and considered chess to be only a hobby, he achieved second place in the contest.

Aside from his studies during the academic year, Arnold was busy with his part-time job of twenty hours per week at the college library, his contributions as editor of the *Ha-Adouth—The Witness* newsletter and his work with the M.Y.F., speaking at various churches on Sundays. Yet, he still found time to write prolifically to Mary Ann. His letters were sometimes up to thirty-eight pages long, as he shared his thoughts with her on a myriad of subjects. Because they corresponded with such regularity, their written exchanges at times touched on some very personal matters.

During the summer of 1964, Arnold and Mary Ann did not have much of an opportunity to see each other. The five-year cycle of the Memory Camp had ended, and Arnold was not going up to the campsite that summer. Instead, he would be in New York City, working at the World's Fair. Mary

Ann, on the other hand, planned to be in upstate New York with her mother and siblings at their house near the campgrounds in the Adirondack Mountains. So, they made plans to meet toward the end of the summer. Meanwhile, they continued to write to each other, progressively sharing more and more on a personal level as time went on. Soon, their friendship took on a deeper meaning for Arnold as he contemplated the future.

God had so richly provided for Arnold again during his second year at Shelton College, just as He had done during the first year. When Arnold went to the business office to settle his bill at the end of each semester during his second year, he found that the Lord had already taken care of it, each time with a little extra left over to be applied to the tuition of the following semester! He was amazed at the various means through which God had supplied all his needs exactly according to the promise in Philippians 4:19. His heart was filled with gratitude that the Lord honored his decision not to reveal his own personal needs to anyone but to trust God alone to supply them. The Lord had indeed come through for Arnold's financial needs and brought glory to Himself by revealing His faithfulness to the one who put his entire trust in the Great Provider.

Summer at the World's Fair

God's timing for the sake of Arnold's Scripture training was impeccable. The five-year Memory Camp came to a close at the end of summer 1963, and the World's Fair commenced in April 1964. It was scheduled to run until October and again over the same period in 1965. The site was the Flushing Meadows Corona Park in the Borough of Queens. At that time, New York City had the largest Jewish community in the world, and the ABMJ saw this event as a great opportunity to reach the Jews with the Gospel of Jesus the Messiah. Had the Memory Camp cycle started a year later, the fifth year program, which would have landed in 1964, may not have taken place at all, as Burl Haynie's attention would have been focused on the World's Fair instead. God certainly foreknew!

Because of the Jews' high interest in education, the ABMJ applied for and procured floor space in the Hall of Education. The fact that a missionary organization was permitted to have a display stand at all was in itself a miracle, let alone in the Hall of Education, despite the initial misgivings of some World's Fair officials to its presence in the latter.

Burl Haynie, with the assistance of another ABMJ worker, had undertaken the designing and construction of the booth. The world's most unusual, revolving clock with the words, "Israel—God's Timepiece," was displayed in front. On the one side was a regular clock displaying the correct time to a split second, encircled with the Scripture verse: *behold, now is the acceptable time; behold, now is the day of salvation.* (II Corinthians 6:2b) On the other was another clock with its hands moving swiftly over a map of the world. Around the border were the words: *it is even the time of Jacob's trouble.* (Jeremiah 30:7b) The piece created a strong visual impact, attracting many visitors.

The ABMJ display booth was located at the most prime location in the Hall of Education. Situated on the upper level right across from the top landing of the escalators, visitors had to pass in front of it to get to the rest of the exhibits on that floor. Right behind it was a *kosher* restaurant. Any Orthodox Jew wanting to have a meal or a snack would have to get past the ABMJ display first. Facing the booth on the opposite side was a bar, which also attracted a lot of foot traffic. About seventy million people were expected to visit the World's Fair during the two seasons, but in the end, the tally was closer to fifty-one million.

A beautiful cabinet exhibited an attractive display of the history and purpose of the Mission. A synchronized sight-and-sound slide series depicting Israel was continuously being shown. A small conference table and chairs provided sitting space where a staff worker could talk with the visitors. Because of the word "Israel" on the revolving clock, many people inquired about the Land, thinking that the ABMJ was an Israeli organization. Special editions of the ABMJ tracts were printed prior to the fair, all done through Burl Haynie's print shop, where Arnold had worked the summer before. Many thousands were given out to the Jewish people, who would have otherwise never entered the ABMJ booth. After the fair ended, it took the ABMJ workers many months to follow up on the new contacts, resulting in scores of decisions for Messiah Jesus.

A minimum of two ABMJ workers manned the booth at all times, from ten o'clock in the morning until ten o'clock at night, seven days a week for the six-month period. Staff members, including Burl, all took turns working an eight-hour shift per day on a roster basis. Arnold's job during the summer of 1964 was to work under Mr. Haynie to help out at the ABMJ stand. He learned his lesson in godliness by watching his mentor take a lot of abuse from the Jewish people, something that was expected to a certain extent. Hollering at the staff, calling them proselytizers, intermingled with a few choice Yiddish words, admonishing them that this was no place to convert Jews, they made it plain and clear that the Mission workers were not wanted there. At times, the Jews would angrily tear up the tracts and throw the pieces into the staff workers' faces. Most of those Jews had suffered through World War II and were thus very much against anything linked with Jesus or Christianity. Being on duty at the booth, Arnold also got some of the abuse dished out.

Totally unexpected was the abuse that Burl Haynie got from some of his fellow workers, who did not agree with his ways or methodology. Arnold never saw his teacher get angry nor have a bad word for anyone. One day, he watched a fellow missionary berate Burl with some severe and not particularly "spiritual" language. Arnold's reaction was to want to deck the man, but Mr. Haynie's response was to calmly look straight into his adversary's face, saying something to the effect that because of what he was feeling inside, he needed to remove himself from the scene and pray through the situation. He did just that. Upon his return, he appeared to be at peace, and nothing untoward came out of his mouth.

Arnold's friend, Bob, also worked at the World's Fair. He was very gifted in electrical works and installed most of the wiring and lighting for the presentations in the booth. For the rest of his time, Bob worked as a janitor for the whole Hall of Education, spending hours sweeping up cigarette butts that were strewn on the floor.

Two beds were placed in one of the rooms on the second floor of the ABMJ building on Throop Avenue in Williamsburg, Brooklyn, where Arnold had stayed the previous summer. The two lads shared the room, keeping each other company. Though Arnold was not chatty, he and Bob discussed a whole raft of subjects about life the way blood brothers did in a family. Neither had much money. However, for a bit of diversion and entertainment, they did manage to get out to a couple of enthralling concerts at the big Meadowlands Stadium, where the U.S. Open Tennis Tournaments took place. One was a Joan Baez concert, and the other featured Bob Dylan. It was a first experience for both lads to be among such a massive throng of people in an electrifying atmosphere.

While staying on Throop Avenue, they had another first experience in their life. One day, a huge street riot broke out in front of the ABMJ building, and they could watch the mobs in progress from the safety of their second-floor window. They had no idea what the riot was about, but were thankful not to be caught up in it. In that era, the area was predominantly an old *Chasidic* Jewish neighborhood, which in later years gradually evolved into mainly a Puerto Rican environment.

Over the summer, Arnold kept in touch with Mary Ann through letters. She had graduated in June from high school in Williamstown, New Jersey, and was staying at her family's home in the Adirondacks, waiting to attend Westminster College in northwestern Pennsylvania in the fall. They hoped to meet up at the end of August at her home in New Jersey, before the new semester began in September for both of them.

Year in Cape May, New Jersey

By the time Arnold entered his third year at Shelton College in September 1964, the campus had moved from Ringwood in the north to Cape May in the southernmost tip of the New Jersey peninsula. Occupying the site of a former resort hotel on the waterfront right across the street from the beach, it had a large gym, a bowling alley, a swimming pool, a snack bar and many other amenities. While the atmosphere was more conducive to having fun than studying, Arnold was disciplined enough for the serious study of the Bible, making straight A's in all his classes, resulting in a 4.0 grade point average that semester. He had already finished fulfilling the basic requirements for the math courses in the first two years at Shelton, so no longer had any low marks to pull down his average.

After briefly meeting up with Mary Ann and seeing her off to Westminster College, Arnold knew in his heart that there was something deeper there and eagerly looked forward to the next time they would see each other. When Thanksgiving came around, it was too difficult for Mary Ann to arrange a ride to get home. So upon the invitation of a friend in college, she spent the holiday with her friend's family. However, as planned, Mary Ann would be home in Williamstown during the Christmas break, and Arnold would be staying with her family then.

Two months into the first semester without any warning, Mary Ann stopped writing to him. At Christmas 1964, Arnold was stunned to see the change in her. He could not figure out how or why she had suddenly become so withdrawn and turned into this iceberg. No longer was she vivacious or communicative. She simply broke off the relationship, leaving him feeling distraught and sickened.

When it came time for them both to get back to their respective colleges, Arnold was very concerned about Mary Ann's wellbeing and kept in touch with her roommate at Westminster. Two months later in February, the roommate contacted him. Something had happened to Mary Ann, and Arnold had to come quickly. He made a special trip to her college to see what he could do to help. However, Mary Ann wanted nothing to do with him. She gave no explanation whatsoever and halted any and all communication with him. He did not know whether they would ever be together again. Arnold continued to write to her until the end of the second semester in June 1965, without receiving a single reply. After that, he also stopped writing. As perplexed as he felt, he had to accept the painful reality that their relationship had come to a dead end. He grieved at the prospect of never seeing Mary Ann again. Yet, he knew in his heart that he needed to move on and try to forget her in due course.

NOW THAT THE SHELTON CAMPUS HAD MOVED TO CAPE MAY, it was too far for Arnold to join Ruth Wardell and the M.Y.F. on Sundays. However, he still stayed actively involved as editor of the *Ha-Adouth—The Witness* newsletter and joined the group every once in a while to minister at various churches closer by. Meanwhile, he found a place of worship in a nearby area called Rio Grande and began attending the Sunday morning services at Grace Gospel Chapel. There, Arnold met a Gentile couple by the name of Charles and Eva Cattell, who lived in Wildwood, New Jersey, not far from Cape May. When they heard that he was the one and only Messianic Jewish student on campus, they invited him over for lunch. From then on, they opened up their home to Arnold and even let him use their car. They had several children, the oldest being the same age as Arnold, and treated Arnold like one of their own, calling him "son," while Arnold called them "mom" and "pop." Their children called him "brother," and Arnold in turn called them "brothers" and "sisters," treating one another just like siblings.

Charles Cattell was a milk deliveryman. The family did not have much money, but used what they had toward giving to the youth ministry at their home church. A very outgoing, youth-loving couple, the Cattells owned a large house along a saltwater canal. Teenage believers from the surrounding churches were often invited to their home. One weekend in early May 1965, Arnold's M.Y.F. group, including his close friend, Bob, descended upon their house for two days of fun and relaxation.

On Saturday after a scrumptious lunch of lasagna, *matzah* ball soup, and *gefilte* fish, the teenagers went bowling in the afternoon. The next day, they went to minister at Arnold's church through their music and guitar. About thirty other Shelton College students were in attendance. One girl gave her testimony, and Arnold closed with a message from Romans chapter 11. Later, after a big meal including a delicious main course of *kosher* roast beef at the Cattells, the youth group went to visit Arnold's campus. They were very surprised to see a resort hotel environment utilized for a college. All too soon at the end of the afternoon, it came time for the group to journey back to their home base.

Because the Cattells lived nearby, Arnold had a place to stay during all his breaks between semesters. He felt at home with them and very much a part of their family. With Mary Ann's abrupt termination of all communication with him even as he continued to write to her, the Cattell family's love and acceptance was God's wonderful provision of encouragement and support as a means of soothing the soreness and confusion of his heart.

In fact, although Arnold had personally experienced the truth of Matthew 10:35 regarding the division between a man and his father, he could also testify to the truth of Jesus' promise of restoration in this life for the losses incurred for the faith:

Yeshua said, Verily I say unto you, There is no man that has left house or brethren, or sisters, or mother, or father, or children, or lands, for My sake and for the gospel's sake, but he shall receive a hundredfold now in this time, houses and brethren and sisters and mothers and children and lands, with persecutions; and in the world to come eternal life. (Mark 10:29-30)

After being expelled from his home in California and starting college, Arnold was "adopted" for all intents and purposes by three different sets of families— not in the legal sense, but in every practical way. By the time he was in his third year at Shelton in Cape May, he had three different house keys on his keychain. The first was for Ruth Wardell's house in Levittown on Long Island, New York. To Arnold, she was his spiritual mom, whom he affectionately called Mom Wardell. She gave him a key to her home to make it easier for him to come and go whenever he needed. The second was for the house of Bob Futoran's family in Washington, D.C. Every now and then, Bob and his parents would come up to Cape May to see him. During vacations and breaks, Arnold would go down and visit them. Bob's parents were used to "adopting" people. Because Arnold was like a brother to Bob, he was accepted as part of the family and given a key to their home to come and go as he pleased. The third was for the Cattells' house in Wildwood, New Jersey. They were like a family to Arnold, and he felt free to stay with them whenever he had a break from school. Arnold was very much a part of all their lives and accepted as a member of each of these families. God had truly restored to him families in this life, over and above all that he could have hoped for or imagined.

SOON AFTER HE HAD BEEN "ADOPTED" INTO THESE FAMILIES, Arnold was confronted with an unusual proposal from his own father. Henry decided to take his first trip to Israel on his own to visit his two brothers and three sisters.[18] It had been nearly nineteen years since he had last seen most of his family members, when he fled for a second time from Poland in 1946. Scarred from the ravages of World War II, Henry had suffered mentally and emotionally from the loss of his other siblings who had perished in the Holocaust. Now that so many years had passed since he settled in America, Henry longed to see his remaining five siblings and their respective families. So, he went to visit them for several weeks. On his way back from Israel in April 1965, he stayed with some friends in New York City and asked to see Arnold. On the surface, Henry appeared to have finally relaxed his policy of total silence, so Arnold went to New York City to meet with him. In an attempt to turn his son back from the path that he had chosen, Henry had

---

[18] As previously explained on pages 41 and 42, they were Henry's uncles and aunts, but since he grew up with them, they referred to one another as brothers and sisters.

devised a scheme of bribery. Getting straight to the point, he put forth a proposal that he thought would be irresistible to his son. He offered Arnold payment for all his college tuition, a car, plus other things, on condition that he would give up his faith. Since renouncing his faith was something Arnold simply could not do, he graciously declined his father's generous offer.

Though Henry continued to be very strongly opposed to Arnold's messianic beliefs and was worried that his relatives in Israel might cut him off from the family, if they got wind of his son's unacceptable convictions, he wanted to somehow find a means to relent his ironclad policy of silence toward him. Seeing that his son would not compromise his beliefs, Henry nonetheless extended a small gesture of reconciliation by inviting him to visit the family in California that summer. Surprised but thankful, Arnold gladly accepted the invitation, all the while hoping that his father would not retract or change his mind in the interim.

ASIDE FROM HIS PERSONAL CONCERNS FOR MARY ANN, Arnold discovered that he also had to deal with a massive crisis at Shelton College. By the end of that academic year in June 1965, Shelton had undergone a huge split. The president of the college had left Cape May to go down to Florida to start a new college called Clearwater Christian College on a new campus. Most of the faculty went with him. Although officially the college made the split sound like a religious issue, the real reason was due to personality conflicts. Shelton College ended up losing its accreditation, which meant that the students would not be able to graduate with a recognized degree.

Arnold immediately began looking into other Christian liberal arts colleges to see if his credits from Shelton would be accepted. Other colleges did welcome students to transfer to their campus. However, instead of being their last year, the seniors were required to study an extra year on the new campus to graduate. This simply did not suit Arnold, as he had already fulfilled all the requirements for his combined double major in Hebrew and Hellenistic Studies at Shelton in the three years. Besides, he did not want to spend a fifth year in college.

The only college that accepted all his credits in order for him to graduate with one year of study on its campus was Cedarville College in Ohio. However, it did not offer the same majors as Shelton did in Hebrew and Hellenistic Studies. At Cedarville, Greek was offered as a major, but Hebrew was only part of the elective courses. The only major that could be applicable for Arnold was the Pre-Seminary major. He would have to take a few extra courses during his senior year there, but Cedarville College accepted all his Shelton credits to count toward that major.

Thus in June 1965 at the end of his junior year, Arnold walked into the business office of Shelton College for the last time to settle his bill. Again to his joy and delight, he discovered that God had once again faithfully arranged for the entire bill to be paid up with some money still left over in his account! However, since he was transferring to Cedarville College, he lost the surplus funds in the wash. True to His Word, God had supplied all his needs and had come through for him in amazing ways. Arnold's heart overflowed with gratitude to the Lord.

HEADING OFF TO NEW YORK CITY that summer of 1965 to work a second season with Burl Haynie at the World's Fair, Arnold met up with Bob Futoran at the ABMJ building on Throop Avenue, where they would be rooming together again. This was the last season for the World's Fair to be held in New York City, and it would be another busy summer.

One day, a first-year student from Shelton College by the name of Cathy Hubbard happened to come by the ABMJ booth. She was a dynamic, Gentile believer with a special interest in Jewish ministry in the Middle East. Before enrolling, she had read about Arnold in the ABMJ's *The Chosen People* magazine and looked him up when she came on campus. Through Cathy, Arnold had come into contact with her roommate, Mary Ann Sleichter, also a Gentile believer. In contrast to her classmate, Mary Ann had no interest in Jewish ministries and was studying toward an education major. From time to time, Arnold spoke with her. It turned out that he was the first Jew she had ever met. He informed Cathy about Shelton's precarious position and suggested that both she and Mary Ann make plans to transfer to Cedarville College, which had agreed to accept all Shelton College students without question.

In September 1965, about twenty students in total transferred to Cedarville College. Although it appeared to be a "fluke" that Cathy Hubbard had run into Arnold that day at the World's Fair, God foreknew His plans to use him to impact the future life direction of Mary Ann Sleichter. While the transfer to another college for his last year may have seemed like a totally unnecessary disruption to his education, it ended up being for Arnold's best as he was soon to find out.

SUBSEQUENT TO HIS FATHER'S UNEXPECTED INVITATION, Arnold altered some of his summer plans. Instead of working the entire time at the World's Fair, he decided to take one month off to go home and see his family in August. To defray his travel costs, Arnold found a one-way car delivery job for part of the trip. A company that had sold a car to a buyer in Oklahoma at a special rate was in need of someone to deliver it. The company paid all the fuel costs for the mileage; in essence, Arnold got a free ride all the way to Oklahoma. After dropping off the car, he took a Greyhound bus for the rest of the way to Los Angeles.

In the years after Arnold had left home upon his high school graduation, three more sisters were born to the family, but he had not seen any of them until this visit. Prior to his departure, his mother had shown signs of pregnancy. Lynda was born in November 1962 about five months after Arnold went away. He had only heard about her birth in one of his brief phone calls home. Lynda was now almost three years old. The other two youngest sisters were identical twin girls, Judy and Julie, born nearly two and a half years after Lynda. They were almost six months old when Arnold first saw them.

Henry had made some changes to the corner building on Robertson Boulevard. The larger of the two storefronts on the ground floor now housed his own photography shop. He had moved his business from Fairfax Avenue shortly after the existing tenant's lease had expired. The smaller unit next to it continued to be rented out to the same artist. With the addition of the younger siblings to the family, Adele could work alongside him at the storefront, while being available to the children whenever needed.

One thing that had not changed about Henry was his all-consuming devotion to chess. In fact, he seemed to have become even more obsessed with the game. He grabbed at every opportunity to display his intellectual prowess over his opponents on the chessboard, playing with great intensity and a strong passion to win. His moods still appeared to be very erratic, often dipping into periods of extreme self-doubt and anxiety. It was clear to Arnold that his father's experiences through all the difficult times in the Soviet Union and Europe had taken a heavy toll on his psyche, causing him to be irritable and unable to relax.

Arnold's brother, Eddie, and his sister, Margaret, were both in their teens, and Arthur was already in elementary school. Since they had not bonded with him in the past, they did not relate much to Arnold during his visit. In many ways, their oldest brother was like a stranger to them. Nevertheless, the overall visit went well without incident. Therefore, it was all the more perplexing when the father-son relationship took another negative nose-dive after Arnold returned to the East Coast. Henry once again reverted to his policy of total silence for no apparent reason. Arnold was thankful that at least he got to go home and see his three youngest sisters and the rest of the family. Over the next several years, sometimes he was allowed to make contact; at other times, he was forbidden. That was how the situation remained. He never knew when the door would be open and when it would be closed. For the most part, it remained closed, and Arnold had to endure the silence treatment as a general rule.

ONCE BACK IN NEW YORK CITY AT THE END OF AUGUST 1965, Arnold joined his M.Y.F. for the ABMJ's Annual Summer's End Conference. It was a very fruitful and inspiring time. Right afterwards, he went down to Wildwood, New Jersey, to stay with the Cattells. During the first weekend in September just before the start of the new college semester, about nineteen members of the M.Y.F. converged upon the Cattells' home to enjoy a fun and relaxing get-together. After lunch on Saturday, they went diving off the back porch into the saltwater canal. In the evening after dinner, they took a stroll along the Wildwood boardwalk by the beach.

It was a full house, and bedtime found the girls sleeping upstairs and the boys sleeping downstairs, with the two dogs and one cat somewhere in between. The following morning, the group conducted a worship service at the Cattells' home. It was attended by several national as well as international visitors, bringing the total number to forty-two there for the noonday meal. It was a miracle how the hostess managed to prepare all the food! In the early afternoon, the group enjoyed free recreation. Some went canoeing on the canal, while others lazed around on the banks along the back porch. Later, the group tried to surprise Arnold with a birthday party. Among the gifts he received were two pairs of pants, a pair of Bermuda shorts, and a transistor radio. It was a way for the group to help celebrate his upcoming birthday before he went off to his new college in Cedarville, Ohio. Arnold had a great time, and it was a much appreciated, delightful send-off to his last year in college.

Burl Haynie very kindly came down to Wildwood to drive Arnold to the Shelton campus in Cape May to retrieve his belongings that had been placed in storage for the summer. Once they loaded his things into the car, they drove up to the old ABMJ building on Throop Avenue in Brooklyn. From there, two college mates, who were also transferring to Cedarville College, gave Arnold a ride all the way to Ohio.

The past year in Cape May had been filled with the unexpected. So much had taken place. In many ways, it was a confusing year for Arnold with the issue of Mary Ann Morrow as well as Shelton's loss of accreditation. Yet, God in His grace had opened up another college for him and was so faithful in providing for all his financial and other needs. With a grateful heart, Arnold looked forward to his last year of college and what God had in store for him there.

Transfer to Cedarville College

For Arnold, attending Cedarville College was like a breath of fresh air compared to Shelton. The environment was very pro-Jewish, with no anti-Semitism on campus. The college adhered strongly to Dispensational Theology, believing in a consistently literal interpretation of Scripture, particularly with regard to Bible prophecy, and held to a clear distinction between Israel and the Church. Again, Arnold was the only Messianic Jewish student on campus. Yet, he was not considered an enigma nor subjected to any anti-Semitic harassment the way he had been at Shelton.

The positive sentiment toward Jews became apparent to Arnold already during his first week on campus. The dormitory that housed the single male students was located on the far end of the college grounds, about a mile from the main campus center. Having no car, Arnold walked both ways at least twice a day. One afternoon, the campus police officer spotted him walking back to the dorm and stopped to give him a ride. Upon learning Arnold's name, the "campus cop" realized that this was the one and only Jewish student on campus, whom he had heard about. He got very excited, chatting non-stop until he dropped Arnold off.

The next morning, Arnold found himself unexpectedly awoken by the "campus cop" standing to one side of his bed in his dorm room. This officer had just started working at the college that fall and had sold his house prior to moving to Cedarville. He told Arnold that he had set aside the tithe from the sale of his house, but had not yet donated it. After a night of prayer, he felt God leading him to give a portion of that tithe to Arnold for his tuition! God had moved the heart of this "campus cop" such that Arnold's tuition for his first semester would be completely covered! How marvelous was His provision!

Cedarville College had a strong Baptist background with ties to GARB, or the General Association of Regular Baptists. While the theology of the college was fine, their actual practice of the spiritual life in that era was quite legalistic with a narrowly set "norm" for what one could or could not do as a "Christian." Fortunately, Arnold's personal experience at Cedarville turned out to be very positive all around. He enjoyed his interaction with the professors in his major. One of his favorites was Professor Robert Gromacki, who took a personal interest in the students. There was a lot of good discussion in Professor Gromacki's classes, and Arnold took as many classes as he could under him. Having already fulfilled all the required courses for his combined double majors at Shelton, he needed only a few extra credits at Cedarville to meet the criteria for his Pre-Seminary major. He thus had more leeway to choose the classes he enjoyed.

Arnold also thoroughly immersed himself in Cedarville's campus life. Once he started college, he had chosen to forego playing the violin due to the lack of spare time. He had also given up chess as a hobby—playing perhaps only once every three or four years—since it was too time-consuming. At Shelton, he did not participate in any extracurricular activities. However here at Cedarville, Arnold found time to step into the role of photography editor of the college yearbook. Photography had always remained a hobby for Arnold, having been taught by his father while still in Brooklyn on how to develop black-and-white photos in the darkroom. In Europe, cameras were very rare and expensive, but in the United States, they were more common. After the family had moved out to California and Henry had set up his own photography store with newer equipment, he gave one of his old cameras to Arnold when he was fifteen. Except for the times when he was away at the Memory Camp, Arnold did not engage in photography in high school. Now that he was at Cedarville, he wanted once again to pursue his hobby.

Among the close friends he made at Cedarville was Mary Ann Sleichter, whom Arnold already knew from Shelton. Others included Carol Simonetti who later married Mike Hamilton, Arnold's best friend at Cedarville. Sharon Tallman who later married Joe Hollaway were both also part of his inner circle. It was a close-knit group of friends, and Arnold remained in touch with all of them up to the present day. For him, Cedarville was a great college, where he spent one of his happiest years of undergraduate studies.

DURING HIS SENIOR YEAR AT CEDARVILLE, Arnold had more contact with Mary Ann Sleichter, now a sophomore in her second year. He noticed that she had a very teachable spirit. So, he began to get together with her more often to pray with her and to help her study the Word. Theirs was a purely platonic relationship. Arnold was a senior, an upper classman, and her mentor. Even during their first year of acquaintance at Shelton, he had already told her about his relationship with Mary Ann Morrow during that period.

One of the most important lessons that Mary Ann Sleichter learned from Arnold was in the area of trusting God for her finances. At that time, she was very much lacking in funds. Her financial situation was so tight that she asked the college for special permission not to have to take her meals at the college cafeteria. She worked part-time as a waitress at a diner within walking distance from the campus and was able to get some of her meals there for free. Arnold would come to the diner from time to time to talk to her and to encourage her. Whenever he came in, Arnold always ordered a "two-cents plain," which was basically a glass of seltzer or soda water. Mary Ann figured it was only fizzy water with bubbles, so she never charged him for the drinks. Only after she had moved to New York City years later did she realize that a glass of seltzer was to be charged and chided Arnold for getting away with free seltzer for a whole academic year! Since then, it became a standing joke between them about Arnold always ordering a "two-cents plain."

Arnold had a full meal plan at the college cafeteria. Because he was not a morning person, he usually skipped breakfast and slept in. However, from the time he learned about the dire financial situation of Mary Ann, he made a special effort to get up to go to the cafeteria to make a sandwich for her at breakfast. Since he did not eat breakfast, he figured that he could give his meal to her instead. So, after wrapping the sandwich in a paper serviette, he held it out in one hand as he stood outside waiting for her by the cafeteria door. She would approach and pick up the sandwich from his hand as she kept walking past without stopping. That was how she managed to get her meals that year.

Encouraging her to pray and trust the Lord to provide, Arnold shared with her God's promise in Philippians 4:19: *And my God shall supply your every need according to His riches in glory in Messiah Yeshua.* It was a totally new truth to her, but she was willing to put it to work and prayed for God to supply. Soon, she began finding blank envelopes in her mailbox with cash amounts of ten or twenty dollars in them. She later found out, of course, that it was Arnold who had placed the envelopes there. However one time, she experienced God's provision in a totally unexpected way. Out of the blue, she received a check of one hundred dollars in the mail from her older brother and her sister-in-law. She had never asked them for any help, and they had never before sent her any money. Married with young children, their finances were also tight. One hundred dollars was a lot of money in those days, so for them to have sent the check in her time of dire need was sure evidence of God at work.

For her major, Mary Ann had many papers to write. Arnold began recommending this book or that book on Jewish people, Jewish culture, or Jewish history for her to read and use as a basis for her papers. Prior to meeting Arnold, she had never before been exposed to anything Jewish. As she read all those books, she became more and more interested in Jewish people. Soon, Arnold suggested that they study the Bible together one-on-one, with Mary Ann in a disciple role. It became a pivotal time for her as she studied the Scriptures under his private teaching. She began to grow and mature in her faith. They met once a week, usually at the college print shop on campus, where Arnold worked as the photography editor of the yearbook. Since he had a key to the office, they could study there in quiet and discuss the Bible without disturbing anyone else. Years later, Mary Ann remembered Arnold habitually carrying his briefcase to those discipleship sessions, wearing a *yarmulke* on his head.

Arnold also initiated a student prayer group that met regularly to pray for Israel. They called themselves "The Friends of Israel." On one occasion, Arnold took the group as tourists to visit a local Jewish synagogue in the area to show them what the Jews did in their worship. It was very informative. On Sundays for their worship service, Arnold and the group attended a church nearby. Once a month or so, they would be invited to someone's home for a meal. At Passover, Arnold demonstrated the *Seder* meal to illustrate the connection of how that ceremony foreshadowed the redemptive work of Messiah Jesus.

During the academic year, Arnold worked part-time at the Cedarville College library as he had done at Shelton. He continued to contribute articles to the *Ha-Adouth—The Witness* newsletter of the Messianic Youth Fellowship. For the Christmas and Easter breaks of his last year in college, he went "home" to stay with the Cattells. It was always good to be there, since he felt so comfortable to be part of that family.

ARNOLD MADE STRAIGHT A'S IN ALL HIS COURSES AT CEDARVILLE. At the end of the last semester, he walked into the business office to settle his final bill, so that he would be allowed to graduate. To his utter astonishment, his account was zero, balancing out absolutely evenly to the very last penny! The exact amount he needed had come in to cover all his tuition and he now owed the college nothing! How he praised God in his heart for having so faithfully provided the funding for his entire college education! Arnold was left in awe of God, *Jehovah Jireh*, who could truly be trusted to supply all his needs, which had remained private and undisclosed to anyone else. This confirmed that God indeed was in total control.

At last, his graduation day arrived on the 28th of May 1966, and this time he attended the ceremony, surrounded by the people who loved him. Ruth Wardell and Burl Haynie made a special trip to come and celebrate this momentous day with him. His close friends from college including Mary Ann, Carol, Mike, Sharon, and Joe all came to support him at his graduation. They were two academic years behind Arnold and had all grown close to him in the past year. These were his friends in the inner circle with whom he did things and could talk on a deeper level. They knew him in more personal depth and were there to support and stand by him. Arnold maintained contact with them to the present day. Ironically, Cathy, who was initially interested in Jewish missionary work, was the one who had lost touch with Arnold. In the end, she decided not to go into Jewish ministry after all.

There were about one hundred and fifty to two hundred students in his graduating class. Arnold earned a Bachelor of Arts degree graduating with a Pre-Seminary major and a grade point average of between 3.8 and 3.9, just slightly short of a perfect 4.0 grade point. His low grades of the basic required math courses at Shelton College had pulled down his overall average. Although officially his major from Cedarville was Pre-Seminary Studies, in actuality Arnold had earned enough credits for a double major in Hebrew and Hellenistic Studies, which he had already completed in the three years at Shelton. So, for all intents and purposes, he graduated with a double major in Hebrew and Hellenistic Studies.

Mom and Pop Cattell could not make it to the ceremony, but they placed an announcement in their local newspaper, which many readers most likely would have perceived to be a misprint. Underneath his graduation picture was a caption that read: "Mr. and Mrs. Charles Cattell announce the graduation of their son, Arnold G. Fruchtenbaum." What a special gesture of love it was for the Cattells to publicly present Arnold as their son! It truly warmed his heart to know that indeed just as Jesus had promised, fathers, mothers, brothers, sisters, and houses were literally restored to him in this life.

Arnold's college years became a positive experience after he transferred to Cedarville College, a fine institution of higher learning. In that period, it was a college of about eight hundred students in total. Since then, it has grown and expanded to become Cedarville University, offering a master's program and with a total student body of several thousand. Arnold summed up his college experiences in an article for the newsletter of the M.Y.F.

> All in all, if the right Christian college is chosen, the Hebrew-Christian could look back to many wonderful events, experiences and friends, which could not have been possible if he were not Jewish. His years in a Christian college become a vast area of opportunity to fulfill his individual responsibility to Hebrew-Christianity.[19]

As expected, his own family was not there for his special occasion. Another scenario that he had come to terms with this past year was Mary Ann Morrow's break-up with him. Thus, when he got a card from her to congratulate him on his college graduation, he did not know how to take it. Not wanting to be involved only to be hurt again, Arnold simply ignored her card and did not respond.

---

[19] Excerpt: *Ha-Adouth—The Witness*, April-June 1966

DURING THE COURSE OF HIS SENIOR YEAR AT CEDARVILLE COLLEGE, Arnold's thoughts had turned to the future and what he would be doing upon his graduation. He knew that he wanted to continue his biblical studies and applied to Dallas Theological Seminary. However, he also had a long-standing desire to take some time off to go and study in Israel. He had never been there, but having studied so much about what took place in biblical times, he wanted to experience living in the Holy Land and to get to know the area that God had promised to His Chosen People. He really wanted to see in person the many historical sites mentioned in the Bible so that everything in the Word would come alive for him.

Having come across a unique master's program in Jerusalem in the specialized area of Hebrew Studies offered by The American Institute of Holy Land Studies, Arnold applied to participate in the fourteen-month program. The cost was $2,400, equivalent to ten times the amount in present-day currency. It included the roundtrip airfare, tuition, as well as room and board. The full amount had to be paid upfront while still in the United States. Arnold applied for financial aid in the form of a grant, but did not know if he would qualify for any funding. Again, he prayed and looked to the Lord for His provision, as he otherwise had no means to pay for his studies. In faith, he left the situation in God's hands.

After the graduation ceremony, Arnold stayed behind for about three weeks to work at the Cedarville College library to earn some cash, while waiting to see how his funding would work out for his studies in Israel. Up until then, he had cumulatively saved $800 from his work over the past three summers through the ABMJ and from his library work during the recent weeks. With the total cost at $2,400, it still left him $1,600 short. Not knowing how he would pay for his studies, he continued to pray privately to the Lord to provide. Just ten days before he was due to board the plane to Israel, Arnold received an official letter from the United States government, informing him of its decision to award him a grant of $1,624 on condition that it be used only for studies undertaken in Jerusalem. Naturally, he was more than happy to comply! When he applied for financial aid to the American Institute of Holy Land Studies, the institute, being an educational entity of American origin, submitted its application for a U.S. government grant on behalf of those students in need. The government granted a lump sum to the institute, which in turn parceled out the grant in varying amounts to individual students. Although it was the institute that decided on the specific amount of $1,624 for

Arnold, the official letter announcing the grant came directly from the U.S. government. Arnold was elated because this was a non-repayable grant and not a loan, so he was not required to pay back any of it when he finished his studies. With the $800 that he had saved plus the $1,624 grant that he received, the total amount was enough to pay for the full cost of the program leaving $24 to spare! This was truly a gift from the Lord. God was not too early, but He was surely never late! As a reminder of the Lord's wonderful and miraculous provision, Arnold kept the letter still to this day.

Prior to the end of his senior year at Cedarville College, Arnold had also received a letter from Dallas Theological Seminary confirming his admission. With the opportunity to go to Israel now a reality, he wrote to the seminary to request a deferment of his enrollment to the following year upon the completion of his studies in Israel. His deferment was approved, and Arnold was all set to go.

Knowing that he would be living in Dallas upon his return, Arnold made arrangements for his personal belongings, consisting mainly of about one hundred books, to be stored at the local ABMJ office while he was away. The "campus cop" lent Arnold a van. Accompanied by his friend, Mike, Arnold drove the long distance south to Dallas, Texas, to store his belongings, and together they drove all the way back to Cedarville.

Prior to his departure for Israel, the Messianic Youth Fellowship, with the help of Ruth Wardell, held a heart-warming farewell party for Arnold at the old ABMJ building on Throop Avenue in Williamsburg, Brooklyn, where there was a gym on the second floor. The group played a good game of basketball before enjoying a delicious dinner of chicken and other tasty dishes. It would be at least fourteen months before they would see him again. They spent time, sharing about the months that lay ahead for Arnold and wished him well with their thoughts and prayers.

Studies Abroad in *Eretz Yisrael*

Almost as soon as Arnold arrived in Jerusalem, he was swept into the daily routine of classes. For a ten-week period starting in July 1966 until mid-

September, he would be taking an intensive Modern Hebrew course at the *Ulpan* of the Hebrew University. In college, Arnold had learned to read Classical Hebrew used in the ancient biblical texts, but did not know how to speak Modern Hebrew. The *Ulpan*, denoting an institute or a school for the intensive study of the Hebrew language, was initiated after the creation of the State of Israel, when the new country faced a massive influx of Jews from many parts of the world. It was a means by which to help the immigrants acquire the basic language skills in order to integrate as quickly as possible into the social, cultural, and economic environment of their new homeland, thus sharing a common bond and identity.

Students on the six-month program were not required to take the language course and only attended courses conducted in English at the institute. For those on the yearlong program, such as Arnold, the Hebrew course at the *Ulpan* was a pre-requisite, as half their regular classes were taught at the Hebrew University, west of downtown, about half an hour's bus ride from where Arnold lodged. So, for six hours per day for ten weeks, Arnold completely immersed himself in assimilating the language.

About a week after his arrival, he wrote an enthusiastic letter to Ruth Wardell, sharing his new experiences and observations.

The books you have read concerning the building of a 20th century Israel are by no means exaggerated. I have only been in and around Jerusalem, but already I can see the truth and Jerusalem is considered poor in comparison to Tel-Aviv and Haifa. I have spent hours upon hours walking around the city of Jerusalem and its suburbs and I have found many unusual and beautiful spots.

I have had a week at the *Ulpan* at the Hebrew University (a most beautiful campus) and the Hebrew is really intensive. Within a ten-week period, they expect us to be able to speak, read, and write Hebrew well enough to attend the University classes. WOW! There are about 300 students at the *Ulpan*—200 Americans, 75 French and 25 from various other parts of the world including England, Mexico, etc.

I live about seven blocks from the Mandelbaum Gate and about four blocks from the border. I am two blocks away from the Mea Shearim section where all the *Chasidim* live.

```
I found a Hebrew-Christian church, which to my surprise
had about 30 Jewish believers gathered together.²⁰
```

The compound of the American Institute of Holy Land Studies was on *Ha-Neviim* Street, or the "Street of the Prophets," about a block from the heart of downtown Jewish Jerusalem and four blocks west of the city border that divided Jerusalem between Israel and Jordan. Constructed in the 1800s of natural stone, two large connecting buildings functioned as one large structure, comprising the classroom and the sleeping quarters. In the front, a relatively high stonewall separated the compound from the street. The structure consisted of three stories plus a complete basement. The director of the institute and his wife lived on one side of the third floor, and the married student couples lived on the other. The second floor was reserved for the single women. Some of the single men stayed in one section of the ground floor, while the rest occupied the basement. The kitchen, dining hall, library, and classroom were all located on the other side of the ground floor. About twenty students, all from the United States, took part in the program and lodged on the premises.

Courses at the institute were taught in English. There was no fixed faculty. Some of the professors came from the Hebrew University, while others were brought in from Tel-Aviv. Most of the professors were not believers, but all the administrators and staff of the institute were. Because he was on a foreign student visa, Arnold was not allowed to do any part-time work while in Israel. Hence, he could simply enjoy being a student, soaking in all that was taught. As the fee for the entire program had been paid up front, Arnold needed only a bit of pocket money to take the bus, buy a few textbooks and toiletries and pay for other incidentals. Again, God was faithful in supplying all that he needed, as checks were sent to him from people in the United States whom he did not even know.

Once the summer language course at the *Ulpan* ended, the other classes began in mid-September. The two courses held at the Hebrew University comprised archaeology as well as biblical studies, based on the Old Testament Book of First Samuel. The other two courses at the institute consisted of Israeli history, both ancient and modern, and historical geography, exploring

---

²⁰ Excerpts: *Ha-Adouth—The Witness*, June-September 1966

what transpired on the land and the background of why history occurred in particular locations.

The archaeology course included two weeks of fieldwork, digging on-site at Tel Gezer, situated halfway between Jerusalem and Tel-Aviv on the western side. It was about half an hour's drive from where Arnold lived, so he commuted for the duration of the fieldwork. The class undertook an exploratory dig, the preliminary stage prior to the real excavation. Their goal was to locate the site of the Solomonic Gate. Much to the students' excitement, on the very last day of their dig, they finally pinpointed the location of the basic foundation of the Solomonic Gate!

For the historical geography course held at the institute, the class went on a total of three short, one-day field trips and two longer, five-day trips. During the first semester, they hired a driver with a large vehicle, similar to a military truck. On hot, sunny days, they drove with the canvas rolled down so that they could see more of the countryside as they rode in the open air. On the longer, five-day trips farther out into the country, the group lodged in youth hostels. During the second semester when the group was down to seven students, they traveled in a camper van owned by one of the students, in which they were all able to fit.

As soon as he had completed his language course at the *Ulpan*, Arnold was ready to look up his father's siblings. Technically, they were his grandaunts and granduncles, but for all intents and purposes, to him, they were his aunts and uncles. His relatives could not speak any English, and Arnold remembered very little Polish or Yiddish, so there would have been no way to communicate with them until after Arnold learned to speak Hebrew. In biblical times, the Jews spoke Hebrew, Aramaic and Greek, but in recent centuries, the Ashkenazi Jews spoke mostly Yiddish and the Sephardic Jews spoke mainly Ladino. Both groups also spoke the local language of their country of residence.

In one of Arnold's brief phone calls to his mother before he left the United States, she had given him the address of his father's siblings so that he could look them up. Henry himself did not want him to contact the relatives. However, Adele told Arnold to visit them anyway, without waiting for his father's permission, which would never come. His relatives all lived around the Tel-Aviv area, over an hour's drive northwest of Jerusalem. One early Friday afternoon, Arnold took a bus from downtown Jerusalem to Tel-Aviv and transferred onto another bus to Holon. Finding the address of the apartment where one of his relatives lived, he knocked on the door. Not having phoned or written in advance, no one was expecting him.

When the door opened, it was his Aunt Chumah standing there, looking questioningly at him. Before she could ask him anything, Arnold said to her in Hebrew, *"Shalom, Ani Arichek,"* which meant, "Hello, I am Arichek." Stunned for only a split second, she recognized his name and burst out screaming. Flinging her arms around him and hugging him, she was overcome with emotion and absolutely overjoyed to see him! Inviting him in, she phoned her other siblings, and they all came over that same afternoon as soon as they heard the news. There were two uncles, Yaakov and Yehoshua, and three aunts, Chankah, Genya, and Chumah, who had all endured and survived the Holocaust and eventually made their way to Israel one after the other. Except for three of their children, who were born in Poland and quite young when their parents left, the rest were all born in Israel. Thus, Arnold would also get to know his cousins during his time in the Land.

They spent the remainder of Arnold's visit catching up with news about the family in California and in Israel. They were so excited and full of questions, wanting to know what brought Arnold to Israel, what he was doing here, how long he would stay, and so on. The relatives all agreed that Henry was right to leave Poland when he did in August 1946 and acknowledged the accuracy of his sixth sense concerning death and danger. Arnold knew that his father never regretted not going to Israel, believing that life would be much easier for immigrant families in America, which had a lot more amenities and plenty of opportunities to get ahead in life for anyone who was willing to work hard. Daily living in Israel was a struggle. To do simple shopping for everyday needs required going to separate stores for different items, and it was time-consuming.

Except for his Aunt Chumah, the others had not seen Arnold since he was a little child back in Poland. Yet, they showered him with so much love and affection, as if they had known him all his life. The relatives had all lost their faith in Judaism due to the Holocaust and had become very secular. It did not matter to them what Arnold's beliefs were. He was their nephew who had come from afar to visit them, and that was all that counted. Besides, Arnold had not come as a tourist, but rather as a student in *Eretz Yisrael*, and he was most heartily welcomed. Arnold was grateful to be accepted by the Fruchtenbaum family in Israel, and it warmed his heart that he felt right at home in their midst.

The weekend flew by very quickly, and all too soon, it was time for Arnold to return to the institute in Jerusalem. Of course, he left with an open invitation from his relatives to come and visit whenever he had a free weekend. From then on, he visited them on most of the regular weekends, staying usually with Aunt Chumah's family. Two other families also had a spare room for him. Wherever he stayed, the members of the other families always came over to see him, as they all lived in the general vicinity near Tel-Aviv in the Holon and Petach Tikva areas. To visit them, he would leave Jerusalem around noon right after his classes on Friday, arrive in the Tel-Aviv area in the early afternoon, stay overnight, and come back to the institute on Saturday evening.

Due to Sabbath restrictions, businesses, schools, and public transportation would shut down from three o'clock on Friday afternoons until sundown on Saturdays, whereas on regular days, the public buses operated all night. All the household grocery shopping had to be done before the Sabbath began. Messianic groups met on Saturdays instead of Sundays. The regular week for work and schools began on Sunday mornings and lasted until Fridays at noon. Classes were held on Sundays, the way they would normally take place elsewhere on Mondays. With no public transportation available on the Sabbath, people were encouraged to take walks, go to the parks or beaches, or spend time with their families.

Arnold discovered that it was more efficient to take a *sherut* taxi than a bus to go to the Tel-Aviv area and also for his return after the Sabbath ended. These were "shared" taxis that took up to five people heading in the same direction outside of Jerusalem. They cost a lot less than regular taxis and had more flexibility than the buses. As soon as the *sherut* taxi filled up with five people, it would take off.

Regardless of which family Arnold was visiting, there would be an endless stream of food coming out of the kitchen. His aunts cooked a variety of dishes in huge quantities way over what they could possibly consume. They fed him constantly, filling his plate to overflowing to the point where Arnold had to make a special effort to stop them. Their priority was to make sure there was always plenty to eat. Having been deprived of food for many years during the Holocaust, food became very important to them. Habitually making an over-abundance of food subtly compensated for their subconscious fear of future deprivation.

Arnold was truly well taken care of. Not only did his aunts feed him, they also did his week's worth of laundry for him. Arnold felt very pampered. Liking to wear flip-flops for their comfort instead of proper shoes, Arnold always came to visit in them. Aunt Chankah thought that Arnold could not afford any shoes, so during one of his visits, she took him out to the shops to buy him a new pair. The next time Arnold visited, she was surprised to see him wearing flip-flops again. It eventually came up in their conversation that Arnold preferred flip-flops for comfort, not because shoes were unaffordable. He figured that Aunt Chankah simply enjoyed buying him shoes as a way of showing him her love and care. His reasoning was that if she would have asked him in the first place why he did not wear any proper shoes, he would have told her.

Aside from the field trips taken for his historical geography class, Arnold also had free time to explore the country on his own with a fellow student, Gary Fisher, a Gentile believer who had been in the same senior year as him at Cedarville College. When Arnold told him about the fourteen-month program in Israel, Gary was very interested and also applied and received a grant. They ended up rooming together at the institute.

With all his previous studies of the Word of God, Arnold had already developed a deep love for *Eretz Yisrael* even before he had seen it. Now that he was here, he wanted to get to know the Land in a special way, in as much detail as possible. As a student with virtually no money and dependent upon the public transportation system, it was not going to be easy for Arnold to get around. However, God answered his heart's desire and provided for him in a most creative way. Shortly after arriving in Jerusalem, Gary bought a Vespa, a two-seat motor scooter, and they used it to travel around the country. Every free day and during the longer weekends and semester breaks, they explored other areas in greater depth.

Arnold bought a large map of Israel, and as Gary drove the motor scooter, he navigated from the back. They were determined to go down every paved street and alley, trace every old and new dirt road and follow each to the very end to see what there was to discover. They traveled in all seasons, even during the times of rain, as they were not about to let the weather interfere with their desire to get acquainted with the Land. For the most part, the weather in Israel was much like that of southern California, warm and sunny. Only once every three or four years did it snow in the mountains. Normally, between mid-October and mid-April, there would be rainfall, but otherwise, the weather was sunny and dry. During one of their breaks, Arnold and Gary took the Vespa and went down to the southern port of Eilat on the edge of the Red Sea. Because the weather was so warm in the winter, they could sleep out on the beach at night in their sleeping bags, thus saving on costs.

In another letter that he sent to Ruth Wardell, Arnold wrote about his travels and the places he planned to see.

> I am doing a lot of traveling around the country. My roommate has a motor scooter and we are traveling all over Israel on it... December 23-27, I'll be in Jordan. Please pray, since the border situation is extremely tense. I hope to be allowed to go down and take pictures of Samua. This is the Jordanian village the Israelis destroyed a few weeks ago. The first two weeks in January, I will be going to work in a kibbutz called Amir. I have relatives there and it is very far north in Galilee on the Syrian border. I purposely picked a border kibbutz, since it is also a defense kibbutz and it would make things all the more interesting... We have three weekends planned in the Galilee area plus a number of one-day trips to coastal areas. We have a private cabin where we can stay at the Sea of Galilee for only one dollar a night. I am really getting to know the country inside out.[21]

The trip to Jordan during the Christmas break of 1966 was an eye-opener for Arnold. Among many other interesting sites in the country, for the very first time he had the opportunity to visit the ancient city of Petra, carved into the rose-colored rocks. From his studies of biblical prophecy, he believed that this would be the place where the persecuted Jews would flee to for safety during the Great Tribulation and where the Second Coming of Jesus the Messiah would take place.

One of Arnold's relatives worked in the secretariat of Kibbutz Amir close to the Syrian border in the far northeastern part of the region of Galilee. The position of secretary of the *kibbutz* was the highest position in the organization and good for a two-year term, before it had to be transferred to another individual. The *kibbutz* system was straight, pure socialism, leasing a

---

[21] Excerpts: *Ha-Adouth—The Witness*, October-December 1966

piece of property from the government, working the land and sharing the profits among the *kibbutz* members. Some groups ended up financially quite well off in this system. Arnold and Gary were accepted right away without having to be on a waiting list, due to Arnold's connections. The two lads were able to live on the *kibbutz* and do volunteer work for two weeks during their semester break at the beginning of January, picking several varieties of citrus fruit including oranges, lemons, and grapefruit. Starting early at seven o'clock in the morning, they would work until noon. After lunch, their time was free to go on their exploration of the surrounding areas on the motor scooter. On the weekends, they explored the area around Tiberias in the region of Galilee, staying at a private cabin for only one dollar per night. Both Arnold and Gary made the commitment to get to know the Land as much as possible during their stay in Israel. By the time the program ended, they had practically covered the whole country on the Vespa. Prior to the Six-Day War, Israel was much smaller, so they were able to accomplish their goal. After the war, they had only a couple of months left in Israel, and much of the newly gained territory was closed to visitors. However, they did get a cursory knowledge of what later became known as the West Bank. Thus, they really did get to know the entire Land of Israel!

EVEN WHILE HE WAS IN ISRAEL, Arnold continued to write for the *Ha-Adouth—The Witness* newsletter, submitting many interesting articles for each issue. He exchanged numerous letters with Ruth Wardell, describing the glorious time he was having. He also kept in touch with Burl Haynie through letters. In the past, his mentor had phoned him regularly, but calls to Israel were too expensive, so instead, they wrote to each other. Arnold felt very grateful that Mr. Haynie had driven him to the airport to see him off. Even as time had ticked away after Arnold's college graduation, without knowing if he would get the funding to go, his teacher had stood by him, encouraging him to trust the Lord to provide in His time and in His way. Now that he was actually living out his long-standing desire to see his beloved Holy Land, Arnold wanted to share as much of his experiences as possible with Burl Haynie through his letters.

A few weeks after he started writing his mentor in the summer of 1966, Arnold was very surprised to receive a letter from Mary Ann Morrow, who was spending the summer at her family's home in the Adirondacks. Apparently, she had gotten his address from Mr. Haynie who happened to be in the area. Even after the ABMJ ceased to sponsor the Memory Camps, he rented the campsite at his own expense to teach. Although Arnold had written his letter in print format, Burl still could not make any sense out of it. Being left-handed, Arnold's handwriting could be quite illegible, so Burl needed Mary Ann's help to decipher the letter in order to read it.

Now, Mary Ann asked Arnold if he would be willing to write to her about Israel, the people, the culture, current events, and so on. Arnold felt quite hesitant, but eventually decided that he would write to her only with factual information on Israel and nothing personal. He did not want to get drawn into anything that would complicate his life and hurt him again. So, for the rest of his stay, they corresponded about topics regarding Israel.

Eyewitness Account of the Six-Day War

The day after Israel's nineteenth Independence Day celebrations, tensions began to mount when a newspaper article on the 15th of May 1967 reported that Egyptian troops were moving into the Sinai and amassing near the Israeli border. On the 16th of May, Egypt's President Nasser ordered the United Nations Emergency Force—stationed in the Sinai as a buffer between Israel and Egypt after the Sinai War in 1956—to withdraw from the area. Two days later, Syrian troops were preparing for battle along the Golan Heights. Thereafter, the Arab media had a heyday with propaganda, proclaiming the strength of Arab unity in the total annihilation of Israel and the destruction of Zionism. On the 22nd of May, Egypt closed the Straits of Tiran and set up a blockade to all Israeli shipping and incoming supply lines bound for Eilat. As tensions escalated, Arnold saw sandbags piling up all around Jerusalem. While nothing was made public in Israel, he knew that war would soon be at hand and detailed a personal blow-by-blow account of his experiences.

```
Sounding very much like another war chapter out of the
Bible, Israel and Ishmael entered into their third war in
the past 19 years. Once again, battles took place in such
ancient places as Shechem, Bethlehem, Hebron, Jericho, the
Jordan River, and Sinai. Jerusalem, the scene of many,
```

161

many battles in her ancient history, was once again a place of battle, and it was the only city in Israel to be actually hit by the war. Otherwise, the whole war was carried out inside Arab territory.

From the day Nasser ordered all U.N. troops out of Egypt and closed the Straits of Tiran to Israeli ships and shipping, Psalm 83 reads like the latest newspaper with all the current events in the Middle East. The English broadcasts coming in from the Hashemite Kingdom of Jordan sounded like a paraphrase of the fourth verse: "...Come and let us cut them off from being a nation; That the name of Israel may be no more in remembrance." (Psalm 83:4) I listened to Jordanian broadcasts declaring how the war of destiny had finally arrived and now the Jews would be driven to the sea and Israel would be destroyed once and for all. One by one, each Arab state declared their support for Nasser. Never did the Arab world seem so united, and even Hussein, the king of Jordan, who had been a bitter enemy of Nasser, flew to Egypt and made a defense pact putting Jordanian troops under Egyptian command. "For they have consulted together with one consent; Against You do they make a covenant." (Psalm 83:5) Even the list of nations involved fit the modern situation:

Edom, Moab, Ammon	– Jordan
Amalek	– Sinai
Philistia	– Gaza Strip
Tyre	– Lebanon
Assyria	– Syria and Iraq
Hagarenes	– Egypt

These verses are not to be taken as literally fulfilled in this Arab-Israeli war. I am only using them as an application. When the war finally began, I found myself praying the words of the first three verses: "O God, keep not You silent: Hold not Thy peace and be not still, O God. For lo, Your enemies make a tumult; And they that hate You have lifted up the head. They take crafty counsel against Thy people and consult together against Thy hidden ones." (Psalm 83:1-3)

From the time Nasser closed the Straits of Tiran, it was obvious to me that war would soon come and I never doubted that it would come. The American Consulate advised all Americans to leave the country and to many Christians, this became a testing period. It made me sick to watch so many Christians in the country panic and flee. Here was a golden opportunity for Christians to be a testimony of their faith and to some extent undo the damage done by the phony Christians throughout the centuries; but instead, they let the opportunity slip through their fingers and as Israelis looked on in disgust, many Christians fled. Those that did stay earned a good name for themselves as Christians and did much to help, to the great appreciation of the Israelis. From the beginning of the crisis, I made my choice to stay. I felt this was the will of God and my duty as a Jew and a Christian.

On Monday morning June 5th, I took a bus to the Hebrew University to attend 8:30 class, but upon my arrival, I learned that the class had been cancelled and that the war with Egypt had begun in the Sinai. I boarded a bus to return to my room at the American Institute of Holy Land Studies located only about four blocks from the Jordanian-Israeli border. About halfway home, an alert came over the radio whereupon everyone had to get off the bus. I made a dash for home not really knowing what was going on.

I returned to my room and began working at my desk. At about eleven o'clock, I heard the Jordanians four blocks away open up with machine gun and cannon fire as the Jordanian shelling of Israeli Jerusalem began. For the first few minutes, I listened to the shells whistling over the roof of the American Institute and exploding somewhere in the distance. The war with Jordan had begun. I ran down the hall of the basement, which was now to be used as a shelter. We quickly let our Jewish neighbors run into the house to the basement, until we found ourselves overcrowded with 75 people consisting of men, women and children; religious and non-religious Jews.

Our overcrowded conditions were to remain that way for the next three days and three nights. I took these people under my care trying to comfort many who were afraid, with quotations from the Old Testament to show that God will not allow the Arabs to destroy Israel, although He allows them to suffer another war. I played with the children who seemed to be oblivious to the war no matter how close the shelling came. The people organized themselves into kitchen and laundry brigades and every night a *minyan* was formed as the Jews once again implored God to save them from this latest onslaught.

Meanwhile, Syria and Iraq joined the war. Jordanian shelling of Israeli Jerusalem continued all day Monday and halfway through the night. At about one o'clock in the morning, the building directly across the street from the American Institute received three direct hits, hard enough to shake our building and causing some plaster to fall. In the morning I ventured outside and saw that all the buildings around us were hit, but the Lord kept our building from receiving any direct hits and not even a window was broken.

By the end of the first day of war (Monday), the Israeli forces virtually destroyed the air forces of Egypt and Jordan and greatly damaged the forces of Syria and Iraq. Israeli troops pushed into the Sinai drawing Egyptian troops away from Israeli borders. The entire Gaza Strip was in Israeli hands except for the city of Gaza itself. On the Jerusalem front, Israeli artillery knocked out Jordanian gun positions by the middle of the night and from then on, all shelling went from the Israeli side to the Jordanian side. Israeli Jerusalem was not to be hit again while the war continued hand-to-hand four blocks away.

On the second day of war (Tuesday), the Old City of Jerusalem was surrounded by Israeli troops, all of Sinai was in Jewish hands and the city of Gaza fell. The third day of war (Wednesday) saw the ancient names of Shechem, Bethlehem, Hebron and Jericho once again under Jewish control as the West Bank fell. Then, the Old City was in Jewish hands. The fourth day of war (Thursday) saw Egypt submitting to a ceasefire as Israeli soldiers had begun washing their feet in the Suez Canal. The war with Syria continued until the sixth day when Syria also submitted to a ceasefire; then Israeli troops were within 20 kilometers from the Syrian capital of Damascus. By Sunday morning, the third Israeli-Arab war was over with an Israeli victory that amazed the world with its speed and precision.

When news first came that the Old City of Jerusalem was in Israeli hands, the joy of the Jews knew no bounds. Hugging and kissing, laughing and weeping, leaping and dancing seized the Jews, religious and non-religious alike. When news first came concerning the recovery of the Wailing Wall, the remnant of the Jewish Temple destroyed by the Romans in 70 A.D., Jews in our shelter let me know that the next Sabbath they will be praying at the Wailing Wall which has seen an absence of Jews since 1948. Now that the Temple Mount was once again in Jewish hands, talk sprang up all over Jerusalem concerning the rebuilding of the Jewish Temple.

Walking outside, after the war with Jordan was over, I saw a car pass by with the words "Rebuild the Temple" painted on its side. One Israeli soldier told me that we still had one wall of the Temple (Wailing Wall) and all we need to do was build three more walls and a roof and we would have our Temple back. All this talk about the Temple must have caused some concern in the Rabbinate, for soon thereafter, they issued a decree that the Temple Mount was off limits to Jews except for the Wailing Wall, since the area was desecrated. The area is to remain off limits until the Messiah comes and the Temple is rebuilt. The implication was that the Temple is not to be rebuilt until the Messiah comes, but this new rabbinical decree can be reinterpreted.

In Mea Shearim, the ultra-Orthodox quarter of Jerusalem, messianic speculation reached a new peak. One group in Mea Shearim actually claimed that the Messiah would be the grandson of their leading rabbi. Another group came out and said that their Messiah must either come this *Shavuot* or on the *Shavuot* seven years from now. Since the Messiah failed to come this *Shavuot*, He must come on the *Shavuot* in 1974. While most religious groups have abstained from setting any messianic dates, the capture of the Old City has caused messianic speculation to run high among all religious groups. They now speak of the Messiah coming not in the distant future but as coming any day now.

When the Wailing Wall was opened to Jews on the first day of *Shavuot*, 200,000 Jews made the pilgrimage and I went with them. I saw Jews, men, women and children praying before the Wailing Wall, kissing the huge stones and crying. The area around the Wailing Wall had been greatly cleared. In later walks around the city, I watched them tear down walls, which at one time had marked the Israeli-Jordan border. I watched land mines being exploded in the area that had been "no man's land." Telephone and electricity lines were being connected between the two sides of the once divided city. Whatever else Israel may return to the Arabs, it is obvious that she had no intention of returning the other half of Jerusalem. The whole city is to be kept under Israeli rule and public works are continuing at full speed to reunite the two halves of the city in every way, never to be divided again. When the Chief Rabbi blew the *shofar* at the Wailing Wall, his words were, "This year in Jerusalem, ancient Jerusalem."

So what significance does this all have for the Hebrew-Christians? We must realize that a great event has taken place in the history of our people. Many of us have been preaching and teaching for years that someday the Jews will get the other half of Jerusalem and now we have watched this event come to pass in our day and literally right before my own eyes. Though we must guard against any speculation about the rebuilding of the Temple, we at least realize that the possibility and opportunity now exists which did not exist before the war. We are now more than ever before to watch the events taking place in Israel, for God will once again begin to deal with the Jews as a nation and the signs of the times are around us.

Another result of the war of special interest to the Hebrew-Christian is the upsurge of messianic speculation and Jews here in Israel are looking for the Messiah to come really soon. Has there ever been a better time in the

history of our people to broadcast by voice and pen of the
true Messiah of whom we know? That the Messiah they are
expecting any day now is to be found in the person of
Jesus Christ? That salvation is not to be found by a
pilgrimage to the Wailing Wall, or in the rebuilding of
the Temple, but in the placing of one's faith in the
Nazarene?[22]

From beginning to end, the entire war lasted less than six days—132 hours and 30 minutes, to be exact. In fact, the duration was much shorter on two out of the three fronts. On the Jordanian side, the war lasted only three days and on the Egyptian side, only four days. On the Syrian side, the war extended to the sixth day only because the actual fighting on the front there took place on the fifth and sixth days of the war. Among the three wars fought between Israel and the Arab nations since the formation of the State of Israel in 1948, this war was the most dramatic in its speed and execution. From the outset, Arnold witnessed the efficiency of the Israeli military. As soon as the siren rang out signaling the outbreak of war, the military, per standard procedure, confiscated the public bus that Arnold was riding that morning, in order to transport the soldiers to their designated assembly points. The swiftness with which the Israelis ended the war with its astounding victory could only be attributed to the mighty hand of God protecting His Chosen People. Arnold gained an even deeper appreciation for the truth of God's promises to the Jewish people.

This stunning Israeli victory was to cause a depressive mood in the Arab world for many years to come, resulting in increased tensions between the Arab countries and the Western world. The Arab weakness compared to Israeli efficiency would not soon be forgotten. Although military casualties were high in Israel with a total of nearly seven hundred and eighty soldiers dead, civilian casualties were minimal. In comparison, the death toll of Jordanians, Egyptians and Syrians combined was over twenty times that number. By the end of the war, Israel had conquered enough territory to more than triple the area it controlled prior to the war.

Among the students, Arnold was the only one who could speak fluent Hebrew and thus, the only one able to communicate with the neighbors to let

---

[22] Excerpts: *Ha-Adouth—The Witness*, July-September 1967

them know about the movements of the soldiers outside. For the first three days, Arnold was on bread duty, as there was not enough food in their building to feed all those people for that many days. When the trucks drove by, Arnold had to run out onto the street to get the satchels of bread distributed by the soldiers. He was safe as long as he was within the compound behind the high stonewall facing the street. During the few minutes that he ran out to the trucks, he was exposed to possible stray shells hitting him, but God kept him safe.

A total of seventy-six people from the neighborhood, including Arnold, all congregated in the basement of the American Institute, where showers and toilet facilities were available. With no windows, they could function only by artificial light and fortunately, electricity was available the entire time. Rooms that served as the sleeping quarters for the single men were now used to accommodate all the people. There was enough space in each of the rooms for people to sit and lie down flat without being too cramped. It was anyone's guess how long the war would last.

The building next door was a hospital, and all the wounded soldiers in the vicinity were taken there. On the first day or so, the civilians had no idea what had transpired in the war, but by the second day, they heard that the war was going well. The government did not want to make it public knowledge that on the first day, within three and a half hours, the Israelis destroyed virtually the entire Egyptian air force. By the third day, the government announced that it was all clear. The neighbors went back to their homes. Arnold no longer had to be on bread duty, but was asked to be on-call as an ambulance driver in case they needed him to transport the wounded. However, the war had ended so quickly and decisively that in actuality he was not required to do any ambulance driving.

To the Jews, the most exciting result of the war was the recapture of the Old City of Jerusalem that had been occupied by the Arabs. The two halves of the City of Jerusalem became officially reunited on the 29th of June 1967, once again becoming one city in Jewish hands under Israeli control. Arnold had witnessed a truly momentous historical event, one that had major biblical implications. Everyone was caught up in the excitement and fervor of regaining the Wailing Wall of the Second Jewish Temple that was destroyed by the Romans in A.D. 70.

Out of the total number of students at the American Institute, more than half had left Israel to go back to the United States even before the war broke out when tensions first began to rise. Arnold made the personal decision to remain. The neighbors near the institute all knew that they were a Christian group and thus, had never communicated with them before. After the war, the neighbors became very friendly with Arnold, because he had taken such good care of them, when they came to the designated shelter. The fact that the American Institute building was the only one in the neighborhood that did not receive any direct hits from the enemy cannon fire was in itself a testimony to God's power and protection over this Christian group. The ice had been broken, and the neighbors' attitude toward the group changed noticeably. They realized that these were American students who could have left the country, but risked their lives to be there to help the Israelis. So, Arnold got invited to their homes for a meal here and a meal there, as they tried to express their appreciation for what he had done for them. However, the relationships did not progress enough to the point of being able to witness to them, because his classes resumed shortly after the war with only about two months or so left in the semester.

Arnold was able to complete his master's program with a full 4.0 grade point average for his papers, midterms, and finals. The students who had left before the war got "Incompletes" for their grades. With the fourteen-month study program in Israel coming to an end, it was time for Arnold to leave. His sojourn in the Holy Land had taken place at a most unique juncture in Jewish and biblical history. This caused him to yearn even more deeply in his heart for opportunities to share the salvation message of *Yeshua Ha'Mashiach* with his fellow Jews.

Penniless upon Arrival

When Arnold returned to the United States at the end of August 1967 from his graduate studies in Israel, he was totally penniless. He did not know how he was even going to pay for the bus fare out of the JFK Airport into downtown New York City. Having experienced how the Lord had provided for him in such amazing ways in the past and having lived through the Six-Day War, witnessing God's awesome power at work, Arnold knew that he could trust Him to supply what was needed for his next step: *...for your Father knows what things ye have need of, before ye ask Him.* (Matthew 6:8b) Much to his grateful relief, Burl Haynie, on his own initiative, came and met him at the airport. In one of his letters to Burl, Arnold had given the inbound flight number, time, and date of his arrival back to the United States. However, he had not specifically asked his mentor to come and pick him up. He was simply going to take a bus into New York City to get to Burl's place. Yet, here was his teacher at the arrival gate! With praise and gratitude in his heart, Arnold rejoiced once again at how God had come through for him.

Arnold stayed with Burl in his little efficiency for a few days, during which time he went to talk with Dr. Daniel Fuchs, head of the ABMJ in Manhattan. As a result of their discussion, Arnold landed a part-time job at the ministry in Dallas, where he had stored his belongings before going to Israel. He would be doing deputation work in the southern region to raise support for the whole Mission and would initially be trained by the head of the ABMJ office in Texas.

Given that Arnold would be a part-time worker for the duration of his seminary studies, the ABMJ paid for his flight down to Dallas. Here again, God so generously supplied the means for Arnold to get to where he needed to go. Without a penny in his pocket, all of his needs had been met from the time he stepped off the airplane at the JFK Airport in New York City until his arrival in Texas.

At first, Arnold inherited an existing list of churches, prepared by his ABMJ predecessor. He thus started taking meetings mainly in Texas and Oklahoma. On very rare occasions, he went farther afield to such places as Denver, Colorado. Usually, Arnold would leave on a Saturday night, speak on Sunday morning and evening, and return on Monday. His part-time work did not interfere with his classes, as Monday was a day off at the seminary. Most of the students were frequently ministering out of town on Sundays, so having Mondays off allowed them time to travel back. Once a week, Arnold also led a Bible study group on his own time for people from the nearby area.

DTS, or Dallas Theological Seminary, adhered to Dispensational Theology and was biblically conservative. Founded by Dr. Lewis Sperry Chafer in 1924, it was a seminary only for men until sometime in the 1990s, when it was finally open also to women. It emphasized expository Bible teaching and pioneered one of the first four-year degrees in theology, the Th.M. or Master of Theology. A shorter degree of three years, the M.Div. or Master of Divinity, was also available, designed for students who had transferred from other seminary programs.

Aside from a Bachelor of Arts or a Bachelor of Science degree, there were no special pre-requisites to enter either of the two master's programs. No prior Bible background was necessary, although one had to be a believer before enrolling. Those who had no Greek previously were required to take what was colloquially called Baby Greek for no credit. Others, like Arnold, who already had an extensive background did not have to take elementary Greek and could go straight into Greek Exegesis. Normally, Hebrew 101 was required as a course, but Arnold tested out of Beginning Hebrew, so could also immediately start Hebrew Exegesis. Basic Bible courses were available for those who had no prior formal training. Being at the graduate level, all the courses were very intensive. A total of six different majors were offered, including Hebrew and Old Testament, Greek and New Testament, Bible Exposition, Church History, Christian Education, and Systematic Theology.

To operate as a private institution, DTS depended upon the students' tuition and individual gifts or contributions from various churches. Unlike secular institutions of higher learning, private Christian seminaries were not as well endowed. The salaries of the professors at the seminary were much lower than those of their counterparts at secular universities. Many professors also simultaneously served as pastors of churches and thereby received a second salary to supplement their income. Other professors, such as Dr. J. Dwight Pentecost or Dr. Charles C. Ryrie wrote books from which they got royalties. A few were independently wealthy, having a family inheritance from which they derived their income. One of those professors essentially taught for free, getting paid one dollar for the entire academic year.

Arnold's studies were funded partly by a scholarship offered to him by the ABMJ in the amount of $250 per semester, equivalent to ten times that amount in today's currency terms. The scholarship continued every semester for all his years at the seminary. The rest of Arnold's tuition was financed by his part-time job with the ABMJ.

For the first few months, Arnold lived in the dormitory on campus until an opportunity arose to live off campus. A student, whom he befriended, worked part-time for the CMA, or Christian and Missionary Alliance, and had become friends with the pastor of a church he was attending. In addition to his pastorate, this man also happened to receive an offer to take on the role as district director of the CMA. The offer included a parsonage, thus the house where he was previously living became available for rent. Because of their friendship, the pastor rented his house to this student for only $50 a month.

It was a big place with three bedrooms, too large for one person. So, the student invited Arnold plus two other students to share the house with him. Each person ended up paying a tiny sum of $12.50 per month to live there. Arnold got a private room to himself and continued to eat his meals at the cafeteria on the seminary campus. The house was in a good location in an upper-middle class neighborhood in a nice community and was very conducive to studying. Arnold certainly could not have gotten a better deal than that for the price he was paying. What an amazing and unexpected gift from the Lord!

SHORTLY AFTER THE FIRST SEMESTER STARTED at the seminary in September 1967, Arnold received a letter from Mary Ann Morrow. It was a very personal letter in which she disclosed some deeply private information, indicating that she wanted to get involved again. Her letter brought back a collage of memories. Arnold had been led to believe in his last year at college that their relationship was a dead issue, but now it seemed to have revived. Although he was open, he did not want to be hurt again, as the pain was simply too enormous to bear.

So, on her birthday in late September, Arnold phoned her. By then, Mary Ann was in her last year at Gordon College, just north of Boston, Massachusetts, having transferred there the previous academic year. In that phone conversation, they decided that they needed to see each other again face-to-face to talk through her intentions. Arnold invited Mary Ann to fly down to Dallas to visit him in December during the Christmas break, and she agreed to come.

Mary Ann Morrow's Story

When Mary Ann's father died on the seventh of August 1962, she was still very bitter over the way the church leaders had treated him and her family prior to his death. After Reverend L. Joseph Morrow had been diagnosed with skin cancer and given one year to live, he made sure that the older children knew what was going on, but his wife, Olive, went into denial and would not hear of it. In March that year, he had gone to the Roswell Park Cancer Institute in Buffalo, New York, to have surgery and returned home to the manse in Kenmore to recuperate. One day, while he was still at home recovering, the leadership of the church came to the house. Mary Ann's expectation was that they had come to pray with her father, to find out how he was doing, and to see if they could offer some support. To her fury, they came instead to talk about his work schedule and to find out when he would be getting back to the office! She knew that their insensitive mindset was not a reflection of the way her father had taught them in the church, so it was all the more infuriating to her.

Two months later in May, her father was hospitalized with a stroke. The cancer had metastasized to the brain. Even with rehabilitation, he knew that he would never regain his ability to speak. It was all the more devastating, as his entire livelihood was dependent upon oral communication. He came home for a day visit from the hospital, fully aware that his time was running out. Not long after that, he slipped into a coma and remained hospitalized until he died.

With her father's death, Mary Ann personally suffered two losses. She had said her own "good-bye" to her father the night before. When her mother got the phone call about his impending death in the early morning hours of the following day, she took Mary Ann's older brother with her to the hospital and instructed Mary Ann to stay at home with her two younger sisters and pray that her father would live. Her mother simply could not emotionally accept the reality of the situation. Mary Ann felt a huge burden of guilt, because she knew that her father would not live and such prayers would be futile at that point. She was angry that her mother refused to see the reality that God was taking him home to Heaven, where he would be free from pain and the devastating effects of the malignant melanoma.

Mary Ann's mother sent her to stay at a girlfriend's house that night, supposedly to make room for arriving relatives. However, this was contrary to all family traditions of staying together. To Mary Ann, it felt like the ultimate rejection from her mother who had trouble accepting her since her birth. While Mary Ann was absent, her mother collapsed both physically and emotionally, requiring a doctor's care. Her aunts and uncles intervened and brought Mary Ann back home. These events contributed to Mary Ann's anger at God for taking the "wrong" parent.

Because her father was a minister and well known in the community, the viewing of his body took place at the funeral home prior to the church service. His twin sister had made burial arrangements right outside of Philadelphia. The leaders of the church, who could have cared less about him, came through the line past the casket offering their phony platitudes. To Mary Ann, what they uttered were all lies, and she was seething with fury. At one point, it appeared that she might explode. A woman from the church, who had been very good to her parents in the past, took her out of the room for a while.

Through the many people who had come, God showed Mary Ann that her father had been a gifted counselor through the years, especially one-on-one. He had honored the confidentiality of his ministry, and no one knew all that he had kept to himself. Mary Ann was very moved to hear of the positive impact that he had made in the lives of various people in the Buffalo area as well as in the counties of Clinton and Essex in New York.

During the viewing, the leadership very inappropriately asked her mother how soon the family would be moving out of the manse. That was the last straw for Mary Ann. She never wanted to set foot in a church ever again! The following summer when her mother was cooking for the fifth Memory Camp in 1963, despite her bubbly, fun-filled demeanor on the surface, underneath the veneer, Mary Ann was still smoldering at the church elders' treatment of her family. While the lads helped out in the kitchen, Mary Ann noticed that both Arnold and Bob displayed a joy in their spiritual life that she did not possess and wished that she did.

One day, Arnold walked over to her family's house, and they sat on the porch and talked. Mary Ann shared about her reaction to the elders and her negative conclusion about men in general. Arnold could see that she was angry, but asked her not to lump him with the other men of the world, to give him a chance to be his own person and not to presume to know who he was. That conversation helped to clear the air for them.

Thereafter, they had many opportunities to interact with each other. To encourage her interest in various Jewish topics, Arnold shared his papers written in college. At times, he made topical entries in her notebook. He even began teaching Mary Ann a bit of Hebrew. They enjoyed each other's company immensely. Before he left to go back to college, Arnold had written "Miriam Hannah Tomorrowbaum" on the cover of her notebook. They did not talk about what it meant, but a seed had been planted. Each knew the implications. In the fall during Mary Ann's senior year in high school, they wrote to each other long-distance, and a writing friendship developed.

A few weeks after her father's death in August 1962, Mary Ann's family moved from Kenmore, New York, to Williamstown in southern New Jersey. An aunt had offered the family the use of half of her duplex, rent-free. So, the family made their home there for many years and continued to come up to their house in the Adirondacks each summer. For Thanksgiving and for Christmas 1963, Arnold visited and stayed with her family in Williamstown.

During her last two years of high school, Mary Ann joined Youth for Christ and sang in choirs. Though outwardly appearing compliant, her participation in these activities masked her ongoing internal conflicts over her experiences as a minister's daughter. Many congregants expected her to be a role model for the other children, chiding her more than the others when they misbehaved. While her own parents were not legalistic, she was exposed to many believers who were and who expected her to live by their rules. She continued to distrust many church leaders. In this context, Mary Ann's encouragement in the faith came mainly from the loving support of her mother's youngest sister, who provided the stability she needed in her later teenage years.

Reverend L. Joseph Morrow began his ministry as a Presbyterian minister in New Jersey where he met and married his wife, Olive. Being very evangelical, he frequently gave a Gospel invitation at the end of the Sunday evening services. The leadership objected to this, so he looked for a church and area where he could be free to preach the Gospel and teach the Bible as the true Word of God. Securing a position at a community church in Essex County, New York, he also served two other smaller communities plus the county nursing home. In addition, he had a strong interest in outreach to teenagers and children.

Rose Burnham heard about this new minister in the area, also known as Pastor Joe, and contacted him. All her previous requests for a pastor to start a children's camp on her site had been declined. In Pastor Joe, she found a kindred spirit in wanting to provide a Bible camp for underprivileged children who otherwise had no means to go to a camp anywhere. They also shared a belief in spreading the Gospel to every people on earth—including "to the Jew first."

Rev. Morrow and Rose proceeded to prayerfully prepare Camp Heathcote for active use. Complying with New York State and Adirondack Park Agency regulations, finding volunteer help at the Plattsburgh Air Force Base and among Christians in both Clinton and Essex counties, and securing basic foods through government provision, it was finally possible to open the camp for two weeks each summer for many spiritually-hungry, local children.

Besides the Bible classes, the children engaged in crafts, played games, and learned how to swim. On several nights, Rev. Morrow built a bonfire either in a clearing on the north side of the buildings or on the beachfront of Trout Pond on the west side of the property. The children enjoyed a time of singing and worshipping the Lord around the bonfire. Upon his invitation to receive Jesus into their heart and give their life to Him, the children threw a stick into the fire as a symbolic gesture of their decision. It was in this manner in the clearing on the north side that Mary Ann was saved one summer night at the age of seven or eight. God's Holy Spirit had touched her heart that evening through the gentle blowing of the wind in the trees nearby, reassuring her that God cared for her and that He would always be with her. When her father extended the invitation, she, too, threw a stick into the bonfire to mark her commitment. While Mary Ann had prayed many times before as a child, it was that night which marked the true beginning of her spiritual life.

Very early on, Rose Burnham was so impressed with Pastor Joe's work that she gifted him with a house plus one acre of land around it, offering to sell it to him for the legal price of one U.S. dollar! The house was situated on the main road about half a mile from the campsite. Rose wanted to make sure that even after their move to Kenmore, the Morrow family would have a place to live nearby, so that Rev. Morrow could continue to carry out his work with the local underprivileged children every summer. The Children's Bible Camp took place in early July, leaving a couple of weeks for Burl Haynie and the lads to prepare the campsite prior to the start of the Memory Camp in early August. Thus, every year, the family came to stay for most of the summer and had free access to the private lake.

While the Memory Camp was designed for the Jewish teenagers connected to the ABMJ, the general evening study and worship sessions were open to children of friends or staff. Rev. Morrow often brought Mary Ann and her siblings there, because Burl Haynie was doctrinally sound and imparted excellent biblical teaching. By exposing his children to this approach, he wanted to reinforce the importance of connecting with other believers who, like him, taught the Bible as the true Word of God and who also believed in taking the Gospel to the whole world. He had a special love for the Jewish people and taught his children how the Jews were God's Chosen People. He instilled in them the importance of reaching the Jews with the message of Jesus the Messiah. From early on, Mary Ann learned to love all peoples of every culture, highly aware of their need to hear the Gospel. She developed a strong interest in the Jewish people, reading widely about their history, culture, the Holocaust, stories of survivors, and other related topics.

Even though Rev. Morrow was committed to the Presbyterian denomination, he was very evangelical and avoided taking his family to liberal congregations when away from his parish. So during the summers, he would frequently introduce his children to Baptist churches, where the truth of God's Word was expounded. Sometimes he would bring them to baptisms at Trout Pond during the Children's Bible Camp or to the evening gatherings at the ABMJ's Memory Camp. He was not blind to the fact that there was an undercurrent of anti-Semitism in the local community. When Burl Haynie brought up a group of Jewish teenagers from New York City to the Memory Camp, the anger of the people was not lost on him. He did not care about their attitude. Neither did Rose Burnham. Sharing her dream for the campsite to be used for the local children as well as the Jewish people, Pastor Joe pictured it as a place that inspired the study of Scripture and quiet contemplation, while soaking in the natural beauty of the surroundings. The students could sit on benches facing Trout Pond, while the teachers faced away from the lake as they taught and expounded God's Word. He hoped that someday there would be a conference center on the campsite for outreach to the Jewish people. This vision was also shared by Burl Haynie, who prayed continuously for its reality.

IT WAS NOT POSSIBLE for Mary Ann and Arnold to see each other the following summer of 1964, because Mary Ann was at her family's house in the Adirondacks and working, while Arnold was assisting at the ABMJ booth at the World's Fair in New York City. In those days without interstate highways, the drive took at least ten hours one-way from the campsite to New York City. To help out Mary Ann's mother at the end of the summer, Arnold offered to drive Mary Ann from their home in New Jersey to her college in northwestern Pennsylvania. Westminster was a Christian liberal arts college with a Presbyterian background of a more liberal perspective. He would find a way

177

to get to her house, borrow her mother's car to drive Mary Ann, and then return the car before heading off to Shelton College.

As it was toward the end of August, Arnold talked Mary Ann into attending the ABMJ's Annual Summer's End Conference in Manhattan. He also encouraged her to seriously consider water baptism by full immersion. She agreed, and Dr. Daniel Fuchs, who had baptized Arnold exactly two summers earlier, conducted the ceremony. It was a very memorable occasion, and she was very glad to have taken this wonderful step of obedience.

When he dropped her off at her dormitory in college, Arnold gave her an iron as a gift. To Mary Ann, it was not a very romantic gift but a thoughtful and practical one. By this time, they both had deep feelings for each other and knew in their hearts that they would someday be married and have a future together, but nothing was said at that stage. Arnold left to return the car before making his way to his college to start his junior year.

In hindsight, it was a huge mistake on Arnold's part not to have given Mary Ann any kind of verbal indication on how he felt about her. In all his letters to her after the fall semester began, neither did he communicate in writing any of the feelings he had for her. Without that much-needed reassurance, particularly in light of how angry and negatively she felt toward men in general, Mary Ann did not know how to face the hurtful disapproval from her mother or how to deal with any of the other issues that assailed her during her first year in college. Deep in her heart, she knew that her father had cared very much for Arnold, feeling such compassion toward his difficult situation at home that he had even offered to have him come and live with the family in Kenmore during his last year of high school. Burl Haynie wisely counseled against the suggestion, knowing that in less than a year, Arnold would leave for college, thus relieving some of the pressures he faced at home. For Arnold to go and live with a Gentile minister's family in the interim would in no way sit well with his parents.

Her mother, on the other hand, did not approve of Arnold, and Mary Ann felt the sting of her disapproval very strongly. If only she could have had some type of verbal or written indication from Arnold, she would have known better how to deal with the situation and been more secure. Finding it too hard to go home for the Thanksgiving holiday in 1964 because of financial constraints, Mary Ann went to stay with one of her college friends, whose family had extended her an invitation to their home.

Her father had clearly raised the children without prejudice. In their home during the last four years of his life, both parents had lovingly cared for very young foster children of mixed racial heritage. After his death, the move to New Jersey to be closer to her mother's family suddenly exposed the siblings to unexpected racism. They were shocked to hear their mother express such attitudes for the first time. The prejudice was first against the African-Americans, then the Italians, and not that far behind, against the Jews. Determined to remain free from prejudice, they faced many emotional challenges along the way, which took a heavy toll on Mary Ann.

Toward Christmas 1964, she had become very withdrawn. Having listened to some very bad advice, and with no verbal or written reassurance from Arnold of his love for her and of their plans for the future, Mary Ann backed off from the relationship in a big way. When Arnold came to the duplex in Williamstown at Christmas, he was just stunned and sickened to see the dramatic change in her. She had suddenly turned into an iceberg and appeared to have shut down. Not knowing how to explain anything to him, Mary Ann simply stopped communicating. She herself did not understand what was going on inside her or how she was feeling. Rather than complicating matters, she just broke off the relationship with no explanation, leaving Arnold distraught, confused, and hurt. Still, he remained very concerned about her welfare and stayed in touch with her roommate.

By February 1965, Mary Ann had fallen deeper and deeper into depression, but no one else knew, because she did not let her grades slip or skip any classes, nor did she stop reading her Bible. Yet, that was not sufficient for her to understand the effects and subtleties of the spiritual battlefronts. Her depression grew steadily worse. It got so bad that she started planning her way out of her misery. Her roommate and some friends had gone off to an event one evening, and Mary Ann was ready to take her own life. For some reason, her roommate and friends came back early. Realizing what Mary Ann intended to do, they took her immediately to the pastor of a church, who met with her, prayed for her, and gave her the name of another pastor who had been trained in counseling.

It was at this juncture that Mary Ann's roommate contacted Arnold, who immediately came out to her college to see how he could assist. However, Mary Ann completely pushed him away. Perplexed, Arnold went back to his college and continued to write to her. Mary Ann did not reply to any of his letters, as she was going through her own emotional rollercoaster and spiritual valley of depression. By the end of that academic year in June 1965, Arnold's letters also stopped.

There was no more communication between them during the following academic year while Arnold was at Cedarville. Meanwhile, Mary Ann was trying to figure out what was going on inside her, unable to make any sense out of her own situation. However, when Arnold was about to graduate from college in June 1966, Mary Ann decided to send him a congratulations card with a short note enclosed to show that she cared about his special day. She got no reply back. Since Arnold had already come to terms with the break-up, he did not bother to answer.

During the summer of 1966, when Arnold was already in Israel, Mary Ann went with her family to their house in the Adirondacks. Burl Haynie happened to be up there around the same time and came to her house with a letter that he had just received from Arnold. He asked her to please help decipher Arnold's illegible handwriting for him. Mary Ann did not really want to read the letter, but since Mr. Haynie needed it to be done, she agreed to help. In the process of "translating" that letter, Mary Ann felt something stir within her, and an interest was sparked in her to correspond with Arnold again. While she did not understand what was going on inside her, it was evident that God was using that letter to reconnect the two of them. A little flame had been rekindled.

Mary Ann took the address from the letter and wrote a short note to Arnold in Israel, asking if he would be willing to write to her about his observations of the country, people, culture, and current events. Arnold responded with a fair amount of reluctance, but agreed to do it, and they started corresponding. This time, Mary Ann decided to hold nothing back, writing about whatever she thought and however she felt. She decided to tell him everything about what had happened to her, so that in the future, Arnold could never say that he did not know. She chose to reveal her struggles and recurrent depression, how and where she was seeking help, and how she was learning to deal with her spiritual battlefronts.

For her third academic year in September 1966, Mary Ann had transferred from Westminster College in northwestern Pennsylvania to Gordon College, a non-denominational, Christian liberal arts college north of Boston, Massachusetts. She had also switched her majors. Initially, she wanted to become a physician and entered college as a pre-med student, thinking that she was well on her way to that goal. However, during her second year at

Westminster, Mary Ann had to accept that as much as she liked medicine, she did not have enough physical stamina to make it through the grueling steps of internship and residency required in the program. So instead, she chose a tri-major at Gordon College, encompassing theology, philosophy, and psychology. She enjoyed every minute of her studies, although she was still depressed and tried to keep to herself. If she said a little too much about her condition, her roommate would sanctimoniously respond that Mary Ann should just pray about it, as if she had not done so already. The Lord, in His grace, supplied a very wise counselor at Gordon, who gave her a lot of support. God even sent her a chipmunk! Watching the little creature, Mary Ann noted that regardless of how much it scurried around to do different things, it was still the same chipmunk. She realized that no matter where she went, she still remained the same person. Depression happened to be a recurrent cycle in her life. She could not change the fact that she was in it and recognized that there was a lot more to depression than what she could understand at the time. It was therefore up to her to unconditionally accept herself the way she was and to receive the help that God provided.

With this in mind, she wrote Arnold a very personal letter during his first semester at Dallas Theological Seminary to let him know that she wanted to become involved again. When Arnold phoned her on the 25th of September to wish her a happy birthday, it set off a desire to see each other to talk face-to-face regarding Mary Ann's intentions. So, they made plans for her to fly down to visit Arnold over the Christmas break of 1967. Meanwhile, they continued to correspond.

Their letters soon began to take on a deeply personal tone about all kinds of private matters, discussing a whole raft of concerns. They both wanted to be crystal-clear on where they stood on different issues. They also wrote about what each one expected in a marriage and what it meant to them. Mary Ann learned that Arnold spoke in churches at least two weekends a month, primarily in Texas and Oklahoma and occasionally in Louisiana. She would have to deal with his regular absence from home, if they were to be together in the future. This time, they strove to lay things out in the open and to communicate to each other without reserve.

Proposal and Wedding

It was a big risk for Mary Ann to fly down from Boston to Dallas to see Arnold. Unlike him, she had not traveled much, having lived most of her life in the New York-New Jersey area, traveling only as far west as Ohio and as far south as Maryland. Her mother did not want her to go to Dallas, because she still did not like Arnold. However, it was Mary Ann's own decision, so she went ahead regardless. The moment she stepped off the plane, Arnold knew in his heart that he was still deeply in love with her. In contrast, Mary Ann was not an instant decision-maker, needing time to think and pray through things. Arnold had arranged for her to stay in an apartment of one of the couples he knew from the seminary. They made plans to go out to dinner the next night. He showed her the house that he was sharing with the other three students, and they just sat around and talked, while Arnold showed her the pictures he had taken in Israel.

Suddenly, Arnold asked her, "Do you love me?" Mary Ann had said before that she considered the words, "I love you," to be so serious that she would never say it to any man unless she was prepared to marry him. Neither would she ever kiss a man without the intention of marrying him. Mary Ann thought for sure that Arnold would have remembered what she had said to him in the past. So, she replied, "Kiss me," and with that kiss, she had agreed to marry him! Their plan was for her to come down to Dallas after her graduation and work for a year before their wedding in mid-1969. Very happy and excited, they phoned home to share their news. Arnold called his family first and spoke to his mother. She conveyed to Arnold that his father's only concern was that his future wife must not be a German-born Gentile. Mary Ann then spoke to them, her first contact ever with Arnold's parents. Next, they called her mother, who was not at all happy about their engagement.

Arnold jokingly chided Mary Ann that she had spoiled the proposal for him, because the next night after their dinner date, he had intended to ask her to marry him. Mary Ann retorted in the same manner that it was his fault, since he had asked her if she loved him, knowing what the phrase, "I love you," meant to her. So, they bantered for quite a while and had fun with it. In Arnold's typical sense of humor, he would later tell people that he and Mary Ann went out on their first date only after they got engaged!

Mary Ann knew in her heart that God's hand was upon them, as she had experienced the Lord's confirmation in several ways. Had Arnold lived in the same household in their teenage years, they would have been more like brother and sister. Further down the road, they most likely would not have looked at each other in terms of a possible marriage relationship. Also, Arnold had wanted to marry a Jewish girl, but he and Mary Ann hit it off so well at the campsite that his friend, Bob Futoran, had always assumed that they would get married one day. Though Gentile and not Jewish, Mary Ann did have a deep interest in Jewish culture and was a dedicated believer. Besides, Arnold had been so exceedingly fond of her right from the very start.

Years later, Mary Ann also recalled a prayer she had offered as a child, that if she were to get married, she would like a man who had his birthday on the same day or the day after hers. That prayer had long been forgotten until she thought about Arnold's phone call on her birthday. She realized that he remembered it only because hers was so close to his. Arnold was born in Siberia on the 26th of September, three years before Mary Ann's birth on the 25th. It occurred to her that if the time zone differences between Siberia and the East Coast of the United States were taken into account, they would have been born on the same day, three years apart! This illustrated how the Lord had taken into consideration even the details of a child's prayer and answered it. God indeed had His plan for their life and foreknew that they were meant to be together.

After the visit in Dallas, they drove up to her home in New Jersey to visit her family before she returned to Gordon College. When she had enough time to pray and think about what had transpired, Mary Ann realized that she was not cut out to go to live and work in a strange city while not being married. By letter and by phone, she let Arnold know how she felt. He told her, in that case, he would not have enough time to earn the money to buy her an engagement ring. Mary Ann did not care about the ring. The important thing was for them to be together. So, Arnold agreed to work something out. He would visit her at Gordon College in about a month's time to talk in person about the details.

IT WAS RIGHT IN THE MIDDLE OF A MILD WINTER, when Arnold arrived in early February 1968. Mary Ann's younger sister, Beth, was also attending Gordon College as a freshman and rooming with her. Because of Mary Ann's lack of stamina, the college allowed her sister to be her roommate, which came in very handy. For his visit, Beth conspired with Arnold behind the scenes without Mary Ann's knowledge. One of her professors lent them a car, so that they could drive to a very nice seafood restaurant in Gloucester on the oceanfront to have dinner. After a great meal while having coffee, Arnold said he had to go to the car to get something. When he came back, he had his raincoat draped over his arm and sat down again. All of a sudden, he pulled out something like an ice cream cone in wrapping paper and gave it to her. When Mary Ann unwrapped it, there was a fragrant carnation inside.

Carnations were one of Mary Ann's favorite flowers. The first carnation was white with a little love note inside, which she pulled out and read. He had written a poem, relating the color of the carnation to Mary Ann in some way. Next came a succession of cones with different colored carnations and a note in each one. Then, Arnold handed her a fifth cone with a blue carnation. Mary Ann thought that he had picked it because of the color, knowing that she really liked blue. While she was admiring the flower, Arnold asked if she was going to look for the note. Not seeing any note sticking out, she pressed open the center of the petals to look for it. To her complete astonishment, she found a diamond ring! Absolutely caught off guard, Mary Ann went into shock, as she was not at all expecting an engagement ring. What a fantastic surprise!

Usually, it was the bride-to-be who determined the date and time of the wedding. Instead, Arnold pulled out his agenda book with his summer 1968 schedule already filled up. The only two-week period that he felt could be workable for him was to forego a trip that he and Burl Haynie were planning to take together to the Middle East, visiting the seven ancient churches in Turkey, ancient Babylon, and so forth. Mary Ann knew how much Mr. Haynie meant to Arnold, so she asked him if he really wanted to give up the trip. Arnold said that he did, so they phoned up Dr. Daniel Fuchs, head of the ABMJ, to see if he could conduct the wedding ceremony for them at the chapel in the headquarters building. The date chosen for the wedding was the 29th of June 1968.

When news spread around Gordon College that Mary Ann was engaged to someone attending Dallas Theological Seminary, one of Mary Ann's professors, a strong believer in Covenant Theology, became quite upset. To him, there was something wrong with the seminary, due to its adherence to Dispensational Theology. He admonished her that she was doing a terrible thing. She let all that talk go by the wayside, as she was convinced that the professor had no clue what he was saying. Very shortly, she developed a severe case of mononucleosis and was sent home from her college for a whole month. She stayed in touch with her professors in order to be able to still graduate in June. Eventually, Mary Ann was well enough to go back to college and realized more than ever what a blessing it was for her to have her sister, Beth, as her roommate.

Choosing Beth to be her maid of honor and her youngest sister, Kathy, along with a close friend from Gordon to be her bridesmaids, the wedding plans got underway. Her mother would be making Mary Ann's wedding dress and veil, plus the other dresses. She did not have the money to pay for the wedding, but neither Mary Ann nor Arnold had expected her to. They simply pooled together what resources they had, mostly from Arnold's work, and got things set up.

A few weeks before her wedding day, Mary Ann obtained her Bachelor of Arts degree from Gordon College. After packing up her things in the dormitory room, Mary Ann went home to New Jersey. There, she had her dress fittings. All the while, her mother was still trying to talk her out of marrying Arnold, not having gotten over her anti-Semitic prejudices and preconceived notions about him.

As the wedding day approached, Ruth Wardell, whom both Arnold and Mary Ann affectionately called Mom Wardell, entered the picture. Mary Ann had to get her blood test done, obtain the marriage license and organize the catering, the flowers, and other arrangements in Manhattan, so she went to stay with Ruth for about a week on Long Island. While it was their first contact, Mary Ann soon realized just how much she needed to be with this wonderful woman of God. Her time with Ruth both comforted and invigorated her. They were like a couple of schoolgirls having a sleepover. Every morning and evening, they chatted about all kinds of things, sharing their thoughts about their relationship with the Lord. Ruth's ministry and especially her personal relationship with God—always starting the day with Him and doing everything wholeheartedly for His glory—left a permanent impact upon Mary Ann's spiritual life. She admired Ruth's generosity of spirit for taking Arnold into her home, giving him a key to her house, and doing so much for someone who was not even a blood relative. In her life, Mary Ann's mother had not been there much for her. Sadly, their relationship became even more strained with her mother's disapproval of Arnold.

ABOUT THREE HUNDRED INVITATIONS WERE SENT OUT to their families, relatives, and friends. Adele Fruchtenbaum had offered to make the wedding invitations, a gorgeous shining blue on a white background. When Mary Ann saw the design in her favorite color, she knew immediately that she would like her mother-in-law in person. Arnold's family did not attend the ceremony. The official reason given was that it would be too expensive to come from California with all the children. While this was true, the real reason was that they did not want to be in a wedding, which expressed faith in Jesus as the Messiah. In actuality, there would be a blend of traditions in their Messianic Jewish wedding ceremony.

Mary Ann had asked her brother, Bruce, and her friends to take lots of pictures during the wedding, as she and Arnold could not afford to hire a professional photographer. Ruth Wardell, who was overseeing the catering, enlisted the help of Mary Ann Sleichter, Arnold's friend from college days, who, in the interim, had changed her name to Miriam and was now working for the ABMJ. Miriam's task was to ensure delivery of the food from the delicatessen, lay it all out, and to look after the coffee and tea. Ruth, along with several others, also decorated the chapel with the flower arrangements. It had just recently been refurbished with freshly paneled walls, new pews and luxurious red carpeting. While the renovation was unrelated to the wedding, its completion was very timely for Arnold and Mary Ann's special day, a wonderful gift from the Lord.

On the day of the *kiddushin*, or "wedding ceremony" in Hebrew—Saturday the 29th of June 1968—Mary Ann was able to get ready on one of the upper floors. Outside, the early summer day was warm and sunny. Inside, there was an air of joy and excitement. When the music began, Dr. Daniel Fuchs, who would be presiding over the ceremony, was already standing under the *chuppah*, the traditional Jewish canopy held by four poles. Walking single-filed in alternate male-female order, the two ushers and Bob Futoran, the best man, then stood to the left of the *chuppah*, while the two bridesmaids, each carrying a lighted candle with flowers and ribbons at the base, and the maid of honor stood to the right. Arnold, the *chatan*,[23] followed to stand under the *chuppah*. Last came Mary Ann, the *kallah*,[24] who had asked her brother to

---

[23] Hebrew for "groom"

[24] Hebrew for "bride"

walk her down the aisle. When they got to the door of the chapel, she had an inner dialogue. She reminded herself that if she continued to walk down that aisle, this would be it. There would be no turning back. If she did not feel sure or felt that she should not be doing this, then now was the time to turn around and walk out of there. Not too many brides had that sort of inner dialogue, but for Mary Ann, it was a very important way of confirming within her heart that she was doing the right thing before the eyes of God. No one else's opinion mattered to her. She genuinely believed that she and Arnold were about to do the right thing, in accordance with God's will. So, she continued to walk down the aisle to stand under the *chuppah* next to the groom.

Arnold had written the entire ceremony, encompassing elements from both the Jewish and the Christian traditions. Dr. Fuchs opened with a blessing to the groom first and then to the bride. He then proceeded to the prayer and the wedding address, after which the best man poured some wine from the bottle into one of the two goblets to give a taste to the groom and then to the bride. Next, the *ketubah*, or "wedding vows" in Hebrew, were said. The best man and the maid of honor stepped under the *chuppah* behind the groom and the bride respectively, to serve as witnesses while the wedding rings were exchanged. Dr. Fuchs said more prayers and gave the groom and bride a betrothal benediction. The best man then poured another glass of wine into the second goblet to give a taste to the groom and then to the bride. After that, the best man wrapped the second goblet in a cloth serviette and placed it next to the left foot of the groom for him to break. The shared taste of wine from the second goblet symbolized a foretaste of the new life ahead, and the breaking of the glass goblet symbolized the destruction of Jerusalem in A.D. 70. It was a Jewish tradition that even on a Jew's happiest day—his wedding day—he was to still remember Jerusalem.

Years later, when giving his testimony, Arnold with his usual splash of humor recounted that moment. He affectionately characterized Mary Ann as one stubborn individual, whom he had to court for seven years before she agreed to marry him. To him, the seven years indicated that he had worked just as hard for his wife, as Jacob, his forefather in the Old Testament, had worked for his. That fact alone concerned him considerably, because Mary Ann had two sisters! In the Old Testament story of Jacob, he had worked seven years to marry Rachel, the love of his heart. Only after the fact did he discover that he had been deceived. Instead of Rachel, it was Leah, Rachel's older sister, whom he had been given as his wife. Jacob married Rachel a week later, but had to work yet another seven years to pay for that privilege. (Genesis 29:16-30)

In a Jewish wedding ceremony, the marriage was sealed at the moment the groom broke the glass goblet under his left foot. Prior to that, he was free to change his mind and walk away, but once the glass was broken, there would be no turning back. So, when the best man placed the goblet next to his left foot, Arnold admitted with a great sense of humor that he took a quick peek behind the veil to make sure that it was the right sister he was marrying! Only then did he shatter the glass goblet with his left heel, thereby sealing the marriage. The groom then lifted the bride's veil and gave her a kiss in the presence of the two witnesses and walked out arm-in-arm, as husband and wife, followed by the other participants. It was a beautiful and moving ceremony. The guests then all went to the reception hall upstairs to celebrate this happy occasion.

There was plenty of food from the delicatessen, including a variety of cold-cut meats, several different kinds of salads, an assortment of savory finger foods and other refreshments, all beautifully laid out. Partway through, Ruth noticed that the food would soon run out, so she sent Miriam and the other helpers to the deli across the street to get some more. The guests all seemed to have a wonderful time, some who met for the first time, after having heard so much about one another.

About one hundred and fifty people were in attendance. On Mary Ann's side, her whole family came, plus a lot of her friends. On Arnold's side, Bob and his parents, Ruth Wardell, Burl Haynie, the Cattells, the ABMJ family, the M.Y.F., and Miriam came to celebrate and wish them well as a couple. He was not alone. His "adopted" families, friends, and the people who loved him were all there to support and bless him. Since the time that his father had disowned him, God had placed caring people in his life to meet his various needs. In Jesus the Messiah, Arnold truly lacked no good thing.

Now, God had given Arnold the gift of a wife, someone with whom to share his life and love of Jesus. The 29th of June 1968 marked not only the first day of their married life together, but also the one-year anniversary of the official reunification of the two halves of Jerusalem as one city under Israeli control for the first time since A.D. 70. God's providence had been clearly evident in the Six-Day War, and His hand was equally real in the way He brought Arnold and Mary Ann together. This timing was another symbolic confirmation of God's blessing upon their life—two individuals joining together as one. The year 1968 also celebrated the twentieth anniversary of the establishment of the State of Israel as a new nation in May 1948. What a special and blessed day!

AS THEY WERE GETTING READY TO LEAVE at the end of the reception, Mary Ann knew in her heart that they were embarking on a very unique life journey together. She recognized that they were entering into a new territory of life that was foreign to both, given the differences in culture between them. At the same time, she felt that they would also be experiencing the blessings of a very special and loving life adventure.

For their honeymoon, Arnold and Mary Ann spent the first three nights at a hotel suite in Albany, north of New York City. Along the way, Arnold introduced Mary Ann to several nice restaurants. She tried her first-ever French onion soup, which surprisingly, she liked. Arnold was quite adventurous when it came to food and wanted his new bride to share a taste of some of his favorite dishes, particularly French gourmet cuisine. They drove the rest of the way to her family's home in the Adirondacks. Once there, Mary Ann made spaghetti, the first meal she cooked for them as a couple. Growing up, due to minimal funds, casseroles and pasta were a big part of her family's diet. They spent the rest of their time walking along the serene lake at Trout Pond, enjoying the beauty of nature around them, and soaking in the peace and tranquility of the surroundings.

Upon their return, they both worked at the ABMJ headquarters in Manhattan for the rest of that summer. As soon as his first year of seminary ended in early May 1968, Arnold had already started full-time for the ABMJ in New York City, doing deputation work for the summer. After taking two weeks off for his wedding and honeymoon, Arnold resumed what he was doing. Mary Ann performed general tasks at the ABMJ headquarters. For their accommodation, they were offered an apartment to housesit for the summer. It was God's wonderful provision for them as newly-weds.

Toward the end of the summer, after finishing up their work at the ABMJ, they drove down to Williamstown, New Jersey, to Mary Ann's family home to pack her things into a U-Haul trailer to drive down to Dallas. In the packing process, they came across a smoothed-out rock that Mary Ann, as a child, had picked up on the seashore, which held a lot of sentimental value for her. Arnold announced that they were not going to take the rock with them, since they did not need the extra weight. However, Mary Ann had kept the rock all those years and was definitely not prepared to part with it now, not for Arnold, not for anyone.

So, they had their first significant fight as a couple over the rock. There had been arguments before, but never a fight like this. In the majority of cases, Mary Ann would give in to what Arnold wanted, but in this case, she stood her ground. She knew that Arnold had no understanding of the emotions attached to the rock, in how and where she had found it, and why it was so important to her. The rock was a part of her life, and she was not about to give it up. When Arnold pursued his viewpoint, Mary Ann decided that for all she cared, he could go down to Dallas by himself. If the rock did not go with her, then she would not go either! If she could not fully explain it enough for Arnold to see her position, then it did not matter to her. She was going to dig in her heels and not concede, and she never regretted her stance. Over the years, some other believers who had heard about the story criticized her for not submitting to her husband's wish, but Mary Ann figured that no one was perfect and continued to keep the rock to the present day.

ONCE THEY GOT TO DALLAS, they unpacked their things in the apartment that Arnold had found for them earlier. Shortly thereafter, they left for California to visit his parents. Upon arriving in Los Angeles, Mary Ann felt quite nervous and unsure about how she was going to greet everyone. When she entered through the front door, she decided to give each of them a hug and greeted Arnold's parents as "mom" and "dad." It seemed that Henry took an immediate liking to her, so much so that within the hour, he left the apartment and came back with a gift he bought for her, an expensive gold watch! Mary Ann was totally taken aback by this unexpected gesture, but composed herself enough to thank him for it. Arnold made it very clear to Mary Ann that she should accept the gift. Arnold's sister, Margaret, gave her father a hard time, teasing him that he never gave *her* a gold watch.

Due to Arnold's beliefs, his siblings did not know how to relate to him. Eddie and Margaret never talked to Arnold about his activities in the ministry. If they happened to be in the same room, they chitchatted about superficial things. Even though they were very secular in their worldview, they were still very opposed to anything relating to Jesus. Hence, they never asked Arnold about his work, and he came to accept that this was the way things would be with his family. He had moved past the stage of sadness, once he was expelled from home, as he knew that he would never be allowed back as part of the family the way it used to be in his childhood.

While Henry liked Mary Ann very much from the outset, he still did not talk directly to his son. Whenever Arnold and Mary Ann were both in the same room, he would stay and talk with his daughter-in-law. As soon as she went to the kitchen or another room to get something, he would immediately leave the room as well.

Prior to their visit, Mary Ann had been asked to bring along her wedding gown and Arnold's tuxedo. Henry wanted to take pictures of them in his studio downstairs. So, Arnold and Mary Ann changed into their wedding attire. Some were formal shots in the studio itself, while others were taken outside in the backyard. From the numerous photos, Henry planned to pick out the ones to be developed and blown up to a larger size, and then send them to Dallas as soon as they were ready, but Arnold and Mary Ann never received them.

A while later, they found out what had happened. Within a day or two after they left, something had come up in his parents' conversation with regard to Arnold's beliefs, his seminary studies, and what he was doing. Henry apparently exploded into a fit of rage and was furious that his first-born son still refused to come back to his senses. In his angry outburst, he made sure that the pictures he took never got developed and enlarged. Except for a few proofs that Adele managed to salvage, he had destroyed all the films.

Since then, Mary Ann had learned that her father-in-law may seem fine on the surface whenever she was there with Arnold, but once they left, it was anyone's guess what would happen. His emotions were like a seething cauldron of boiling rage ready to erupt at any given moment. Most of the time, Adele felt as though she were walking on eggshells around him. Throughout the years, she had always been caught in the middle between her son and her husband's tempestuous episodes, often in a bind with no audacity to contradict Henry's allegations against Arnold. Wanting peace at all costs, she would go along with whatever he decreed in order to placate him.

Adele often suffered the brunt of his anger, when he ranted and raved implacably over the slightest mention of what Arnold was up to. Perhaps, that was why she never asked Arnold any questions or discussed what he was doing or what he believed. She never allowed any of their talks to cross that boundary and would immediately shut down the conversation even at the slightest allusion to the subject.

The fact that Henry genuinely liked his daughter-in-law was a gift from God. Considering that she was a Gentile Christian, his positive attitude toward her defied human logic. Mary Ann also got along well with her mother-in-law. In later years, she discovered why Arnold never notified his parents in advance if they were in the area and wanted to drop by for a visit. She learned that if he phoned ahead of time, Adele would more than likely tell him not to come. From her vantage point, it always meant trouble for her afterwards. Henry's moods were just too unpredictable.

By the time their visit came to an end in California, it was nearly the start of the fall semester at the seminary. Arnold and Mary Ann returned to their apartment in Dallas, Texas, to begin a new life there. While Arnold attended his classes, Mary Ann would be working once she found a job. Arnold had three more years left to go at Dallas Theological Seminary before he graduated. They looked forward to discovering what God had purposed for them in their life together.

Dallas Theological Seminary

For the duration of his studies, Arnold and Mary Ann lived in the same apartment, conveniently situated near the seminary, right by a bus stop on a major route to downtown Dallas. Consisting of two bedrooms—one of which functioned as Arnold's study and office—plus a combined living and dining room, a small kitchen, and a bathroom, it cost $225 per month. Mary Ann found a full-time job at the accounting office of an insurance company in the city center, where she worked until Arnold's graduation. Being in such close proximity to public transportation, it was easy for her to catch a bus to work every day. Arnold could also get to and from his classes easily, but spent most of his day at the seminary.

As a married student residing off campus, Arnold's tuition came to $300 per semester, equivalent to at least ten times that amount in today's currency terms. He could pay for most of it with the $250 scholarship per semester from the ABMJ. The rest of his tuition and fees, their rent and other living expenses were paid out of Mary Ann's full-time salary and the money from

Arnold's part-time job with the ABMJ, doing deputation work. During this period, Arnold did not see the kind of miraculous provision from God the way he previously had in college and in Israel, as their combined earnings were enough to cover all their needs.

Before applying to DTS, Arnold had researched a myriad of seminaries to make sure he found one that adhered to Dispensational Theology rather than Replacement Theology. Upon checking the background of the professors, he discovered that most who were Dispensationalists had graduated from DTS. So, he decided to go to the source and do his studies there, choosing the four-year Master of Theology program, with a major in Hebrew and Old Testament. He very much enjoyed Dr. Charles C. Ryrie's Systematic Theology courses, realizing only too late that it would have been the more practical major for him. The professors in his Hebrew and Old Testament courses were too enamored with details. For instance, in a Hebrew course called "Pentateuch," the class got stuck in Genesis chapter one for the entire semester, instead of reading a lot of Hebrew while going through all the five Books of Moses. Hence, Arnold chose not to enroll in that class the following semester. He ended up fulfilling the basic minimum courses required for his major and spent the rest of his time taking as many electives in Systematic Theology as he could under Dr. Ryrie.

A large number of graduates from DTS ended up in teaching roles or pastorates. With his knowledge of Hebrew and Greek, plus his earlier training from Burl Haynie, Arnold could take apart a Scripture passage, analyze the actual meaning of the Hebrew or Greek words, and expound on the passage based on the literal text and its context. In doing so, he followed the premise that "a text apart from its context is pretext"—a principle taught by his mentor who had learned it from Dr. David L. Cooper, although it was unclear whether or not Dr. Cooper had originated it himself. Already, Arnold's path for the future seemed to be well set in the direction of teaching.

During his first year at DTS, Arnold was the only Messianic Jew on campus. By his second year, another Jewish believer, Barry Leventhal, had enrolled in the fall. Barry had visited the seminary during the spring of Arnold's first year. At that time, Barry had already been accepted and just wanted to come and take a look around the campus, so Arnold took him out to lunch. In his third year, another Jewish student, whom Barry had known from his college days, also enrolled at DTS, so in total there were three messianic believers at the seminary prior to his graduation.

Aside from being Jewish, Arnold and Barry had other things in common. Both were married to blond, Gentile, Presbyterian believers whose first name began with Mary. Both liked Chinese food and went out to lunch together almost every day during the semester, often to a Chinese restaurant, where the generous portions were tasty and cheap. At other times, they went to different diners close by or to a Jewish deli. They also liked to frequent the IHOP, International House of Pancakes, located a couple of blocks within walking distance from the campus.

Out of the total chapel sessions held at the seminary on Tuesdays through Fridays, the students were allowed to cut sixteen per semester, averaging one cut per week. Each student was assigned a specific seat at the chapel and marked as absent if not in the seat. Arnold and Barry used to cut up to the maximum number of times allowed. The chapel sessions usually lasted an hour with ten minutes free before and after, adding up to an hour and twenty minutes, giving them plenty of time to take off to the IHOP, eat, and get back to their classes. They enjoyed each other's company and soon became best seminary friends. They talked about all kinds of things and shared a common sense of humor. Barry learned a lot from Arnold regarding Messianic Jewish beliefs during his first year at the seminary. A new believer of just a couple of years and having grown up in a more secular Jewish home, Barry at that time had nowhere near the kind of prior Bible training that Arnold had already received.

THE HEAD OF THE ABMJ IN DALLAS generally spoke in churches within the nearby Dallas-Fort Worth vicinity, while Arnold took the more distant churches in Texas and Oklahoma, flying there and back on most weekends. Over the summer vacation period, Arnold worked full-time away from home for one full month straight at a time, mainly in Oklahoma, doing more of the same. Only once during his seminary days did he experience a complete break from his usual routine, when he went to Mexico for one week as part of a class on missions, spending time mostly around the ancient monuments and Aztec sites.

On the weekends during the academic year when Arnold was away, Mary Ann would attend the Northwest Bible Church in Dallas as her place of worship. Once during the summer, she took a bus to visit him in Oklahoma over a weekend.

194

In the course of a week, Arnold could sometimes be teaching at seven different locations in the evenings and would base himself at the same motel as the central point. He soon became a regular motel dweller, a pattern that continued throughout the latter years of his life. From those early days, Arnold began to prefer staying in motels rather than in someone's home. He found it easier to study, write, or prepare for his evening meetings, as he would have no distractions in a motel. Not being much of a sightseer, he could get a lot done this way.

Starting from his second year at DTS, Arnold began pulling together his own itinerary for his ABMJ deputation work, contacting new churches by advanced cold, phone calling. His sphere of meeting venues began to grow and expand, and many new doors were opened. For the last ten minutes of each meeting after teaching the Bible, he routinely made a presentation on the ABMJ, after which a free-will offering was taken up. People could commit to pray or to provide regular financial support or both. The funds raised went directly to the common pot of the ABMJ, which were then distributed according to the needs of each branch. He also began taking meetings at the ABMJ office in Dallas and continued to lead a local Bible study group once a week on his own time.

One summer, in addition to his deputation work, Arnold had to drive some young teenagers from the Dallas area up to Honey Brook, Pennsylvania, to attend Camp *Sar Shalom*. Because Mary Ann was working full-time all year round and Arnold was also working full-time during the summers, they had very little free time to take a vacation. For the most part, they spent their few vacation days at home in Dallas. At best, they occasionally managed to take a week off to go and stay at Mary Ann's family home in the Adirondacks to relax and enjoy the beauty.

That same summer en route to upstate New York, they stopped briefly to see Mary Ann's mother in New Jersey. She whispered a question in her daughter's ear, asking her whether she was happy. When she thought about it, Mary Ann realized that she was indeed very happy. About a year after she was married, her brother even commented to her that he did not think it would ever happen to her, but that he thought marriage had been good for her. Somehow in the interim, Mary Ann had softened from the tough stances she had taken after her father's passing.

IN GENERAL, SEMINARY STUDENTS were expected to finish their studies first before they could be ordained. However, Arnold wanted to advance the timing and be ordained as soon as it was feasible. Toward the end of his second year, he inquired into the possibility at the church where he had worshipped while attending Shelton College in Cape May, New Jersey. Five pastors from the core fellowship group of churches got together to examine him for several hours, after which they discussed among themselves whether or not to grant him ordination. The approval was unanimous.

Grace Gospel Chapel of Rio Grande, New Jersey, then organized a special service on the third of September 1969, to which they invited Burl Haynie to give the ordination address. Mr. Haynie used his own paraphrase of First and Second Timothy, addressing Arnold as his disciple just as the Apostle Paul had addressed his disciple, Timothy. Not only had he been Arnold's teacher and mentor, he was always there for all of his special occasions and milestones, while Arnold's own family never was. Mary Ann, the Cattells, the rest of the church members, and the pastors all attended the ceremony. Once ordained, Arnold could henceforth be addressed as a Reverend and serve as a pastor if he so desired, but that was not his calling in life. An ordained minister could legally officiate at weddings, funerals, and other legal ceremonies. Thus, after receiving his Certificate of Ordination from Grace Gospel Chapel of Rio Grande, New Jersey, Arnold soon began to perform messianic wedding ceremonies, starting from his third year at seminary.

By his fourth year of studies, Arnold began working on his thesis as part of the requirements for graduation. On top of his regular classes, where he had to keep up his grades, take tests, write papers and prepare for pop quizzes interspersed throughout the year, Arnold now had to write a master's thesis. He chose to work on the Hebrew word, *kan'a*, composed of three possible meanings: to be zealous, envious, or jealous. His thesis turned out to be around fifty pages long, all on the study of that one word.

Graduation day soon dawned, and Arnold was ready to obtain his Master of Theology degree. Between fifty to sixty students graduated that year. The banquet, which included a formal dinner, took place on Friday evening, the day before the actual ceremony. The speeches were all geared toward addressing the students' many non-believing family members. At the official ceremony held on Saturday, the seventh of May 1971, the graduates were dressed in full regalia in their caps and gowns. The entire student body was required to attend. Thus, Arnold's best chum, Barry, was there to cheer him on. Of course, Mary Ann came to celebrate as well. Since Dallas was so far away, many of Arnold's friends from the Northeast could not make it to this graduation, and, as had been the case in the past, neither was his family in attendance to help celebrate this happy occasion. Notwithstanding, the ceremony was a full-blown celebration with many speakers and lots of singing, intended to be a joyous time for all the graduates and their families.

After four long years, Arnold had achieved yet another milestone in his preparation to go into Jewish ministry. God had been so faithful to provide for all his needs to arrive at this juncture. With anticipation, Arnold and Mary Ann looked ahead to what God would accomplish in and through their lives over the next phase of their journey.

PART IV

~ *Ministry* ~

For we are His workmanship,
created in Messiah Yeshua for good works,
which God afore prepared that we should walk in them.

(Ephesians 2:10)

A fter their first year of marriage, both Arnold and Mary Ann felt the need and the burden to go to Israel for one year to see what type of ministry the Lord might have for them there. With this in mind during the remaining two years of Arnold's seminary studies, they began to save and plan for their trip. They decided to put aside enough money to buy a brand new Volkswagen camper van directly from the manufacturer in Germany, with the view of traveling around Europe first and then continuing onto Israel to minister to the Jewish people as the opportunities arose.

The camper van would allow them the freedom to travel at will and provide readily available and free accommodation. In the planning process, they happened to spark the interest of four other people, together comprising quite a diverse group. The two young women from Oklahoma were familiar with the ABMJ ministry and had heard Arnold speak during one of his deputation tours in their home state. One of the two young men was a fellow student of Arnold's at DTS. The other knew one of Mary Ann's younger sisters, who were both attending Gordon College at the time.

Originally, Arnold and Mary Ann were supposed to go to Israel under the ABMJ for one year. Their regular monthly salary would have been enough to live on during that period. However, complications arose that caused Arnold to leave the ministry by the time he graduated. Thus, their potential income could no longer be counted on. Still, they both felt the Lord's call to press ahead to Israel. The big difference was that they would now be going purely on a faith basis, as their visa status prohibited them from working to earn an income while in the Holy Land.

After putting their belongings in storage, they flew from Dallas to New York City where they met up with the other four people. Together they flew on Icelandic Air, offering the cheapest airfare to Luxembourg, where Arnold picked up the new Volkswagen van. Because he had pre-arranged its purchase and payment, it was waiting for them at the airport. After filling out and signing the papers for the transaction, he drove off in it with the rest of the group as passengers.

Although the camper van came equipped with a little kitchenette, it was not conducive to cooking for a group. Instead, they used the cooking facilities at the campsites to prepare their meals. Along the way, they sometimes ate at restaurants, experiencing the local foods and culture.

Like a regular mini-van, the camper van could comfortably seat the group including the person driving, allowing plenty of space for the six to travel together during the long drives around Europe. At night, the seats could be folded down to turn into a bed for Arnold and Mary Ann. The other four slept in the big tent that came with the van, which they had to set up. At some campsites, small cabins or bungalows could be rented at a very cheap rate. From time to time, the rest of the group stayed in those.

They visited France, Holland, Spain, Portugal, Germany, Switzerland, Italy, Austria, Yugoslavia, Greece, and Turkey. Arnold did all the driving and enlightened the group with his knowledge of the history and significance of many places. Mary Ann enjoyed all the travels. While in Austria, she bought herself a traditional dress from Tyrol, with puffed sleeves and a tight waist, which she wore often. She even braided her hair and wound them in circles around her head, the way the young women did in Austria and looked quite the part.

The month-long trip in Europe went by very quickly. Before touring Turkey, it was time for the two young men to fly to Israel to start their classes at the American Institute of Holy Land Studies in the same graduate program that Arnold had completed four years earlier in 1967. Now located in Mount Zion overlooking the Hinnom Valley, the campus itself occupied the historic grounds and buildings of a school that was built over one hundred and twenty years earlier, resting atop portions of the Herodian Wall, with the site of the Essene Gate at one corner. The surroundings were very conducive to the study of the history and geography of the Holy Land. Over the years, the institute continued to grow and develop, later becoming known as Jerusalem University College.

The rest of the group found their way to the archaeological sites of the seven churches in Turkey, mentioned in Revelation chapters two and three, and discovered that the Hebrew word, *alma*, still meant "virgin" to the Turks. Finally, they loaded the camper van onto an old Turkish passenger ship and sailed to Haifa, Israel. The ship took about four to five days to reach the port. Since Westerners did not normally travel on that type of local vessel, the voyage turned out to be quite a unique experience for the four of them. Once they got to Israel and cleared customs, the group continued to travel through Israel for another month. As tourists, Arnold and Mary Ann obtained a three-month visa and did not have to pay any duty on their van. Arnold already knew the Land well and was thus able to show the group many biblical sites, normally not visited on regular tourist trips. After a wonderful time in *Eretz Yisrael*, the two young women flew back to the United States.

BEFORE THIS TRIP, Miriam Sleichter, who had kept in touch with Arnold since his graduation from Cedarville, mentioned to him that the CMA, or Christian and Missionary Alliance, had rooms to rent. As an ABMJ worker, she had spent a year in Jerusalem on the "Israel Apprentice Program" between the summers of 1970 and 1971 and had lodged in the CMA building. Arnold and Mary Ann decided to check out the possibility once they arrived. It just so happened that the CMA had taken over the two connecting buildings on the "Street of the Prophets," after the American Institute had moved its campus to Mount Zion shortly after the Six-Day War in 1967. Coming full circle in a sense, the vacancy now available to them was exactly the same basement room, where Arnold had lived during his student days!

Arnold informed the couple in charge of the CMA work that he had the funds to pay the rent for only a couple of months with no guarantees for future payments. The wife stated, "Then we'll see how God will provide." So, Arnold paid the $50 for the first month's rent. All those lodging in the basement had to share the common kitchen facilities on the same level. It was not easy for the married couples to live that way, but this was what was affordable at the time, so Arnold and Mary Ann made the best of the situation. In God's providence, they ended up living there for two years.

When Arnold was a student in Israel four to five years earlier, he had noticed the fragmentation among the believers, with no real united effort. There was also no place where an Israeli believer could go and obtain any kind of formal Bible training. Although a seed was planted in his heart, Arnold did not formulate any concrete plans to address the need. He did not give it much further thought and merely let it simmer somewhere in the recesses of his mind. Back then, he was fully committed to spending the rest of his life serving with the ABMJ.

This time, Arnold discovered that the Messianic Jewish situation had undergone significant improvements. A local congregation had been founded, called the Messianic Assembly of Jerusalem, located about two blocks from the CMA building where he and Mary Ann were lodging. It consolidated and encompassed four or five smaller congregations, one of which Arnold had known and attended during his student days in Israel. The leadership consisted mainly of untrained men with a few trained men, including Warren Graham—the head of the CMA work in Jersualem—whose wife, Linda, supervised the building.

It soon became apparent to Arnold that he needed to focus his ministry efforts on the discipleship of individuals, one-on-one. Among those under his tutelage was a new believer, a young American Jewish man by the name of Lloyd Carsen, who lived just across the hall from them. Arnold taught Lloyd the Bible privately for one year. Lloyd was very keen to learn, asking Arnold a series of questions non-stop about the Bible while following him around. One time, there was something that he did not understand in the second chapter of Joel, so he leaped out of his chair and went straight to the bathroom where Arnold was taking a shower. In his enthusiasm and without thinking, he shouted out his question to Arnold through the door above the sound of the running water. Arnold's gracious and calm response was that he could not answer, because he did not have a Bible in the shower! Lloyd later went to work for the mission organization, Jews for Jesus, in Los Angeles, after changing his name to Tuvya Zaretsky, the last name being the family name in Europe.

At the end of their first three months, Arnold and Mary Ann were able to get their visas extended for a further nine months. Mary Ann began learning basic Hebrew and could soon do the grocery shopping in the local language. When they had been in Israel for six months, they both committed to staying on for a second year, once their first year was completed.

Close to Christmas 1971, they received a visit from Ruth Wardell and a fellow worker, Eleanor Bullock, from the ABMJ in New York City. The two-week trip to Israel was a reward granted to them, marking their twenty-five years of mission service since 1946. Arnold and Mary Ann were delighted to see them, and to the thorough enjoyment of the ladies, their visit culminated in a private tour around Israel. Fifteen years had transpired since Ruth had led Arnold to Jesus the Messiah. Now, Arnold was the more knowledgeable one of God's Word and was eager to show her all the biblical sites of the Holy Land while explaining the significance of each location. The four traveled together in the Volkswagen van during the day. At night, Arnold and Mary Ann slept in the camper van, while Ruth and her co-worker stayed in hotels. All in all, they had a wonderful time together.

DURING THEIR FIRST YEAR IN ISRAEL AS A COUPLE, Arnold and Mary Ann had to trust God and rely completely on His providential care to miraculously provide for them. The Lord proved Himself faithful in surprising ways. Whenever they needed to pay the rent, get gas for the camper van, buy food, or pay the bills, the money was there, even though they adhered to their policy of not telling anyone about their personal needs. Their funds came through many unique channels, often from people they had never met to this day. They once even received a check from a Catholic nun in the United States! How she had heard about them in Israel was beyond Arnold and Mary Ann.

By the time their first year in Israel drew to a close in the summer of 1972, Arnold and Mary Ann faced a dilemma. If they stayed in Israel continuously for over one year, they would be required to pay duty on their camper van. The cost amounted to two hundred percent of the value of the vehicle itself, too much money for them to afford besides making no financial sense. The solution was to take the camper van out of the country, travel around Europe for a couple of months, and then return to Israel with it. That way, upon re-entry as tourists, they could again declare the vehicle and pay no duty. It worked out to be considerably cheaper to travel around Europe and come back.

Prior to their temporary leave from Israel, Arnold wrote to Miriam Sleichter to see if she would like to join him and Mary Ann on their trip around Europe, just the three of them. Miriam readily agreed, flew in from New York City, and met up with them in Vienna, Austria. Together, they toured for six weeks through Western Europe, including Italy, France, Spain, Portugal, Belgium, Holland, and even Andorra and Liechtenstein plus other areas. The camper van had a pop-up roof under which a hammock-like bed could be set up, and Miriam slept there. For ease of reference, they dubbed it the "upstairs." Miriam had no privacy. Neither did Arnold and Mary Ann, who slept in the camper van "downstairs."

Staying at the various campsites, it sometimes proved difficult to find hot water for washing up. Being summer, it was not too bad. However, one of Arnold's challenges was to shave with cold water without nicking himself. After a few attempts and getting little cuts here and there on his jaw, he shaved less and less frequently and eventually decided to grow a beard just for the summer. Much to his surprise, Mary Ann really liked it, so he never shaved it off, keeping a beard ever since that summer of 1972.

All too soon the six weeks came to an end, and Miriam flew back to the United States while Arnold and Mary Ann returned to Israel by ship as they had done the summer before. They had no hassles bringing in the camper van for the second time and did not have to pay any duty on it as tourists. They were able to continue lodging in the same room in the basement of the CMA building and looked forward to their second year.

TO BECOME MORE PROFICIENT IN HEBREW, Mary Ann enrolled in a formal language course at the *Ulpan*. She also learned many worship songs, singing them a cappella to minister to the Hebrew-speaking congregation where they attended. The congregants could hardly tell that she was not a native speaker when she sang in Hebrew.

Arnold's one-on-one discipleship was so effective that more and more believers requested some type of formal Bible study or training. Thus, starting their second year, he established a mini-Bible institute, under the guidance and sponsorship of the local Messianic Assembly of Jerusalem. The students comprised Jewish believers mainly of American and Israeli backgrounds plus a couple of British individuals. A vacant room in the CMA building served as their classroom. They met three evenings per week for five weeks straight, took a four-week break, and then continued for another five weeks of studies and so on. Classes were taught in English. Separately, Arnold also conducted home groups in English during his own private time on alternate evenings.

Arnold spent part of his free daytime hours preparing the lessons and tending to his other ministry duties. He soon began to develop a course entitled "The Life of the Messiah from a Jewish Perspective." At DTS, he had taken an excellent course from Dr. J. Dwight Pentecost called "The Life of Christ" utilizing the book, *Harmony of the Gospels,* by A.T. Robertson. Arnold had noted that there was no Jewish rabbinic background or any Jewish frame of reference for that time period. Being a Gentile believer, Dr. Pentecost simply did not have the Jewish upbringing or training to delve into that realm. The course Arnold developed was very basic and still in its infancy. Even so, it provided more expository teaching of the Word than what the students had been exposed to before. More importantly, it was taught within a Jewish frame of reference, providing the much-needed background information to help better understand the issues during the period that Jesus was on earth.

In his remaining free time, Arnold began working on the draft of his first book, *Hebrew Christianity: Its Theology, History, and Philosophy*, which he dedicated to Mary Ann. In the book, he clearly laid out the definition of a Jew, a Gentile, a Christian and a Hebrew-Christian and surveyed the biblical position and basis for the Messianic Jewish distinctiveness. The manuscript was sent to the ABMJ, but it never got there. Arnold did not know this until he returned to the United States; hence, he resubmitted it. While it was being reviewed, he was contacted by the Southern Baptist Convention to present a manuscript on Jesus as the Messiah. Since the subject matter was very familiar to Arnold, he did not have to do any outside research to pull the text together. He completed the first draft in record time, needing only about a week or two. Thus, *Jesus was a Jew* became the first among all his writings to be published in 1974 in the United States. He dedicated the book affectionately to Ruth Wardell. Shortly thereafter, a publisher was found in the United States for the manuscript of *Hebrew Christianity: Its Theology, History and Philosophy*. [25] Canon Press, the book division belonging to the same publisher of the *Christianity Today* magazine, produced the first edition of this book the very same year.

On the weekends, Arnold and Mary Ann drove their camper van to explore the historical places in the vicinity. During the four-week breaks in between the five-week teaching sessions, they traveled farther into the countryside, visiting the many biblical sites in the new territories gained during the Six-Day War. In those days, things were rather quiet, and they could move about freely everywhere. Arnold again made it a premise to go down every paved road and dirt alley, noting down the areas of interest that could be worthwhile to show others.

They also went regularly to the Holon and Petach Tikva areas near Tel-Aviv to visit Arnold's relatives. Given that his surviving aunts and uncles were from the Holocaust generation, Arnold was interested in tracing their individual stories and recording their experiences. He also wanted to include the stories of those who perished, in order to record whatever information was known about how, when and where they died. For this endeavor, he visited his relatives about once a month or more to tape-record his interviews with them, which were conducted in Hebrew. It was important for Arnold that those family members would be remembered. [26]

---

[25] Today, this book is sold under the title, *The Remnant of Israel: The History, Theology, and Philosophy of the Messianic Jewish Community*.

[26] Decades later, David S. Turner compiled the accounts of the individual members of the Fruchtenbaum family and wrote down their stories in the book, *When Your Face Was Your Destiny*, published by Ariel Ministries.

IN THE LATE SUMMER OF 1972, Arnold and Mary Ann received a second visit from Ruth Wardell. This time, she had organized a group of fifteen current and past M.Y.F. members from the United States, ranging in age from the mid-teens to the early twenties. Using his own camper van plus a rented mini-van driven by Lloyd, Arnold took them around on a comprehensive study tour all over Israel for five weeks, which he considered to be adequate time to see the biblical sites at a good pace, including one rest day per week. The young people slept in several large tents already set up at the various campsites, while Ruth had her own pop-up tent. Thus, they visited the whole country at minimal expense.

During stops along their travels, the group often came into contact with local Israelis. One of the M.Y.F. members brought along his guitar and played many worship songs for the group to sing. Some songs were in Hebrew, which frequently drew a small crowd of local Israelis, curious to find out more about these young people. This gave Arnold an opening to speak with them, thus indirectly witnessing to them.

Frequently enjoying a good laugh, the group began teasing Arnold as to why they had never heard him sing before. He assured them that it was because he was tone deaf. Not easily deterred, they continued to badger him. So, Arnold finally relented and began singing, "This Land is Mine," the theme song of the movie, "Exodus." All the way through, he sang every single note off key, bellowing out the last word on such a long flat note that the young people all burst out laughing. It was so hilarious! They definitely got their fix, because after that number, they never again asked Arnold to sing.

The Bible verse that Ruth had given the group prior to the trip was First Thessalonians 5:18: *in everything give thanks: for this is God's will in Messiah Yeshua to you-ward.* One time near the Sea of Galilee, the group had pooled together their money, about fifty cents each, for Arnold to go to the nearby stores to buy bread, yoghurt, and other breakfast items. While waiting, they encountered droves of flies zooming about. They were good sports and lived out their Bible verse for the day by giving thanks even for the flies.

Other people soon began to contact Arnold, asking him to show them around Israel for shorter periods. Sometimes, he took them on walking tours around the city of Jerusalem for one or two days over the weekends. Other times, he led shorter tours around the Land. Even a former classmate from his seminary days, Tim Timmons, and his wife, Carol, came to Israel. They brought along three people whom Tim was discipling, and together, the seven of them traveled on a short tour around the country.

One of the most memorable tours that Arnold conducted took place toward the end of 1972. On this tour, he spent a few days with a missionary from Wycliffe Bible Translators, who had brought along two of his native converts from West New Guinea, known today as Irian Jaya. The missionary was very impressed with the biblical sites, while the two converts—one of whom was a tribal chief—were even more impressed at the way the Israelis supposedly built their "straw" huts! Just observing their reactions alone was enough to give Arnold a tremendous sense of reward and gratification to be able to show them *Eretz Yisrael.*

Toward the end of their second year in Israel, Arnold took his students from the mini-Bible institute on a five-week study tour of Israel. Around twenty people traveled in Arnold's own camper van, a rented mini-van and the car belonging to the head of the CMA. Arnold's camper van certainly came in very handy for all his tours in Israel.

WITH A VERY FRUITFUL ONGOING MINISTRY, Arnold and Mary Ann committed to staying a third and fourth year in Israel. However, close to the time when they needed to renew their visas, they received a letter from the Department of the Interior requesting Arnold to come to their office for an appointment. When he went to the bureau, the authorities advised him not to bother to apply for their visa renewal, since the government would not be granting them an extension. Arnold realized that word had gotten around about his teaching ministry at the mini-Bible institute, and this had angered certain religious groups. The local "Pharisees" of the day made sure to apply enough pressure upon the government to finally ask the Fruchtenbaums to leave.

The second largest newspaper in Israel, *Yedioth Ahronoth,* got wind of the story and wrote quite a prominent article about the real reasons behind the refusal to renew their visas. Though many of the facts were wrong, the thrust of the article was on the point. While Arnold and Mary Ann had done nothing illegal nor broken any laws, it was very clear that the religious groups had become alarmed at the impact of Arnold's teachings. The local "Pharisees" had succeeded in exerting heavy pressure upon the government in such a way as to get Arnold and Mary Ann expelled.

Sadly as a result, they were forced to leave the country at the end of their second year. It was especially hard, knowing full well that once they left, the mini-Bible institute would be discontinued. At that juncture, no one else was available to take over the program. It had been a very effective ministry up to that point, and the students had gained a vast store of knowledge from studying the Bible under Arnold. Disappointed at this turn of events with only two months left before their visas expired, Arnold and Mary Ann prepared to leave. They decided that this time, they would drive through Europe all the way to the U.K. and take an ocean liner back to the United States, keeping their camper van with them.

An artist living in the same CMA building traveled with them across Europe that summer. During their stay in Jerusalem, this Jewish lady had painted two portraits of Mary Ann, which they brought back with them to the United States. Since that time, those two paintings have continued to grace the walls of their home. In early September 1973, the lady was dropped off in England. Once Arnold and Mary Ann reached the port of Southampton, Arnold went to the customs office to fill out the paperwork to have their van transported back to the U.S. on the same vessel they would be taking. They spent that night in a motel, costing fifty dollars, an exorbitant amount of money for them at that time, but worth the splurge. The next morning, they boarded the huge ocean liner, Queen Elizabeth 2, and set sail toward the United States.

Arnold and Mary Ann enjoyed the great meals on board. The QE2 was a very nice, ultra-modern ship, a major contrast to the old freighter that had carried Arnold and his family to the shores of America some twenty-two years earlier. In those days, Arnold could never have imagined how his life would turn out over the next two decades. The closest he ever got to a luxury ocean liner on that first voyage was when the Queen Mary sailed past the old carrier with impressive speed. At that time, Arnold certainly would never have envisioned himself on an ultra-modern, luxury liner like the QE2.

More astounding was how inconceivable it would have been back then for Arnold to even contemplate the idea of ever believing in the "Gentile Christian" Jesus as his Jewish Messiah. Yet, here he was, many years later, returning to the United States after having ministered to the Jewish believers in Israel for two years and having imparted to them a wealth of in-depth knowledge about *Yeshua Ha'Mashiach* from the Word of God. Arnold marveled at God's calling upon his life to bear spiritual fruit that would last for eternity. As the QE2 sailed toward the United States, his heart swelled with thanks and praise at how wonderfully God had provided for him and Mary Ann during their time in Israel.

Reluctant Obedience

Upon returning to the United States in September 1973, Arnold and Mary Ann drove their camper van from the East Coast across the country to Seattle, Washington, to get reacquainted with the people they had known in the past. They then continued to California to meet up with Ruth Wardell, who meanwhile had transferred to the ABMJ office in Los Angeles. While in the area, they stopped to see Arnold's family. In the eleven years since his expulsion from his parents' home, this would be his third visit, the most recent with Mary Ann five years earlier. Henry's silence policy was still in place, although on the odd occasion, Arnold was allowed to make contact. On this visit, they were keen to see how much his three youngest sisters had grown. They also looked forward to spending time with Arnold's maternal grandmother, Emma Suppes, who had gotten out of the Kazakh A.S.S.R. in 1969 to come to the United States to live with the family in California.

During their time in Los Angeles, they heard that war had broken out in Israel on the sixth of October 1973 on *Yom Kippur*, the holiest and most solemn day of the Jewish religious year. The war began when a coalition of Arab forces, mainly Egypt and Syria, launched a surprise attack on Israel as a reaction to their territorial losses and humiliation of the Six-Day War in 1967. The *Yom Kippur* War lasted for nearly three weeks, ending in a ceasefire on the 25th of October, after Israel successfully recaptured most of the areas that it had lost at the start of the war. While both sides suffered many casualties, the Arabs lost more lives. The surprise element from the Arab side, however, demonstrated that Israel was not militarily invincible, having its pockets of vulnerabilities.

From California, Arnold and Mary Ann made their way back to Dallas to pick up their belongings that were in storage while they were in Israel. They then drove through the states of Texas, Georgia, and Tennessee to catch up with their friends, before continuing onto their destination, New York City.

At the end of their six-week road trip, they sold their camper van, as they would have no more need of it.

Although it was a great disappointment for Arnold and Mary Ann to be forced to leave Israel, they noticed a most wonderful change in the United States. The Holy Spirit had been doing a tremendous work among young Jews in the intervening years. Through the "Jesus movement" of the 1970s, unprecedented numbers were coming to faith in the Messiah, rivaling that which was recorded in the Book of Acts. Such an explosion of new Jewish believers was marvelous, but because of their minimal knowledge of the Word, the young people got swept up in all kinds of non-biblical spiritual movements. Arnold realized the crucial imperative for Jewish ministries to provide sound biblical teaching to new believers, balancing evangelism with ongoing discipleship.

When the ABMJ offered Arnold the role of managing editor of publications, he gladly accepted, anticipating that he would have many opportunities through the Mission to teach the Bible, in concert with his main editing work. As God's providence would have it, Arnold was to work on *The Chosen People* magazine—the cover of which was given to his mother by Theo Burgstahler at the D.P. Camp in Ulm, Germany some twenty-four years earlier, triggering a series of events leading to his salvation. Now, coming full circle, he rejoined the staff of the ABMJ at the beginning of November 1973 to work full-time on the same monthly magazine.

During the two preceding years, many changes had taken place at the ABMJ. The existing headquarters building in Manhattan and the old ABMJ building on Throop Avenue in Brooklyn had both been sold. The printing and mailing operation was outsourced to Burl Haynie, who had resigned in September 1972 to work independently on a contracted basis for the Mission. He had secured a rental space in Zarephath, New Jersey, at the Pillar of Fire school property and purchased the printing and mailing equipment directly from the ABMJ for his own workshop.

By the time Arnold started working at the ABMJ, the headquarters had already relocated to Englewood Cliffs, New Jersey. Mary Ann was also employed there, performing clerical accounting duties. They rented a two-bedroom apartment in New City, New York and commuted to work, driving across the state line to New Jersey every day during the workweek. They both kept busy, especially Arnold, who also conducted a Bible study group in their home once a week.

In addition to his full-time work at the ABMJ, Arnold took courses part-time at the Jewish Theological Seminary in New York City during the second semester and through the summer of 1974. It was the main place of training for rabbis of Conservative Judaism. In September of the 1974-75 academic year, Arnold got his course credits transferred to New York University, where he began studying part-time toward his doctorate. The equivalent of three years of resident classroom studies was required in the Ph.D. program, before Arnold could start working on his dissertation. By going to classes part-time during the 1974-75 academic year plus the summer of 1975, along with the transferred credits, he was able to fulfill the requirements for the first year of resident studies.

In his role as managing editor, Arnold was responsible for the layout, but was not the final decision maker regarding the contents of the publications. He reported to the head of the Mission, Dr. Daniel Fuchs, who maintained the final right to edit what could or could not go into print. After one year, Arnold was appointed as editor. In this capacity, he theoretically had the authority to make the final decision, but in actuality, Dr. Fuchs retained the right to the final editing.

Aside from the occasional conference or the odd church meeting, the only other opportunity for Arnold to intensively teach the Bible was the one time in 1974, when the ABMJ allowed him to lead a study tour to Israel. The main emphasis of the ABMJ seemed to have veered heavily toward evangelism with barely any focus on discipleship, thus lacking the same balance that there used to be in the past. Hence, things did not go as Arnold had hoped in terms of plentiful Bible teaching opportunities through the ABMJ. A number of other factors had also come into play, some of which grieved Arnold, regretfully leading to his eventual resignation in late 1975.

DURING THE TWO YEARS of working at the ABMJ, Arnold saw the critical need for a more focused and disciplined approach to the Bible training and discipleship of new Jewish believers, but had no intention of starting up a new ministry organization. Hence, when the head of the CJF, or Christian Jew Foundation, offered him a position as a teacher on the ministry's radio program, "The Christian Jew Hour," he jumped at the opportunity, figuring that he would have more free time to teach the Bible intensively in other settings as well. The CJF was a large and well-to-do Jewish ministry located in San Antonio, Texas, founded about twenty-five years earlier. It comprised around fifteen full-time staff members, its own publications, and a major radio ministry with broadcasts through approximately seventy-five radio stations across the entire country. Thus, Arnold and Mary Ann moved down to San Antonio and settled in a house they managed to purchase.

As associate director, Arnold started out at the CJF with a two-week teaching program, which he handled all on his own. A parameter was given to him to ensure that the topics he covered did not overlap with the broadcasts recently aired. Otherwise, he was free to choose any biblical topic he wished, as long as he taught it within a Jewish frame of reference. He prepared and taught one third of all the programs, while the founder and head of the organization taught the other two-thirds. The work was immensely enjoyable. Since the CJF had its own studio, Arnold could record a whole week's worth of programs in one sitting, consisting of five twelve-minute segments. He normally prepared his materials in outline form, teaching impromptu from the wealth of Scripture knowledge already memorized in his head. In doing so, he usually accomplished the recordings in only one take, rarely having to do any retakes, thus requiring only about an hour and a half per sitting.

The other part of Arnold's job description was to travel to Bible conferences at various churches to speak. This was where he thought he would have more free time and flexibility to teach the Word, which was his deep-felt passion. Unfortunately, the founder of the CJF turned out to be a very controlling individual. He did not allow Arnold to take on more than five local, outside teaching engagements per year, even though Arnold was receiving many more invitations. He even tried to control which church the Fruchtenbaums were attending on Sundays!

Thus, Arnold ended up spending the rest of his time at the office doing administrative paperwork and answering correspondence, all of which he found to be tedious. While he really enjoyed teaching the Word via the radio programs, he felt increasingly frustrated by the restrictions placed upon his other teaching options.

Fortunately, before coming on board, Arnold had negotiated to take two summers off during the first couple of years of work at the CJF. He planned to continue taking classes at New York University to fulfill the resident class requirements for his eventual doctorate degree. Since Mary Ann was not working at the time, she could spend that summer there with him. For their accommodation, they had an offer to housesit for a family who would be away for the entire summer and needed someone to look after their house. By the same token, they also found someone to stay at their house in San Antonio during their absence. Arnold thus spent the summer of 1976 engaged in intensive study at New York University, fulfilling the second year of required resident classes. The following summer of 1977, he flew up by himself. Mary Ann had found a job by then, working full-time in the accounting office of a chain of cafeteria restaurants and could not go with him. She stayed behind at their house in San Antonio, and Arnold once again found a place to housesit while he completed the third and final year of resident studies required for his Ph.D. degree. The next step was for him to write his doctoral dissertation.

WHILE WORKING AT THE ABMJ AND THE CJF, Arnold had come to recognize the pressing need for a new and distinctive Bible teaching ministry to the Jews that centered on evangelism as well as discipleship. Other couples with a connection to Jewish ministries had separately approached him at different times with similar concerns and even indicated to Arnold that they would be willing to work with him if he would set up such a ministry. Although the idea persistently tugged at him, he kept putting it off from year to year. His reluctance stemmed from not wanting to deal with all the bureaucratic headaches and administrative complexities of setting up such a tax-exempt, non-profit organization. He much preferred working as a paid staff member of an already existing Jewish ministry. As the need brewed in the back of his mind, Arnold prayed and did a lot of serious thinking about it. Meanwhile, his frustrations with the teaching restrictions at the CJF continued to mount, and he grew increasingly restless. More detailed discussions with the various couples ensued during the summer of 1977.

Clearly, God was not going to let the idea simply drop. Arnold recognized that the Lord was nudging him to step forth in a new direction, having prepared him all along for a distinctive ministry to the Jewish people. Patiently and persistently, God had been calling him, yet Arnold had consistently avoided the issue. Finally, he could resist the Lord no longer and resigned from the CJF in November 1977.

Several of the men attending Arnold's adult Sunday school classes at Wayside Chapel, the Fruchtenbaums' home church in San Antonio, were very supportive of his concept of a new ministry to the Jews. One of them, Ben Wallis, happened to be a lawyer. Submitting to God's call, Arnold went to seek legal counsel from him regarding all the ins and outs of setting up a ministry organization. He learned that Ben was prepared to handle all the complex legal paperwork involved in the incorporation of such a tax-exempt, non-profit entity. All Arnold had to do was to provide a draft constitution and fill in a number of standard forms. The rest would be up to the lawyer.

Normally, approval for such a request could take up to six months or longer. Yet to everyone's sheer amazement, the incorporation and tax exemption status came through within just eight days of submitting the application! Never before had the lawyer obtained any legal approval so quickly with no hitches along the way. Indeed God's hand was evident throughout the whole process, a true testimony to His sovereignty overruling the entire situation. With incredible speed, Ariel Ministries was born on the first of December 1977! Completely in awe, Arnold joyfully took this miraculous result as a confirmation that he was on the right track with this new endeavor.

From its inception, the governance of Ariel Ministries was through a board of directors consisting of five men including one in the role of chairman. They were all deeply committed believers. Due to its very limited resources at the outset, the ministry began its operations in Arnold's home, converting two of the bedrooms upstairs to Ariel offices. One very large room at the far end of the hall was to be used for Arnold's office, containing his library. Apart from a desk and a chair toward the back of the room near a window, the remaining walls were lined with shelves and shelves of books. The other office, just atop the stairs on the left-hand side, was reserved for a future secretary.

As Ariel was a faith-based ministry, it depended solely upon the incoming financial gifts for its support. Arnold had to rely totally on the Lord, trusting God to provide for the ministry's needs. Even though Mary Ann was not part of the staff at Ariel Ministries and was still working full-time at the accounting office of a chain of cafeteria restaurants, she nonetheless helped out by setting up the bookkeeping system. She made sure that an efficient procedure was put into place for the processing and receipting of the donors' monetary gifts.

During the first month of December, Arnold worked by himself as the only staff member of Ariel Ministries. Within only one month of starting, the ministry had received enough income with a solid, monthly, committed donor base to be able to bring a secretary on board. Charmaine O'Neill, who also worshipped at Wayside Chapel with her husband, Mark, was able to take a huge administrative load off Arnold's shoulders while he concentrated his efforts on his itinerant teaching ministry.

Even with a secretary to assist, Arnold still arranged his own speaking engagements by cold phone calling and contacting the various churches himself. Aside from teaching the Word of God, his goal was to make Ariel widely known so that enough ongoing financial support could be raised for the new ministry to become stabilized. From the outset, Arnold booked himself quite heavily in terms of taking church meetings in different states. His ministry travels took him away from home about twenty-five days a month. As Mary Ann was still working full-time, she could not travel with him during the first year of Ariel Ministries. For the most part, Charmaine worked alone in the office. On the remaining days of the month when he was not traveling, Arnold rarely spent more than three consecutive days back at the office. It tended to be more sporadic, a day here or a day there. So, when he was actually in town, the work pace became very intensive and hectic for Charmaine.

Arnold was extremely organized and productive with the use of his time during his travels. He carried with him all the reference materials that he needed for his research on a particular book he was writing or on a subject he was studying at the time. Usually, he brought along two hard suitcases to check-in plus two carry-on bags. One of the carry-on bags contained his Dictaphone, files of office work, and letters from ministry supporters. Questions on a myriad of Bible topics would flood into the office. Arnold made sure that he personally responded to all his individual correspondence, dictating his replies for Charmaine to type up.

On one such teaching trip, Charmaine's husband, Mark, got his first induction to Arnold's repertoire of suitcases when he drove him to the airport. As Mark went to stow the suitcases into the trunk of his car, he could barely lift them off the ground. The suitcases were so heavy that he momentarily thought they were filled with either huge rocks or cement blocks! In his amazement, he asked Arnold how he could ever manage to maneuver all the pieces of luggage by himself on his travels. Arnold replied that all he had to do was to get Mark to carry his suitcases to the check-in counter, and from there on, he would find himself a little trolley to push his carry-on bags all the way to the departure gate and get on the plane. Easy!

Since most of Arnold's meetings were scheduled in the evenings, he had most of the daytime free to stay in his motel room to study or to write. Thus, he got through an enormous amount of work on every trip. As he finished using certain materials, he posted them back to the office. After each segment of his travels, his suitcases became lighter and lighter. Before heading home, he definitely had a lot less to pack in his luggage.

Quite early on, the various aspects of the ministry fell quickly into place, with several missionary couples coming on board within the first few years. The overall progress was very encouraging. Ariel's policy was to keep its donor list strictly confidential, never to send out any heart-wrenching appeal letters to drum up support, and not to charge any honorariums nor obligate the hosts to pay for travel expenses. The only thing Ariel Ministries requested was for the host church to take up a freewill offering at the end of the teaching session. In all its years as a faith-based ministry, never once has Ariel ever had to turn down a speaking request within the United States due to a lack of funds for travel expenses. God was always faithful to somehow provide the means. Over the years, the ministry's unswerving adherence to this policy has been a great testimony to the principle it upheld that "God's work done in God's time will never lack God's support."

Living in San Antonio

By the time Ariel Ministries was into its first year of operations, Arnold and Mary Ann had been living in their house in San Antonio for over two years. Given that they would be staying there for a while, they decided in the early part of 1978 to have some renovations done to their house to better suit their ongoing needs. It was a good-sized, two-story brick house with four bedrooms upstairs, two of which functioned as Ariel offices. The downstairs included a living room, a family room behind it and a master bedroom plus a bathroom off to one side. Off to the other side of the living room was a kitchen with a tiny breakfast nook.

A contractor was hired to renovate the master bedroom and bathroom spaces, and to add a new dining extension to the small existing nook. Upon completion of the two new wings, the ground floor configuration would become u-shaped. The house had a huge backyard, which was a delight for Mary Ann. She truly enjoyed puttering around in the garden, planting plenty of colorful flowers and tending to the young shoots.

Because Arnold and Mary Ann frequently had other people staying in their home, they wanted to have some private space to themselves to be alone whenever they needed a break. In the process of enlarging their wing of the house, the bathroom was completely redone and covered in light blue tiles, Mary Ann's favorite color. It included a new heart-shaped bathtub with golden swan fixtures to boot! Arnold was a romantic at heart and had a high idealistic view of marriage. Deeply in love with Mary Ann, he enjoyed wooing and romancing her. The newly renovated bathroom was one of the many arenas through which he expressed his romantic notions. The renovations were timely, as Arnold and Mary Ann would be celebrating their tenth wedding anniversary toward the end of June 1978.

Within the first few years of their marriage, Arnold started working on the manuscript for his book, *Biblical Lovemaking: A Study of the Song of Solomon*, which largely expounded on the ideals of love between a husband and wife as God intended it to be. Such was the unconditional love that he wanted to always have for Mary Ann, in addition to honoring, respecting, and protecting her. His devotion to her was apparent to those around him. One time at a poolside gathering to which they were both invited, an acquaintance, who had not noticed them coming in together, asked Arnold where Mary Ann was. As Arnold looked across the backyard through the crowd to point her out, his face lit up when he spotted her, beaming proudly with love and delight as though he were showing off his beloved queen.

The new dining room extension could amply accommodate a very long dining table. Arnold and Mary Ann wanted to invite a large number of guests for celebrations, such as Passover *Seders* and other traditional Jewish feasts. From time to time, Charmaine and her husband, Mark, were invited over to share an informal meal with the Fruchtenbaums on a social level, which they both enjoyed very much. Arnold took pleasure in cooking Jewish food, including *matzah brie, latkes*, and *matzah* ball soup. He also liked to try his hand at cooking French gourmet dishes, one of his most favorite cuisines. Normally, he prepared the main course, carefully following the recipe and instructions from a cookbook, while Mary Ann whipped up the accompanying dishes, mostly a mixture of mashed potatoes and rutabagas and a variety of salads.

On those social occasions, Charmaine noticed that Arnold was very different from what he was like at work. Because of his frequent travels away from the office, once he was in town for a short interlude, he strictly focused on the business at hand with utmost intensity in order for them to get through all the work that required their attention in the ministry. In contrast, when Arnold was relaxed on a social level, he was very jovial and witty, displaying a dry sense of humor with his Jewish "rabbi" jokes that triggered many belly laughs.

MARY ANN WAS VERY FOND OF CATS. Surprisingly, so was Arnold. When he was a youngster living in Brooklyn, his family once adopted a stray kitten that he loved very much. His parents were not too fond of pets, but let him keep the kitten nonetheless. One day, as the little kitty was running across the street, it was killed in the midst of oncoming traffic, which left Arnold heartbroken. Mary Ann, on the other hand, had grown up with cats in her family household and took great pleasure in having them around.

Shortly after they got married, Arnold and Mary Ann started adopting kittens. The kitties were mostly from a litter, but sometimes they took in strays. For the kittens to grow up together, they always had a minimum of two and occasionally up to seven at the same time. When they lived in Jerusalem, they took in one of the wailing alley kittens and named it *Yirmiyahu*, Hebrew for Jeremiah, after the weeping prophet.

When they moved to San Antonio, Texas, they brought with them their cats, B.B., short for Boston Blackie, and her mother, Amnona. By the time Arnold and Mary Ann had settled into their own house, the mother cat had disappeared, leaving B.B. behind. B.B. grew into a rather unusual cat, unlike any other. She habitually enjoyed a certain sunny spot in one of the rooms upstairs for her afternoon snoozes. When the room was later transformed into Charmaine's office with a desk right over her favorite spot, B.B. was undeterred. Not about to sacrifice her daily nap, the persistent feline paid regular visits to the office to claim her spot to snooze away, totally oblivious to the work activity around her.

Sometimes, B.B. exhibited such peculiar behavior that it led Charmaine's husband, Mark, to conclude that she was "possessed," secretly dubbing her "Beelzebub" instead of Boston Blackie! On one social occasion, Charmaine and Mark were among the many guests who were invited over to celebrate the Feast of *Purim*. Before the meal was served, the guests were in the living room, listening to Arnold's lecture on how God, through Esther and her cousin, Mordecai, delivered His Chosen People from total annihilation at the hands of their Persian enemies. In strolled B.B., halting suddenly in her tracks as though struck by a lightning bolt. She seemed confused as to how to get through this morass of strangers to where her food dish was kept in the garage. Then without any warning, she launched herself into the air with one long swoop all the way across the room, landing for a split second onto a lady's lap by the edge of the couch, before ricocheting off with another grand leap to make her escape through the kitty door to the garage. B.B. was quite a frightful sight, catching everyone off guard, especially the dear lady, who let out a terrified scream, as this massive ball of black fur hurtled in her direction at breakneck speed! The guests were in stitches with laughter at this unexpected acrobatic performance.

IN BETWEEN HIS TRAVELS while living in San Antonio, Arnold was able to carve out a bit of time from his ministry schedule to take care of a very important personal matter. The situation in Siberia at the time of his birth did not permit for a *brit milah*, Hebrew for "circumcision," nor was a *mohel* available to perform it.[27] Therefore, Arnold was never circumcised as a baby. Until recently, he had moved from place to place without being able to put down any roots for a prolonged period. Now based in San Antonio, although still traveling quite heavily, he finally had the opportunity to schedule an appointment with a specialist in urology to perform the surgery. Under the Abrahamic Covenant, it was necessary for a Jewish male to be circumcised as a sign of his Jewish lineage. Even though Arnold had become a believer in Messiah Jesus and was part of His Body, the true Church, he was still obligated to uphold the requirements of the Abrahamic Covenant, which was an eternal one for the Jewish people.

Arnold and Mary Ann developed some good friendships with other believers from Wayside Chapel. Most of them attended Arnold's adult Sunday school classes and were among those whom he invited over to the house to participate in celebrations of various Jewish feasts. One of the men discovered that Arnold liked playing racquetball for exercise, and soon, they began playing together. When his travels increased exponentially with Ariel Ministries, Arnold found it easy to pack a racket in his suitcase, just in case he found someone to play with. Highly skilled at the game and extremely competitive by nature, he played to win. Most of his opponents noted that his desire to dominate every single game became like an obsession. If he lost, he

---

[27] The noun *mohel* is derived from the same verb stem as *milah*, "circumcision." So while *brit milah* refers to the covenant of circumcision, the *mohel* is a professional circumciser.

was gracious about it. However, he would immediately schedule another game just so that he could win the next time. On the days that he did not have an opportunity to play, Arnold would go jogging for several miles to keep fit.

He also continued to keep in touch with his close friends from the past. After college, his good friend, Bob Futoran, pursued a military career in the Air Force. During the time that Arnold was attending seminary, whenever Bob was on his way to a new posting, he would stop by Dallas to meet up with Arnold. They would go out to dinner at a nice restaurant and talk about all kinds of things, catching up with what was going on in each other's life. It was Arnold who introduced Bob to Japanese food for the very first time at a traditional Japanese restaurant in Dallas, where they sat on the *tatami* floor and ate from a low table using chopsticks. Even though Bob had been to Japan on his postings, he had not yet ventured out to try the *sashimi*, or raw fish, and the *sushi* seaweed rolls. By contrast, Arnold was quite adventuresome when it came to trying out different types of food. Aside from French gourmet, he also enjoyed German food, especially the veal schnitzels, as well as Chinese and Japanese cuisines.

After Arnold and Mary Ann settled in San Antonio, and Ariel Ministries had been up and running, Bob stopped through San Antonio every now and then to visit with them. He remembered going over to their house one time for a wine tasting session. On a social level, Arnold embodied the *joie de vivre*. He enjoyed life, good food, parties, and a hearty laugh. Like most people, he embraced the basic comforts of life. He believed in giving people what they were due and was not interested in living in a one-room hovel, eating breadcrumbs.

Arnold's other close friend, Miriam Sleichter, was now married to Sam Nadler, a Jewish believer, and living in San Francisco, California. Together, they served with the Jews for Jesus organization as part of its singing tour group called "The Liberated Wailing Wall." As such, they traveled around the country to evangelize and minister among the Jews. From time to time, Miriam's group stopped in San Antonio en route to other venues and stayed overnight at the Fruchtenbaums' home, enjoying their hospitality.

Once the renovations were completed on their house, Arnold and Mary Ann opened up their home to receive people to come and stay with them whenever the need arose, thus extending their hospitality. It seemed as though there was a steady stream of people in and out of the house, and the spare bedrooms upstairs were occupied most of the time. In his younger days,

Arnold himself had been on the receiving end of much gracious hospitality from people who had taken him into their homes. Mary Ann's childhood home was a loving haven for the foster children whom her parents cared for. Hence, they both wanted to make their home available to any believers who needed a temporary place to stay. It was one of their ways of sharing God's love and care. However, neither Arnold nor Mary Ann could have ever imagined whom God would soon be sending their way to live with them permanently.

Endearing Connection

One Sunday evening in the late spring of 1979 when Ariel Ministries was in its second year, Arnold received a phone call at home from his mother in California. After they talked for a while and hung up, Arnold informed Mary Ann that they needed to make a decision within the next few hours. Things had gotten utterly unbearable for Adele, and she was at the absolute end of her tether. The ongoing conflicts between her husband, Henry, and her mother, Emma Suppes, had escalated to a boiling point. Adele had no other recourse but to ask Arnold if his grandmother could come and live with them in San Antonio.

Having just finished refurbishing one of the extra guest bedrooms upstairs, there happened to be a spare room available in their home. Arnold and Mary Ann referred to the room as the "prophet's chamber." The inspiration came from a story in the Bible of a Shunammite woman who prepared a room in her house for Elisha the prophet, a man of God. Their original desire for the room was to make it available for believers directly involved in ministry work, who were passing through town or needed a place to stay short-term.

As Mary Ann thought about the situation over the next couple of hours, she concluded in her heart that it was no accident that they had just refurbished the room. She was convinced and firmly believed that God must have intended the room for Arnold's grandmother. Normally, she liked to take her time to think and pray through a situation before making a decision. However in this case, she quickly agreed with Arnold that of course Emma could come and live with them. What puzzled her, though, was why Adele put forward the request only to Arnold and her, and not to the other siblings, like Eddie, Margaret, or Arthur, who were already on their own and residing in the local vicinity. Would not the closer proximity make it easier for Arnold's mother and his grandmother to see each other more frequently? To Mary Ann's bewilderment, those questions somehow never got answered.

When Emma heard that Arnold and Mary Ann had opened up their home to her, she was so delighted that she immediately went about packing to get ready to move. So, Adele informed Arnold that she would be flying in with his grandmother the very next afternoon! Inwardly in shock at the immediacy of their arrival, Mary Ann felt as though in a daze. Not being the keenest of housekeepers, she experienced dire stress, as the house was in a rather messy state. Very early the next morning, she enlisted the help of Charmaine, and together, they scrambled frantically to get the house all cleaned up before her mother-in-law and Arnold's grandmother arrived in the afternoon. Given the lack of time, they simply gathered all the clutter and hauled the mess up to the attic as a temporary measure. It would be the first time that Adele ever visited them in San Antonio, and although the house was not in spic-and-span shape, it was now at least orderly and presentable.

NEARLY TEN YEARS HAD ALREADY PASSED since Emma Suppes first stepped foot on American soil in 1969. Not long after the family had settled in Brooklyn, her daughter, Adele, reconnected with her by mail after many years of disrupted communication. In California, it took a number of years before Henry was able to establish and operate his own photography store on their premises. When the family's life and income stabilized enough, Adele began the long and arduous process of filing the necessary paperwork to get her mother out of the Soviet Union, without ever telling her husband what she was doing. She patiently but determinedly waded her way through the morass of documentation required. The wait for approval seemed interminable, but Adele persevered. At long last the day finally dawned, when Emma Suppes was granted the coveted approval to immigrate to the United States.

For the very first time in her life, she flew on an airplane across the Atlantic Ocean and landed in New York City to be transferred onto a domestic flight to Los Angeles. Adele asked Arnold if he could go and meet his grandmother at the airport. He agreed. At that time, Arnold and Mary Ann had been married for over a year and Arnold was just into his third year of studies at

Dallas Theological Seminary. It did not pose a problem for him to take a couple of days off to make the trip, except that he needed to figure out how to communicate with his grandmother, who spoke only Russian and German. One of the ABMJ workers in the New York City area, Eliezer Urbach, spoke Russian, so Arnold asked if he could serve as the interpreter. With this all set up, Arnold flew from Dallas to New York's JFK Airport, where he met up with his interpreter, and together they waited. When Emma Suppes finally came out of the international arrivals, Arnold saw his grandmother for the very first time, recognizing her by the photos that he had seen of her. An indescribable rush of emotions surged through him as he went up to greet her and introduce himself. Despite not speaking the same language, he felt an immediate connection to her. When he went to check on her connecting flight, he noticed that she was booked on a flight that would make four stops en route across the country. He changed the booking to a direct, non-stop flight leaving New York City later, but arriving into Los Angeles earlier than her original schedule. Once the details were rearranged, Arnold phoned his mother in Los Angeles to let her know. It was only then that Adele informed her husband that his mother-in-law was coming to live with them!

Over thirty-two years had passed since Arnold's mother and grandmother last saw each other. So much had transpired in each of their lives in the span of those decades. Now in her late sixties, it was a big adjustment for Emma to come to the United States, a foreign country with a new language and culture. It was all a lot for her to take in as she met her son-in-law and the grand-children for the first time.

Years earlier, many changes had taken place in the household on Robertson Boulevard. When the twin girls were born and more space was needed, Henry converted the other apartment upstairs—which had been rented out to tenants up to that point—combining the two to create one large spacious apartment for the family. He segmented off a portion on the street side, reserving it for use as his photo studio. He then leased out the storefront on the street level and moved his own business upstairs to his newly renovated photo studio, where he focused primarily on professional studio shoots. Adele no longer had to help out in the storefront business downstairs, so she was able to spend more time taking care of the younger children at home.

Henry had made these changes, due in part to the effects of his diabetes. While he could see just fine during the daytime, he suffered a loss of his night vision and was unable to function in the darkroom at the storefront to develop films. By focusing only on professional studio shoots, Adele could help with the proofs and final development of the few chosen photos, which required minimal time. Because of his poor eyesight, Henry eventually lost his driver's license and was subsequently declared legally blind. With no other means to earn a living, Henry was placed on a medical disability program that provided social benefits from the government.

Even with the additional rental income from the two storefronts downstairs supplementing the disability allowance, the total was still insufficient for the family to live on. Thus, Adele had to pick up the reins. She found a coffee shop about a mile away from the house, which she rented and operated. Although Henry was indirectly involved, the daily work fell largely upon Adele's shoulders alone.

By the time her mother came to live with the family in 1969, Adele was already working full-time at the coffee shop. Much of the conflict between Henry and his mother-in-law revolved around the family situation. Emma simply could not understand why her daughter had to work so hard on her own, while her son-in-law slacked off and occupied himself mainly with playing chess. Because Adele had to go very early in the morning to open up the coffee shop, it was Emma, the grandmother, who looked after the three younger girls to get them ready for school.

From the start, the relationship between Henry and his mother-in-law had been a rocky one, and it got progressively worse. The growing sense of animosity between them was reciprocal, and no amount of appeasement from Adele seemed to calm either one. When Arnold and Mary Ann visited the family shortly after they returned from Israel in the fall of 1973, they wondered why his grandmother never sat at the same table to eat with the family. She would wait in the kitchen until the meal was over and then do the dishes, as though it were her regular contribution. No matter how much she was encouraged during their visit, Emma simply could not be persuaded to join the family for a single meal.

BEFORE MARY ANN HAD TIME TO PREPARE ANYTHING ELSE THAT DAY, Adele arrived at the house with Arnold's grandmother, now in her late seventies. Some of Emma's things were in a suitcase, but her other belongings were wrapped in a big patchwork quilt with the four corners pulled to the center of the bundle and tied in a knot. Mary Ann had never seen anything like that before. Maybe that was the way people carried their belongings in

Kazakhstan. Within the first twenty-four hours, Mary Ann went out and purchased a couple of dictionaries—one in Russian and English and another in German and English. Since she had taken a few classes of German back in school, she still had a vague recollection of some words, which helped at times to communicate without the aid of the dictionaries. However, Adele asked Mary Ann not to learn any Russian, so that her mother could use what little English she knew and learn more.

Adele stayed for about a week to help her mother settle into her new environment. By this time, Grandma Suppes—as she was now called—had already lived in Los Angeles for about ten years and had established her own routine. Adele informed Mary Ann what Grandma wanted to do, such as shop in the grocery store and make her own meals separately, and how she liked to have her hair done. Adele also fixed a specific time to phone her mother from Los Angeles every Sunday, so that they could speak to each other in Russian.

After Adele left, Grandma Suppes settled quite comfortably in her new home. Although her bedroom was upstairs just down the hall from Charmaine's office, she spent most of her time downstairs. While a very private person, she was still very personable to Charmaine. She cooked delicious Russian food and would often bring some upstairs for the secretary to sample at lunchtime. Charmaine once commented that she was gaining weight just by smelling the aroma of Grandma's delicious cooking!

Because Arnold was traveling so frequently out of town for ministry purposes, he never had time to do any maintenance work on the house or in the yard. Charmaine's husband, Mark, would come over from time to time to help with the trimming and pruning of the trees in the backyard. One day, just as Mark was pruning a tree, Grandma Suppes came rushing out of the house, gesturing wildly at him to stop cutting down the tree. She was a very spirited lady, robust and full of spunk, not someone to be messed with. Mark tried to explain in easy English combined with a bit of pantomime that he was simply trimming the tree, but Grandma could not be convinced. She crossed her arms and adamantly stood her ground, as if preparing for a standoff. Finally, she went and got Mary Ann, who, with the help of a dictionary, managed to get her to understand that Mark was not chopping down the tree.

During the time that Grandma Suppes lived with them, Mary Ann needed to phone Adele only a few times to clarify things in Russian. One such incident concerned B.B., the cat. Over a period of time, B.B. had developed a problem with dairy products, but Grandma Suppes continued to give her milk. B.B. could not digest and break down the milk and got diarrhea each time. As a result, the veterinarian advised Mary Ann to eliminate dairy products from B.B.'s diet altogether. Having grown up in the Soviet Union where cats were part of everyday rural life, and dairy products were the norm for a cat's diet, Grandma Suppes could not understand what the problem was. Mary Ann felt as though she were banging her head against a brick wall, trying to explain why it was not permitted. She ended up phoning Adele for help. Even though her mother-in-law did not agree with the veterinarian, she had to communicate the verdict to Grandma, who finally relented, because she really liked B.B. and did not want her to be sick.

Grandma Suppes had a sixth sense about people. Friends of Mary Ann would sometimes stop by to visit, and ninety percent of them did not meet her standards. Interestingly, those whom she liked were all believers, while the rest just did not pass the mark. She had a deep suspicion and fear of people in general, but of strangers in particular. Even though she had done nothing wrong, she had been sent to a Soviet prison camp and relegated to working at hard labor in the Kazakh A.S.S.R. for almost a decade during the reign of terror under Joseph Stalin. In that era, people there spied on one another and reported any and everyone at random to the Russian Secret State Police. Living in San Antonio, Grandma was always afraid that the neighbors might report her to the government of the United States, resulting in her being deported back to the Soviet Union. No matter how many times she had been reassured that this was not the case here, nothing seemed to carry any weight with her.

Arnold and Mary Ann habitually had various people living in their house. One of their guests was somewhat inquisitive and began asking Grandma Suppes a series of basic questions, such as where she was born and where she lived and so forth. Even these were too personal for her liking, and she ended up in a total state of panic, claiming that he was going to report her, that she would be deported and that she was not safe there any more. She was absolutely terrified and regardless of what Mary Ann said to her, she would not calm down. One day, she was shivering all over, and it appeared as though every cell in her body was infused with fear. Not knowing what else to do, Mary Ann phoned Adele and explained that she and Arnold had known this couple for a number of years, and they most certainly had nothing to do with the government of the United States. Only after Adele had explained all this to her mother in Russian, did she very slowly begin to relax a bit.

At the same time, Adele advised Mary Ann to tell her guests in advance not to ask Grandma any questions. Never having lived under a totalitarian regime, Americans had no experience of the type of ongoing fear that she had constantly lived with. On the other hand, it was impossible to convince Grandma that the questions posed to her were not at all invasive.

DURING THE SECOND YEAR OF ARIEL MINISTRIES, Mary Ann resigned from her job at the accounting office of a chain of cafeteria restaurants, primarily so that she could travel more with Arnold. It appeared unlikely that his extensive travels away from home would abate anytime soon, so she tried to accompany him as much as possible. Also, a number of health issues had cropped up, some requiring surgery or special tests to be done. The rest of the time she could be more available at home for Grandma Suppes. Due to his extensive travels away from the home base, Arnold, on the other hand, did not have much time to spend with his grandmother. Besides, they could not communicate in a common language, although Grandma Suppes probably understood a little more English than she had let on. Arnold cared very deeply for her and had an abiding concern for her safety, comfort, and welfare. He wanted to make sure that her needs were always met and showed her a great deal of kindness. There were times when he experienced moments of frustration with her, but in an affectionate sort of way. In his heart, Arnold felt a deep and endearing connection to her, as Grandma Suppes was the only living grandparent he had.

Progress in Outreach

Back in 1973 shortly after Arnold began working full-time with the ABMJ in Englewood Cliffs, New Jersey, he became acquainted with Dan Rigney, who at that time was heading up the ABMJ mission work in Baltimore, Maryland. One day, Dan approached Arnold to ask for his help in setting up a one-week Bible study camp the following summer of 1974 for a group of new Jewish believers, mostly high school students, whom he had been mentoring. Funded by the ABMJ, the program was intended to be a special one-time discipleship event only. As for the venue, Dan and Arnold both thought of the Camp Heathcote property in the Adirondack Mountains of upstate New York, the location of Burl Haynie's Memory Camp for five summers.

Before her death in 1969, Rose Burnham had turned the camp property over to a local association of five pastors, called the CEEA, or the Clinton-Essex Evangelical Association. Sadly in the interim, the camp property itself had fallen, by and large, into disuse. It had been a long interlude of eleven years since 1963, when Arnold last attended the Memory Camp. Now, he would be back—not as a student this time, but as a teacher of the Word.

The group of fifteen, including staff, benefited so immensely from the teachings in 1974 that Dan and Arnold decided to repeat the program the next summer, extending it to two weeks. Hence, Arnold prepared materials on more biblical topics. The response was so positive that Dan and Arnold once again decided to run the camp the following summer, expanding it even further to three weeks of teaching. The attendance increased to around forty. By the end of summer 1976, the Bible study camp had been running for three years in a row. After giving it further thought, Arnold decided to press forward to continue a fourth season in 1977. While the ABMJ had been willing to continue funding all the camp costs until this season, it would be their last year of involvement in this particular type of camp ministry.

When the following summer rolled around in 1978 for the fifth season, Ariel Ministries had already been launched for about eight months. As the ABMJ was no longer funding the program, Ariel Ministries ran the study camp under its own banner that year. It was now called the Ariel Discipleship Camp. That year, Arnold sat down with two other believers with a seminary background, and together they came up with a five-year study curriculum for the camp. Since then, the summer discipleship program became a regular annual feature of Ariel Ministries.

After five years of renting the campgrounds for the program from the CEEA, Ariel Ministries was offered a lease to the property starting the summer of 1979 for ninety-nine years at the price of one dollar per year! The ministry would now have full control over the campsite and be able to develop it as a study camp for Jewish believers. As a tribute to Rose Burnham on whose heart God had laid a burden to reach the Jewish people, Ariel

Ministries decided to change the name of the campsite to Camp *Shoshanah*, a Hebrew word meaning "rose."

ARIEL MINISTRIES HAD MADE NUMEROUS STRIDES by its third year as Arnold continued to witness the outworking of God's amazing provision and protection. Besides meeting its material needs, God had blessed the ministry's work in evangelism and discipleship. Arnold was convinced that the progress achieved thus far was a direct result of the many faithful prayers offered on Ariel Ministries' behalf. The ministry had grown to such a point that it required more office space than the two rooms it occupied in the home of the Fruchtenbaums. A suitable place was found in a small industrial complex in a non-descript building on the corner of Colwick and Nakoma Streets of San Antonio.

It soon became obvious to Arnold that more Home Office workers were needed to meet the administrative demands of an expanding ministry. A new, part-time paid role was created, which soon developed into a full-time position of receptionist-secretary, and Charmaine was then promoted to administrative assistant. With Arnold on the road much of the time, it was Charmaine who oversaw the daily running of the Home Office. A few times per week, two regular volunteers assisted—one to process the study tapes and the other to handle the bookkeeping.

The ministry's outreach was expanding rapidly. Since the autumn of 1978, Dan Rigney and his wife, Arlene, had joined Ariel Ministries as missionary workers heading up the Ariel Baltimore Branch in Maryland. In early 1980, a couple based in Bergen County, New Jersey, joined the ministry. The same year, another couple started a local messianic congregation under the Ariel umbrella in Los Angeles, California. In early 1982, another couple joined part-time to help out the Ariel Los Angeles Branch due to its rapid growth. By the fall of 1983, this couple started up the Ariel San Diego Branch also by planting a local messianic congregation. Both congregations later went independent within the stipulated timeframe of five years. Meanwhile in the spring of 1981, a non-staff couple volunteered to start up a branch in Seattle, Washington, which closed down a few years later when the couple moved to Portland, Oregon, where a similar volunteer work was set up.

New initiatives in evangelism and discipleship were actively pursued. By the fall of 1982, a new radio ministry was launched, followed by a new division called the Ariel Ministries Press. By underwriting the publication of all of

Arnold's books, the ministry could retain the copyrights as well as maintain full control and flexibility to manage the quantity and timing of printings. It seemed that God wanted all of the net proceeds to go to the ministry rather than to an outside publisher. These funds would then help bring on board more missionary workers. Within a short span of time, the volume of book stocks increased beyond the space capacity of the Home Office, so the ministry eventually rented a mini-storage room nearby to house them.

SINCE THE INCEPTION OF ARIEL MINISTRIES, Arnold's speaking schedule had filled up quite quickly. About five years into the ministry, his engagements were already forward-booked for two years out. Instead of Arnold contacting the churches to seek out teaching opportunities as he had done in the early days, it became the other way around. Notwithstanding his full speaking itinerary, he still had to somehow carve out time to work on his doctoral dissertation for New York University.

Arnold faithfully carried on with his commitments, resting in the knowledge that...*it is God who works in you both to will and to work for His good pleasure.* (Philippians 2:13) He was very serious about honoring all his teaching engagements and, if at all possible, avoided having to postpone any meetings for whatever reason. Throughout the years of his ministry, it was clear that God's protective hand was upon him, keeping him healthy and safe, enabling him to fulfill his commitments.

Out of all the places in the United States that had opened up to Ariel Ministries, the one area that Arnold had least expected was Hawaii. After his resignation from the Christian Jew Foundation, Arnold and Mary Ann took a much-needed two-week vacation trip away from home in early January 1978. Many times in the past, Mary Ann had expressed her desire to go to Hawaii. So they decided to take their vacation there, visiting four islands, which they enjoyed immensely.

While there, Arnold made contact with two or three fellow Dallas Theological Seminary graduates who were living in Hawaii at the time. Although he had not planned on a speaking itinerary or any teaching ministry while on vacation, he was invited on the spur of the moment to hold a couple of Bible conferences to expound the Word of God from a Jewish perspective for the local community of believers. Soon, invitations to teach in Hawaii began to mushroom. From then on, Arnold and Mary Ann returned to minister every year for about six weeks each time. Eventually though, as

Arnold became busier with his increased travel schedule, it was no longer possible to commit to a yearly teaching itinerary in Hawaii. For the fourth teaching trip in 1982, he decided instead to send Dan and Arlene Rigney, who were very well received. From the following year onward, Arnold and Mary Ann returned to Hawaii once every two years.

Early on, they had been teased about their ministry trips to Hawaii. What others did not realize was the hectic daily schedule that Arnold followed in his teaching engagements. Most other speakers usually went for a two-week teaching tour, but in actuality spoke only once or twice and used the rest of the time for full-scale personal recreation. This type of behavior did not engender much respect from the local Hawaiians. In marked contrast, Arnold would teach and minister every day for two months straight, sometimes speaking at several different churches on the same day. He was even willing to go to remote islands. Wherever there were people willing to learn, Arnold was willing to go and teach, no matter how small the turnout might be. After each meeting whether it was during the daytime or evening, the Fruchtenbaums always made themselves available to meet with individuals or small groups as often as the people wanted. They would go to a restaurant nearby and answer a myriad of questions on the Bible, while enjoying fellowship. Once it was clear that Arnold and Mary Ann were indeed there to minister God's Word to the people rather than for their own personal pleasures, the local community's initial wariness turned into deep appreciation. As time went on, a number of churches added Ariel Ministries to their mission budget, and the ministry also gained a lot of support from individuals.

Unplanned Ministry in Warsaw

In the spring of 1980, two and a half years after Ariel Ministries was launched, Arnold had a rare opportunity to take a personal trip to Poland. Barry Leventhal, his close friend from seminary days, was working on his doctoral dissertation at Dallas Theological Seminary on the subject of the Holocaust. Barry was spending the late spring and summer of 1980 abroad, using Munich as his base in Germany to research the *Shoah*. Barry wanted to visit some of the German Nazi extermination camps in Poland as part of his firsthand research in gathering information and data and asked if Arnold would like to join him.

The origins of Arnold's family on his father's side traced back to Poland, and he himself had lived there for a short interlude in 1946 before he turned the age of three. Over the years, he had heard many stories about the Fruchtenbaum family from his surviving relatives in Israel and wanted to visit his family's hometown of Pultusk to see for himself what might still be left of his heritage. Back in 1967 at the end of his studies in Israel, Arnold had planned to fly via Poland en route back to the United States. However, the Six-Day War had erupted, and diplomatic ties between Israel and the Soviet Union along with its satellite countries, including Poland, were broken. All the flights from Israel to Poland were cancelled indefinitely, so Arnold's stopover plans could not materialize. This time, he was very keen to join Barry.

Because their visit was a personal one, Arnold and Barry had not made any plans to teach or minister in Poland, but it appeared that the Lord had other intentions. Unbeknown to them, God had been preparing in advance to use them as His answer to the prayers of a fervent Polish Gentile believer in Warsaw. At that time, Poland was still a communist country, and they found themselves unexpectedly involved in a covert teaching ministry among a small group of dedicated Polish Christians, who had a heart for the Jewish people.

Earlier in the year, I mentioned in a letter to a friend of mine who works for Operation Mobilization that I was planning to go to Poland. One of the jobs he performs is to smuggle Christian literature behind the Iron Curtain, so he had several contacts in Poland, especially with one woman that had a special interest in Jewish people. So during his next trip to Poland, he told the woman about our plans to come. All he knew was the date that Barry and I would be arriving, but did not know any more than that. I did not know that such a contact had been made.

When Barry and I arrived at the Warsaw airport, to our surprise, we were paged on the intercom. My first thought was that there might be some trouble, for as far as I knew, no one in Poland knew that we were coming. As it turned out, this woman, whom we shall call Mrs. P., had been at the airport for about six to eight hours having our names paged as each plane arrived from the West. Finally, she got the right one and we met at the airport where she explained how she had learned that we were coming. Mrs. P. had been a member of the Polish underground during World War II and was forced to watch while the Germans burned the Warsaw Jewish ghetto to the ground. She was frustrated that nothing could be done about it. Still later, after the war, she was forced to watch other tragedies hit the Polish Jews under the communist regime until the majority of the Jews were finally forced out of Poland in 1968.

She has since then gathered a group of disciples composed mostly of young Polish people and she spends a lot of time teaching them about the Jewish people and God's program for them. She also spells out the details of the tragedy of Polish Jewry. She has been able to place these young people into jobs where they can be of help to the few Jews still living in Warsaw. She has been doing some writing for the Polish church to point out their faults in the tragedy of the Jews and has put several tracts together for the purpose of witnessing to both Jews and Gentiles in Poland. In fact, everywhere we went together, she found opportunities of witnessing and leaving tracts with the people she talked with. She had been praying for years that God would send a Hebrew-Christian to Warsaw to teach her little group, and now God seemed to doubly answer her prayer, as suddenly two Hebrew-Christians arrived. While she had had many Western believers come through and teach her group, this was the first time the group was taught by Hebrew-Christians.[28]

After the Germans were defeated at the end of World War II, the entire country of Poland fell into the hands of the Communist Party. At the time Arnold and Barry took their trip in 1980, Poland was still under a communist regime. Many of the buildings in Warsaw, dating back to the pre-war days, had not yet been repaired from the damages incurred during the war. Even

---

[28] Excerpts: *Ariel Ministries Newsletter*, November 1980

the hotels were old and somber, lacking many of the modern amenities that were taken for granted in the West. A sense of oppression and restrictiveness hung in the air like a wet blanket over the population, and their lack of freedom could be felt tangibly everywhere. This became even more evident when they were invited to Mrs. P.'s apartment to meet her young Polish disciples in secrecy under the cover of darkness at night, stealthily climbing the stairs, the tension palpable in the air until they were safely inside behind locked doors.

After we checked into our hotel, Mrs. P. took us to the area where the Warsaw Ghetto once stood. Nothing much is left. The Germans had so totally destroyed the area after the Jews revolted that it needed to be rebuilt and is now composed primarily of new apartments, but this time without Jews. Only a memorial to the Jewish revolt reminds anyone, that at the time, Warsaw rivaled New York City as a major center for the Jewry... That evening, she brought us to her apartment where her little group of disciples had gathered. The apartment building pre-dated World War II, and much of the war damage has never been repaired. We had to ascend six flights of stairs in total silence, for we were warned that an informant was living one floor below Mrs. P. If he were to hear any English at all, he would notify the police immediately.

Barry and I were asked to give our testimonies, which were recorded, and Mrs. P. translated line by line from English to Polish. Barry's testimony went smoothly without a hitch, but mine had to be censored several times over, since nothing negative could be said about the Russians or positive about Israel, both of which play a role in my testimony. All in all, it was a unique experience...

The next morning, we drove fifty miles north of Warsaw to the town of Pultusk, where the Fruchtenbaums originated. Mrs. P. agreed to come along to serve as our interpreter. I had been given two addresses of two houses where the Fruchtenbaum family had lived, but upon arrival we discovered that the communists had changed some of the names of the streets. Where they had not changed the street names, they did change some of the house numbers. But thanks to Mrs. P. who made several inquiries at local

residences and then the town hall, she finally found
someone who knew the original names as well as the new
names.

   Largely through her help, we were able to find both
houses where the (Fruchtenbaum) family had lived and the
Jewish rabbinic school where my great-grandfather taught
the Scriptures. However, the synagogue where he worked had
been destroyed by the Germans. We even ran into the son of
the landlord who rented the house to my family, and he
still remembered all the various names of the family
members. My family in Israel had warned me about him, that
he might be somewhat dangerous because his father was a
violent anti-Semite, and he seemed to share the same
feelings. But, apparently, with no more Jews in Poland, it
was no longer a problem.[29]

Although meeting Mrs. P. in Warsaw was totally unforeseen, it was very providential. Without her help, Arnold would not have been able to locate the houses or the streets on his own, due to the language barrier. His surviving relatives in Israel, who had lived and grown up in Pultusk, in particular Aunt Chankah, had explained to him what the two houses on the same street looked like. He found them exactly as they had described. A huge deluge of mixed emotions coursed through his being, engulfing him like a tidal wave as Arnold pictured his big, loving family living their daily life in the two houses in close proximity to each other, going to the Jewish school, shopping at the *kosher* butcher store, and attending the synagogue.

Many feelings were going through my heart and mind as I
remembered all the many stories that my father, uncles,
and aunts told me about the life of the Fruchtenbaum
family in this town. These are feelings I shall never be
able to adequately express in words or in a newsletter.[30]

Tragically, the peaceful life of the Fruchtenbaum family in the little town of Pultusk had come to an abrupt end, never to be restored again. Without the war, none of the family members would have perished, and life would have

---

[29] Excerpts: *Ariel Ministries Newsletter*, November 1980
[30] Excerpts: *Ariel Ministries Newsletter*, November 1980

continued normally for them in this town. A wave of nostalgia and a sense of loss washed over Arnold. Seeing the place with his very own eyes made the family history become more real, the tragedy more poignant. Once a thriving Jewish community, Pultusk was left devoid of Jews after the war. Like the fate of hundreds and hundreds of *shtetls*[31] located in Poland, Hungary, Czechoslovakia, Austria, and other parts of Europe, Jewish community life was completely eradicated here.

After heading back to Warsaw that evening, Barry and Arnold again met at Mrs. P.'s apartment and taught the Scriptures to her group of disciples. The message that they studied together on the Abrahamic Covenant, "How to Destroy the Jews," somehow seemed a befitting theme after what had happened to the Jews of Poland during the Holocaust in World War II. Arnold wanted to know how he could be of assistance to Mrs. P.'s valiant efforts in teaching her disciples about God's Chosen People.

> We asked Mrs. P. if there was anything we could do for her. She emphasized that she did not need any money, since she receives sufficient support from friends in various places. Her main problem is getting literature that is usable in Poland, since she is not permitted to hand out literature that has been printed anywhere in the West. Unfortunately, most printed materials do have it stated as to where it was printed. Because much of her literature has to do with a special sensitivity to the Jewish people of Poland and the condemnation of the Polish church for its failures, many organizations refuse to have it published. So, I told her to get the material ready and Ariel Ministries will publish it for her and not have anything on there to show where it has been printed. So, at least we can do this much of a ministry behind the Iron Curtain.[32]

After spending a good part of a day at the death camp of Treblinka, Arnold and Barry returned to Warsaw that evening. For most of the following day, after a brief stop at the Warsaw Jewish Cemetery, they drove south in their

---

[31] Yiddish for "small towns"

[32] Excerpts: *Ariel Ministries Newsletter*, November 1980

rented car to a hotel in Krakow, which served as their base to visit Auschwitz and Birkenau. After a lengthy visit of these two extermination camps the next day, they returned to their hotel in Krakow to spend the night. The following morning, they turned in their rented car and took a flight back to Warsaw.

> At the Warsaw airport, we were again met by Mrs. P. We had about a five-hour layover before we were to catch our plane out of Poland, so she took us to downtown Warsaw for a little more fellowship and some tea and refreshments.
>
> By Polish law, Polish money is not permitted to be taken out of the country. But neither were we allowed to exchange it back into U.S. dollars. We had quite a bit of money left over, but we had no desire to turn it over to the Polish government. So, just before we cleared passport control, I stuffed most of our leftover money into an envelope and handed it to Mrs. P. She would have never accepted it, but by the time she realized what was in the envelope, we had already gone through Passport Control and there was no way she could return it to us.
>
> I am praying about the possibility of returning to Poland sometime next May or June. There are still a few places I would like to check out. I also want to make contact with this Polish Christian group and spend a lot more time teaching than we did before...[33]

Arnold's hopes of returning to Poland the following year to bring more teaching to Mrs. P.'s group of disciples did not materialize, due to many factors. The labor force in Poland was in turmoil at the time. As usual, the Jews were blamed for the problems, even though there were scarcely any left in the country. Once again anti-Semitism reared its ugly head and was on the rise in Poland. The communist government cracked down on the people and declared Marshall Law in 1981, which severely restricted the activities of the population.

Notwithstanding, after Arnold returned to the United States at the end of his trip in spring 1980, he did follow through with his offer to Mrs. P. and

---

[33] Excerpts: *Ariel Ministries Newsletter*, November 1980

managed to get some Christian literature published in Polish for her, which did not carry any identification marks.

> We have since sent the work she wanted done to our printer, and as soon as the printing is completed, we will ship all these things to a contact I have in Austria. He, in turn, will smuggle the literature into Poland. In light of the recent events in Poland over the last year, especially with the rise of Polish anti-Semitism (as always in Polish history, whenever there are any problems like the recent ones, the Jews have been blamed—and they have been blamed again), getting this literature into Poland is very crucial.[34]

In February 1982, Arnold again wrote a short update on the status of the Polish tracts. The printing of the materials had all been completed, and it was now a matter of waiting for the right opportunity for the tracts to be smuggled into the country as soon as it was feasible.

> In previous newsletters we announced that we would attempt to publish Polish tracts for our contact, Mrs. P., in Warsaw. We are happy to report that these tracts have been published and printed by Ariel Ministries and are ready to be taken into Poland at the earliest opportunity. Because of Marshall Law, the borders are sealed at the moment, and getting the literature into Poland will be impossible. As soon as Marshall Law is lifted, attempts will be made to get the literature into the country.[35]

---

[34] Excerpt: *Ariel Ministries Newsletter*, June 1981
[35] Excerpt: *Ariel Ministries Newsletter*, February 1982

Visiting the Past in Poland

In his heart, Arnold knew that visiting Treblinka would not be easy, and he was comforted to know that his friend, Barry, would be there with him. Treblinka was a death camp hidden away in the remote forests of northeastern Poland near the Bug River, a tributary of the Vistula River. During the war, the Vistula River served as the demarcation line dividing Poland between the German Nazis to the west and the Soviets to the east. This was enforced until the sudden German invasion of the Soviet Union in June 1941, when the entire territory of Poland fell under Nazi rule. It was only in early 1942 that the Germans put their "Final Solution" in place, aimed at the total destruction of the European Jewry. All the extermination camps were located in Poland, mostly in the former Soviet-occupied zone of the country. Treblinka, in operation from July 1942 to August 1943, was dissolved in late October 1943, completely ceasing by November.

After arriving in their rented car at Treblinka, some sixty-odd miles from Warsaw, Arnold and Barry spent the afternoon looking around. Neither said much to the other as they walked about the grounds, each drenched in his own dazed silence, trying to take it all in. Arnold noted the evidence of the attempts by the Polish communist government to cover up the truth concerning the mass extermination of the Jews at the camp, as if those barbaric acts against the European Jewry could somehow be obfuscated by a camouflage of convenient forgetfulness.

In walking around the area and looking at the various memorials, it was obvious that the Polish communist government has attempted to hide the fact that it was mainly Jews who were killed... Crosses were displayed everywhere, and memorials emphasized the death of Poles rather than Jews. Only on one stone was a Jewish star to be found and admitting what had happened. But Poland has over and over again tried to revise history, emphasizing that it was Poles and not Jews who died. Again, it is impossible to describe the feeling a Jew gets, especially a child of the Holocaust, as he walks around such an area. There is a somberness, but at the same time a desire to

```
cry out against such acts of wholesale murder and
destruction.³⁶
```

The visit was an extremely heavy one for Arnold, especially since very likely some of his own family members had been murdered at Treblinka. As a child of the Holocaust, Arnold could hardly imagine what it was like for his relatives to find themselves in this horrific place. So many questions surfaced all at once as Arnold's thoughts exploded in the labyrinth of his pent-up grief. He wondered what was going through their minds at the time and how traumatized they were. What and whom were they thinking about? How much did they suffer before they breathed their last? Such unfathomable anguish from such unprecedented cruelty caused something immense to swell up inside Arnold. He wanted to wail and holler out against this unspeakable atrocity, this utter injustice and this cold-blooded, wholesale destruction of innocent lives.

Anti-Semitism never ceased. Pogroms were still rampant in Poland even after the war, which forced Arnold's own family to flee the country in August 1946. The Arab invasion immediately following the creation of the State of Israel in 1948 stirred up and ignited a fury of anti-Semitism around the region. A vicious wave of anti-Semitism also surged through Europe after the Sinai War in 1956. Israel's quick and decisive victory in 1967 over the Arabs in the Six-Day War caused anti-Semitism to reach new heights in the area. Further bolts of hatred sprang up after the *Yom Kippur* War in 1973 that attempted to crush the Jewry. To protect their lives, most of the remaining Jews in Poland elected to emigrate at that point, leaving behind only about eight thousand of their people. By 1980, the total Jewish population in Poland dwindled down to about five or six thousand, out of which approximately four thousand lived in Warsaw. Only about five hundred of them attended a synagogue regularly, as most of the Jews had lost their faith in Judaism after the war. It was indeed a serious indictment against the Polish people and their country, which earlier in the same century had a Jewish population of over three and a half million.

Ending their visit, Arnold and Barry drove back to Warsaw. The next morning on their way south to Krakow, they decided to stop at the old

---

³⁶ Excerpt: *Ariel Ministries Newsletter*, November 1980

Warsaw Jewish Cemetery on the outskirts of the city, where Arnold's great-grandfather had been buried. To enter the cemetery, the men were required to cover their heads, usually with a *yarmulke*, as a show of respect. Arnold had hoped to locate his great-grandfather's grave, but the scene that greeted them was shocking. Neither one could have been mentally prepared for what they saw. To a Jew, a cemetery was a holy site, but the Germans had grievously desecrated the place during World War II, and the Poles had allowed the cemetery to fall into disrepair, leaving it derelict for many years.

The grounds were unkempt with overgrown grass and trees everywhere. The cemetery had also been vandalized. Many tombstones were knocked down and smashed, and broken pieces were strewn all over. The terribly dilapidated condition in which Arnold and Barry had found the old cemetery reflected the disdain and total lack of respect that the Polish people maintained toward the Jews and their traditions. It epitomized the ongoing anti-Semitic attitude, prevalent even to this day.

Before World War II, there were hundreds and hundreds of Jewish cemeteries around the country. However, the Germans destroyed most of them during the war, hauling away the tombstones to build roads. A large portion of the tombstones of the Warsaw Jewish Cemetery was still standing intact, possibly because enough paved roads already existed around the city, and the tombstones were thus not in great demand. In its prime, the Warsaw Jewish Cemetery was one of the largest in Europe. It covered eighty-two acres of land and housed between 100,000 to 250,000 graves and tombs. During the war, mass graves were dug in this cemetery, so it was impossible to accurately count the dead that were buried there. Because the Nazis had destroyed most of the documentary records of Warsaw's Jews, those remaining tombstones were the only evidence left that served as a kind of lasting archive.

With literally tens of thousands upon thousands of grave markers at the huge site, it was not feasible in the short span of time that Arnold had available to locate the gravesite of his great-grandfather. The sheer size of the cemetery alone would have required many days, if not weeks, of searching to find it. Arnold felt a deep pervading sense of sadness to see the place in such a state of disrepute. However, just being physically present there and knowing that his great-grandfather was laid to rest somewhere within the confines of this cemetery, gave him a sense of connection to his family roots in Poland.

THE REST OF THE DAY was spent in driving south to Krakow. Arnold and Barry planned to visit the extermination camps of Auschwitz and its sister camp, Birkenau, the most famous of all the death camps, responsible for killing the largest number of Jews in one location.

For Arnold, the visit to Auschwitz and Birkenau was highly emotionally charged. In contrast to Treblinka where most of the buildings were damaged in the fire, the twin camps of Auschwitz and Birkenau were far more extensive. Upon entering the grounds, one could see the famous sign in German that read, ARBEIT MACHT FREI, literally "work makes free," a sardonic deception. Numerous structures in these camps including many barracks were left standing and were open for visitors to view. The electrified, barbed-wire fences, with warning signs in German enclosing the enormous compound, were still intact. While what was left of the remaining structures was nothing more than mere empty shells, those who perished in the cataclysmic genocide, though forced into silence by their deaths, nevertheless seemed to cry out from the ashes.

Because the Nazis had destroyed many of their records, it was impossible to pinpoint the exact number of victims at the camps of Auschwitz and Birkenau. Figures of the total death toll of the Jewish prisoners ranged from over one million to four million, eventually with 1.1 million being the more commonly accepted number of Jews who were exterminated there. The figure was equivalent to about one-third of the Jewish population of Poland at that time. In the latter part of the war, the camps of Auschwitz and Birkenau became the epicenter of the Nazis' "Final Solution" of the Jews and the site of the largest mass murder of human beings in modern history. Aside from being the center of the heartless, systematic annihilation of the Jewish people, Auschwitz was also the site of the imprisonment of many hundreds of thousands of forced slave laborers from various countries that the Germans had annexed. Auschwitz operated from late May 1940 until late January 1945, when the Soviet troops liberated all the camps in the surrounding vicinity.

Both Arnold and Barry were deeply haunted by the unimaginable horror that the victims would have undergone. They walked about in anguished silence, stunned into mute incomprehension, each lost in his private thoughts. Hardly anyone else was around. The day was leaden and overcast, with dark ominous clouds hanging overhead, the gloominess somehow befitting the atmosphere of the camps. They spent quite an extensive amount of time that day at both Auschwitz and Birkenau, which were located four kilometers, or about two and a half miles, apart.

They struggled to grasp the colossal magnitude of the heinous crimes committed against the Jewry. The victims walked into the camps as healthy, living human beings and exited the buildings as swirls of black smoke through the chimneys of the large incinerators, their ashes then dumped into the nearby river. Arnold recorded his impressions.

> Again, it was obvious that there was a full-scale attempt to downplay the fact that it was Jews who died there. For the most part, it tried to give the concept that it was Poles and other Eastern European nationalities that were killed at these camps. The one Jewish pavilion was the smallest of them all with no form of advertisement whatsoever. All the other national monuments were well labeled and obvious. The Jewish one was out of the way, and we had to search for it. All the glory went to the Soviet Red Army, which finally liberated these camps! Again, I had that same feeling of somberness and a desire to cry out at the same time. It took a satanically depraved intelligence to have come up with a system like this.[37]

As Arnold and Barry walked around the grounds, it boggled their minds to realize how deeply entrenched anti-Semitism was in Poland, which was reflected in the way the government tried to mask the atrocities committed against the Jewish people. In the afternoon, a group of school children were brought to the grounds, perhaps on a field trip for their history class. They appeared to be light-hearted in this dismal place, with their soft drink bottles, chatting away, seemingly oblivious to the significance of what had taken place in these extermination camps. Their disrespectful attitude was inappropriate, out of place, juxtaposing sorely against the sufferings of those who had been helplessly murdered in cold blood. Yet their chaperones made no attempts to properly steer their behavior. It was disheartening for Arnold and Barry to note that the younger Polish generation was much more anti-Semitic than their German counterparts.

---

[37] Excerpt: *Ariel Ministries Newsletter*, November 1980

Partway through their visit around the grounds, Arnold and Barry walked in different directions to spend a little bit of time alone. Barry wandered off to the outskirts of the camp, where he found ponds near the sealed boundaries of the campsite. He stuck his whole arm into the murky waters to the level of his shoulders and could still scoop up the black ashes from the pond, ashes from the remains of those who were gassed in the chambers and then incinerated in the furnaces. It was a stark and grim reminder of the sufferings of the Jewish people.

As Arnold roamed the grounds by himself, his thoughts drifted to his family members, whom he had never met. Yet he felt a special sense of bonding and connection to them, not only because they were his relatives, but because of the collective suffering of the family members as a result of the war. A number of his relatives were also likely murdered at Auschwitz and Birkenau. Some of them had children. Shuddering at the evil, Arnold wondered how the children died and if they were spared from being subjected to the cruel and twisted medical experiments. Arnold felt disconsolate as more questions gnawed at his mind. Suddenly, a plethora of emotions pummeled him like a gigantic tsunami. He had an urge to scream out against these despicable acts of horror against the Jewry and the senseless loss of innocent lives.

As the visit to Auschwitz and Birkenau drew to an end, there was just one other thing that Arnold wanted to do before heading back to Warsaw. He wanted to look up a Jewish believer living in the town of Auschwitz, whose name he had obtained prior to visiting the death camps.

> I had been given the name of a Hebrew-Christian in the town of Auschwitz, but learned that he had died a year earlier. It is an irony of history that the last Jew of Auschwitz should turn out to be a Hebrew-Christian... The next morning we turned in the car and flew by a Polish airline back to Warsaw. The engines died three different times as the plane moved down the runway, but it finally lifted off into the air and managed to land safely in Warsaw, probably largely due to the silent prayers of Barry and myself.[38]

---

[38] Excerpts: *Ariel Ministries Newsletter*, November 1980

The visits to the death camps were emotionally draining, and Arnold and Barry were both left with very heavy hearts. Yet, they were deeply moved by the words of one inmate's inscription on a wall of one of the camps, still echoing in their minds, reflecting the deep faith of the one who clung onto the goodness of God despite the grievous plight of the Jews about to be sent to wholesale destruction:

> I believe in the sun when it is not shining.
> I believe in love even when feeling it not.
> I believe in God even when He is silent.

Arnold knew and understood from the Scriptures that God had not abandoned His Chosen People. The God of Abraham, Isaac, and Jacob, the same yesterday, today, and forever, had a plan and purpose for His own. The Messiah in the Person of God's Son, Jesus, had already come. Through His sacrificial, substitutionary death on the cross, He had paid the penalty for their sins, in order to redeem them. Sadly, *Yeshua's* own Chosen People did not receive Him. Nonetheless, having been resurrected from the dead, Jesus would come again to rule and reign on this earth during the Millennial Kingdom yet future. Every promise of blessing, including the Promised Land, which God had made to His Chosen People through the Abrahamic Covenant, would be fulfilled, when the Times of the Gentiles[39] became complete. Not a single promise would fail. Arnold longed for the Jewish people to turn to Jesus the Messiah, and receive Him into their hearts as their personal Savior and Lord. Once again, he yearned for his surviving family members to come to faith in Messiah Jesus and put their hope and trust in the One through whom they could find eternal life.

---

[39] More information on the "Times of the Gentiles" can be found in the first chapter of Dr. Arnold G. Fruchtenbaum's book, *The Footsteps of the Messiah.*

Initial Study Tours to Israel

When the visit to Poland ended, Arnold flew to Israel to prepare for his intensive five-week Israel Study Tour, set for the last week of May to the end of June 1980. All twenty-seven spaces were filled. A week prior to the group's arrival, Barry flew to Israel to join Arnold. Together, they checked that all the arrangements such as lodging, restaurant reservations, and transportation were in good order. After the tour, Barry would spend the summer in Israel to continue his research on the Holocaust.

The official program for those five-week study tours evolved from informal beginnings. As a student before the Six-Day War, Arnold noticed that the tourists usually saw very little of the authentic sites in Israel, spending much of their time at the traditional sites. At that stage, he had no plans to conduct any future tours. Some years later, when he and Mary Ann were living in Israel, Arnold had led two long five-week tours around Israel—one for Ruth Wardell's group of young people from the M.Y.F. and the other for the students from the mini-Bible institute. Interspersed, he also conducted a number of shorter trips for people who had requested them.

While leading his students, an interest was sparked in Arnold to utilize mini-vans for his tours in the future. Since each vehicle held up to nine people including the driver, he could comfortably manage three vans, allowing a maximum of twenty-seven individuals per trip. Having driven down just about every paved and dirt road in Israel, Arnold knew his way around the country, especially the biblical sites. During his work at the ABMJ upon returning to the United States, he had led a special study tour to Israel in 1974. Thereafter, when Ariel Ministries was launched, Arnold began leading a five-week Israel Study Tour once every two years during the even years. In those early days, the cost amounted to only $200 to $300 per person, as the campsites cost each individual only one dollar per night. When eating out in restaurants, the participants paid for their own meals.

The 1980 tour was by far one of the best groups Arnold had ever led around *Eretz Yisrael* up to that point. Particularly rewarding was the group's enthusiastic response, propelling him to go out of his way to ensure that they would see and experience more. Arnold's love of the Land of Israel was infectious, and his detailed background on each of the sites brought them all to life.

Prior to the tour, each participant was sent a handout with the protocols and list of things to bring, plus a list of books and reference materials to read ahead of time. Once they were in Israel, they were given the outline notes from which they had to study and do their pre-assigned reading and homework every night. The pace of the five weeks was usually very regimented, as each day was jam-packed with many places to see. The participants got up very early and returned to the place of lodging just before the evening meal. After dinner, the group attended a debriefing session during which Arnold showed them a map of the places they had seen, reviewed the biblical background of those sites, and answered any questions. He then gave a lecture about the places they would see the following day. The group was expected to take notes and study up on the sites with daily reading assignments before the visits.

The pace being so intense, Arnold allocated one free day per week for the group to rest up. The conditions were at times rather rugged, and the participants had to be fit to keep up with the itinerary. Often the lodging was in a *kibbutz*, where communal tents had already been set up over wooden frames, sleeping six people per tent. Showers were located in a separate structure, while communal cooking areas for the campers were in another facility. It was certainly not a luxury tour by any means.

During this trip, it so happened that there were a few terrorist incidents in the Hebron area, but the group was never in the vicinity when the attacks occurred. Nevertheless, it was a unique experience to be in the country simultaneously as these events unfolded. This particular tour was special in that two Ariel Ministries couples were able to join the group, including Dan and Arlene Rigney from Baltimore, Maryland, and Gregg Hagg and his wife from Bergen County, New Jersey. Barry served in a pastoral role to ensure that any personal needs or problems in the group could be addressed and met. After the trip, Dan Rigney produced a T-shirt with a humorous saying printed on it, which reflected his sentiment regarding the intensive pace of the tour: *I went to Israel with the Frucht and survived!* By then, many people had been referring to Arnold as the "Frucht," literally meaning "fruit" in Yiddish and German. Obviously, the "Frucht" was also a shortened version of his last name. Since that time, Ariel Ministries ensured the availability of that T-shirt to participants of the study tours.

After the tour, Arnold usually stayed on for about a week to make contact with his relatives living near the Tel-Aviv area. During that week, he usually also made arrangements to meet with a few Messianic Jewish groups that he was acquainted with to encourage and minister to them.

While each intensive five-week tour was characterized by its own unique moments, the subsequent one that Arnold led in the spring of 1982 was quite beyond the ordinary.

During the months of May and June, I led one of my five-week study tours of Israel. It turned out to be one of the most unusual trips I have ever led, and strange things happened. One example of these "strange things" is that one of our participants lost his wallet at the bottom of the Sea of Galilee. A couple of days later as he was swimming, he found it waiting for him in the water.

Another time, two of our vans were broken into, and several of the participants lost their cash, traveler's checks, passports, jewelry, and other legal and important documents. One day later, as we were traveling to a new base, all of the stolen property, with the exception of the cash, was found sitting on the side of the highway. Everything else had been recovered and was in good condition. The entire group broke out singing a praise song to the Lord right there on the highway...

A few days later, as I was taking the group on a tour of the northern border of the vicinity, the PLO opened artillery fire and shelled Jewish settlements in the Galilee and Lebanese villages in South Lebanon. The trouble began just as we were standing at the Lebanese border looking toward the city of Tyre... It was certainly evident to everyone there just who was firing at whom first.

I knew from past experience that the Israelis would only tolerate the shelling so long and earlier had spotted Israeli military equipment starting to move northward. As the shelling got worse, the camp director approached me to give us the option of leaving for safer ground. I refused and told the authorities that as long as I had the choice, we would stay right where we were. The group had wanted me to share my testimony, so as the rockets exploded continuously from the PLO guns, I shared my testimony about how I found my Messiah and then sent everyone to bed.

Around midnight, I was awakened by a strong knock on the door. The Israeli military authorities had come into the camp and ordered all non-Israeli citizens to leave the area. When I asked why, the answer I was given was that the military wanted us out of shelling range of the PLO. I had been in these situations before and knew that PLO shelling alone would not cause them to force us to leave the area. The real reason was that the Israeli military intended to move into Lebanon to put a stop to the PLO once and for all and would do so within 24 hours. We packed up all the vans, and at two o'clock in the morning, I had to find new accommodations. We finally found them twenty miles south in the city of Acco. As we drove towards the south, we could see a lot of heavy military equipment making way towards Lebanon.

The next morning, the news confirmed my suspicions: Israel had invaded Lebanon to destroy the PLO's ability to harass the Jewish settlements of the Galilee and Lebanese settlements under Saad Hadad. The travel schedule for the day was to take us into the border areas where the artillery duels were going on with the PLO and would put us back into PLO range. I decided to stay with the schedule, and we spent quite a bit of that day in border territory. We again could hear shelling by the PLO guns. Though the main roads were blockaded, I knew the country well enough to find my way around the blockades, so the group saw everything I intended to show them that day, though in a roundabout route. But throughout the day, we could see miles of military equipment moving towards Lebanon and it was obvious that this was not going to be a one-day military mission as in the past, but almost a full-scale war.

Once I completed the tour as scheduled for the northern areas, we moved south and traveled in other parts of the country far away from the war zone. I stayed on in Israel after the group left to visit with my relatives and Israeli believers that I know. A number of my relatives and a number of Israeli believers had been called into the

army and were fighting in Lebanon. You can praise the Lord
that, as of this writing, none of the Israeli believers
called into battle have suffered any casualties.

It was sickening to see how the Western news media,
especially the American news media, reported the war. It
was very one-sided and anti-Israel. They failed to report
how the Lebanese citizens themselves welcomed the Israelis
as liberators from the PLO. While the news media reported
on civilian casualties, they failed to report that much of
the civilian casualties were caused because the PLO was
deliberately using civilians as shields. They also highly
inflated the actual casualty figures as well as the
refugee figures. One news report I heard stated that there
were 600,000 Lebanese refugees in South Lebanon. That is
more than the entire population of South Lebanon. They
never even bothered to report how Israeli construction
groups came in immediately after an area was cleared of
danger to repair much of the war damage in cities such as
Tyre and Sidon. [40]

Two years later in the spring of 1984, Arnold conducted two types of tours to
Israel. The first was a three-week tour in conjunction with another Jewish
ministry, for which Arnold served as the teacher. Colloquially called a
"Schlepper's Tour," it was an easier type of trip with a larger number of spots
available. Participants traveled in an air-conditioned tourist bus and stayed in
kibbutz guesthouses, similar to American motels. The other tour was the
normal intensive five-week Israel Study Tour during even years, which
Arnold led with the help of Barry, who was there part of the time.

---

[40] Excerpts: *Ariel Ministries Newsletter*, November 1982

Discipleship of a *Minyan*

In early 1982, as a result of the Ariel board's vote for Arnold to cut back on his travel schedule, he had a bit more time in San Antonio to devote to regular discipleship activities. Hence, interspersed between his speaking engagements around the country, he started a local men's discipleship program under the Ariel Ministries umbrella. It was initially designed to be a one-year course, meeting three times per week on Thursday nights and on Friday and Saturday early mornings. Classes were held in the conference room on the new Ariel premises. A number of the men attending the course were from Arnold's adult Sunday school class at Wayside Chapel. He simply announced the availability of the program, which was limited to ten people. Those interested were to approach him about the details and then, together with him, make a decision if they would like to be part of the group.

In the Jewish culture, the minimum number of men required to form a *minyan* to pray or to hold worship services in the synagogue was ten. Here, Arnold was following the same concept, except that he would personally teach and train the handpicked men, so that they, too, could one day disciple others in a similar fashion.

Some may have had preconceived notions of what the program would be like. Once the course got underway, they soon realized that the content was way over their heads and super intensive. Arnold was a very demanding professor and did not tolerate any slack or nonsense. Teaching at a seminary level, he expected the students to take copious notes and to do serious studying on their own in preparation for each class. He definitely did not like to have his time wasted. Lecturing at a fast pace, he covered an enormous amount of material per class. Even his answers to questions were clipped, very short, and succinct.

It soon became obvious that Arnold wanted only serious students in his class. Those who were not prepared to put in the time and hard work simply did not last the distance. For starters, two out of the three classes per week began very early at five o'clock in the morning! That immediately weeded out those men who were not totally committed to serious learning. Although by nature Arnold himself was not a morning person, he made a concerted effort for those early sessions and was always prepared and alert in his classes.

Serious, strict and disciplined, he expected everyone to be on time. He himself was extremely punctual, starting right on the dot and ending exactly within the allocated timeframe. If a student arrived late to class a total of three times, he was automatically disqualified from continuing the program. Unfortunately, one of the men fell asleep during an early morning session and was asked to leave the class and subsequently lost the privilege of continuing with the group.

The men knew the value of what they were learning. After having heard more than enough of the simplistic sermons preached from some of the pulpits up to that point, they found that Arnold's teachings with the Jewish frame of reference made so much more sense. Their knowledge of the Bible was further enriched through the various word studies that Arnold taught and also required them to undertake. Choosing one word and following it through the Old Testament and the New Testament every time the word was mentioned, they learned its symbolic, metaphorical, or literal meanings within its Scriptural context. To fulfill the assignment, the men had to dig deeply into the Bible.

One of the men was assigned the word "star." After spending a lot of time writing up his word study, he thought that he had done a brilliant job. However, Arnold took his study and in essence, ripped it apart in front of the entire class. Highlighting the word from when it was first mentioned in the Bible, then word-by-word, line-by-line in the context of the passage, Arnold demonstrated exegetically exactly what the word said, not what the pastor thought it said or what it might have meant in the modern Gentile context, but precisely what was written in the Holy Scriptures.

Arnold also showed them that a word, such as "star," could start out meaning one thing in the Old Testament, but end up meaning something very different in the New Testament. It appeared that the student's write-up on the word was nowhere close to what it truly meant. As difficult as it was to sit through the class while his work was being shredded into pieces, he knew that he was under the tutelage of a great teacher. He was astounded anew at the depth of Arnold's knowledge of the Hebrew and Greek texts, his profound grasp of theology, and the wealth of his understanding of what the Word of God truly said. Arnold's style followed the Jewish circular way of thinking, always very logical in his teaching, going from the known to the unknown, reflecting the great style of the Apostle Paul.

Although the discipleship program was initially designed to be a one-year course, it ended up taking two full years to complete. While Arnold was supposed to have cut back on his travels, the many requests for him to teach at various churches across the country necessitated him to be away from home more frequently again. Because he could not meet every week, the classes took place as and when he was in town on any of the Thursday evenings, or Friday and Saturday mornings. Hence by necessity, the duration of the program was extended to two years. In the end, five out of the ten men completed the course. One of them was Charmaine's husband, Mark, who went on to teach the Sunday school classes at a local church. Others took various active roles in their local fellowships, while still others formed a new congregation where they all preached and taught on a rotating basis. Some twenty years later, two of the men became members of the Ariel board of directors. It was Arnold's aim to disciple the men and get them well grounded in the Word of God, so that they in turn could teach others, thus perpetuating the making of disciples among both the Jewish and Gentile believers.

One incident stood out in Mark's mind, very clearly illustrating that Arnold considered himself to be Mark's Bible teacher and mentor. A good while after the course had ended, there was a gathering at which Dr. Charles C. Ryrie, professor of Systematic Theology at Dallas Theological Seminary, was in attendance. Dr. Ryrie happened to be Arnold's favorite professor at seminary. Mary Ann went up to make introductions. When it came to Mark's turn, Mary Ann referred to him as Arnold's "student." Mark found it interesting, because he and his wife had socialized with the Fruchtenbaums as friends on a regular basis, while they were living in San Antonio. Even so, it appeared that Arnold viewed Mark first and foremost as his disciple, the way Burl Haynie had looked upon Arnold.

The discipleship program had made a profound impact upon the five men who persevered to the end. All five happened to be Gentile believers and would never again view Scripture the same way they did prior to the course. They learned how to rightly divide the Word of God and saw the plain meaning of the passages within their proper context. They derived from the text what the Scriptures really said rather than imputing interpretations that veered off the mark. More than ever before, they became increasingly cognizant of the fact that "a text taken out of context is a pretext." Most importantly, they learned and experienced firsthand what discipleship was all about and went on to emulate and replicate the process with their own disciples. Arnold's approach was similar to the way *Yeshua* trained His disciples. The men considered themselves very privileged and blessed to have been under the direct tutelage of Arnold. Many years later, they realized just how fortunate and blessed they were, as Arnold never again gathered around himself a group of ten men to whom he personally taught the Bible in such an intensive and concentrated fashion for a focused period of time.

While Arnold was a very strict and demanding teacher, he still exhibited a sense of humor and often caught people off guard with his witty remarks at the most unexpected but opportune moments. Mark recalled a funny incident that illustrated the dry sense of humor that characterized Arnold so well. One early morning just as he drove up to the Ariel Home Office at about a quarter to five, he found Arnold sitting in his car with his door slightly ajar, listening to the radio. When Mark approached him and asked him what he was doing, Arnold replied with a sense of satisfaction that he was listening to a Bible teacher whom he could listen to all day long. That teacher on the radio turned out to be the one and only Arnold himself!

Apart from being a tough but very gifted Bible teacher, Arnold was relaxed and fun to be with at parties and other social settings. In all the years that Charmaine worked with him, she never once recalled seeing him get angry or lose his temper over anything. He was very even-keeled and disciplined, almost with a sense of detachment, pausing to think and reflect before responding to any given situation. He hardly ever reacted to any outward circumstances. The only time that Charmaine could remember seeing Arnold visibly upset over something was at the start of a long weekend in New Orleans, Louisiana.

Arnold and Mary Ann plus another couple along with Charmaine and Mark were all going to spend a getaway, social weekend in the city. Arnold had made all the hotel reservations for the group. He and Mary Ann plus the other couple had gone ahead earlier in the day. Charmaine and Mark would follow, flying in later that evening after work. The other couple fetched them at the airport when they landed. Upon entering the lobby of the hotel, Charmaine was surprised to see Arnold at the front desk, looking very unhappy. Even though he had made the bookings himself, the hotel seemed to have messed up the arrangements and did not have any room reservations in their system for Charmaine and Mark. Arnold was very displeased and not impressed at all with the hotel as he engaged in an intense discussion with the staff.

For the very first time, Charmaine discovered that when Arnold was upset, his voice tended to sound slightly more assertive and he talked at breakneck speed. His accent became even more pronounced, rendering it practically impossible for the hotel personnel to understand him. In the end, suitable accommodations were arranged, and they all had a very enjoyable weekend together. As usual, Arnold was an excellent host, showing the group around many sites and introducing them to the wonderful food of New Orleans.

Sorrows and Losses

In May 1983, Mary Ann had a rare opportunity to visit with her mother and her siblings. After her youngest sister, Kathy, left home for college about a decade and a half earlier, her mother had moved out of the duplex in Williamstown, New Jersey, to live permanently in their house in the Adirondacks. Olive's sister needed the duplex back at the time, so moving to upstate New York to their summer home was pretty much her only option. It was a freehold house with no mortgage owing and very low property tax, so it was financially manageable for her. At least in recent years, Olive's negative attitude toward Arnold had finally changed for the better, after his first book got published. From then onward, she felt that she could refer to her son-in-law as a writer, which in her mind was a legitimate profession, and she stopped objecting to Mary Ann about Arnold. On the same trip, Mary Ann also attended her fifteenth-year class reunion at Gordon College in Massachusetts, which she thoroughly enjoyed.

Shortly after her return in early June, Arnold and Mary Ann were confronted with a serious personal situation. Grandma Suppes, who had been living with them for over four years, was stricken with cancer of the pancreas and hospitalized for surgery. Because the bleeding could not be stopped after the operation in the morning, she underwent a second surgical procedure that same evening. She was then kept in the intensive care unit for over a week. For a while there, it looked as though she would not survive, especially since she had also caught pneumonia. However, much to Arnold's relief, Grandma Suppes did rally and was subsequently moved to the intermediate care unit for another week, and finally to a regular room. The doctors hoped that she could be released within two weeks. As for her prognosis, they gave her anywhere between two months to two years to live.

Mary Ann had notified her mother-in-law immediately about the impending surgery and asked the hospital to search among its staff for German or Russian speakers. Fortunately, Grandma's doctor was fluent in German. Adele quickly made arrangements to cover her absence from work and care for the family at home, and flew from Los Angeles to San Antonio to be with her mother. While she and Mary Ann spent several weeks together at Grandma's hospital bedside and at home, the two became very close. Adele also got to see the various forms of support that came from friends of her son and daughter-in-law.

Arnold had always felt a deep affection for his grandmother. Despite not having a common language to communicate to each other, a strong bond existed between them. Although he was not able to personally share the Gospel message with her, he had once given her a Russian and a German Bible plus several tracts in those languages. Still, he was unsure whether or not she had clearly understood the Good News. Her eternal destiny was the foremost concern on Arnold's mind, a burden that anguished his soul. His heart yearned for her to come to salvation in Messiah Jesus, to believe in Him, and to know the Lord's saving grace. In an issue of the *Ariel Ministries Newsletter*, he asked the dedicated prayer supporters around the country to pray that his grandmother would recover enough to be able to think clearly and that God would send a believer who could speak either Russian or German, in order to clearly present the Gospel message to her.

While Grandma Suppes was in the regular room recovering from her surgery, she unexpectedly began to suffer from delirium and slipped into a coma. By the grace of God, Arnold was able to find a German-speaking minister who happened to be in San Antonio on an exchange program at that time. After meeting with him to make sure that he was a true Bible believer, he felt reassured enough to bring this minister to his grandmother's bedside. In answer to the prayers offered on her behalf, she emerged out of her coma and delirium for a very short interlude. Holding her hand, the minister clearly explained the Gospel to her in German. At this point, Grandma Suppes appeared to understand what was being said to her, but unfortunately, was no longer able to respond verbally and barely in any other way. Nevertheless at certain moments, especially when the minister talked about Jesus, he could feel Grandma Suppes squeezing his hand ever so slightly. That was on the last day she was lucid. Within hours, she slipped back into her coma and died a few days later, less than two months before her eighty-second birthday.

For the first hour or so after her death, Arnold went into deep shock. It did not seem real that his beloved grandmother had just passed away. She had every fighting chance to make it. After the second surgery, the doctors had given her between two months to two years to live. So why did she die so soon, so unexpectedly while still in recovery? Something very strange had transpired in her mind, almost like a self-fulfilling prophecy. Grandma Suppes firmly believed—as did most elderly Russians—that there was only one reason for a person to enter a hospital, and that was to die. She was in her early eighties and had been in great physical shape, strong and robust, and could still engage in hard, physically taxing labor that would put most young men to shame. Yet, it was clear that the cancer had widely metastasized in her body. Grandma Suppes had expressed to Mary Ann in previous years that she did not want to die alone. God answered beautifully by bringing her daughter, Adele, her grandson, Arnold, and his wife, Mary Ann, all to her side—each expressing their farewell and remaining present until she breathed her last.

Arnold had never personally experienced the death of a family member before. When he eventually came out of his shock while alone with Mary Ann in their bedroom, all of his inner anguish and pent-up sorrow suddenly erupted, coming to the fore. For the first time in his adult life, Arnold wept openly. It was as though a dam had been broken inside him. His tears just welled up from within, gushing forth uncontrollably, his intense throbbing pain assaulting his inner being. By nature, Arnold was a very private person, not prone to showing emotions, and in his own words normally did "not emote." Yet, he experienced such an overwhelming sense of loss and inner desolation that no words could be found to express his profound sorrow except through his tears. He had a congenial relationship with his grandmother and shared an understanding with her that did not require words. When she fell ill, he even postponed his speaking engagements, so that he could be there for her.

More than anything else, Arnold had longed for her soul to be saved. Now that Grandma Suppes was gone, there would not be a second chance for her to make a decision regarding her salvation in *Yeshua Ha'Mashiach*. Although the German minister had clearly presented the Gospel to her, Arnold could not tell if she had personally taken the opportunity to receive Jesus as her

Messiah. He could not truthfully say from his heart that he knew for certain that she had accepted *Yeshua* as her personal Savior on that day. He would have to wait until the other side of eternity to find out. The thought of the possibility of his grandmother not being in the presence of the Lord was inconceivable and simply too painful for Arnold to bear. Grief overpowered him like a tidal wave, and a burning pain pierced his heart.

A COUPLE OF MONTHS AFTER HIS GRANDMOTHER PASSED AWAY, Arnold was scheduled to present a paper in Newmarket, England. It was toward the end of August 1983, at the second international gathering of the Lausanne Conference on Jewish Evangelism. Arnold was thankful to the Lord that Mary Ann felt well enough to travel with him on that overseas trip. Still grieving deeply, it was good for them to be away together in a totally different environment for a change of scene. After the conference ended, Arnold taught at the London Messianic Fellowship for three days in early September. A Jewish believer familiar with his teachings had set up this meeting at his congregation. It was the first time for Arnold to teach the Scriptures in England. His Jewish frame of reference was so well received that he was invited back for another meeting in the fall of 1985, which he fulfilled. In August 1986, he returned to the U.K. again to present another paper at the third international Lausanne Conference on Jewish Evangelism, held this time in Easneye, England.

Upon their return to the United States in September 1983, the state of Mary Ann's health had become a cause for concern and weighed on Arnold's mind. For a long time, Mary Ann had been battling with an enzyme deficiency, known as lactose intolerance, prohibiting her from partaking of any foods containing dairy. Since there were no cures, it was something that she had to learn to live with for the rest of her life. In addition, Mary Ann also developed an allergy to chicken, which further limited what she could eat. It definitely altered the way she planned and cooked her meals, having to take into consideration the restrictions her conditions imposed upon her. To complicate matters, she was also dealing with endometriosis, causing her a lot of pain in the pelvic area.

One of the reasons Mary Ann had resigned from her full-time job during the second year of Ariel Ministries was so that she could travel more with Arnold on his speaking engagements across the country. Her role was to minister to the various churches through singing Jewish worship songs a cappella in Hebrew. However, in the last year or so, she had not been able to travel as frequently with Arnold as she would have liked, due to her sub-optimal health. Usually, members of the host church would invite them to stay in their homes. Quite often, the meals that were served contained ingredients that Mary Ann was no longer able to eat, inevitably causing much awkwardness for the hosts. It was embarrassing for Arnold and Mary Ann to have to send detailed instructions on dietary restrictions beforehand. As guests, they felt that it was too much of an imposition upon the families who desired to be their hosts. It was simply easier to stay in motels and eat their meals at restaurants. That way, Mary Ann could at least maintain control over what she consumed.

Because of the pain caused by the endometriosis, her time away with Arnold was reduced to about half of what it used to be in the past. It became more practical for her to stay at home to rest and relax, while serving in her ministry of personal counseling with people living in their home or with many others from the Messianic and Christian communities. She could also enjoy gardening and looking after their cats.

Just as Mary Ann was appearing to adapt to her conditions and doing well, other health complications cropped up, requiring extensive surgery in the months before the end of 1983. In one operation lasting over three hours, she had three procedures done at the same time—a hysterectomy, an appendectomy, and a restructuring of her intestines. Two surgeons worked on her in the operating room. Ironically, one was a Jew and the other an Arab. Her recovery was much slower than what the doctors would have liked.

Aside from the physical toll, Mary Ann also suffered from the psychological and emotional effects of the hysterectomy. It was a very sad day for her, knowing that after the procedure, there would be no possibility of her ever bearing children. Both Arnold and Mary Ann very much wanted to become parents. For years and years, they had tried, but their efforts had come to naught, as Mary Ann simply could not conceive and get pregnant. Still, they had remained hopeful until the hysterectomy. The operation seemed so final, representing a death to their dream. It was a loss that cut deeply into their souls and a test of their faith and trust in the Lord's sovereignty over their lives. Even though they were denied their heartfelt prayers, Arnold and Mary Ann believed that God still loved and cared for them. They looked to Him for solace and comfort as they mourned their plight. In their time of grief, they knew that they could entrust the Lord with their suffering in their childlessness and took comfort in God's Word: *Weeping may tarry for the night, But joy comes in the morning.* (Psalm 30:5b) In the ultimate analysis, they were certain that God foreknew what was best for them and clung to His compassion and faithfulness. It was in the midst of these difficult circumstances that Arnold turned forty years old.

There was always the option of adoption, to which they gave serious consideration. By the time Mary Ann underwent her hysterectomy, it was clear that Arnold's heavy travel schedule was not going to abate any time soon, so it did not make any sense for them to go that route. Years later, the wisdom and foreknowledge of the Lord for their particular situation became even clearer as Mary Ann's health began to falter. It would have been a huge burden for her to have to take care of children in her state of weakening health.

For many months after her three-pronged surgery, Mary Ann experienced consistent pain, sometimes so severe that it got beyond the point of endurance. She returned to the hospital in the spring of 1984 for extensive testing. The doctors finally determined that the femoral nerve was probably entwined in scar tissue causing the pain. One suggested wearing a TENS unit—transcutaneous electrical nerve stimulator—to block those nerve signals. Though awkward to wear, the TENS unit significantly diminished the pain over the following months. Still, Mary Ann was obliged to cancel her trip with Arnold to Israel in the spring of 1984.

A few days before Arnold returned from Israel, Mary Ann started having severe abdominal pains and was rushed to the hospital. The doctors found an intestinal blockage likely caused by the adhesions from her hysterectomy. They decided to observe her for three days to see if the obstruction would clear up—it did not. Hence, another surgery had to be performed in early July 1984. Arnold arrived back from Israel after midnight in the wee hours of the morning on the very day of her scheduled procedure. He praised and thanked God that he was able to get back in time to be there for his wife. The surgery itself went very well, and Mary Ann recovered fairly quickly, resulting in no further need of the TENS unit. She even made it to Camp Shoshanah for about a week and a half in late summer and really enjoyed herself.

LOOKING BACK

~ *Life in Pictures* ~

to walk worthily of the Lord unto all pleasing,
bearing fruit in every good work,
and increasing in the knowledge of God;

(Colossians 1:10)

First Steps

Top: Arnold (Arik), less than six months old, in Tobol'sk, Siberia.
Bottom Left: Arnold, under two years of age, in Ukraine.
Bottom Right: Arnold and his mother Adele in Lodz, Poland.

First Vehicles

TOP LEFT: Arnold riding in a wagon in Hofgeismar.
TOP RIGHT: Arnold riding a tricycle with a playmate in Hofgeismar.
BOTTOM: Arnold's first car, a go-cart, at the D.P. Camp in Gabersee.

The Family Grows

Top Left: Arnold with his mother Adele and baby brother Edward (Eddie) at the D.P. Camp in Hofgeismar in 1948.
Top Right: Arnold in the arms of his father (1946).
Bottom from left to right: Arnold, Margaret, Edward, and mother Adele.

Finding Messiah

TOP: Hanna and her father, Theo Burgstahler, in Ulm.
MIDDLE: Arnold's spiritual mom, Ruth Wardell.
BOTTOM: Dr. Daniel Fuchs baptizing Arnold, August 1962.

Early Life as a Believer

TOP: Arnold listening to Ruth Wardell teaching the Scriptures (ca. 1957).
MIDDLE: Trout Pond at the site where the Memory Camp was held.
BOTTOM: Arnold practicing his violin (ca. 1957).

TOP: M.Y.F. group shot with Ruth Wardell. Bob Futoran is standing behind Arnold. This picture was taken in 1965 at the Cattells in Wildwood, NJ, near Cape May.

MIDDLE: ABMJ booth, World's Fair in New York City (1964-65).
BOTTOM: Bob Futoran and Arnold fixed a meal for Mom (Eva) Cattell in Brooklyn at the ABMJ building where they lodged (1965).

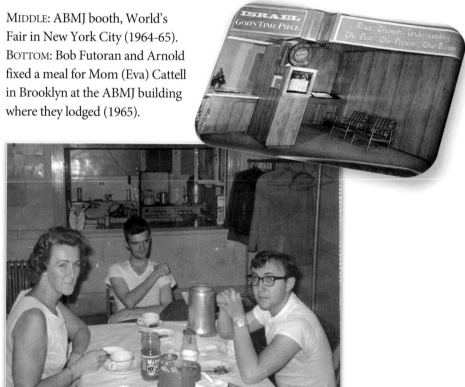

Influential Men

Top: Theo Burgstahler (left; ca. 1960). Dr. Charles Ryrie (right; ca. 1970). Bottom: Burl Haynie (1959) flanked by Eleanor Bullock (left) and Ruth Wardell (right).

Arnold and Mary Ann

Camp Heathcote becomes Camp Shoshanah

TOP LEFT: Original kitchen/dining/teaching hall of Camp Heathcote (1974), which became Camp Shoshanah in1978.
TOP RIGHT: Israeli dancing at the lecture end of the hall.
MIDDLE LEFT: Arnold breaking bread during *Shabbat* (early 1980s).
MIDDLE RIGHT: Dan and Arlene Rigney, former co-directors of Camp Shoshanah's summer program, enjoying their *Shabbat* dinner.
BOTTOM LEFT: Ruth Wardell teaching the youth at Camp Shoshanah (1982).
BOTTOM RIGHT: Mary Ann and Arnold.

Attire

Top Left: Arnold sporting a Texan hat at the Pre-Trib Conference in 2013.
Top Right: Arnold in a suit and tie (1974).
Bottom Left: Ruth Wardell and Arnold both dressed for *Shabbat* (2005).
Bottom Right: Arnold in his library wearing
a leisure suit (2005).

Israel Study Tours

Top Left: T-Shirt given to all participants of Arnold's Israel tours.
Top Right: The T-shirts are also worn by those who are yet to go to Israel "with the Frucht." From left to right: Matthew, Rachel, and Rida Lipsey.
Bottom: Arnold started to lead tours to Israel in the 1970s. This picture was taken on one of those early tours on top of Mount Sinai.

TOP: Arnold visiting the "survivors" of the Fruchtenbaum family in Israel (1974).

MIDDLE LEFT: Arnold with the leader of Ariel Canada, Jacques Isaac Gabizon, on a more recent Israel trip in 2013.

MIDDLE RIGHT: Arnold's tour guide mode.

BOTTOM: Arnold in front of the Madaba Mosaic Map (2013).

Connections

Top: Arnold and two of his teaching chums—Mottel Baleston (left) and Dr. Barry Leventhal (middle)—at Camp Shoshanah (2014).
Bottom: Mary Ann and Ruth in 1975 and 2005.

Conference Speaker

TOP: Arnold with other speakers at the AMC Messianic Conference in Los Angeles, 2006. From left to right: Arnold, Dr. Alan Poyner-Levinson, Peter Koziar, Steve Shermett, Mottel Baleston, Sam Nadler, Douglas Friedman.
BOTTOM: At the Pre-Trib Conference in Dallas, 2014. From left to right: Dr. Randall Price, Beverlee Price, Dr. Charles Ryrie, Arnold.

To the Uttermost Ends of the Earth

TOP LEFT: Arnold in front of one of the many guard towers that used to mark the border between East and West Germany (2012).

TOP RIGHT: Arnold with Rita and Ivan Nagy, the leaders of Ariel Hungary, in Hofgeismar, Germany (2012).

BOTTOM LEFT: Arnold teaching in Japan (2012).

BOTTOM RIGHT: Two Kiwis in New Zealand posing as Mottel and Arnold (2001).

Top Left: Arnold teaching in Hawaii (2013) . . .
Top Right: . . . and in Poland (2014).
Bottom: Camp Shoshanah experiences stiff competition on the other side of the globe when people in New Zealand gather at a camp to study under Arnold and his co-teacher, Mottel Baleston (2001).

TOP: Arnold walking towards the remains of his favorite hotel in Christchurch, NZ, which was destroyed by an earthquake in 2011.
MIDDLE RIGHT: Arnold with Ivan Nagy visiting an Orthodox synagogue in Budapest, Hungary (2012).

MIDDLE LEFT: Arnold enjoying dinner at the Herzliya Pituach beach in Israel.
BOTTOM: The Manna International staff who, for years, has organized Arnold's tours to Australia. Left to right: Phyllis Stock, Jocelyn Betfort, Heather Tupper.

Where It All Began

Camp Shoshanah is where it all began: Arnold's love for Mary Ann (top left); Mottel Baleston's, Michael Gabizon's, and Arnold's teaching careers (top right, in order from left to right) with Camp teacher, Bob Morris (to the far right); Arnold's lordship over the bell (middle left); his baptizing ministry (middle right and bottom).

Top: Master of the Aaronic blessing (2013).
Bottom: Bob Dylan fans par excellence—Arnold and Mary Ann at Camp Shoshanah in 2013.

Ariel Ministries in Texas

Though his library of many thousands of books is an integral part of his home in San Antonio, Texas, Arnold's main office is at the headquarters of Ariel Ministries. Here, he also has a chance to hold seminars (middle left). Below and on the next page are pictures showing a few of the treasures one finds there.

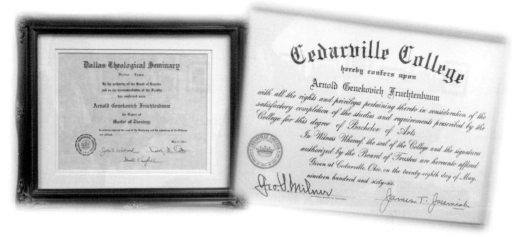

Dallas Theological Seminary

Cedarville College

TOP: Two of Arnold's degrees of higher learning.

BOTTOM: A book in the making. These stacks of papers are only a fraction of what went into the books about the life of Messiah from a Jewish perspective.

PREVIOUS PAGE: A few artifacts and paintings found in Arnold's office. The portrait at the top right corner depicts Arnold's paternal grandfather, Yitzchak Meir Fruchtenbaum.

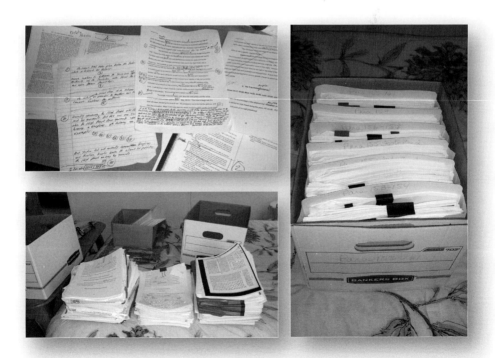

Ariel's School of Messianic Jewish Studies

Top: Gary Demers and Arnold breaking ground for Ariel's School of Messianic Jewish Studies (2005). Bottom: Arnold teaching one of the many courses offered at the school. Though this picture was taken during Camp Shoshanah's summer program in 2011, the classroom setting is the same for the yearlong curriculum.

PART V

~ *Expansion* ~

So then neither is he that plants anything,
neither he that waters;
but God that gives the increase.

(I Corinthians 3:7)

I t was understood that San Antonio, with a very small Jewish population, was to serve only as a temporary location for the Ariel Home Office. The original intention had been to establish the headquarters in an area more densely populated with Jews. From the end of 1982 until the Home Office was eventually relocated to southern California near the Los Angeles area in December 1984, the Ariel board of directors changed the final location and moving date several times due to a number of variables.

During this interval, Arnold faced extra pressure with regard to the ministry's tight financial situation. The recent, unfavorable stock market conditions had adversely affected many supporters who were no longer able to honor their commitments. The move out to California would incur large one-time expenses and further destabilize the ministry's precarious circumstances. Yet in faith, the ministry proceeded with its plans.

So much had yet to be done—the sale of Arnold's house in San Antonio, finding a new one in southern California, searching for suitable office space for Ariel Ministries, and hiring new staff for the Home Office. Arnold extended a generous severance package to Charmaine and also wrote her an excellent letter of recommendation for her potential future employment. While the decision of Charmaine and her husband, Mark, to remain in San Antonio, was not what Arnold had hoped for, he understood. Both he and Mary Ann had also grown very fond of the vibrancy of San Antonio with its modern skyline and charming edifices. They, too, would greatly miss their life and friends there that they had come to appreciate so much. In particular, it would not be easy for Mary Ann to be uprooted from San Antonio.

By faith, the Fruchtenbaums listed their San Antonio house on the market on the first of September 1984, trusting that it would be sold prior to the purchase of their future home. They had been to southern California twice before to look around, but had not found anything suitable for the Ariel Home Office or for themselves. So in October 1984, they returned for the third time, praying for a successful outcome. The Lord granted them a very knowledgeable real estate agent, who took them to the town of Tustin in Orange County, adjacent to Los Angeles County. They viewed a large office space in a modest business park on Parkway Loop, priced considerably lower than other places seen on previous trips.

While a five-year lease was agreed upon, Ariel Ministries did not have enough funds left in its coffers to cover the relocation expenses, much less the first and last months' rent stipulated in the lease. Regardless, the board went ahead and signed the necessary papers, trusting that "God's work done in God's time will never lack God's support," and presented their needs to the Almighty in fervent prayer. Ten days before the actual move, the Lord provided all the necessary funds through a large monetary gift! It was cause for great rejoicing to see God's answer just in the nick of time.

As for their own home, Arnold and Mary Ann had seen nothing that met their needs. Houses in southern California were a lot more expensive and comparably smaller in size than in Texas. They realized on their third trip that they simply had to decide upon a house, even if it may lack some of the features that they had desired. Ideally, Arnold wished to have one big room to accommodate all his books, but he accepted that the library might have to be split up between two separate rooms, even three.

Thankfully, the Lord intervened in a most wonderful way. He again provided a very capable real estate agent who knew how to ask just the right questions beforehand to determine their needs. By the time they got to Orange County, the agent had already looked at various houses herself and had picked out the ones that she thought might be suitable. One house in the town of Irvine, based on a "Plan Six" floor plan, seemed to fit the bill. It consisted of enough bedrooms for them to accommodate other people, plus a very large room with plenty of wall space to house Arnold's entire library and even extra space for future expansion!

In that one week alone, two out of the three "Plan Six" houses had already been sold. It was obvious that "Plan Six" homes were in great demand in Orange County, as there had not been even one for sale during their first two trips. On top of the desired features, the house in Irvine was located only six miles from the new office in Tustin, so they decided upon it right away. Unfortunately, they immediately ran into a snag. In Texas, when one put down earnest money as a deposit for a house, the purchase would be conditional upon the sale of the buyer's old home. Such a conditional clause was not acceptable in southern California, so they could not proceed with the final price negotiations until their house in San Antonio got sold, which would provide the down payment for the new house. Otherwise, no broker would be willing to arrange a mortgage. From a human standpoint, the new house would be long gone by the time all was said and done. Hence, if they were to purchase this house, God would certainly have to divinely intervene to make it happen, and He did!

Without their prior knowledge and absolutely by complete surprise, Arnold and Mary Ann received a generous offer of help from a totally unexpected source. The Lord moved the heart of a supporter of Ariel Ministries to personally lend them the necessary amount for the down payment, totally interest-free! The personal loan was extended with the understanding that Arnold and Mary Ann could take their time and wait until their house in Texas got sold first before paying it back.

Over the next two months while waiting for the closing date, more snags occurred along the way, but the Lord overruled in every instance. With the final approval of the Savings and Loan Company, the house purchase was closed on the fourth of December 1984. What a wonderful testimony of the Lord's marvelous provision and care, another occasion for Arnold and Mary Ann to praise and rejoice in the Lord!

Meanwhile, God also provided an answer to another much-needed prayer request. In addition to Arnold's new administrative assistant, Sylvia Mendelson, a Jewish believer, the Lord also brought other staff to join the Ariel Home Office in Tustin. The full-time position of receptionist-secretary was filled as well as the part-time position of processing tapes and typing manuscripts. A volunteer couple assisted in their spare time, with the husband serving as the office equipment handyman while the wife handled the bookkeeping.

Since the launch of Ariel Ministries seven years earlier, it was the first time that Arnold was physically present at the Home Office for so many weeks in a row. His last scheduled engagement in 1984 was on the 20th of November, and his calendar thereafter was free for seven weeks from any ministry commitments. A lot of things needed to be handled at the new office. In addition, he wanted to help Mary Ann unpack and settle into their house, as well as look for a new home church, which they found at a community church in Newport Beach. Upon moving in, they hired a carpenter to custom-build bookshelves all around the large room that was to serve as Arnold's library. Life was very hectic for a while.

Once they got a bit more organized, Arnold and Mary Ann planned on taking a personal vacation at the start of the following year for some much-needed rest and relaxation. They decided to combine their trip with Charmaine and Mark in Hawaii, since Charmaine had received an all-expenses paid trip for two as part of her severance package from Ariel Ministries.

Since the four of them had socialized together in the past for evening get-togethers or long weekends away, it was easy for them to find complementary interests and mesh their rhythms on this trip. Arnold was very relaxed and fun to travel with on those personal trips and refreshingly resourceful in discovering new places to see and things to do.

Upon returning home to the West Coast, Arnold strove in earnest to complete his doctoral dissertation toward his Ph.D. from New York University. He had been researching his subject for over eight years starting the last year of his resident studies and had been using his little Dictaphone while on his travels to record his way through a portion of his first draft. Much of the rest of the draft remained handwritten, as he could only work on it sporadically here and there, never having any blocks of time at home to work on it. Despite the geographical distance from California, Charmaine, who continued to live in San Antonio, volunteered to type up Arnold's dissertation on her IBM electric typewriter.

RESIDING IN IRVINE, CALIFORNIA, meant that Arnold and Mary Ann were located not too far from the city of Los Angeles in the adjacent county. It had been twenty-two and a half years since Arnold had been expelled from his parents' home. Only recently, after his six younger siblings had all grown up and left home, did his father's silence policy and prohibition against Arnold making contact come to a permanent end. By the time Arnold and Mary Ann began living in California, Arnold was free to visit his parents' home at will. At least on the surface, the father-son relationship appeared to have been somewhat restored, although there was always an undercurrent of hostility and animosity toward Arnold's belief in Jesus. For the most part, Henry talked only with Mary Ann during their visits. As it had been in the past, his moods were very unpredictable, so it was difficult to gauge how he would react in any given situation.

Adele often ended up on the receiving end of the brunt of her husband's erratic moods. After a visit, if Henry felt unhappy about something that had been said, his temper would explode on her when they were alone, unleashing a tirade of pent-up emotions. However, he seemed to genuinely like Mary Ann and was always nice to her, which was a great blessing from the Lord.

Soon after Arnold and Mary Ann had moved into their home, they arranged to host an open-house get-together for Arnold's family to come and visit for a day. His parents and all his siblings were invited. Some of his brothers and sisters were already married by then, and they brought along their spouses. The interaction between Arnold and his family was rather stilted, as the siblings all skirted around the main issue—that of Arnold's faith in Jesus—and engaged only in superficial chitchat. His two younger brothers were the most antagonistic toward his beliefs. They had always regarded him as the strange, older brother, the odd one out, and took absolutely no interest in what he did in the ministry.

On this particular occasion, after Arnold's parents left the get-together and got back home, Henry exploded with his furious ranting and raving yet again, no holds barred. This time, Adele had endured enough and was not going to just take it from him. For the very first time, she talked back to her husband and told him to stop. She pointed out to him that Arnold was the only one among the siblings who would be willing to take his father into his own home in Henry's old age, when and if she could no longer take care of him. With that fact out in the open, he backed off a bit and temporarily curtailed his bad temper and his tirades against his son.

In contrast to the tentative experiences with his family, Arnold's warm and close relationship with Ruth Wardell was the exact opposite. One of the great joys for Mary Ann in moving to southern California was her proximity to Ruth, who had been transferred to the ABMJ office in Los Angeles some twelve years earlier toward the end of 1972. From time to time, Mary Ann was able to meet with her for lunch and catch up on each other's news. Having had health issues in recent years and especially after her hysterectomy, Mary Ann was susceptible to occasional bouts of depression. With none of her own family members living near her, she was grateful to have Mom Wardell—a fellow believer—to turn to for comfort and support.

SINCE MANY PEOPLE COULD NOT TAKE SO MUCH TIME OFF to go on his intensive five-week Israel Study Tours in even-numbered years, Arnold, with the support of his friend, Barry Leventhal, led two short two-week trips in the spring of 1985, each with twenty-four spaces available. Earlier in the year, Barry had stepped into the role of chairman of Ariel's board of directors after having served as a board member for a number of years. The itinerary of the second tour promised to be especially interesting with the additional side visits to the cities of Rome and Athens.

Prior to the start of these short study tours, Arnold planned on visiting Jordan with a few other people on a private trip. Due to her health issues,

Mary Ann had missed out on several previous trips to Israel with Arnold, but this time, she felt well enough to go along. Joining them would be Barry, Gregg Hagg—the missionary worker from Bergen County, New Jersey—and one other couple, friends of Ariel Ministries. Together, the six would take twelve days to travel through Jordan, studying the East Bank of the Jordan River from a biblical, historical and geographical perspective.

Arnold was very enthused about all his upcoming travels. For him, the highlight of this private trip would be the journey to Petra, which he had not visited since the end of 1966 when he was a student in Israel. Petra, also known as Bozrah in the Bible, was the place where Arnold believed that the Jews would be fleeing to during the Great Tribulation and the location where the Second Coming of Jesus the Messiah would take place. He looked forward to seeing this special site again.

By the late spring of 1985 before the Fruchtenbaums left on the trip, their house in San Antonio still had not yet been sold since its listing in the fall of 1984. It posed a very difficult financial situation for them on the personal level, because they had to make two house payments every month. On a ministry salary, it was particularly challenging to keep up with the double payments and make ends meet, all the more so during those periods when Arnold took salary cuts and postponements of reimbursements. Little could he and Mary Ann have imagined then just how long the house sale process would take.

Power of Prevailing Prayer

For reasons that only God foreknew, the entire publication process of Arnold's original version of the book, *The Footsteps of the Messiah: A Study of the Sequence of Prophetic Events*, dragged on for more than five years. From the time that the typed manuscript was ready at the end of 1977, a number of mishaps and complications arose one after another until the book finally rolled off the press at the end of 1982. No one could have conceived that the long delays causing the initial disappointments turned out to be God's way of linking Arnold to an incident in his past.

In early 1984, one of the largest publishers in West Germany had picked up the book and inquired if they could publish it in German. With ample finances, they could do their own translation in-house and handle all the marketing. The book would be put out in two volumes, targeted for release at the end of 1984 and the year after, respectively. True to form in early 1985, the first volume of the German edition entitled *Handbuch der biblischen Prophetie I* became available on the West German book market, followed by the second volume in early 1986. Both books spread rather quickly throughout the country. Arnold was subsequently asked to write another book entitled *A Dictionary of Bible Prophecy*, which the publisher aimed to translate and produce in the German language only.

Shortly thereafter, out of the blue one day in February 1985, Arnold received a letter written in English from a woman living in West Germany. In it, she informed Arnold that her husband had come across the German edition in a bookstore. Walking along a street, the title in the display window caught his eye. Not familiar with the author, but knowing that his wife was interested in prophecy, he bought the book for her. She immediately recognized the author's last name as being the same as that of a family she once knew at a D.P. Camp in Ulm in 1949. Not aware that Arnold's first name had been changed from Arichek, she asked if he was from the same family that she and her father had known back then. She listed the first names of his parents and his two siblings born in Germany and gave her own father's name as Theophil Burgstahler.

When Arnold read the letter, he was absolutely amazed that this woman was Hanna, the daughter of Theo, the German Lutheran minister who had befriended his parents at the D.P. Camp in Ulm! When Theo had found out that Arnold's family was planning on immigrating to America, he was the one who had given Adele the cover of the October 1949 issue of *The Chosen People* magazine, published by the ABMJ in New York City. The rest was history.

Only about six years old at the time, Arnold could not personally remember Hanna and her father. After becoming a believer, he slowly began to piece together some of his family's history. When he learned about the German Lutheran minister and his daughter, he really wanted to find the family, so that he could let them know what had transpired in his life since. Due to his family's many moves from one D.P. Camp to another and their subsequent journey to America, unfortunately, all contacts had been lost.

Still, Arnold held out hope and continued his search. Whenever he conducted seminars, lectured at conferences, or taught at Bible colleges and seminaries in the United States and Canada, he would always be on the lookout for students from Germany. He would ask them to see if they could somehow find the Burgstahlers or at least locate an address for him, once they returned to their home country. Some had invested a considerable amount of effort to do so, but their search somehow always turned up empty. Arnold would receive a letter notifying him that they were unable to find anyone with that last name. Eventually as the years went by, the search appeared to be futile, so he simply ceased his pursuit of finding them. Disappointing as it was, he decided that it would only be in Heaven, where they would have any kind of reunion.

Now suddenly, Arnold was holding a letter that was written by the very same person whose family he had been trying to locate for so many years! He replied immediately, followed by a whole series of correspondence back and forth. He found out that Theo Burgstahler had passed away some twenty years earlier in the mid-1960s and that Hanna was now married and living in a town about three hours' drive from the city of Frankfurt. It was little wonder over the years why those German students could not find anyone by the last name of Burgstahler. Hanna, who was the only child of Theo and his wife, had changed her last name to Künstler, when she got married to Manfred, a chartered public accountant by profession.

Plans were made to meet that summer of 1985. Since Arnold was scheduled to conduct two short trips to Israel in the late spring of that year, and Mary Ann was going to be traveling with him, they arranged to visit Hanna and her husband on their way back to the United States from Israel. They would extend their stay at the Frankfurt airport hotel and drive a rented car to go and see the Künstlers for a couple of days. There was no adequate way to express Arnold's eager anticipation as he joyously looked forward to their reunion, after a lapse of nearly thirty-six years since his family last lived in Ulm.

This would not be the first time for Arnold and Mary Ann to be in Germany. About five years earlier, between the end of December 1979 to early January 1980, Arnold taught at an English-speaking military church in West Berlin, and Mary Ann had gone with him. Now, they would be back to Germany once again, but this time for very special, personal reasons!

After a relatively uneventful three-hour drive from Frankfurt, Arnold and Mary Ann succeeded in navigating their way to the house where the Künstlers lived. It was a momentous occasion for Hanna, as she stepped outside to welcome Arnold and Mary Ann. Being a rather conservative German and aged somewhere in the mid-fifties, Hanna was very formal in the way she greeted them. She calmly shook their hands, with no outward display of emotions, introduced them to her husband and then invited them into their home. Hanna's reserved manner in no way diminished the overwhelming plethora of emotions that welled up within her at that moment. She was very, very deeply moved, having thought that she would never find out what had happened to the Fruchtenbaum family, let alone live to witness this day.

Arnold was equally moved. He could hardly process all his thoughts and emotions that swirled within him in that instant, when he finally met Hanna face-to-face again. He marveled at the way God had engineered the circumstances all those years to bring him to this point.

Their reunion was extremely meaningful with so much to share and reminisce together. Arnold learned that while at the D.P. Camp in Ulm, his father had asked Hanna and her father, Theo, to be Arnold's godparents. What an astonishing discovery! Henry, known as Chaim back then, had been an ultra-Orthodox Jew, who had lost his faith in Judaism by the time he had escaped to the Soviet Union. Considering how vehemently he had opposed Arnold's belief in Jesus later on, it was a total mystery how Henry could have made such a request to the Burgstahlers in the first place. The idea simply astounded Arnold. Perhaps, being the impulsive and emotional person that Henry was, the Burgstahlers' caring friendliness may have momentarily disarmed him toward them. The request might have just been his way of expressing his appreciation and gratitude to Theo and his daughter for befriending his family. In many ways, Theo and Hanna were the first Gentile believers that had ever shown any kindness and good will to the family, and their love for the Jewish people came across as truly genuine. During the nine months that Arnold's family lived in Ulm, Theo and Hanna had visited them at their living quarters a number of times.

It was entirely possible that Henry may not have clearly understood what being a godparent was all about. In the turmoil of the aftermath of World War II, he may have simply wanted to arrange for someone to look after his first-born son, if anything should ever happen to himself at the D.P. Camp. His request might have also been an expedient one, knowing that his family was not going to remain in Ulm for very long, surmising that once they left the country, Theo and Hanna would be under no obligation to uphold their commitment.

Whatever the reasons, Henry could not have known how seriously Hanna had undertaken her role, praying earnestly for Arnold's salvation every single day from then on. Interestingly, she felt deeply compelled to pray fervently for Arnold, but did not feel the same sense of conviction for the rest of his family. When Theo fell ill and was hospitalized, Hanna asked him before he died, whether or not she should continue praying for Arnold, since she would never know if the prayers would be answered. Her father's advice was for her to persevere in her prayers and to never give up, because some day she would know.

If only Theo could have lived to see how marvelously the Lord had answered Hanna's faithful prayers! Without fail, she had prayed for Arnold every single day for the past thirty-six years. She continued to pray even though she had no knowledge of his whereabouts, or what had happened to him. Now, God had openly rewarded her and answered Hanna's prayers over and above all that she could have ever hoped for or imagined. What an absolute blessing it was for Hanna to discover at last that Arnold not only had been saved, but he had gone on to head up an effective and distinctive ministry to the Jewish people!

Hanna was totally overwhelmed at the chain of events and the fruit that had grown out of the tiny seed that her father had planted so long ago through that one magazine cover. Only a sovereign God could have brought about something so amazing. It was evident that Arnold was God's chosen fruit from the beginning, and through the salvation of this one Jewish boy, thousands more Jewish and Gentile lives had been blessed and changed. Hanna was deeply grateful that her father encouraged her to continue praying. The reunion that day was a tremendous testimony to the mighty power of prevailing prayer!

Manfred's English was very good, while Hanna's was less fluent. Yet, Arnold and Mary Ann were able to communicate with them freely on a deep level. They spent a lot of time reminiscing about the past and felt the presence of the Holy Spirit very strongly in their midst. Arnold was deeply impressed and moved that Hanna had specifically prayed for him for so many years. He was the only one in the family that had become a believer. Their hearts were brimming with awe and gratitude to the Lord for His grace in their lives and for enabling them to meet again in such joyous circumstances. It was truly God's gift from on high.

During the two-day visit, the Künstlers showed Arnold and Mary Ann around Ulm and also took them to see the resting place of Hanna's father. It was heartening that even in the midst of the Nazi regime, there were Germans like Theo who truly loved the Jewish people. Theo even testified at the Nuremberg Trials against the Nazis after the end of the war. It was a very touching experience to be standing at the gravesite of the man whose gesture of kindness to Arnold's family had started a chain of events that led to his faith in Jesus the Messiah and continued to have ripple effects in the Kingdom of God until the present time.

The Künstlers took them to visit the former army barracks that had once served as the D.P. Camp for the Jews after the war. They saw the building where Theo had first made contact with Adele in their small quarters with little Arik standing by her side. Apparently, a Jewish man was living in those very quarters now. As they walked away from the compound, Hanna noted that it would have warmed her father's heart to see a Jew living there at present. Hitler could never have dreamed that there would be Jews still living in Ulm in 1985!

What a privilege for the four to spend time together, sharing many things from the past and discovering a poignant bond in the present. Like them, the Künstlers had also remained childless. Though convinced in their hearts that God in His sovereignty had permitted this condition in their lives, it was nevertheless sad and very painful for the couple. From the depth of their being, Arnold and Mary Ann could relate to them on this matter, for they, too, had been greatly grieved over their own childlessness.

Their brief two-day visit came to an end all too quickly, and it was soon time to say good-bye. Leaving with a feeling of warmth in their hearts, Arnold and Mary Ann were thankful for Hanna's testimony as living proof of the power of prevailing prayer in leading many to salvation.

Very soon after they returned to California, Arnold and Mary Ann rejoiced to hear that Hanna and her husband wanted to begin volunteering their time for Ariel Ministries in Germany. The Künstlers slowly started translating some of the manuscripts and newsletters into German and became involved in the distribution of the Ariel study materials and tapes. It was wonderful how in the latter years of her life, God had blessed Hanna with this new opportunity in His service.

Through Hanna's faithful prayers for Arnold over so many years, he had come to salvation in Messiah Jesus and eventually started Ariel Ministries. Now, Hanna was involved in that ministry in Germany! In a way for Hanna, life appeared to have come full circle. Her faithfulness was a powerful testimony to the amazing way in which God answered her prevailing prayers in His time, in His way, turning certain delays into His appointments. For Arnold, he could now clearly see God's hand and purpose for all the setbacks in getting his book, *The Footsteps of the Messiah: A Study of the Sequence of Prophetic Events*, published. The long years of delays were well worth the wait, as they indeed turned out to be God's vital means of connecting Arnold to a pivotal link of prayer in his past.

Safety and Protection in the Land

Through his study tours, Arnold was keen to show people the Land of Israel the way it ought to be seen, as opposed to visiting only the popular traditional sites. At the same time, he could assess firsthand what was happening politically on the ground. The media's portrayal was largely negatively skewed and did no justice to the actual situation of safety in Israel. By gauging the spiritual state of the Jewish believers around the country, it helped to shape Ariel's future ministry activities in the Land.

Although all the available spaces had been filled at the start of the year, as soon as the American bombing of Libya occurred in mid-April 1986, about half of the group cancelled their reservations just two weeks prior to departure. While Israel was geographically located hundreds of miles on the other end of the Mediterranean, people were still fearful of possible retaliation against Americans overseas and were unwilling to take the risk. Arnold was very disappointed at the lack of objectivity, as Israel itself was a very safe place, probably more so than most American cities. The group would be flying non-stop via El Al Israel Airlines, the most security-conscious airline in the world. Whatever the reasons for not going to Israel, Arnold believed that fear ought not to have been one of them.

Even with the group's size dwindling down to about twelve people, the 1986 intensive five-week Israel Study Tour went ahead anyway. As usual, Arnold arrived about a week or so earlier to ensure that all the prior arrangements were in good order. This time, Mary Ann again felt well enough to come to Israel with him. It turned out to be a very good trip and completely safe. In fact, they had an added benefit of shorter days on the road. It took far less time to move around a substantially smaller group, leaving more free time each day after the sightseeing part ended.

This 1986 trip stood out as being very distinctive from the others—Arnold's parents had come along! They, of course, were not on the study tour, but came to visit the many relatives on Henry's side of the family. It had been forty years since Adele had last seen most of her husband's surviving family members back in 1946 in Poland. For Henry, it was a different story. After the family had settled in California, he had gone to Israel on his own in 1965 to visit his siblings. After that, he went back a second time in recent years to see them again.

Arnold vividly recalled how his father's second trip had come about. It was shortly before he and Mary Ann moved to Irvine, California, while still living in San Antonio. By that time, although Henry's silence treatment and prohibitions had pretty much ended, their relationship was still rather strained. In one of the rare conversations with each other, Henry unwittingly disclosed how nostalgic he was to see his family in Israel again, but had lacked the necessary resources to go. At that point, he had been legally blind for many years and was receiving a disability pension, so funds were very tight. Arnold responded by saying that he could get his father a free roundtrip ticket if they would travel over to Israel together. Surprisingly, Henry agreed without any objections. What he did not realize at the time was that Arnold was going to pay for his father's ticket out of his own pocket. Had he known the truth, he would never have accepted to go.

Years earlier, when Henry began speaking to him again, Arnold had committed in his heart to honor his father in spite of his opposition to his son's belief in Jesus as the Messiah. If Henry persisted in his unbelief, therefore destined to an eternally lost condition, Arnold still resolved to make his life on this earth as comfortable and enjoyable as possible for him. As an adult, he had great compassion for his father, fully aware that his earlier life as a Jew in Europe had been wrought with hardships—filled with flights, near escapes, and attempts at sheer survival. Arnold even purposed in his heart to take his father into his own home, if need be, and care for him the way he had done for his beloved, maternal grandmother. He also wanted to make sure that his father got to see the relatives in Israel again. Because Henry's siblings were Holocaust survivors, the reunions were particularly poignant and special, all the more so, now that they were in their old age.

Arnold had arranged to meet his father at the JFK Airport in New York City. He would wait for Henry to disembark at his arrival gate, and together they would transfer to the international terminal to catch their flight to Israel. Unbeknown to Arnold, Ruth Wardell just happened to be in transit to another flight and was in the same waiting area when Arnold got to his father's arrival gate. Taken completely by surprise yet joyful at this unexpected encounter, Arnold quickly informed Ruth about the situation. Knowing that his father would not be too pleased to run into the woman who had initially led his son to Jesus, he apologetically asked her if she would mind not being seen with him. Arnold did not want anything to trigger off his father's erratic temper, especially after having invested so much effort in his attempts at fostering a tenuous line of communication in their precarious relationship. Ruth understood Arnold's awkward dilemma and quickly removed herself to another corner. It had been over twenty-five years since Henry had last seen her in person, and it was highly unlikely that he would have recognized her among all the other people. Nevertheless for Arnold's sake, it was better for her to be cautious, so she graciously blended into the crowd. However, from her vantage point, she could still see all the comings and goings through the different arrival and departure gates.

When the arrival gate opened and all the passengers filed through, she watched Arnold go up to greet his father. As soon as Henry saw him, he came toward his son, and much to Ruth's surprise, they hugged each other. It was a very touching, poignant moment as father and son embraced. Very moved by what she saw, Ruth felt in the same instant that perhaps the seeds of healing in their relationship were beginning to germinate. Aware of Henry's severe harshness toward Arnold all those years for his faith in Messiah Jesus, she was deeply grateful to the Lord for having allowed her the gift of witnessing this very precious moment between father and son.

Upon arrival in Tel-Aviv, Arnold and his father went their separate ways. Arnold had to immediately turn his attention to checking on all his arrangements for the tour. As for Henry, his siblings met him at the airport and whisked him off with them to their home. After visiting for a few weeks in Israel, he returned to the United States on his own.

This time in 1986, Arnold had once again paid for the roundtrip flight tickets out of his own pocket without his parents' knowledge, and they all traveled over to Israel together. Ever since her mother had passed away, Adele—being an only child—had none of her own family left. Visiting her husband's family would be good for her, as they could communicate in Yiddish or Polish together. Living in apartments with very little spare room, it was difficult for the relatives to accommodate both Henry and Adele during their visit. So, Arnold also paid for their lodging at the same *kibbutz* guesthouse just outside of Jerusalem, where he and Mary Ann were initially staying. During the first week while Arnold was busy finalizing the tour, Mary Ann shuttled her in-laws back and forth in a rented car between the guesthouse and their relatives' place. One time, Arnold did the driving for them through the Galilee and the Golan Heights. Surprised at how well he knew the Land, Adele asked Mary Ann how Arnold knew all those turns he had to make.

Wanting to do some sightseeing around Jerusalem and the surrounding areas, Henry asked his siblings to recommend a good tour guide. They chidingly told him that his son was the best they knew. Arnold's three aunts had once taken part in one of his Jerusalem tours and knew firsthand how good he was. Caught in an awkward bind, not able to back away from their recommendation, Henry and Adele joined Arnold's tour for a few days while they were in the vicinity of Jerusalem.

Henry seemed quite impressed with his son's knowledge of the history and geography of the area, and could tell that Arnold knew the Bible very well. As their relationship was still somewhat strained due to Henry's strong stance against Arnold's beliefs, they did not talk much to each other. However, if they found themselves among other people in the group and were expected to carry on a conversation between father and son, they simply exchanged neutral comments about mundane things such as the weather or the pick-up time for the next site visit.

It was a very unique, once-in-a-lifetime experience for Arnold to have his parents sit in on one of his evening lectures. They were certainly not obliged to attend, and yet they did. Afterwards, however, they made no comments whatsoever about the lecture. Arnold was not sure whether or not his teachings would bring about any long-term spiritual results, but it was certainly encouraging that they were exposed to biblical themes, which they otherwise would never have heard. It had always been Arnold's prayer that his family members would come to a saving knowledge of the grace of Jesus the Messiah. Perhaps, in hearing the teachings, there may have been a slight chance that Henry's stance might have softened a bit. Of course, there was no way of knowing, and Arnold could only hope. In many ways, it turned out to be a very good trip. The country was very safe, and the group encountered no difficulties along the way.

Arnold was pleased to see the progress that an Ariel couple was making in Israel. Because of the restrictions against foreigners entering openly as missionaries, Noam and Joan Hendren had immigrated to Israel years earlier and were now citizens. Orthodox Jews were very antagonistic toward any type of Christian work and had plenty of clout to pressure the government to expel those whom they considered damaging to Judaism. Laboring in the Lord's service in Israel required much patience and perseverance. Although the seeds of mission work had been planted in the hearts of this couple back in 1979 in Dallas, Texas, and a branch in Israel was eventually launched in mid-1982, it took several more years of hard work before the ministry slowly started becoming fruitful in mid-1986. When Arnold and Mary Ann had met up with them the previous spring, the indications of how they were doing then were already very encouraging. Due to the sensitive nature of any kind of Messianic Jewish work in the Land, Ariel Ministries wisely remained discreet, reporting about this couple's ministry activities only in vague terms in the newsletters to its supporters.

BEING WELL AWARE OF ALL THE NEGATIVE REPORTS of widespread violence and turmoil in Israel, particularly the unfavorable news regarding the Arab uprising in the West Bank and the Gaza Strip, Arnold personally wrote in advance to those who had signed up to go on the next tour in 1988. He wanted to reassure the people with his firsthand, well-informed views that the entire country was not in imminent danger and that they did not need to have any fears about their safety while traveling in the Land.

Indeed, the "calamity" so thoroughly portrayed by the various news outlets does not do justice to the situation in Israel. Though it might seem that the entire country is aflame, the fact is that the conflict has been localized to small areas of the West Bank. I do not foresee any

difficulties during our tour. More importantly, the
accounts of general turbulence obscure another vital
current event—one that is truer and even further-reaching:
Jewish believers living in their homeland continue to
acknowledge Jesus as their Messiah, and Ariel Ministries
continues to witness and play a part in this blessed
display of God's grace. And, we know that though the land
and people of Israel will undergo a season of destruction,
they are not consigned only to "calamity," but rather to a
future and hope of peace and salvation through Messiah
Jesus.[41]

Fortunately, the cancellations on this particular tour were quickly filled up
with new applicants, reaching its maximum capacity of twenty-seven. The
year 1988 marked the fortieth anniversary of the birth of Israel as a nation in
May 1948. It was also a special year personally for Arnold and Mary Ann, as
they would be celebrating their twentieth wedding anniversary toward the
end of June that year. Except for minor variations here and there, the itinerary
around the country remained pretty much the same, with none of the
essential spots eliminated from the tour.

As usual, I went to Israel a few weeks ahead of the group
to make sure all arrangements were in order. Then, to test
the waters, I drove alone throughout the West Bank, even
through the "dangerous" cities of Nablus (Shechem) and
Hebron. The drive was pleasant enough, except for one
stone thrown at my vehicle in Shechem. It was a bit tenser
than normal, but hardly as explosive as the news media
would have the public to believe. The tour went pretty
well as planned, with a few minor adjustments here and
there. While we were traveling through the West Bank, we
did get stoned on three occasions—the first of which
shattered a window in the last of our three vans. On
another occasion, we were given a private military escort
through certain areas of the West Bank until we left them
to take a different route from what the officers had
wanted us to travel (some tour members fondly referred to

---

[41] Excerpts: *Ariel Ministries Newsletter*, May 1988

this maneuver as "ditching"). We bypassed only one area—Gaza—due to increased tension there. But, this was certainly not a major omission, as there are no archeological or historical sites within that city.

I pray that those influenced by the media to avoid Israel will reconsider, because the country is basically a very safe place to travel. We praise God that everyone was protected and that, except for the incidents already mentioned, the trip went smoothly. In fact, the tour was quite eventful and, as always, a great learning experience.

The Arab uprising necessitated some rather "interesting" adjustments in other areas. Through all my years of visiting and living in Israel, I have cultivated friendships with certain Arabs. They have come to trust me, and this proved quite valuable. For example, all Arab stores close down during certain hours of the day as part of the uprising.

Naturally, this might have prevented our group from seeing these shops. But on this trip, my friendship with one Arab storeowner in the Old City of Jerusalem and another in Bethlehem allowed us access. I made arrangements with both to allow the group in and then shut the doors behind us so that the stores still appeared closed. This occurred even though Arab terrorists have been known to destroy the shops of those merchants who disobeyed orders. At the Bethlehem store, one Arab worker, who has known me for several years, joined the tour to serve as an escort. As we proceeded toward the southern part of the West Bank to Hebron—which is rather tense—our friend's Arabic came in very handy. My friendship with Arabs was also helpful in Nablus, where I usually make a lunch stop for the group. Because this particular restaurant was scheduled to close at certain hours, the Arab owner arranged for the meal to be served to our

```
entire group in the privacy of his own home. Here, we were
treated to musachan, a special Arab chicken dish.⁴²
```

Since the Fruchtenbaum's expulsion from Israel fifteen years earlier in 1973, Arnold had not spoken at an Israeli congregation. During this tour in 1988, he had a rare opportunity to speak on two separate occasions at two different congregations in Jerusalem. The first was at an Arab congregation that the Christian and Missionary Alliance had established inside the Old City of Jerusalem. Arnold had known this CMA missionary for many years and was invited to speak. Despite the high Jewish-Arab tension prevailing at the time, there was no tension between Arnold and this Arab group, since they had their common faith in Jesus. Arnold enjoyed a good time of fellowship with the Arab believers. The second took place at an English-speaking congregation, the Jerusalem Christian Assembly, founded by a Canadian minister. It was probably one of the largest congregations in Jerusalem, if not the largest in the country, comprising both Jewish and Gentile believers. They met to worship at the local YMCA, providing some exposure to the unbelieving community around them. It was encouraging to see this congregation starting a Hebrew-speaking ministry as well.

Outside of Jerusalem, another teaching opportunity came up in Jaffa, sponsored by the Beit Immanuel Study Center, where Arnold taught a Bible school class. A local ministry in Jaffa asked him if he would be willing to come out on a yearly basis to conduct a two-week seminar. Though an exciting opportunity, the financial situation at the Ariel Home Office rendered it prohibitive at that stage, as it would be a costly venture for the ministry. It thus became a focus of prayer for Arnold and the ministry as they sought the Lord's guidance in this matter.

God's protective shield clearly abounded on the Israel Study Tour of 1990. While the *Intifada* uprising may have appeared to be wreaking havoc in the Gaza Strip and reaching a fever pitch in some areas of the West Bank, the rest of Israel was safe for travelers. In total, they drove over several thousand miles, stopping at more than two hundred sites. Among the participants was the Ariel receptionist-secretary, Stacie Knable, now also editor of the *Ariel Ministries Newsletter*. Others included an older lady in her late sixties, a young

---

⁴² Excerpts: *Ariel Ministries Newsletter*, Winter 1988/89

Bible college student from Canada, a sixty-year old man recovering from brain surgery, and many more. Despite the divergence in backgrounds, they all had a common bond: their belief in Messiah Jesus. They also shared an unparalleled zeal to study the history and geography of the beautiful Land of Israel and to examine God's Word on His plans—past, present, and future— concerning *Eretz Yisrael*.

One of the highlights of the trip was climbing the historic mountain to the top of Masada. For many Israelis, it was considered a sort of "rite of passage." The narrow, dirt snake path, lined with a foreboding barbed-wire fence near the top, had to be scaled by foot at four o'clock in the morning to beat the blazing Negev sun. It was a major feat to get to the top. For Arnold, it was as easy for him to make the climb as it was for a goat to trot up a mountainside. Wearing his trademark flip-flop sandals and knee-high socks, it was all par for the course. He had walked the path more than a few times before!

On this tour, the participants got to witness a fascinating exchange. Arnold took them to visit Bethlehem Bible College, established for and operated by Arab believers. While there, Arnold donated dozens of his books to the college. The group heard an enlightening firsthand account of the Palestinians' experience in the occupied territories. This illustrated the bond of fellowship among believers in Messiah Jesus, regardless of their backgrounds or other differences. The associate dean of the college warmly received the group and openly conveyed his perspective as an Israeli-Arab. He later wrote a letter to Arnold to thank him for the visit.

> Greetings in the name of our Messiah. I would like to commend you for extending your hand to us and to the Bible College by your personal visit and contribution of books and also for introducing your tour group to us. There are not many messianic believers that are willing to have Arab believers share with the group. The tendency is to give a one-sided picture… I'd like to inform you that your effort has had an impact on the Arab believers… I want to encourage you to keep on in your efforts.[43]

---

[43] Excerpts: *Ariel Ministries Newsletter*, Fall 1990

Through the Trying Years

Running the Ariel Home Office out of Tustin, California, during the first few years of relocation proved very challenging for Arnold. While the ministry's monthly income had held steadily from the supporters' faithful giving, the general cost of living in southern California was about triple that of Texas, thus sharply increasing the ministry's ongoing operating costs. Faced with numerous financial hardships, all staff salaries had to be halved in the interim. Only one missionary staff couple felt the need to resign due to the pressing financial situation. It was an amicable parting with no hard feelings on either side.

In late September 1987, a major earthquake suddenly hit the region with shattering force. The walls and floors of the Ariel Home Office shook visibly. Thankfully, no one on the staff was hurt. A little over a month later in November 1987, the stock market crash of Black Monday occurred. Many supporters of the ministry lost a large portion of their investments and thus were unable to honor their committed giving.

By the time Ariel Ministries reached its tenth-year anniversary in December 1987, its financial situation looked bleak. It became necessary to adjust the policy regarding the missionary workers. Instead of being on salary, they would now need to raise their own support. It seemed as though the ministry was precariously treading water with many close calls, barely surviving from one financial "crisis" to another. The next few years were very trying ones for Arnold. Yet, the ministry did not send out any emergency appeal letters to its donors. By prayer and supplication, it turned only to God through Messiah Jesus to provide.

Ariel Ministries also suffered from external harassments. Some strong adherents to Judaism formed anti-missionary organizations, often led by a rabbi, to counter all Messianic Jewish activities, especially the message of *Yeshua Ha'Mashiach*. According to such a group, "one named Arnold G. Fruchtenbaum is notorious for all the harm he has done to the Jewish people." Arnold was mistakenly considered a *meshumad,* or "apostate" in Hebrew, and wrongly perceived as a traitor to Judaism and the Jewish people. The tactics of those opposition groups were aggressive in nature. If there were any consolation, it was the knowledge that Ariel Ministries was indeed effective in its labor among God's Chosen People, with at least one Jewish person coming to faith in Messiah Jesus every quarter. God's grace and His blessings were evident upon the collective endeavors of the ministry's missionaries, for which Arnold was truly grateful to the Lord.

Apart from these strenuous challenges, God was opening up doors of opportunity for Arnold to teach the Word from a Jewish perspective in Gentile Christian churches, some with large audiences. Ariel Ministries was also progressing in both evangelism and discipleship among the Jewish people. Yet in their personal life, Arnold and Mary Ann faced very trying circumstances. Thus far, their house in San Antonio had remained empty and unsold since September 1984. This was very unsettling and particularly difficult for them financially. The high cost of living in southern California combined with Arnold being on a half-salary caused a huge strain in their ability to sustain their two mortgage payments. Moreover, Arnold felt extremely uncomfortable about the long delay in paying back the personal loan, which they had received for the down payment of their house purchase in California.

In truth, being under the burden of $25,000 in personal debt was inwardly anguishing for Arnold, not to mention the stressfulness of still having an unsold empty house back in San Antonio. Something had to be done. With no buyers in sight, Arnold and Mary Ann gave instructions to have their house temporarily taken off the market to be rented out for six months from mid-October 1986 to mid-April 1987. This helped to bring about a little reprieve, as the rental income could be used to pay the corresponding mortgage. At the beginning of May 1987, the house went back on the market. By then, it had been over two and a half years since the house was up for sale. This time, the asking price was lowered substantially to attract prospective buyers.

Shortly thereafter, an offer came in. A few possible factors could still cause the sale to fall through, but Arnold and Mary Ann were hopeful that the transaction would be finalized in mid-July. Arnold asked the prayer supporters of Ariel Ministries to pray for a successful sale, or if not, then that the Lord would send another buyer. At long last, the next prayer letter of August 1987 carried the great news of their house sale! During the nearly three years of waiting, Arnold and Mary Ann were under tremendous financial strain and extreme emotional pressure. What a relief it was for them to have that burden lifted and to be released from suffering for so long! They could now finally close that chapter.

Arnold and Mary Ann chose to repay the interest-free, personal loan received three years previously with an additional $2,500 as a gesture of appreciation, which their supporters accepted. God had His own sovereign reasons for His timing of events, which at times were hard to discern, but the Lord had proven Himself faithful, and Arnold was elated to clear their debt.

Much to their relief, the Lord had shielded them and restrained them from dipping into their special savings account during the long period when the going got financially very tough. Ever since they got married, Arnold and Mary Ann had set up a separate savings account that they called "God's Account," in which they held their financial offerings to the Lord. They put aside a certain amount of money from each paycheck into that account to be used for God's work. As good stewards, whenever the Lord put it upon their hearts to support a certain mission or ministry, Arnold and Mary Ann would use the funds available in that specific savings account for that purpose. During their trial, there were many times when they could have dipped into that account to bring them some temporary financial relief from their personal struggles, but they remained true to their commitment to use those funds only for the Lord's work.

After more than four years of going on a half-salary, Arnold was only just beginning to receive seventy-five percent of his salary in mid-1989. The ministry still had a long way to go to make up for the back pay owing. As the director, Arnold believed that he should be the first one to take a cut and the last to be paid after everyone else's salaries had been paid up. Eventually after several more years, the ministry was finally able to repay him, making up for all the salary cuts he had taken in the past. Arnold and Mary Ann were deeply grateful for God's faithfulness and His sustaining power to see them through all the trying times, strengthening them to develop a growing dependence upon Him alone.

SINCE MOVING TO THE WEST COAST, Mary Ann's health gradually improved for the better, and so did her overall physical stamina. Though still easily fatigued, she felt well enough to travel with Arnold about fifty percent of the time. Having been uprooted from her well-established life in San Antonio, it took longer than two years before she began to feel somewhat comfortable and acculturated to California. Every once in a while, she succumbed to bouts of depression, causing her to feel isolated. She missed many of her friends back in San Antonio, especially her close friend, Jan. It seemed that she still felt reluctant to fully embrace her new life out West, but was making a concerted effort to integrate.

She began taking some courses at the local university and enjoyed learning new skills in some novel areas of study. Actively engaging in a variety of counseling ministries, she also took a course for volunteers in hospice care. By mid-1987, she was doing quite well health-wise and was working in a hospice care program for cancer patients. She had a personal burden for those dealing with chronic physical or mental illness. She had already helped one family through the process of death, burial and the subsequent period of grieving on the part of the widow.

In late spring of 1987, Mary Ann traveled with Arnold back to San Antonio, where he was leading a Bible conference at their former home church, Wayside Chapel. They both enjoyed the opportunity to renew friendships and to visit the city that was so dear to them. The typical hot and muggy San Antonio weather at that time of the year proved to be a bit too much for Mary Ann, who was very heat-sensitive. She soon recognized that she had actually grown accustomed to the dry and cooler climate of southern California without consciously realizing it.

Because of the fatigue that she had felt from San Antonio's heat, Mary Ann decided to skip Camp Shoshanah that summer and stayed at home in Irvine to rest. A number of people whom she had ministered to in the past at the camp missed her presence. So did Arnold, but their cabin would have been too hot for Mary Ann to withstand the heat.

After initially worshipping at a community church in Newport Beach, the Fruchtenbaums became members of a new, smaller messianic congregation in Irvine, called *Shuvah Yisrael*—"Return, O Israel"—founded by Larry Feldman whom Arnold had known for many years. Mary Ann got involved in a weekly Bible study for women and slowly began to develop new friendships. Having Mom Wardell in nearby Los Angeles for solace and comfort during her bouts of depression helped her to feel less isolated. She really enjoyed having lunch with Ruth and appreciated her loving compassion and listening ear. In the latter part of 1987, Mary Ann's youngest sister, Kathy, and her family moved from Michigan to California. Her husband, George, accepted to pastor a new church in San Diego, about seventy miles south of Irvine. In the nineteen years of marriage, it was the first time that Mary Ann had lived this close to a family member. Delighted to have Kathy nearby, she finally felt a sense of belonging in southern California.

In early June of 1988, Mary Ann visited her family in upstate New York and other relatives in Maine and Ohio while Arnold led his tour in Israel. She attended her twentieth class reunion at Gordon College in Massachusetts and visited Westminster College in Pennsylvania. After a wonderful time of going down memory lane with those she knew back then, she joined Arnold for a time of ministry in Vancouver, Canada, where they also celebrated their twentieth wedding anniversary.

In the autumn of 1990 after nearly six years of living in Irvine, the household experienced the loss of B.B., the grand dame, who died at the ripe old age of sixteen. She had been the "queen of the roost," reigning over her younger cat subjects with an air of disdain. They never lacked a dull moment with B.B. at the helm. Having paid a few begrudging visits to the Ariel Home Office in Tustin, when Mary Ann had brought her along, the staff had all become quite familiar with B.B. and her eccentricities. She was like an icon, a period piece, symbolic of a great bygone era. Her feistiness and energy even in her old age were akin to an old, steam locomotive, dark and shiny, whistling and clanking its way into a station, marking its presence and then rolling away to disappear into the distant mist of history. No one who had met B.B. would ever forget her unparalleled personality. In her own unique way, B.B. had brought joy to the household, and she would be greatly missed.

From "Down Under"

In early 1988, Arnold and Mary Ann decided to take a personal vacation to New Zealand and Australia to just relax and enjoy time together. It had been a long while since they had actually spent a vacation on their own. To maintain their privacy, they wanted to go to a place where Arnold was not known and would not be recognized. Having heard about the gorgeous scenery in New Zealand and the fact that English was spoken there, they planned to rent a car and drive at their own leisurely pace from one city to another while visiting places of interest along the way.

Arnold's close friends from Cedarville College, Joe and Sharon Hollaway, had been serving as Baptist missionaries in New Zealand for a number of years, but happened to be away in the United States that year on furlough. While they were in Auckland, the largest city in the country, Arnold received a phone call at their hotel from a believer whom he did not know. The believer lived in Palmerston North, a city in the southwestern part of the North Island, and was part of a ministry that regularly prayed for Israel. He had somehow heard of Arnold's visit and tracked him down! This triggered an interesting turn of events.

Arnold was puzzled as to how this man could have known that he was in New Zealand, let alone in Auckland. To the present day, he never did figure it out. At the time, it had never occurred to Arnold to ask! New Zealand was a small country in many senses of the word, especially among the Christian community, where word-of-mouth traveled fast. Perhaps the old "bush telegraph" had made its rounds, possibly stemming from Joe and Sharon Hollaway, who might have casually mentioned to other believers in passing about Arnold and Mary Ann's upcoming vacation.

Regardless, this believer asked on the phone if Arnold could please hold some meetings and conduct a few seminars while in New Zealand. So much for being incognito and having some private relaxation time away from ministry work! Yet, how could he refuse? After he spoke in Auckland, Arnold and Mary Ann meandered their way south, stopping to visit some tourist attractions en route, before ending up in Palmerston North, where Arnold taught the Bible, while Mary Ann ministered through her Hebrew worship songs performed a cappella. Quite surprisingly, the believer also arranged for meetings to be held in Wellington, the capital city in the south of the North Island, as well as in Christchurch in the South Island. Consequently, what started out solely as a personal vacation in New Zealand ended up turning partly into a ministry trip, which Arnold could never have anticipated.

The reception to his teaching was excellent, and he was asked to please return to conduct more meetings in the near future. Because of the wonderful and enthusiastic response, Arnold went back in the spring of 1990. A Gentile believer in Christchurch even volunteered to serve as the distributor of the Ariel materials in New Zealand. Hence, all the ministry's study resources became available to the people in the country. This believer was not involved in setting up any of Arnold's speaking engagements, as his function was purely voluntary and not that of a branch. Totally unbeknown to Arnold, the Lord had flung the door wide open to a whole new area of ministry "Down Under." The way the teaching opportunities had come about left no doubt in his mind that it was God's doing. Though the Jews were few in number in New Zealand, God was preparing the Gentile believers there to study the Scriptures within a Jewish frame of reference, so that they could learn about God's plan and purpose for His Chosen People.

In Australia, Arnold and Mary Ann knew no one and were there merely as tourists. In Perth on the western shores, Arnold happened to pick up a magazine containing a devotional article written by a pastor on the six different ways one could be "born again." In the traditional form of Rabbinic Judaism that descended from the Pharisaic Judaism of the New Testament times, the term "born again" had six different meanings: First, it described a Gentile converting to Judaism; second, it was used when a man was crowned as king; third, it described a young man at his *Bar Mitzvah* at age thirteen; fourth, getting married meant being "born again" in one's life; fifth, being ordained as a rabbi carried the same meaning; and sixth, it described a man who became the head of a rabbinic academy. Obviously, all six ways pertained to the physical realm, whereas Jesus gave the term a spiritual connotation in reference to the spiritual rebirth.

Only a Jewish person familiar with the *Mishnah* and the rabbinic writings could have known these teachings. Arnold wondered whether the pastor was a Jewish believer, who might have previously been a rabbi. Intrigued, he phoned the number listed at the end of the article to inquire. It turned out that the pastor was a Gentile believer, who happened to have heard Arnold's teaching on the subject on a radio program during an earlier visit to the United States. Imagine his utter surprise when Arnold announced on the phone that he was the very same teacher on the radio! It was from this totally unexpected point of contact that Arnold's ministry in Australia began. The pastor invited him to return to the continent to teach at several churches. Suddenly out of the blue, Australia also became wide open to Ariel Ministries! Later on, an arrangement was made with Manna International, a Jewish ministry on the ground that volunteered to be the distributor of Ariel's resource materials to the believers in Australia.

No human could have arranged the sequencing and unfolding of events that occurred on this particular vacation trip. The handprint of God was definitely on the outworking of these new ministry opportunities. Except for establishing a presence in Israel, it had never occurred to Arnold to take Ariel Ministries abroad. Initially, he had aspired to plant five mission branches in the United States under the Ariel umbrella in key cities with large Jewish populations on the East and West Coasts. In truth, he would have been satisfied with achieving those goals. Never could he have imagined that Ariel's work of evangelism and discipleship of the Jewish people would one day literally reach across the oceans to such far-off places. More amazing was that he had no inkling or prior knowledge that God was quietly paving the way in His own timing for the ministry "Down Under." Arnold could only praise and humbly thank the Lord for His sovereignty over all circumstances and for directing the future steps of Ariel Ministries.

ONE OF THE MOST COMMONLY ASKED QUESTIONS from numerous supporters of Ariel Ministries in the United States was what Arnold actually did while on the road. Besides teaching at meetings, conferences, or seminars in the evenings and studying, researching, or writing during the daytime, Arnold did not do much else, as he was not into sightseeing during his free time. Being a real night owl, he usually stayed up until two o'clock in the morning to work and then slept in for a while in the mornings before going for his daily jog. The rest of the day was spent in the motel room, working on his writings or preparing his talks, packing a lot into his day.

To practice, he first reviewed his outline and notes, having already memorized the entire teaching session in his head. Unlike many speakers, he never read from a fully written document. Turning on the television set with the volume on mute—using the characters in the shows to serve as his audience—he taught extemporaneously, referring to his outline only every now and again, timing himself in the process. If he went over his time allocation, he would adjust the length of his teachings accordingly. In his candid sense of humor, Arnold often joked about the number of top Hollywood stars whom he had taught over the years, but whose offerings were very poor! He was very organized, meticulous, and disciplined with his time, pacing himself well on his writing projects and scheduling daily things he had to accomplish for the various tape series or different stages of a book manuscript.

Another thing that Ariel supporters often wondered about was what Arnold was really like as a person. There was a certain sense of intrigue surrounding him, because he was somewhat reserved and in general, rather quiet in everyday social settings. In short, he was an enigma to most. One particular incident illustrated Arnold's typical interaction, or lack thereof, with people. An older lady—a supporter of Ariel Ministries and an acquaintance of Ruth

Wardell—offered to give him a ride to another city, where his next speaking engagement was to take place. She was really looking forward to having a few hours alone with him on the road to get to know him personally. Much to her exasperation, she could hardly engage him in a dialogue! Whenever she asked him a question about something, he would reply for the most part with a short one-word answer, either a "yes" or a "no." After several unsuccessful attempts in the first hour at extracting some sort of chitchat out of him, she gave up and drove him the rest of the way in an awkward silence. What she had not realized was that Arnold would have talked with her at length about any biblical subject. He was so passionate about the Word that he could discuss any myriad of scriptural topics for an indefinite length of time, but he simply was not one to freely engage in general everyday small talk.

As a public speaker in ministry work, Arnold naturally had many acquaintances. However, in his own narrow definition, he had only a few friends. In his lifetime, overall there were about ten people whom he considered as friends. Most of them were the close friends he had made while attending Cedarville College, including Mary Ann Sleichter (now Miriam Nadler), Mike and Carol Hamilton, and Joe and Sharon Hollaway. In seminary, it was Barry Leventhal who was a great buddy. Of course, there was Bob Futoran from his teenage Memory Camp days, who was like a brother to him. They were believers in his inner circle, who knew him well from early on and with whom he felt comfortable to discuss and share the deeper things of his life. These were the friends who were there for him and for whom he would be there when needed. If they could not help him for any reason, he knew that it was because it was not possible for them to do so, not because they refused to do so. Arnold himself was a very loyal friend in turn, generous and giving, always ready to help especially in his friends' time of need, with no strings attached. He was not one to express his appreciation of his friends in so many words, but through his actions in what he did for them.

Other important figures in his life were people like Ruth Wardell and Burl Haynie, whom he considered his spiritual mentors. For others in the wider circle of people who impacted his work and ministry, Arnold remembered to show them his appreciation by dedicating his books to them and sending them a copy as a gift. Those who were acquainted with Arnold had an enormous respect for him as a teacher, a believer, and a person. They had never encountered anyone else with such consistent discipline in daily life. Arnold was one of those rare individuals who knew exactly what his calling was in life and who had a plan to achieve those goals that God had laid out for him to accomplish. One of the major goals was to complete during his lifetime a verse-by-verse commentary on all the books in the Bible. A bulk of the research and initial taping work of some of the books had already been prepared within the first ten years of the ministry, but there still remained a lot more to be done.

Arnold arranged his time according to the truth in the Bible about the length of one's life:

The days of our years are three score and ten, Or even by reason of strength fourscore years; ... So teach us to number our days, That we may get us a heart of wisdom. (Psalm 90:10a, 12)

He used an agenda book that allocated one full page to a day. While staying at the home of acquaintances during a speaking engagement in their city, he had left it open on the dining table. The wife of the couple noticed numbers consisting of many digits written on the top corner of each page in consecutive descending order and asked Arnold what those numbers meant. He explained to her that he took seventy years as a basis for how long he would live and calculated how many days he still had left in the Lord's service, all things being equal. As the numbers decreased by one with each passing day, he was able to literally number the days of his life. Once he reached seventy, he planned to note how many days were left before his eightieth birthday and begin the process all over again.

Counting down the days of his life with the full understanding of the consequences of "unworthy" days gave Arnold a fresh perspective on the importance of investing in activities of eternal value. It was a daily reminder not to waste time. This system of keeping track brought to the fore every morning the reality that he had one less day left to live, propelling him to make each of the remaining days count for eternity and not only for time.

Attaining the Doctorate

From the time that Arnold first began researching his dissertation topic until he attained his Ph.D. from New York University in Religious Education with a focus on Jewish Studies, a total of thirteen years had elapsed. As soon as his topic, "Israelology," was approved during his second year of resident studies, he started his research in earnest. Once the courses were fulfilled, the university allowed ten years to complete the doctoral dissertation. Arnold's deadline was December 1987.

Although no longer serving with Ariel Ministries, Charmaine had volunteered to type the first draft in early 1985 on her electric typewriter. The first version of 2,200 pages was way too long for New York University to accept, the average being about two hundred and fifty. To meet the stipulated limit, Arnold went through several traumatic rewrites, agonizing over the many deletions and reductions. A good friend of the ministry, Roxanne Tretheway, had been transcribing Ariel radio tapes on a voluntary basis. She now offered to type the revisions. Roxanne's computer skills came in very handy as she kept up with all of Arnold's rewrites, staying in constant contact with New York University to make sure the shortened version conformed to the required format. A while later, she started volunteering her time at the Ariel Home Office. When Sylvia resigned and left at the end of 1988, Roxanne took over the full-time salaried position of administrative assistant.

The three faculty members on Arnold's dissertation committee, including the chairperson, provided many helpful comments. She encouraged Arnold to persevere and not to give up. The reworking was a painstaking process, causing him problems in meeting his deadline in December 1987. He requested and was granted the maximum number of three extensions, with an absolute final deadline at the end of September 1988. If he failed to complete his revision by then, another extension would not be granted, thus forcing him to abandon the project. Hence, it was of paramount importance to press on toward this finish line. Arnold's final version totaling four hundred and sixty-six pages, though still much longer than the average length, was accepted on the premise that Arnold was writing on a subject wherein little work had been done previously.

One final hurdle remained: he had to pass his oral examination, scheduled for the latter part of November that year. In total, there would be five faculty members on the examining panel, three of whom were the same individuals on his dissertation committee. The other two were professors randomly selected from other departments. The same chairperson, also serving on the oral examination panel, warned Arnold that there would be questions from the two random professors on any number of subjects outside his specific field. Apparently, the panel was allowed to question the Ph.D. candidate on unrelated topics to the dissertation itself.

A list of twenty books on subjects in other fields was assigned to Arnold. Embarking on a reading marathon, he began to get ready. Right in the throes of his preparation, he received a phone call from the university informing him that the oral exam would be held at the Payne Room of the Press Building on campus. When he hung up, Arnold heaved an audible sigh, at the same time chuckling at the hilarious irony of the venue. At least, he still maintained his sense of humor at this stressful time. For sure, the whole rewriting process had been a painful one, but the pain was not going to be over until it culminated in the "Payne" Room!

A couple of days before the oral exam, Arnold flew up to New York City and checked into a hotel near the university, reviewed all his materials one last time, and collected his thoughts in preparation for his big day. It was crucial to pass his orals this time. There was a lot at stake, especially since he was among the last of the chairperson's doctoral students. Her retirement was fast approaching after the end of the year, so Arnold needed to pass. There were three possible scenarios for his outcome. First, he hoped to receive a Pass, leading to a definite Ph.D. Second, he could receive a Pass-Deferred and be given only one more chance to rewrite his dissertation and undergo another oral exam. A new deadline would be set. If he still did not pass at that stage, there would not be another chance. Third, he could receive a Fail, thus having to abandon this dissertation and start all over again on another subject.

Arnold knew that he simply would never have the time to work on a new dissertation due to his heavy travel schedule. He would have to give up his quest for a Ph.D. if he failed. Of the five votes, it took only two Fails or two Pass-Deferreds for New York University to withhold the doctorate degree from a candidate. At this point, his success hinged upon how well he defended his dissertation during his orals. Arnold tried to assess where each professor stood with regard to his contents. One of the three members of his dissertation committee was a believer, so would be on Arnold's side. The other two were neutral. Out of the two randomly selected faculty members, one was a Jewish professor in philosophy and very antagonistic. The other from a very liberal Catholic background had already expressed dissatisfaction with Arnold's conclusions. Arnold was up against some serious opposition and prayed for the Lord to overrule.

Arnold was severely grilled during the orals, which lasted several hours. The Jewish professor attempted to dominate the entire session, clearly intending to expose Arnold and trip him up. He would ask a question to challenge, but would immediately cut Arnold off and move on to the next question, not even bothering to listen to his defense of the topic. He simply wanted it to appear as though Arnold did not know the answers. His antagonism was blatantly obvious, but Arnold had to endure it and respond to all the questions courteously and objectively.

Once the exam was over, Arnold was asked to step outside to the sitting area down the hall, while the panel conferred with one another. All he could do was to pray and trust the Lord for a favorable outcome. About half an hour later, the chairperson came out and said to him, "Congratulations, Dr. Fruchtenbaum." After so many years of hard work, it was a moment to be cherished! Arnold thanked and praised the Lord in his heart for allowing him to achieve this important milestone.

Later, the chairperson recounted the voting process. The Jewish professor could not fail Arnold, because he had answered all of his questions, so he gave him a Pass-Deferred instead. Apparently, the other randomly selected professor had already made up his mind at the start that he was not convinced about the subject. However, when he witnessed the behavior of the Jewish professor and how unfairly he had treated Arnold, he changed his mind and swung over to Arnold's side, giving him a Pass. The two neutral professors on his committee were also convinced by Arnold's answers, giving him a Pass as did the believer. In order for a Pass-Deferred to take effect, the university required two out of the five examining panelists to give such a mark. With only one Pass-Deferred, the final result was in favor of granting Arnold his Ph.D.

Absolutely thrilled, Arnold could not wait to get back home to rejoice over the great news with Mary Ann, but he did not have to wait until then. The chairperson immediately handed him the office phone. Humorously, he informed Mary Ann that when she came to fetch him at the airport, she could call him "Dr. Arnold." By the time he flew back to California, Mary Ann had already called all their family and friends about the terrific news. The degree represented much more than just a new title to Arnold's name. It would allow him greater access to the academic community such as Bible colleges and seminaries and lend credibility in his interactions with publishers and especially with Jewish unbelievers who were apt to question his authority on theological issues.

Graduation day in May 1989 was a joyous occasion as Arnold participated in the ceremony with about twenty other Ph.D. candidates from New York University, all in full regalia. He walked onto the stage as Arnold G. Fruchtenbaum to receive his Ph.D. degree and walked off the stage as Dr. Arnold G. Fruchtenbaum. What an achievement indeed! Mary Ann organized a wonderful party for him in the evening right there in New York City. She invited around twenty people, important at various stages in his life, including Ruth Wardell and Reverend Burl Haynie. It was a very happy occasion filled with fun and celebration.

Many of the guests at the party spoke words of congratulations sprinkled with a good dose of humor. Arnold himself was beaming as he stood behind an informal podium, offering heartfelt gratitude to the Lord, and expressing his thanks and appreciation to those who had encouraged and assisted him throughout this whole arduous process.

It was Arnold's wish to publish his original 2,200-page dissertation in book form. To do so, he needed to cut down the number of pages to about one thousand. Pragmatically, it was difficult to find a printing house that was prepared to physically print such a large work. Hence, he soon began working on a revised medium version. Roxanne once again devoted her spare time to typing the text into the computer.

IN GOD'S PROVIDENTIAL TIMING, the second Lausanne Consultation on World Evangelism, commonly known as Lausanne II, was held in Manila, Philippines, in July 1989. Originally the brainchild of the evangelist, Billy Graham, the previous gathering took place in the mid-1970s in Lausanne, Switzerland, where leaders from various ministries and churches all over the world gathered to explore world evangelism. A separate division focused specifically on Jewish evangelism. Arnold's Ph.D. would lend more credibility to his theological stance on Israel.

Before attending the conference, Arnold and Mary Ann decided to stop en route in Hong Kong, Bangkok, and Singapore for a short, personal vacation. On their way home, they planned to squeeze in a brief, private trip to China and Japan. Arnold had heard about the workmanship of tailors in certain Asian cities. Leisure suits were in fashion and very popular in Texas in the seventies. When he approached a tailor in the United States, he found out that such a suit would cost $700, way too much money for him. This trip to Asia came at a very opportune time, giving him the chance to replenish his wardrobe for work. In Hong Kong, Arnold got three leisure suits tailor-made. Each came with a jacket and two pairs of pants. He also had a similar number tailor-made in Bangkok. The cost of such a tailor-made leisure suit in Asia was equivalent to only $100. After getting his measurements taken, Arnold paid a deposit and was assured that the suits would be ready within a day or two. He could pay the remainder, when he returned to collect the suits. The workmanship was excellent. For the price of one leisure suit in the United States, he could get multiple suits in quality textiles here in Asia. It was a special blessing for him, as these suits would last him a long while to come.

Over the years, many Ariel supporters had teased Arnold about his leisure suits and his flip-flops, which they called "thongs" before the word came to denote something entirely different in the secular world. Arnold strongly disliked wearing regular enclosed shoes. For him, flip-flops with socks were so much more comfortable. Flip-flops were not that unusual in warm climates such as Hawaii or California, but it seemed that only Arnold wore them with socks. When he was in college and did not have much money, Arnold economized by wearing proper shoes only to his classes, so that they would not wear out too quickly. For almost everywhere else, he wore his flip-flops with socks, while studying in his dorm room, eating at the cafeteria, or working in the library. Later on in life, even when he could afford proper shoes, he still wore his flip-flops with socks wherever he could, due to their comfort, whereas for his speaking engagements, he would put on tight, ankle-high Texan boots under his pants. Arnold's infamous flip-flops and socks became such a hallmark for him that he received many hilarious drawings of cartoon caricatures of himself from various Ariel supporters.

A SPECIAL BLESSING CAME ABOUT while Arnold and Mary Ann stayed for a few days in Singapore. As it was their first time there, they had no prior contacts. However, Arnold recalled having once known a Singaporean lad with whom he had worked at the Shelton College library during his freshman year. Swee Wha Quek was a pastor's son, who had come to the United States to study at a Christian college. From Monday through Friday, they worked together at the library. The two traveled together on Sundays, giving their testimonies at churches to encourage people's support of foreign missions. Outwardly, they presented an interesting contrast, with Arnold, a Jewish lad wearing a *yarmulke* on his head, and his college mate, a Singaporean donning his full native garb. Yet, their underlying Gospel message of God's redemptive love and salvation grace through His Son, Jesus the Messiah, was the same. They had spent a lot of time together that year until Swee Wha Quek graduated in June 1963. He went on to pursue further theological studies at a seminary in Philadelphia with the goal of eventually returning home to assume a pastorate in Singapore. Now, twenty-six years later, Arnold finally made it to Singapore and remembered his former college chum. He decided to make a concerted attempt to locate his buddy.

The first thing Arnold did was to scan the local telephone directory. Since English was one of the official languages in Singapore, it made the search a little less daunting. However, much to his dismay, he soon realized that Quek was a very common family name in Singapore, akin to names like Smith and Jones in the United States. Tens of thousands of people shared this last name! Still, Arnold refused to be deterred and persevered with sheer determination in his search for his buddy. In the end, his efforts paid off. Through God's wonderful providence, he finally found the right Quek.

When his former college chum received a phone call from a man with an unusual mixture of strong accents announcing himself as Arnold Fruchtenbaum, he was completely caught by surprise! At the same time, Swee Wha was overjoyed, because just the previous week, he had been to Jerusalem and had made enquiries among his Jewish friends if they knew anyone by the name of Arnold Fruchtenbaum. Now, after so many years, they were brought together once again in a most unique manner that only the Lord could have engineered. God had certainly answered Swee Wha's prayers! Over the years, the Lord had led the two men down different paths and yet in similar ministries.

Swee Wha had indeed followed his calling and returned home to Singapore after his studies in the United States to serve as a minister of an English-speaking congregation called Zion Bible Presbyterian Church. Numbering over eight hundred, his current congregants read about the exciting and joyful reunion between their minister, Reverend Quek, and Dr. Arnold G. Fruchtenbaum of Ariel Ministries, in their Sunday church bulletin, aptly named *The Zion Bulletin*. They enthusiastically listened to Arnold as he taught and expounded a portion of Scripture from a Jewish perspective. More than ever before, they embraced the importance of sharing the Gospel message with the Jews first. They were also treated to a traditional Hebrew melody, which Mary Ann sang a cappella. The church choir was so enraptured that they requested Mary Ann to teach them a Hebrew song. She was of course thrilled to oblige!

Although the Jews comprised only a small community of a few hundred in Singapore, the congregants developed a greater awareness of God's Chosen People, who were dispersed all over the world in the *Diaspora*, some even in their own country. Arnold's visit was a blessing to the congregation, and while the reunion with his former college mate was very brief, they were both thankful to the Lord for having brought them back together again after a long lapse of twenty-six years.

God had truly blessed Arnold's trip to the Lausanne II conference. Not only had Mary Ann felt well enough to accompany him, they were able to take a short personal vacation together in some interesting Asian countries en route. In addition, Arnold had been able to locate his former college chum after so many years. The contacts that were made at the Lausanne II conference in Manila led to some open doors of opportunity later on for Ariel Ministries to minister in distant countries offshore. The conference also provided wider exposure for the work of Ariel Ministries in Jewish evangelism and discipleship of the Jewish people. God's hand was indeed upon the ministry, guiding and directing Ariel's work, and making it known in other countries.

Evangelizing Soviet Jews

At the time that Ariel Ministries was launched, Arnold could never have imagined that of all places, he would one day be evangelizing scores of Soviet Jews congregated in Ladispoli, Italy. For decades, the Soviet suppression of Jewish life and the barring of most emigration had forced the Soviet Jewry into a desperate plight. With the advent of reforms that took hold under Mikhail Gorbachev during the *glasnost* era, the Soviet Union finally unleashed its floodgates in the early 1990s, leading to a mass exodus of Jews in unprecedented numbers. The first year, many hundreds of thousands of people sought to immigrate to Israel, the United States, Canada, and Australia, where they hoped to find safety, liberty, and freedom. In the following years, up to one million Soviet Jews departed to seek refuge elsewhere.

With no direct flights to Israel, they first had to detour to another country to undergo the immigration processing. For this reason, many thousands of Soviet Jewish refugees were gathered in Ladispoli, an Italian seaside suburb just south of Rome, and in other nearby towns, which served as "holding tanks" to house the refugees while they awaited their paperwork. The crowded living conditions in those camps were quite deplorable. Many became discouraged and fearful, while others were pained and embittered about having to leave some of their family members behind in the Soviet Union.

An American Conservative Baptist missionary in Italy, serving as the contact person for Ariel Ministries, was in charge of coordinating Arnold's one-week trip toward the end of January 1990 and arranging for an interpreter. To prepare for this once-in-a-lifetime opportunity, the ministry received very timely and generous donations from its supporters, contributing to the cost of printing ten thousand copies of Arnold's publication, *Jewishness and Hebrew Christianity*, in Russian. Thus far, it was the most effective tract for witnessing to the Jewish people.

Born in Siberia himself and also having experienced life in the D.P. Camps in Germany, Arnold understood the plight of the refugees in Italy. In many ways, he felt as though he had returned to his Russian roots while circulating amid the Soviet Jews. He found himself preaching and personally ministering to hundreds of spiritually hungry people right on the streets of Ladispoli, which would have been inconceivable even the year before!

God was doing a great work among His Chosen People, whom He had not forgotten nor forsaken. After decades of suffering under communist suppression in the Soviet Union, the Jews were hungry for spiritual knowledge and nourishment. Prior to Arnold's arrival, the American missionary experienced a remarkable phenomenon. Jews and Gentiles alike were coming up to him and asking him to tell them about God. They were extremely eager to have an opportunity to learn, and they urged him to please teach them. Never before had he ever experienced Jews begging a Christian missionary to speak to them about God and spiritual matters!

Speaking no Russian, Arnold's messages were all communicated through an interpreter, who happened to be Jewish but not a believer. As Arnold worked in tandem with the American missionary, distributing the tracts and witnessing on the streets, he prayed that many of his fellow Jews would come to a saving knowledge of Jesus as their Messiah. So much openness and fervor for the Word of God was previously unheard of! Not prone to using superlatives, Arnold later described his experience as "fantastic," "tremendous," "exciting," and "amazing." He had the unique opportunity of presenting his testimony and preaching the Gospel to a single gathering of three hundred people, who hung onto his every word. It was the largest group of unsaved Jews that Arnold had ever witnessed to in his entire ministry. In his own words, "The response was unbelievable." Never before had he experienced having Jews running after him, begging for a New Testament! They were so eager to obtain the literature that presented Jesus as the Jewish Messiah that they practically devoured the tracts that were distributed to them. A good number of them received Jesus as their Messiah, and there were others who were very interested and close to making a decision. Just in the short time that Arnold was in Italy, he personally witnessed four refugees receive the Messiah. Only God could have foreseen such an amazing phenomenon.

Not having heard anything about God in the Soviet Union, these people hunger for spiritual things, including information about the New Testament. We were unable to give away our literature and New Testaments fast enough. Almost everywhere we went, as soon as we began laying out our materials, we were literally mobbed by the Soviet Jews. In one case, the van was so swamped by refugees waiting for our tracts and books that we could not even get back to it to replenish our supply. We had to stand idle for twenty minutes until there was enough of an opening for us to return to the van to grab some more materials. This was probably the single most amazing response we had, as our van was literally emptied of all the literature. [44]

---

[44] Excerpt: *Ariel Ministries Newsletter*, Spring 1990

In the span of that one precious week, Arnold was also able to interact with many Soviet Jews on a more personal level, conversing with individuals through his interpreter. The fact that he was a Russian-born native was much appreciated by the refugees and led to more openness in discussions. It was very evident that the Jews hungered to know God personally.

```
I did a great deal of one-on-one witnessing... Almost
every day I had private meetings with Soviet Jews who
invited me into their living quarters and often fed me.
(In fact, the whole week I was there, I only had Italian
food once when I ate out with some friends at a
restaurant. Otherwise all my meals were taken care of by
Russian Jews and they all cooked Russian-style meals, not
Italian)... There is no question that the Soviet Jews are
very hungry to know more about God. Where else do you tell
a group of Jews that they need to accept Jesus, and they
applaud?[45]
```

For Arnold, the week in Italy was the most wonderful highlight of his ministry to the Jewish people thus far. After so many years of the Cold War, the world was finally changing. East and West Germany had moved toward reunification and had become one nation after the fall of the Berlin Wall in late 1989. Communism was being overthrown peacefully in the Eastern Bloc countries, one by one, without warfare. In December 1991, an astonished world looked on as the Soviet Union officially dissolved right in front of its very eyes without a major revolution or bloodshed as had occurred in other historical events in the past. These pivotal moments in history reflected God's sovereignty overruling the affairs of men. The Lord was clearly at work, changing the course of history.

With the influx of Soviet Jewish immigrants to the United States, Ariel Ministries explored the possibility of holding a Russian camp after the regular three-week discipleship program at Camp Shoshanah during the summer of 1990. Dan and Arlene Rigney, who had also ministered in Italy for six weeks in the spring, had made many significant contacts among the refugees. Some had arrived in the United States shortly thereafter. The ministry decided to take the opportunity to offer a Russian camp, which they aptly referred to as

---

[45] Excerpts: *Ariel Ministries Newsletter*, Spring 1990

the "Soviet Jewish Immigrant Week." Neither Arnold nor the Rigneys could have anticipated just how much the outreach meant to the participants and how abundantly the Lord blessed that camp. They certainly could not have imagined that the program would continue to be offered in the following years.

Reciting the *Kaddish*

By December 1991, Arnold and Mary Ann had been living in California for seven years. Because Irvine was a little over an hour's drive from Los Angeles, they were able to go and see Arnold's parents from time to time. About a week or so prior to Christmas that year, they went for another visit.

In recent years, Henry had become even more obsessed with chess—for him, a passionate, all-consuming, professional sport—priding himself in his mental prowess over his opponents. After he could no longer drive due to his legal blindness, his children would drop him off and pick him up at the park. When the last of them grew up and left home, Henry started to take the bus, not wanting to miss a single game. As he got more elderly, in addition to his diabetes, he also developed a heart condition, which did not seem life threatening. Thus, when Arnold and Mary Ann saw him that December, he appeared fine, and the visit took place without incident.

The next day, Arnold traveled to Israel to serve as the tour guide for a group from Project Joshua, a study and evangelistic program for college students, sponsored by the Jews for Jesus organization. Over the years, it had been Arnold's guiding principle to foster a spirit of cooperation between Ariel and other Jewish ministries. When his assistance was requested, he readily agreed. As he had done for the project two years previously, Arnold arrived in Israel a week ahead of time to finalize the preparations for the tour.

The group was scheduled to be in Israel for two weeks, starting from Christmas Day 1991. They would engage in evangelistic outreaches, witnessing on the streets in various cities of Israel on alternate days under the leadership of a staff member from the Jews for Jesus organization in the United States. On the other days in between, the group would be on a study tour with Arnold as their teacher and guide. He was a planner and very organized, counting on things to be on track, almost like clockwork. In reality, life often presented unforeseen circumstances.

On New Year's Day on a *kibbutz* just outside Jerusalem, I found myself repeating Joseph's words to Pharaoh. *"Now therefore let me go up, I pray thee and bury my father and I will come again."* (Genesis 50:5b, ASV)… I received a fax telling me to contact home due to a medical emergency… my 72-year-old father had been hospitalized with a recurrence of heart trouble. Bypass surgery was considered, but he slipped into a coma before that was possible. The last time I saw him alive was December 17th, one day before I left for Israel. I now prayed that my father would live long enough to hear the Gospel one more time.

The next day, January 1st, brought a rarer-than-rare 18-inch snowfall to Jerusalem and another fax to me: my father had died, having never emerged from the coma. In fact, he had undergone six code-blues before his heart finally gave out at 2:00 a.m. on New Year's Day… My mother's message read: "There is no need for you to come home at this time." I could not tell if she was trying to spare me undue hardship, or spare the family possible embarrassment, as my beliefs about Jesus seemed to clash with the traditional Jewish funeral planned for my father. As did my responsibilities: to my family as the first-born son and to Jews for Jesus as their tour guide…My mother's note did not exactly encourage me to pursue the matter, nor was I certain that I'd receive a hearty welcome from my siblings. I prayed for guidance.

With the group's encouragement, I decided to make the trip and return to Israel and the tour the day after the funeral. (Only later did I realize how much my words paralleled those of Joseph, *"and I will come again"*). Still, I knew that actually making it back in time for the funeral would require a miracle. That's when Joseph's request to Pharaoh became my prayer. Not only would God need to overcome a snowstorm, but also these circumstances: El Al has only one daily non-stop flight to New York, and this was peak traveling season. The Lord confirmed my difficult decision by providing the last seat on Friday's 1:00 a.m. flight; He also enabled me to make connections, albeit tight ones, to get me into L.A. two hours before the funeral. Furthermore, He took us safely through snowy roads to the airport in Tel Aviv…

En route to the Galilee, the group dropped me off at the airport 11 hours before my 1:00 a.m. flight. The plane was ready to leave on time, but the door jammed, and it took a half hour to repair. That would cut into my very short layover time at JFK in New York. I again made Joseph's words to Pharaoh my prayer, and seeing how God had worked out all the other details, I knew He would work this one out as well… The plane was able to make up time and we arrived at JFK at 6:05 a.m. only five minutes late. An El Al agent, informed of my special case, rushed me through customs, and I had no difficulty catching my 7:30 a.m. flight. We arrived into LAX a half hour early. Mary Ann picked me up, and we met the family at the Jewish cemetery in plenty of time. It was a cold, rainy day in Los Angeles, appropriate weather for the occasion.

All seven of my father's children were there, along with five spouses (two siblings are single) and three grandchildren. Three of my father's chess partners came as well. The officiating rabbi was informed that I was the first-born, but not of my beliefs. At the internment (a separate ceremony), the rabbi asked me to recite the *Kaddish*, a traditional prayer for the occasion. My father was then buried. The rest of the day was spent with the family at my mother's home, the same home from which I was expelled by my father 30 years ago. The next day, I caught a 7:00 a.m. flight back to Israel, while Mary Ann went to comfort my mother.[46]

The Mourner's *Kaddish*, a traditional Jewish prayer recited at funerals or memorials, is in Hebrew and Aramaic only. Starting with the first phrase in the prayer, it extols the magnificence and sanctity of God's Name. In the middle of the prayer, it continues to laud His Holy Name and His attributes. It acknowledges His sovereignty over all circumstances, even in adversity, and

---

[46] Excerpts: *Ariel Ministries Newsletter*, Spring 1992

ends with a blessing of peace: *...He Who makes peace in His heights, may He make peace upon us and upon all Israel...*

Were his father's ultra-Orthodox Jewish tradition strictly carried out, Arnold's duty as the first-born son would have been to recite the *Kaddish* not only at the internment, but also once a day for a whole year thereafter. In addition, according to the normal Jewish tradition, he was expected to return to the cemetery once again on the first anniversary of his father's death to repeat the Mourner's *Kaddish*. Adele knew that Arnold was leading a tour group in Israel and did not want to impose on him to disrupt the group's itinerary to come home for the funeral. She was also not sure if he could make last-minute arrangements to get back in time, hence the wording in her fax. In the end, she was glad that he made it.

The Jewish tradition was always to bury the dead, never to cremate the body. Henry was buried in a Jewish cemetery that catered to all segments of Judaism from the ultra-Orthodox to the secular. His corpse was dressed in normal clothing and laid in an airtight coffin, which was then placed inside a double vault above the ground. The other side was reserved for his wife who would someday be laid to rest next to him.

Because of the alienation experienced by all of Henry's children due to his terrible temper, not a single one was moved at his funeral. By nature, Arnold, in his own words, did "not emote," and was brought up in an environment where he kept his feelings inside, with no outward emotional response. Inwardly, though, he mourned over his father's eternally lost spiritual state.

```
My father died an unbeliever. It would be tempting to find
a way out for him, and I have seen believers begin to make
allowances upon losing an unbelieving parent. I have seen
others turn around to deny the reality of an eternally
lost condition. I have seen some lose their faith. My own
faith is not shaken, for I have seen and experienced God's
grace too many times and in too many adversities for me to
begin questioning Him now. (Yes, Job, though He slay me,
yet will I trust Him). Nor can I begin to try to twist the
Scriptures to make it easier for my father, though God can
testify that my heart truly bleeds for him. My prayer now
```

is that my mother, two brothers, and four sisters might
come to know the Messiah.[47]

Standing there in the rain with his family members at the Jewish cemetery on that cold, dismal day in January 1992, Arnold experienced a deep anguish in his heart for their souls. He yearned for his mother and his siblings to come to faith in Messiah Jesus, so that they could spend eternity with the Lord. They all lived a very secular life and had no interest in the things of God. The two younger brothers, in particular, were patently antagonistic toward Arnold's belief in Jesus. It was only after he and Mary Ann moved to California that Arnold tried very tentatively to establish some kind of contact with his siblings. Most of his efforts to reach them with the Gospel message came to no avail.

One time when Arnold and Mary Ann were visiting his sister, Margaret, there was a slight lull in their conversation that opened up an opportune moment to share the Gospel. Normally, she wanted nothing to do with the Messiah. On that particular occasion, however, she appeared to be affected by what she had heard. Unfortunately, at that very moment, a neighbor came to the door to ask about something, which had no urgency and did not need to be asked at that point. Both Arnold and Mary Ann knew in their hearts that the spiritual enemy had come and snatched away the seed just planted. Their hearts were very heavy, knowing that such an opening with Margaret was extremely rare. Sadly, the chance did not come up again.

More than ever before, Arnold recognized the urgency of the mission of Ariel Ministries to help reconcile the Jewish people to their everlasting God the Father through His Son, Jesus the Messiah. *For other foundation can no man lay than that which is laid, which is Messiah Yeshua.* (I Corinthians 3:11) It was sobering and frightening that once a person died, it was simply too late to make a decision about the Messiah. Casting his mind back over the years, Arnold recalled that the last time his father would have heard the complete Gospel message clearly presented was the day after Christmas in 1990, a little over a year before he died.

Arnold had the privilege of appearing on a televised show called "Praise the Lord," a Trinity Broadcasting Network program hosted by Hal Lindsey, a

---

[47] Excerpt: *Ariel Ministries Newsletter*, Spring 1992

Gentile believer and author. Hal had a great love and burden for Israel and led many Jewish people to the Lord, including Arnold's seminary friend, Barry Leventhal. It was an open forum to discuss the work of Ariel Ministries in evangelism and discipleship of the Jews, Camp Shoshanah, and the intensive five-week Israel Study Tours. Arnold focused on messianic prophecy and other topics, highlighting the issue of anti-Semitism and gave his personal testimony, all the while presenting the Gospel. Hal Lindsey graciously referred to Arnold as "the number one authority on the subject of Israel." Aired live on the 26th of December 1990, millions watched the show, constituting the single largest audience of Arnold's public ministry, providing Ariel with more exposure than it ever had before. As a result, the Ariel Home Office was inundated with a deluge of phone calls and an avalanche of letters from people all over the country wanting to know more about the ministry.

It was evident that the show had reached and impacted multitudes of lives. Henry was one of the nationwide viewers that day.

> My father "just happened" to be flipping through the
> channels when, to his surprise, he tuned in to his son. He
> called my mother to the T.V. and watched the entire show.
> Besides my part, Hal Lindsey gave a very clear
> presentation of the Gospel from Isaiah 53. My father heard
> it all. But when the interview was over, he turned the set
> off and did not speak to my mother for two weeks (his way
> of rejecting my message). As I view it now, God seemed to
> give my father one last chance to hear the Gospel clearly,
> partly from his own first-born son. But he again
> apparently chose to reject, and I cannot fault God for
> that. A year later, exactly, he went into the hospital and
> shortly thereafter passed away. And, sadly, there is no
> reunion awaiting us in Heaven.[48]

ON THE EL AL FLIGHT BACK TO ISRAEL, Arnold finally had time to collect his thoughts. Henry's death was so sudden, so unexpected. Arnold had hoped and prayed that his father would hear the Gospel message one last time and

---

[48] Excerpt: *Ariel Ministries Newsletter*, Spring 1992

choose to believe in Jesus as the Jewish Messiah before he breathed his last, but this was not to be.

It seemed so ironic that all of Arnold's early knowledge of the Scriptures had come from his father alone, instilling in him a love and zeal for the Bible that never once waned since the age of four. Thirty years later, that same passion had led him to found and establish Ariel Ministries. Arnold tried to picture his father's last moments, replaying the scene in his mind.

> My father had a sixth sense, if danger of death faced the
> family. About one year ago, he had a dream in which he saw
> several members of the family. But only one was distinct:
> his brother, Yehoshua. In that dream, Yehoshua spoke to
> him in Yiddish, saying, "It's all right, Chaim, my life is
> just beginning." My father took that dream to mean that
> Yehoshua was going to die. Two days later, he did. When my
> father first entered the hospital for what was to be a
> somewhat routine bypass surgery… he told a nurse, "I am
> going to die." Shortly thereafter, he slipped into a coma.
> My father had a sense when physical danger was approaching
> and used it more than once to save himself. How I mourn
> that he did not have a sixth sense to warn him of his
> spiritual danger, so that he could save himself by faith
> in his Messiah.[49]

The Bible clearly states: *For the wages of sin is death; but the free gift of God is eternal life in Messiah Yeshua our Lord.* (Romans 6:23) Because of sin, mankind is spiritually separated from God. But in His love and mercy, God made complete provision for the redemption of mankind through the death of His beloved Son, Jesus the Messiah, who shed His blood on the cross at Calvary. It is up to each individual to acknowledge and receive God's forgiveness, in order to be reconciled back to Him through the substitutionary death of Jesus, for *…apart from shedding of blood there is no remission.* (Hebrews 9:22b)

Henry had been exposed to the Gospel and had heard the message of redemption very clearly presented regarding the one and only way to God through Jesus the Messiah:

---

[49] Excerpt: *Ariel Ministries Newsletter*, Spring 1992

I am the way, and the truth, and the life: no one comes unto the Father, but by Me. (John 14:6b) *And in none other is there salvation: for neither is there any other name under heaven, that is given among men, wherein we must be saved.* (Acts 4:12) *Today, oh that ye would hear His voice! Harden not your heart.* (Psalm 95:7b-8a)

Yet mere days before his death, Henry still appeared to have rejected the message. Having chosen not to receive this unfathomable gift of eternal life, he passed away without the Lord into a lost eternity forever. Arnold had to come to terms with the reality of his father's ultimate destiny. He could find his peace only in trusting God: *...shall not the Judge of all the earth do right?* (Genesis 18:25b)

When the plane landed safely in Tel-Aviv, Arnold was able to rejoin the Project Joshua group, grateful to the Lord that he could fulfill his responsibilities as their study tour guide. Because the group's street activities had been scheduled on alternate days, they simply continued to conduct their evangelism work on consecutive days during Arnold's brief absence. Upon his return, he was able to easily make up for the missed touring days by taking them around for several days in a row. Thus, the group got to see all the places originally intended.

After the newsletter containing the article about his father's passing was sent out, the Ariel Home Office received an outpouring of love and condolences for Arnold in his time of deep grief. The staff was reminded of the verses in II Corinthians 1:3-4:

Blessed be the God and Father of our Lord Messiah Yeshua, the Father of mercies and God of all comfort; who comforts us in all our affliction, that we may be able to comfort them that are in any affliction, through the comfort wherewith we ourselves are comforted of God.

One letter was very touching:

```
Your recent newsletter recalled to mind when my dad died
without knowing the Lord. I spent the last two weeks of my
dad's life by his side as he was dying from cancer. Up to
the end, my dad stated he didn't need a Savior… I just
kept thinking there must have been something different I
could have said to change his mind. Now, I realize he had
his chance and chose not to follow… I praise God that He
```

saw fit to allow my mother and stepfather to come to a
saving knowledge of our Lord Jesus.[50]

With a busy year ahead, Arnold focused on the ministry work at hand and
looked to the Lord for strength. His father's salvation had been a constant
subject of prayer in his daily walk with the Lord, even up to the last minute.
For decades, Arnold had developed his own system of keeping track of all his
prayer needs and requests. On his desk in the office, he kept a little recipe box,
containing a stack of three-by-five inch cards. On each separate card, he wrote
out the prayer requests or needs of the ministry, the missionaries, the office
staff, the supporters, his friends, his family, and any other items that the Lord
would lay upon his heart, also noting down pertinent details of each situation.

Every day, he would take a few of those cards in rotating order and pray
through the needs, thus ensuring that he thoroughly covered the issue in
prayer at least once a month, if not more frequently. Once a prayer was
answered, he would remove the card. Quite often, the answers were delayed,
and he would continue to prevail in prayer. In the case of his father, the
answer had come, but not in the way that Arnold had hoped or desired. Sadly,
it was time to remove that card from the box.

In constant communion with the Lord, Arnold did not carve out huge
chunks of time specifically to pray, but rather prayed in his heart while
jogging, driving, or traveling. Conscious of God's sovereignty, omniscience,
and omnipotence, he shared his thoughts and heart with his ever-present best
Friend. On the days that he was at the Home Office, he prayed with the staff at
their meetings. A very private person, Arnold did not share much about his
personal prayer life. Nevertheless, it was clear that he understood the
paramount importance of prayer for the smooth functioning of the ministry
and the growth of his own spiritual walk. Arnold lived out his beliefs in daily
life and upheld everything to God in continuous prayer, including the
salvation of his mother and his siblings.

---

[50] Excerpts: *Ariel Letter*, March 1992

Expanding Horizons

In the 1990s, new areas opened up abroad for Arnold's teaching. The president of a German Bible school, who had read about Arnold through some of Ariel's translated materials, invited him to come and teach for one week in mid-January 1990 and also to speak as one among a number of presenters during a ten-day conference on Israel at a local church. New contacts were made, and Arnold was asked to come back to teach at various churches around the country. Thus, he returned in early 1992 on a three-week teaching trip, after which Germany became a regular destination once every even-numbered year. His subsequent itineraries ranged from one to two and a half months, taking place in the winter months early in the year. On his trip in January to February 1994, Arnold also spoke for the very first time in Switzerland at a church meeting arranged for him in the Swiss-German part of the country.

In the autumn of 1993, a British Jewish believer contacted the Ariel Home Office to inquire about bringing Arnold on a speaking tour through England, which she would arrange for him. Part of a young and dynamic, close-knit co-ed fellowship of believers who had stumbled upon Arnold's teaching four years earlier, the group had been voraciously studying the Bible through the Ariel resource materials. Arnold never ceased to be amazed at how some of his teaching materials found their way overseas. The timing of her contact was like a special personal gift from the Lord, as Arnold had just celebrated his fiftieth birthday.

Thus a year later in late November 1994, Arnold taught in England. Interest was very high, and he ended up with a long list of contact addresses plus a generous freewill offering to take back. On the same trip, a man asked if Arnold could return to the U.K. every two years to teach for a month, which he was more than willing to do. This man subsequently became the sole distributor of the Ariel written resource materials and got partially involved in setting up Arnold's future speaking itineraries, though he did not fulfill the role of an affiliate or a branch. Separate arrangements were later made with another organization to distribute the Ariel teaching tapes in the U.K.

After Arnold's 1990 itinerary around New Zealand and Australia, he began teaching there every odd-numbered year starting in 1991. During the mass exodus of the Jewry from the Soviet Union starting in the early 1990s, many

Jews chose to immigrate to Australia. In view of the timing and the unusual way in which the doors were opened to Arnold's teaching "Down Under," it became clear that the Lord was preparing the Gentile believers in those countries to study the Word from a Jewish perspective to be better equipped to share the Gospel message with the former Soviet Jews who now lived in their area.

At one of the conferences in Australia in 1991, Arnold had an interesting "reunion" of sorts with a Soviet Jewish woman who had first heard his teaching in Ladispoli, Italy, the preceding year. Shortly thereafter, this Jewess and her son and daughter-in-law all accepted *Yeshua* as their Messiah, and the entire family immigrated to Australia. It was so good for Arnold to see her growing in her spiritual knowledge and faith.

OVER THE FIRST HALF OF THE 1990S, new volunteer missionary workers joined the ministry in rapid succession. After many years of being closed, the branch in Seattle, Washington, was revived in mid-1993. In the spring of 1995, an older couple volunteered to set up a home fellowship outreach to the Jews in Athens, Georgia, under the Ariel umbrella. Jacques and Sharon Gabizon launched a new branch in Montreal, a predominantly French-speaking city in Quebec, Canada, in early 1996. By spring, a fully-fledged Ariel mission branch was opened in Brooklyn, New York City. In the summer, a second missionary staff couple moved from northern California to join the team. Furthermore, Arnold's itinerary within the United States progressively widened, bringing him as far away as Alaska in early December 1993. A ministry to inmates across the country unexpectedly evolved, and in early 1996, Ariel Ministries finally entered cyberspace, providing more efficient communication between the Home Office and the missionaries in various branches via E-mail. This opened up another avenue for those wanting to ask Arnold questions on the Bible or on theological points. The turn-around time became much shorter and more economical than using the postal service.

Despite all the progress, Ariel Ministries continued to experience financial uncertainties. Additionally, a massive earthquake struck about two hours' drive away in June 1992, causing tremors as far as Tustin. Within a mere fifteen months in the fall of 1993, a huge blazing fire swept past. In January 1994, another big earthquake hit the area. By fall 1996, enormous wildfires roared across southern California, leaving a trail of destruction behind.

Thankfully, the Ariel Home Office and the staff's homes were spared, and their families were all kept safe.

After moving to California, Mary Ann was able to maintain a close relationship with Arnold's mother and went to visit her often. On one occasion in the early spring of 1995, she was surprised to see Adele reading the Reader's Digest's *Who's Who in the Bible* all on her own initiative! It had always been Arnold's earnest desire to see all his family members come to faith in Jesus the Messiah. However, whenever he broached the subject, his mother, a self-professed atheist, would invariably shut him down. There was simply no way for him to get through to her. He faithfully continued to pray for an opening to share the Gospel message. Perhaps, this was the start of a softening on his mother's part to hear the truth about the Jewish Messiah. Only time would tell.

Fond Farewell

During the third and final week of the 1996 summer discipleship program at Camp Shoshanah, Arnold received sudden notification that his beloved teacher and mentor, Reverend Burl Haynie, had just been promoted to glory at the age of eighty-one. Reverend Tomlin from the Pillar of Fire Church of Zarephath, New Jersey, had phoned Arnold with the news. It was at this church where Burl, a member since late 1972, still taught the Scriptures through the last several years of his active ministry. The funeral was to be held in Amarillo, Texas, where Burl's son, Harold, had moved him the preceding year due to his failing health. Although Arnold was busy teaching the intensive program in upstate New York, there was no way he would miss the opportunity to be there to bid his beloved mentor a fond farewell. Even with such short notice and all the airlines booked with a heavy summer schedule, the Lord ensured that a seat was available to get him there in time for the service.

During the long flight to Amarillo and well into the wee hours of the night in his motel room, Arnold reviewed his memories of the long, thirty-nine year association with his teacher, who had become such an influential part of his life. In his shared farewell service with Reverend Tomlin, Arnold wanted to present a meaningful message to the people who would be gathered at the funeral home. For the first time, he would meet Burl's daughter, Janelle, and his brother, Firman—people whom, until then, he had only heard about.

As the body of Burl Haynie lay in the casket next to where Arnold was standing, he gave a touching tribute in honor and remembrance of his beloved teacher and mentor. He chronicled their association—how they first met, the five-year Memory Camp for young Jewish believers, the discipleship he had received one-on-one, and how much his mentor's teachings had molded his life. Arnold observed how Mr. Haynie had applied the lessons of Scripture to his own daily life in practical ways, thus exemplifying for him how to live by faith through his college years. His teacher had manifested godliness and self-control. Through working at the printing department under him, Arnold learned his lesson in work ethics and to consistently set aside time to study God's Word every day.

Although the frequency of their contacts had decreased in the subsequent years after college, Burl Haynie was always there for Arnold's special occasions. In addition, whenever Arnold was speaking somewhere nearby in New Jersey, Burl would always make the effort to come. Later, after they had both left the ABMJ, they still managed to see each other once a year, when Burl would visit the camp up in the Adirondacks. Over the years, Arnold truly felt that this Gentile believer proved to be a father figure provided to him by the Lord, when his own father had rejected him.

Arnold also reflected upon the wonderful legacy that Burl Haynie had left behind. First and foremost, Arnold was still using the American Standard Version of 1901—affectionately dubbed the "Haynie Bible"—to study and to teach the Word. He also attributed Ariel Ministries' foundational principles of evangelism and discipleship to what his mentor had taught him. From small beginnings, the ministry was now operating through a number of branches in the U.S. with a presence in Canada, parts of Europe, and Israel. Finally, Camp Shoshanah was a result of Burl Haynie and Rose Burnham's shared vision of its purpose as a Jewish Bible camp. Over the years, it was Burl who had unswervingly prayed in faith for the fulfillment of this dream, and Arnold in his own words "had long ago been bitten by the Haynie vision."

On the flight back from the funeral, Arnold spent more time thinking about the last year of Burl Haynie's life. To make sure he was available when needed for anything, Arnold had instructed his office staff to stay in the loop about his mentor. They did a good job and informed him when the reverend was moved back to Texas, after his physical and mental health started deteriorating with the onset of Alzheimer's disease.

I felt that if I did not see him soon, I might never see him again. After camp in 1995, I arranged for a trip to Amarillo just to spend the day with him. He still recognized me at that time. I took him and his son out for a Texas steak dinner, then, spent a good bit of time with him back at his nursing home apartment. There were long periods of silence and some conversation as we reminisced about the people we knew, with him asking me about those he had discipled... (Bob Futoran was always the first one he asked me about). Finally, it was time for me to leave. As I stood up to say good-bye, I'll never forget his last words to me: "It seems you and I are always saying good-bye." I said to him, "We will see each other again." I felt even then that I would never see him again in this life. But I believed what I said—I will see him again, but it will be in glory.[51]

In the early days, Burl was instrumental in the initial work done on the campsite in the Adirondacks during the years of the Memory Camp. While he had witnessed many improvements later on, he did not get to see the number of new buildings constructed in recent years at Camp Shoshanah. He would have been totally elated to see the beautiful, brand new lecture hall that the camp supervisor, Gary Demers, had completed just prior to the 1996 summer session. It was aptly named "The Burl Haynie Lecture Hall," in honor of Burl's vision for a Jewish Bible camp.

Arnold's dream was to someday set up a yearlong Bible school that would accommodate resident students in their intensive study of the Holy Scriptures within a Jewish frame of reference. To ensure that the future of this dream was kept alive, Burl Haynie, in the early part of 1995, donated to Ariel Ministries a total of two hundred acres of land that he owned adjacent to the camp property, which had been gifted to him by Rose Burnham. Camp Shoshanah thus occupied 465 acres in total. The original 265 acres was still

---

[51] Excerpts: *Ariel Ministries Newsletter*, Fall 1996

317

owned by the CEEA, the Clinton-Essex Evangelical Association, from which Ariel Ministries was leasing the property. Now, with the additional tract of land from Burl, the ministry could look forward to further developments and expansions in the future.

Arnold was very grateful to the Lord for having provided him with such a wonderful mentor, teacher, and father figure. Twice before, he had been nominated as one of the nation's "Outstanding Young Men." Both times came as a complete surprise to Arnold, and he had no idea who might have made the submissions. Thinking back, it seemed possible that it could have been Mr. Haynie, who was always so supportive of him, but there was never any hint or clue either way. One thing that Arnold wished he and his teacher had done together was to go on a tour to the Middle East, just as they had planned in 1968, visiting the sites of the seven ancient churches located in Turkey, the site of ancient Babylon, and so forth. His wedding to Mary Ann had taken place during that time instead. Afterwards, somehow there never seemed to be another opportunity available to find a common time to go.

All of Ariel's Bible teachings were still based on the "Golden Rule of Interpretation," studying the Word in its proper context without speculation. As such, his own book, *The Footsteps of the Messiah: A Study of the Sequence of Prophetic Events*, was dedicated to Burl Haynie. Arnold personally presented it to him as a hardbound edition, when it was first published in 1983.

Burl Haynie had finished his course well, keeping the faith while eager for the Lord's appearing. Though Arnold missed his beloved mentor, he also experienced a deep sense of joy, knowing that Mr. Haynie had lived a spiritually fruitful life and was now home in the glorious presence of the Lord. All the wonderful memories of his teacher would live on in his heart, and Arnold would carry on with the legacy that Burl had left behind.

Like that of other believers, Arnold's experience in grieving for the loss of a loved one who passed away as a believer in Jesus the Messiah was very different from grieving for the one who died as an unbeliever. He felt an underlying sense of profound assurance and security in knowing that the believing loved one departed to be with the Lord, which was not the case with the unbeliever who passed into a lost eternity, banished from the presence of the Lord forever. The contrast was clearly evident between Burl's funeral and that of his father's. A note of triumph underscored the reverend's passing, celebrating his life of submission and obedience to God, whereas Henry's death was mourned for its hopeless desolation. For the two men, accepting *Yeshua Ha'Mashiach* or rejecting Him made all the difference in this world and in eternity.

PART VI

~ Passage ~

Blessed be the name of God for ever and ever;
for wisdom and might are His.
And He changes the times and the seasons; …

(Daniel 2:20b-21a)

P rior to going overseas on his long speaking tour during the last two months of 1996, Arnold was comforted to know that Mary Ann would be safe in their home in Irvine. For a number of months now, the house next door had been up for sale. Initially, they hoped that one of Arnold's sisters would purchase it and live next door to them, but she did not want to move to their area. Hence, they prayed for the Lord to send them good neighbors, people who would not be antagonistic toward them for serving in Jewish ministry. To their relief, the house was eventually sold to a nice, young couple with no children, who turned out to be ideal next-door neighbors.

As usual, Arnold's travel schedule in the fall of 1996 had been very hectic right after Camp Shoshanah—teaching the Scriptures in many states around the country as well as in Canada—before heading off to England, Ireland, and Germany. After a very brief Christmas break at home and further travels in the U.S., followed by a month-long teaching tour in Hawaii from mid-January to mid-February 1997, it was soon time to fly to New Zealand and Australia in April.

Unfortunately, Arnold witnessed a very disturbing situation during the entire trip "Down Under." The Toronto Phenomenon had been sweeping through New Zealand with a vengeance, taking the believers by storm, dividing churches, splitting families, and causing general mayhem. Believers were turning away by droves from sound doctrine and looking only to "spiritual experiences" as evidence of their faith. Lacking knowledge of the whole Word while taking a verse such as First Corinthians 8:1b out of context, some wrongly claimed that knowledge of the Word would puff up believers. Those who had once been keen learners of the Bible quickly lost interest in studying the Scriptures. Arnold was disheartened to encounter such strong opposition to his expository teaching coming from the leaders as well as from the lay people of the churches. In general, churches in New Zealand were very liberal and denied the fundamentals of the faith; others were caught up in "the movement." Hence, many believers had no recourse but to leave the church and gather in small house groups to study the Word of God, while searching for ways to be exposed to solid Bible teaching.

The situation in Australia was no better. There, too, people had been burned as a result of the Toronto Phenomenon and other extremist movements. The spiritual state of the Australian churches was in a lamentable condition. Just as in New Zealand, many believers had fallen away from the serious study of

God's Word and were caught up in the "experience of the Lord," displaying very strange and outlandish behaviors. Arnold felt grieved to witness the far-reaching effects and influences of the worst that North America had to offer.

BACK IN TUSTIN, THE PRESSURE ON THE ARIEL STAFF was mounting from the increasing workload associated with the ministry's rapid growth and expansion in the recent years. With the advent of the Internet and plans for a fully computerized system at the Home Office, an enormous load of extra work landed on the staff's shoulders. All the published books plus current ones in the pipeline had to be typed into the new system for ease of editing in the future. This resulted in a massive amount of laborious work in addition to the daily administrative support that the staff had to provide for the missionary workers. The stress from the overload reached almost breaking point.

It was obvious that the operating procedures previously put into place were no longer effective for the current situation. Twice before—once in 1994 and again in 1996—similar scenarios had arisen. Each time, Arnold had stepped in to address the issues, putting certain work procedures into place for more efficiency. However, the sheer volume of extra daily work consistently overwhelmed the staff. This led to other internal issues at the ministry with more serious repercussions. Thus, after much prayer and in-depth deliberation, the Ariel board of directors concluded that a complete reorganization was necessary to meet the ministry's future growth trends. Except for Roxanne's role, all the other positions were redefined, creating major redundancies, shocking the staff. This sudden and comprehensive restructuring of the ministry's operations became an agonizing exercise for everyone involved.

In parallel, there were numerous circumstantial changes in the field among the missionary staff and volunteer workers. The Ariel mission branch in Brooklyn was discontinued; the volunteer worker of the branch in Seattle decided to move on; the older volunteer couple in Athens, Georgia, withdrew from their service primarily on account of health factors; and the Ariel branch in Portland closed down when the missionary worker transferred to the Ariel Home Office. Barry Leventhal, who in recent years had stepped into the role of co-director, saw this as an appropriate time to move on. With health issues cropping up lately, traveling to teach on behalf of Ariel Ministries had become an increasing hardship for him.

The resulting transition, though necessary, was especially painful and anguishing for Arnold. Alongside him, Mary Ann also suffered tremendous inner pain as she witnessed all the upheavals taking place in the ministry. Over the years, she had formed friendships with the staff members at the Home Office—in particular, with one individual there. While Mary Ann's loyalties lay with Arnold and Ariel Ministries, it pained her deeply to lose her friends as a result of the turmoil. Turning to the Lord, she found solace in the words of Messiah Jesus: *In the world ye have tribulation: but be of good cheer; I have overcome the world.* (John 16:33b) She also sought comfort from Ruth Wardell, who helped her to shift her focus onto the One, whom she and the ministry were serving. With more than fifty years of effective ministry experience, Ruth wisely pointed out that none of what was happening came as a surprise to the Lord and that changing and adapting to new situations while maintaining a heart of humility and service was an integral part of one's personal spiritual growth. Mary Ann wrote a personal letter to all the Ariel prayer supporters and asked them to specifically pray for the ministry during this challenging period—that it would be more effective, more efficient, and more extensive once the new organizational structure was put into place.

Throughout all the years of the ministry's existence, there had been difficulties and challenges within the organization from long periods of financial leanness. Though deeply grieved that most of the workers had to be let go, Arnold was nevertheless thankful that he was able to maintain a friendship with some of the former staff members still to this day.

Although major, sweeping organizational changes often came with their associated pain and disruptiveness, the end goal of having a suitable infrastructure to support the missionaries and a more efficient operating environment for the Home Office staff longer term, was well worth the difficult interim period. As Arnold learned over the years, those who got involved in Jewish ministry were, without exception, inevitably subjected to many trials and tribulations. Yet, Jesus the Messiah had overcome the world and could be counted on and trusted to see the ministry through to a new stage of growth. Arnold was fervently grateful for the Lord's protection over the ministry through these tumultuous times. Having had firsthand experience of His guidance and provision in the past, Arnold knew that he could rely on God's wisdom and unchanging faithfulness to support the difficult restructuring of the organization, the forming of the new office team, and the planning of Ariel Ministries' future expansion.

Triple Celebrations

The year 1998 opened with Arnold traveling once again to Germany and Switzerland in the winter months of January and February to teach. He anticipated a busy but promising year ahead in the next phase of the ministry's growth. With the revamped infrastructure in place and new support staff on board, there was an air of expectancy at the Ariel Home Office to see what God would do next. Three special milestones were coming up this year—the fiftieth anniversary of the birth of Israel, Arnold and Mary Ann's thirtieth wedding anniversary, and Camp Shoshanah's twenty-fifth season—all blessings for which to thank the Lord. Arnold was very excited that he would be back in *Eretz Yisrael* to lead his study tour in late spring and to witness the nation's celebrations.

Even with the *Intifada* uprising in the West Bank and the Gaza Strip in 1990, things had been relatively calm during his long tour in 1992 and his short one in 1993. His 1994 tour saw seven repeaters from several previous trips, which felt almost like a joyous "old homecoming." Arnold was grateful to the Lord for the rare opportunities that opened up for him to teach the Word at local messianic congregations. Most of the assemblies were barely self-supporting and did not have the financial means to bring in speakers from outside. Since Ariel Ministries operated on the principle of never charging any honorariums or asking for reimbursements of travel expenses, Arnold was available to teach whenever he was leading a tour. Doing so did not place any extra financial burden on Ariel. On his 1994 trip, he taught at several messianic assemblies—two in Jerusalem, one in Tel-Aviv, and one in Tiberias.

Furthermore, two members of my family requested the Hebrew version of *Jesus Was a Jew* and this took me by surprise. On past trips, I took copies with me, but these relatives were not interested; this time, then I did not bring any with me, only to find out that two family members wanted them. I had to go to a bookstore and purchase copies of my own book in order to be able to present it to them. I would appreciate your prayers that both will read, understand, and come to faith. [52]

In mid-June 1995, a weeklong international gathering of the Lausanne Consultation on Jewish Evangelism, held every four years, took place for the very first time in Jerusalem. Arnold was thrilled to fellowship with about one hundred and seventy workers from various messianic ministries around the world, including many from Israel itself. After that, he led a three-week study tour around the Land. In Haifa, he was featured as the keynote speaker at a Jewish-Arab reconciliation conference, part of a weekend seminar, sponsored by *Musalaha*, a ministry headquartered in Jerusalem. Based on an Arabic word meaning "forgiveness" and "reconciliation," *Musalaha* dedicated its efforts to fostering reconciliation between the Jews and Arabs through Messiah Jesus. Arnold's topic, "What the Bible Teaches about Peace," presented to more than one hundred Jewish and Arab believers, was well received.

Over a ten-year association, Arnold had cultivated a friendship with the founder of *Musalaha*, who was also the academic dean of the Bethlehem Bible College, a training ground for Arab-Palestinian Christians. A regular highlight of the five-week study tours was a visit to the college to expose the group to an Arab-Christian perspective right there in the West Bank. The Arab-Palestinian students always appreciated the groups' visits.

Following the peace treaty between Jordan and Israel toward the end of 1994 when the borders were opened, Arnold added an optional leg of four days to the five-week itinerary starting in 1996. This allowed a visit to the sites in Jordan, including the famous city of Petra, also known as Bozrah in the Bible—the ancient city carved into the rose-colored sandstones—where Arnold believed that Jesus the Messiah would return.

In the autumn of 1994, Arnold's new book, *A Study Guide of Israel: Historical & Geographical*, [53] was published. An exhaustive, unique guide in its genre, it comprised three main sections—the first with basic information about the modern State of Israel and a breakdown of the historical and archeological periods of the Land; the second with the six geographical

---

[52] Excerpt: July 1994 "Thank-You" letter

[53] Today, this book is known under the new title, *An Historical and Geographical Study Guide of Israel – With a Supplement on Jordan.*

regions as outlined by Moses in Deuteronomy 1:6-8; the third with an alphabetical listing of all the specific sites plus their associated facts and events. Arnold dedicated the volume to past and present members of the Fruchtenbaum family and poignantly listed the individual names of those who died in Poland before World War II, those who perished in the Holocaust, those who survived and subsequently immigrated to Israel plus their children, and to his parents who had come to America.

Now in 1998, Arnold would be right there on the ground to witness the jubilant celebrations to mark the fiftieth anniversary of the birth of the State of Israel on the 14th of May 1948, a special moment in the young nation's history. During the span of those fifty years, although the neighboring Arab countries invaded Israel numerous times in an attempt to defeat it, God's protective hand was over the Holy Land.

For the first time, a two-week English-German study tour was organized to take place in early May prior to the regular, long English tour. While Arnold spoke in English, someone else interpreted in German. Two days after the German tour ended, the usual intensive five-week Israel Study Tour began. Ariel's new Eastern Field Representative from Lancaster, Pennsylvania, John Metzger, had the privilege of participating. The group walked through the streets of Jerusalem, visited the *Yad Vashem*—the official Israeli memorial to the Holocaust victims—and passed by the Temple Mount. They visited Hezekiah's Tunnel, still covered knee-deep in spring water, and the Pool of Siloam. They saw the spots where David killed Goliath, where he hid from King Saul, where Samson lived, and where Joshua gained victory over the kings of the south in his conquest of the Land. They traveled to the Hills of Nazareth, Mount Tabor, the Hill of Moreh, and the Hills of Samaria. They visited Mount Gilboa where Gideon fought the Midianites and where Deborah and Barak fought Sisera. At Mount Carmel, the group pictured how Elijah contested the false prophets of Baal. They viewed the Tel of Megiddo, the Tel of Dan, Mount Hermon and much, much more, hardly able to catalog all the places in their minds.

There were also relaxing moments with a less hectic pace, when they could take a dip in the Mediterranean Sea, or float on the Dead Sea. For many, it was a life-changing experience to be in *Eretz Yisrael*. As on the previous trip in 1996, participants could choose to travel for just the first three weeks out of the five, or also join the optional leg of four days to Jordan at the end of the five weeks. Many chose this latter option.

As soon as the tour ended, Arnold flew over to the U.K. at the start of July 1998 for two and a half weeks. He taught at a conference in England, where the attendees had a high interest in God's plan for Israel. A Jewish believer there had come to faith in Messiah Jesus, in part, from reading Ariel's literature! Arnold also spoke during a Sunday service at a church fellowship nearby, where the pastor and several congregants had been listening to Arnold's tapes since the late 1980s. The highlight was a first-ever two-week Bible camp held in the Malverns, England, organized by a British believer, a former attendee of Camp Shoshanah. Participants came from many corners of the U.K., relishing the freedom found in the Lord. Their eyes were opened to the depth of meaning of the Scriptures taught from a Jewish perspective. It was a joy for them to be released from past legalistic bondages and to be truly free in Messiah Jesus.

This year was special for Arnold and Mary Ann in a very personal way, as it was their thirtieth wedding anniversary on the 29th of June 1998! On that very day soon after the Six-Day War in 1967 exactly one year before their wedding day, the Old City of Jerusalem was officially united with West Jerusalem to become one city, now marking thirty-one years of unification. Because Arnold was away overseas until past mid-July, he and Mary Ann postponed their anniversary celebration to a later date. Usually, they went to a very high-end French restaurant or something similar to celebrate their special milestones. So much had transpired in the thirty years of their marriage. Through all the ups and downs, the joys and sorrows, the planned and the unexpected, one thing remained constant in their life and that was their love for the Lord, for each other, and for God's Chosen People.

BACK IN THE U.S., Arnold went straight up to the Adirondacks to celebrate Camp Shoshanah's twenty-fifth season of its discipleship program! There was a distinctive international flavor. For the first time, a Hungarian couple, Ivan and Rita Nagy—on their way home to Budapest from New York—attended the camp. Special moments of thanksgiving and festivities were sprinkled throughout the three weeks of the English-speaking camp, culminating in a scrumptious feast for the Friday evening *Shabbat* meal, plus a most wonderful and totally unexpected surprise. A pastor from the CEEA, Clinton-Essex Evangelical Association, presented Arnold with the deed to the Camp Shoshanah property, making Ariel Ministries the legal owner of the 265 acres of land! Since leasing the property from the Association in 1979 for one dollar per year, Ariel Ministries had invested a substantial amount of funds in upgrading the property. The CEEA recognized this effort and felt that it was time to pass on the ownership of the property directly to Ariel Ministries, selling it for the grand sum of one dollar! This fulfilled Rose Burnham's desire to see the campsite used for Jewish ministry.

The CEEA could not have chosen a better time to present the deed. Combined with the 200 acres that Burl Haynie had gifted to the ministry earlier in 1995, Camp Shoshanah now comprised a total of 465 acres of land, completely under the legal ownership of Ariel Ministries. What a way to mark the twenty-fifth milestone of Camp Shoshanah! As Arnold reflected upon the camp's humble beginnings, he marveled at God's faithful provision throughout all the years. Despite the ministry's tough financial struggles in some years when things were so touch-and-go, the discipleship program at Camp Shoshanah had somehow managed to carry on annually without fail. Arnold's heart overflowed with immense gratitude to the Lord for His great and unfailing mercies and care.

In the fall, Arnold experienced yet another blessing. Two years previously in the spring of 1996, the tape series, *Messianic Christology*, was transcribed into written form by one of Ariel's supporters in Scotland, who freely volunteered his time and effort. The book included a comprehensive study of the thirty-one passages—all essential Old Testament prophecies—concerning the First Coming of the Messiah, plus the Hebrew texts of the relevant passages in the study. Arnold felt so rewarded, when the book was published in the early fall of 1998. Today, it is sold under the title, *Ha-Mashiach, The Messiah of the Hebrew Scriptures*.

Tracing Family Roots

Although Arnold had been back to Poland once before in his adult life to visit his father's homeland, he had never returned to Russia, the land of his own birth. In the spring of 1999, after an extended period of ministry in Hawaii, Arnold was booked to teach for three consecutive months in five different countries, starting with Russia. It just so happened that he had a rare five-day break immediately prior to his busy itinerary, so he decided to begin his long journey by revisiting Poland on a personal trip within that window.

During his first trip in 1980, the country was still under communism. The many rundown buildings reflected the austerity of the era following World War II. In 1989, when democracy won over communism, Poland began to enjoy the freedoms of a capitalist society that existed prior to the war. Now in 1999, after ten years of a free market enterprise, many changes were visible, notably the number of new, modern-style buildings in the big cities. No longer were any damaged structures still standing from the days of World War II. The atmosphere of oppression appeared to have lifted, and an air of contained optimism seemed to permeate the society. Great strides had been made in improving the standard of living.

On this particular trip, Arnold's cousin, Batya, about five years his junior, flew in from Israel to join him. Though born in Poland, she held no recollection of her life there, as she had left at a very young age. Having heard so many stories from her family and relatives about their life in Pultusk, she had always wanted to see those places with her own eyes. This was her first time back as an adult. Even after their move to Israel, her family kept on speaking Polish in their household alongside Hebrew. Arnold wished that his own parents had spoken Polish and Yiddish with him at home, after they had immigrated to America. Because Batya could communicate with the local Poles, her language skills were a great help to Arnold on this trip.

Upon arrival, they first checked into a hotel in Warsaw, which served as their base. They wanted to visit the Warsaw Jewish Cemetery, but unfortunately it was closed due to it being Passover week that year. Hence, Arnold's search for his great-grandfather's grave had to be postponed yet again to another trip. Early the next morning, they planned to drive a short distance north to their family's hometown of Pultusk. Arnold tried to get in contact with Mrs. P., the Polish Christian lady who had been very helpful to Arnold and Barry during their 1980 visit. However, his efforts turned up empty, as she had passed away.

BEFORE WORLD WAR II, over fifty-five percent of the local population of Pultusk was Jewish. Just prior to the Holocaust, approximately eight thousand three hundred Jews lived there. After the German Nazi invasion on the first of September 1939, about eighty-five percent of the town was destroyed, and the entire Jewish community of Pultusk was expelled several weeks later. The town then became incorporated into the annexed territories of Nazi-Germany and was renamed Ostenburg. After the war, the town reclaimed its former Polish name, Pultusk, but hardly a single Jew could be found living there. Since anti-Semitism continued to be rife in Poland even decades after World War II, only those Jews who really did not want to leave Poland were left by the end of the twentieth century, numbering around five or six thousand, about four thousand of whom were living in Warsaw. At the time of their visit, the population of Pultusk comprised 18,000 to 19,000 inhabitants.

Thanks to some contacts with one Gentile family who were business partners of my uncle, we were able to find what we were looking for. Thus, we found the home where my father and his brothers and sisters were raised. We found the synagogue where my great-grandfather taught, though it is now only an empty shell. We also found the Jewish schoolhouse where my family members attended. While the building is still intact, it is no longer the Jewish school it once was.[54]

The big two-story house on the main street by the Narew River, where Henry and his numerous siblings grew up, was rented from a Polish landlord whose family was very anti-Semitic at the time. Arnold and Batya also viewed a smaller house, rented from the same landlord, on the end of another street, where one of Henry's older married siblings had lived. They found the location of what used to be a *kosher* butcher shop, which they had heard so much about, and also located the actual grain mill that Arnold's uncle, Yaakov had once owned.

In many ways, it felt surreal for Arnold to be in Pultusk and actually see the neighborhood, which conjured up recollections of stories that his surviving relatives had recounted. A few of the tales about his great-grandfather, Baruch Simchah Fruchtenbaum, had gotten so embellished over time that they became rather far-fetched. Arnold wondered whether there was any kernel of truth in them at all, but they still remained as legends in the family to pass down to posterity.

---

[54] Excerpt: *On The Road*, September 1999

THE NEXT DAY, Arnold and Batya made their way down south to Treblinka. The proprietor, a young man serving both as a guide and an overseer of the site, took a special interest in them and showed them around all day on a private tour. Although no one could be certain of how or where those other Fruchtenbaum family members had perished, it was very likely that some of them would have been murdered in death camps like this one. It was such a senseless loss of life. A feeling of horror and rage swelled up inside Arnold, wrenching his heart. He wanted to cry out at this epic, unspeakable evil committed against God's Chosen People. No matter how many times he were to visit the extermination camps, the same sense of sheer horror at the heinous crimes against the Jewry would continue to grip his heart and be grimly etched in his mind.

After their poignant visit to Treblinka, Arnold and Batya were also meant to go to Auschwitz. Batya was too distraught and haunted by the trip to Treblinka with its unfathomable atrocities to even contemplate going. She simply could not face seeing yet another horrifying death camp, so she opted not to go. Arnold had been to Auschwitz before, so he also decided to forego the visit this time around.

> Though the trip was intended to be purely personal, I did have with me the name of a pastor with Jewish background in Warsaw. I called him, and he joined us for lunch on our last day. As it turns out, besides pastoring a good sized evangelical church, he also has a small messianic fellowship that meets on Friday nights for a messianic service to which a good number of unbelieving Jewish people attend, since there are few other options for Jewish people still in Poland. He asked me to come back and do a series; so the next time I return, it may be a ministry trip as well as a personal trip.[55]

Arnold and Batya were aware that after the Jews' expulsion from Pultusk, the Fruchtenbaum family had made their way to Vilna, in modern-day Lithuania, where they found refuge. When the Germans subsequently attacked the Soviet Union in mid-1941 and established a ghetto in Vilna a few months later, all the Jews including the Fruchtenbaum family were forced into that

---

[55] Excerpt: *On The Road*, September 1999

confining space. With the aid of local Lithuanians, the German Nazis systematically rounded up the Jewish men in large numbers from the ghetto, brought them to the Ponary Forest, about ten kilometers or six miles from the outskirts of the city of Vilna, and massacred them in cold blood. The forest area, once used for outings and picnics before the war, turned into a killing field. The local townspeople nearby could hear the shootings reverberating through the forest. It was highly probable that two of Arnold's uncles, Tzemach and Asher, as well as Yoseph—the husband of Chavah, one of Arnold's aunts—were shot dead in this way in the Ponary Forest.

Two years later in September 1943, with the final liquidation of the ghetto in Vilna, stronger men and women were herded onto railcars and transported to concentration camps in Estonia and Latvia to work at hard labor. Older men, weaker women, and children were loaded onto cattle cars and deported by rail to various extermination camps in German-occupied Poland, where they were put to death in the gas chambers. Tragically, some of the female Fruchtenbaum family members would have likely been sent to death camps like Treblinka or Sobibor, including Arnold's great-grandmother, Ittah Leah, aunties, Chavah and Adah, and two cousins, Gutkah and Frumkah. Somehow, it seemed ironic to Arnold that the final liquidation of the ghetto in Vilna was completed just a mere two days before his birth in Siberia on the 26th of September 1943. He felt deeply grieved that those family members who perished never lived to see the defeat of the German Nazis or the new life that some of the other surviving siblings eventually found in Israel. What anguished him the most was the fact that none of them ever knew Jesus the Messiah.

When certain archives of the World War II era were opened to the public, Arnold wrote to two different museums in Poland in early December 1990, to find out any information or records on individuals with the Fruchtenbaum name. About six weeks later in January 1991, he received a reply from both, saying that the name did not appear in any of their archived files. Aside from destroying records, the Germans took many with them when they retreated from Poland. Sadly, Arnold's efforts turned up nothing, and it appeared that he would never learn of where and how some of the family members had met their fate.

AT THE END OF HIS PERSONAL TRIP TO POLAND, Arnold headed off to St. Petersburg, Russia, for two and a half weeks, while Batya flew back to Israel.

St. Petersburg was a beautiful, classical city of unsurpassed elegance, crisscrossed with canals and bridges, its streets dotted with great domes of cathedrals, graceful spires, magnificent palaces, and pastel-colored mansions. Some dubbed this beautiful city the "Venice of the north." A vast, needy community of between 150,000 to 170,000 Russian-born Jews lived in St. Petersburg among a local population of over four and a half million inhabitants.

Arnold met up with an Ariel Ministries couple serving there at the time. A messianic congregation had been officially established in March 1998, and Arnold was gratified to see the congregants growing together in the knowledge of the Word. He spent time teaching through an interpreter. The meetings attracted a good turnout with a mixture of Jewish believers and unbelievers, as well as Gentile believers.

Coming back to Russia for the first time since his infancy held special personal meaning for Arnold. The trip was even more memorable with both Mary Ann and his mother joining him. It had been nearly fifty-five years since Adele was last in Russia. The visit was particularly significant and poignant for her, as many memories were stirred up from her childhood days, when she was still living there with her parents.

> Since I had three days free, we went by train and airplane down to the city of Saratov, my mother's hometown. We stayed at a hotel, which was kitty-corner to the house where she grew up. The house is still standing, and it was obvious that my mother looked at it with some deep feelings and some bad memories. It was while they were living in that house that the Russian Secret Police had her father arrested, imprisoned, and eventually shot... and her mother sent to a Soviet prison.[56]

From the outset, Adele made it absolutely clear that she would not attend any of her son's meetings. She had no interest in his ministry work or in what he was doing in Russia. Still, she did get together at times with the Ariel Ministries couple and the other local believers. At least, she got some exposure to Ariel's work and saw a facet of the ministry that she had not known before. Ironically, when Adele took her daughter-in-law to view

---

[56] Excerpt: *On The Road*, September 1999

certain famous Russian artworks, Mary Ann saw several paintings of Jesus by Russian artists, which were far more inspirational than any icons—one even correctly depicting the Herodian stone in Jerusalem! Interestingly, Adele allowed conversations to revolve around the topics of those artworks, whereas she normally would have forbidden any such talking points of a spiritual nature. Overall, it was a very nostalgic trip for her. When the visit ended, she and Mary Ann returned to the United States, while Arnold flew to Israel.

For Arnold, revisiting the past in Poland with Batya helped to trace the history of the Fruchtenbaum family, bringing it to life and rounding out the story on his father's side. By the same token, visiting Saratov gave him a glimpse into his mother's past and an appreciation of her side of his family roots. It was deeply moving to see where she had come from, where she grew up, and how much loss she, too, had suffered in her life under Stalin's regime. On each side of his family, loss of life was incurred because of the fact that either they were Jews in Poland under Nazism, or because as Jews, they were wrongly accused by the Soviet totalitarian communist regime. Yet, Arnold knew that God had not forsaken the Jewry nor forgotten His Chosen People. In His own timing, His plan and purpose for the Jewish people would come to fruition in the Millennial Kingdom yet future. Arnold felt an ever-increasing sense of gratitude to the Lord for His care and protection over his own life since birth—for surviving starvation as a child, for his salvation as a teenager, and for the work that God had called him to do in Jewish ministry.

String of Many Firsts

During the same three-month period overseas in the spring of 1999 after Poland and Russia, Arnold flew to Israel for two weeks to lead a private study tour. Straight afterwards, he went to Japan on a first-ever ten-day speaking tour at the invitation of Harvest Time Ministries, a large non-denominational, evangelical Christian organization based in Japan. It was back in 1989 at the Lausanne Consultation on World Evangelism in Manila, where the head of this ministry, Kenichi Nakagawa, had initially come into contact with Ariel Ministries. He later also heard Arnold speak at one of the gatherings of the

Lausanne Conference on Jewish Evangelism and liked the contents. Eventually, an invitation was extended to Arnold to teach in Japan. With a fully booked schedule, the spring of 1999 was the earliest that he could arrange to be there.

The head of Harvest Time Ministries served as Arnold's host and interpreter, accompanying him to different parts of the country, where Arnold spoke at independent churches. Despite the miniscule number of believers in Japan, Arnold was impressed with their seriousness and strong interest in Bible study from a Jewish perspective. The people were all very attentive and took copious notes. Even with a language barrier, the fellowship was still very sweet. Arnold was pleasantly surprised to meet a Jewish believer and the wife of another messianic believer—both living in Japan—who came to hear him speak. This was indeed a rare and special experience for him, as the Jewish community numbered only around two thousand out of a total Japanese population of over one hundred and twenty-six million.

The response to Arnold's teaching was so positive that he was invited to return the following year to hold another ten days of meetings. He gladly obliged and, from that point onward, taught in Japan on a yearly basis. Harvest Time Ministries soon began translating some of Arnold's manuscripts into Japanese. While the nation was deeply entrenched in Shinto and Buddhist traditions, the believers in Messiah Jesus were very committed to growing in maturity in their faith.

Who could have imagined? When Arnold and Mary Ann visited Japan as tourists ten years earlier, they were both drawn to the country. At that time, they were on a shoestring budget. As everything was expensive in Japan, they survived on eating *gyoza*, a form of Chinese dumpling, much like the Jewish *kreplach*, Polish *pirogi*, Russian *pilmeni*, or Italian *ravioli*, which was very popular in Japan and which they both enjoyed. Since rental cars were also very expensive, they took a number of bus tours to various parts of the country and were captivated by what they saw. Arnold, for one, did not think that he would ever get to visit the country again, let alone teach the Word of God from a Jewish perspective to the Japanese! Yet, here he was! Only an omniscient God could have opened the door to this most unexpected and welcomed opportunity.

That spring of 1999, Arnold also spoke for the first time in Austria, a staunch Catholic country with only a few evangelical churches serving a small number of believers. In total, Arnold spoke at three different congregations, before traveling on to Germany for four weeks. Most German congregations at that time tended to be quite liberal, seeking entertainment and experimentalism over solid, expository Bible teaching. Despite this trend, Arnold found a keen audience in the Brethren congregations and independent churches, thus ending his time in Europe on a high note.

Back in the United States in July, Arnold carried on with his full speaking itinerary in several states before heading off to the Adirondacks to Camp Shoshanah, after which he traveled to Quebec, Canada, on a ten-day speaking tour around the province. Though he had taught in Montreal once before, this would be his first time to embark on a longer teaching itinerary that led him deeper into the outlying areas of this French-speaking province.

Ever since Arnold started traveling on behalf of Ariel Ministries some twenty-one years earlier, he no longer played racquetball regularly, due to the lack of a steady partner. Hence for exercise, he began running three miles a day whenever he was traveling. On that trip, he was jogging one day through the parking lot of a Catholic church in the town of Mont Joli, about eight hours' drive from Montreal, when without any warning, his ankle got twisted.

Suddenly my right foot gave way under me, and my ankle did a ninety-degree turn in the wrong direction. Immediately, I not only lost the ability to do any more jogging, I also lost the ability to walk. Even putting my foot on the ground caused extreme pain. I soaked it in hot water, but it continued to swell. An hour before I was scheduled to speak, it was finally decided to take me to a local hospital to have it x-rayed. The x-ray showed nothing was broken, but the sprain was extremely bad, and I was forced to stay on crutches for the next three days. I walked into the meeting that evening an hour late, but people stayed through it all, and so we were able to finish that conference.

The next day was a long ride back to Montreal. We made it to the church, and then I had to learn how to use the crutches going up and down stairs, since the fellowship hall was on the basement level.

The next morning, I took a flight to Michigan. Since I travel with two carry-ons, trying to deal with these on crutches was going to be a bit unwieldy, so I prayed the night before that if God did not choose to heal me completely, that He would at least allow me to be able to walk, even if with a limp. And so it was. I got up that morning, and the swelling in the foot had gone down enough for me to be able to put my boots on. (I had been going barefoot the previous three days) and apparently the tightness of the boot gave enough strength, so, although I was obviously limping badly, I was able to walk without the use of crutches. So, I left them in Montreal and thanked the Lord...[57]

From Quebec, Canada, Arnold went on to Lansing, Michigan for five days to teach for the very first time at a church where Mary Ann's brother-in-law, George Butler—husband of her youngest sister, Kathy—served as the pastor. Since they had relocated from California a while back, it was a personal pleasure for Arnold to reconnect with the family. The time in Michigan thus seemed all too short.

Arnold's next stop was New York City to attend a special three-day conference sponsored by Chosen People Ministries entitled, "To the Jew First in the New Millennium." Mary Ann was able to join him, and they both very much enjoyed listening to the presentations. Arnold was overjoyed to see so many former Camp Shoshanah participants, now growing strong in the Lord and serving in full-time Jewish ministry. A very rare and touching moment came, when Arnold met up with Molly Fetner Jacobs for the first time in over forty-one years. She had worked with Ruth Wardell in the early days at the ABMJ East New York Branch and had known Arnold before he had come to salvation in Jesus.

Right afterwards, Arnold and Mary Ann went up to their little cabin on the Camp Shoshanah property for a few weeks of rest and relaxation, away from the hustle and bustle of daily ministry. For a long time now, it had become an annual tradition for them to take their vacation up in the Adirondacks to enjoy the serenity and resplendent beauty of the surroundings. The first week of October was usually when the leaves peaked and burst forth with their dazzling autumn colors. They took long drives along the back roads of the area and strolled through the woods, contemplating and soaking up the quietness and nature's breathtaking splendor. No matter how many times

---

[57] Excerpts: *On The Road*, December 1999

they came up here in the fall, they were always enthralled by the magnificence of God's creation. They thanked and praised God for His love and care of His Chosen People and for the camp, which held such special personal meaning for them individually and together.

After the fall break, Arnold traveled to Denver, Colorado. There, he spoke for the first time at a messianic congregation, where the pastor happened to be Chaim Urbach, the son of Eliezer Urbach, who had helped to interpret for Arnold when his grandmother first arrived in New York City in 1969. Arnold had not seen Eliezer for thirty years, and now he was speaking at his son's congregation! For lunch afterwards, Arnold got together with Eliezer, his wife, and their son at a *kosher* Jewish deli, enjoying fellowship together as they reminisced about the past. It was thrilling for Arnold to see the second generation of Jewish believers continuing in Jewish ministry.

WITH 1999 DRAWING TO A CLOSE, the world experienced the end of a millennium and the start of a new one. Arnold spent the first nine weeks of the year 2000 in wintry Germany, covering churches, Bible schools, and conference centers. From there, he traveled to Japan in March for a ten-day speaking tour as he had done the preceding year. After the next two months of a busy speaking itinerary back in the United States, it was time for him to once again lead his intensive Israel Study Tour in May 2000.

Upon his return, he went up to the Adirondacks to teach at the Russian-speaking camp right before the English-speaking one. Ever since the first program was launched for the former Soviet Jews back in 1990—except for one summer when it was suspended in 1993—by the grace of God, it had been offered every year. In between the two programs, Arnold flew back to Los Angeles to attend the wedding of one of his younger sisters, the last of his siblings to get married. This sister married "a nice Jewish boy." Much to Arnold's delight, two other Messianic Jewish believers sat at his table. One was a cousin of the groom, living in Connecticut. The other was a close friend of Arnold's sister. It was interesting that in addition to himself, there was a Messianic Jewish believer from each side of the newlyweds' guests.

BACK IN SOUTHERN CALIFORNIA, Arnold taught at a seminary for two weeks, took his annual break with Mary Ann up in the Adirondacks and resumed his hectic speaking schedule around the country. One day, while he was speaking at a conference outside of Dallas, Texas, during the last weekend in October 2000, he noticed for the first time that something was amiss with the vision in his right eye. Notwithstanding, he carried on with his itinerary to Colorado and then to Los Angeles, where he spoke at a conference all day Sunday. The next day, Monday, he was scheduled to fly out to Europe for six weeks of meetings in Switzerland, Germany, and England. There was simply no time to see a doctor prior to his departure. So, Mary Ann did a bit of research on the Internet and printed out some useful information for Arnold to read and take with him.

Mary Ann had always been interested in medicine and subscribed to various medical journals and reports. Her knowledge was quite extensive, and many times, her friends would call her for a first opinion and then go to a doctor for a second opinion or the other way around. She strongly urged Arnold to find an ophthalmologist during the first stop on his itinerary in Switzerland. Based on what she knew, the large blackened field of vision in his right eye was likely due to a detached retina, which without medical attention could permanently damage his vision. Not wanting to cancel his trip, as many people had been working hard for up to two years to arrange the meetings for him, Arnold decided to press ahead overseas.

Upon landing in Switzerland, the series of events that took place could only be attributed to God's hand orchestrating all the details every step along the way. Even though it was a day off for the specialist, Arnold ended up undergoing laser surgery. Later, once back in the United States, when he had it checked out again, his own doctor confirmed that indeed an excellent job had been done. The cost itself was also very affordable, much less than what the U.S. health system would have cost him. He was so relieved that his eye problem had been taken care of right away. As it worked out, he did not have to cancel any meetings and thus continued to maintain his impeccable record of fulfilling all his speaking engagements. God's timing was perfect, as Arnold did not have any more free days scheduled in Europe after the Swiss leg of his journey. It was a very close call. Had he not had the surgery done when he did, it was impossible to tell what might have happened later on during the trip, or if he would have received the kind of top-notch medical attention that he had in Switzerland.

After a weekend conference in Germany, Arnold flew to the U.K. where he spent about three weeks in England and Wales. He was privileged to take part in the renewal of the marriage vows of a Messianic Jewish couple. It was the wife, who, seven years earlier, had contacted Ariel Ministries to inquire about bringing him over to England for a series of meetings. From then on, she helped to set up meetings for Arnold's teaching itineraries in her country.

Earlier in the year while Arnold was teaching in Germany, he had received a phone call from her husband asking if Arnold would be willing to officiate over the ceremony of their marriage vow renewal. Arnold was more than happy to oblige. The couple had organized a very lovely event, including a fully-fledged wedding plus a delicious dinner for the guests afterwards. It was a beautiful testimony to a spiritually committed marriage. A clear presentation of the Gospel message was shared with the guests, comprising both believers and unbelievers, a blessing to witness.

Shortly after Arnold flew back to the United States, he and Mary Ann took off for a much-needed three-week vacation from mid-December to the first week of January in the New Year 2001. Most of their time was spent in the Death Valley National Park in Imyo County in the eastern part of California, spreading into western Nevada. The park covered nearly four thousand eight hundred square miles. They rented a four-wheel drive and traveled many miles off the beaten track on some rough back roads that had barely been treaded on before.

At times, they would travel the entire day without seeing a single living soul around. They appreciated the peace and quiet found in the desert scenery. The natural wildlife had its own unique kind of beauty, reflecting the splendor of God's diverse creation. They enjoyed seeing with their naked eyes the phenomenal expanse of the clear night skies with millions upon millions of brightly shining stars, sparkling like myriads of diamonds against a black velvet canopy. Without any hint of light pollution, they could even see the distant Milky Way in the far reaches of the galaxy that left a luminous swath across the great expanse. As they contemplated the awesomeness of God's creation, they were reminded of the one true Light of the World, *Yeshua Ha'Mashiach*:

There was the true light, even the light *which lights every man, coming into the world. He was in the world and the world was made through Him, and the world knew Him not.* (John 1:9-10)

God's creation was truly breathtakingly magnificent, and they were awed by the Master's handiwork. They drew strength and refreshment from the exquisite beauty that surrounded them even in the desert places. Their heartfelt desire and prayer was for God's Chosen People to come to know their Jewish Messiah, to put their faith and trust in their Savior, and thereby receive eternal life in the Lord. Renewed through their vacation break, Arnold looked forward to a new year of ministry work ahead, filled with God's blessings and provision.

Shifting Tides

By 2001, a number of changes had taken place at the Ariel Home Office with turnover among the support staff and volunteer missionary couples. Arnold's long-time administrative assistant, Roxanne, who was ready for a change after twelve years of service, left the ministry at the end of 2000, and Donna Wixson took on the role as Arnold's executive secretary.

Arnold began the year by teaching a course for three weeks at Chafer Theological Seminary in southern California. On the two weekends sandwiched in between, he also spoke at two different local congregations. For a number of years now, he had taught twice a year at Chafer as an adjunct professor, usually in the months of January and September. In his musings, Arnold once said that if he had not been called as an itinerant Bible teacher, he would have been content to be a professor at seminary level. Passionate about teaching the Bible from a Jewish perspective, he enjoyed interacting with the students.

Then, it was time for six weeks of hectic ministry in Hawaii. Mary Ann joined Arnold for four of the six weeks. Since autumn of the preceding year, she was able to travel with him more often than had been possible in recent years. Her time in Hawaii was filled with enjoyable fellowship with many believers, some of whom had not seen her in ten years. She also had an opportunity to teach a women's Bible study in Hilo. Her sister, Beth, and niece, Rachel, visited her for part of the time in Hawaii, making the trip doubly special for her.

In late March 2001, Arnold flew down to New Zealand for almost two months of teaching, including a one-week camp, the third of its kind. It had been four years since he had traveled to the country. Much had changed within the local believing community since 1997. At that time, the believers there had been torn apart by the damaging effects of the Toronto Phenomenon. While residual effects still remained, most of the fanaticism had subsided considerably. Many of those who had been victimized came to realize the need to return to scriptural foundations. Though opposition to the teaching ministry still existed, the tide seemed to be shifting toward the deeper things of God. Arnold was encouraged to see that the Brethren churches were growing again. They were among the few churches that had remained unswervingly faithful to the Word during "the movement." Many believers who had previously turned away from the Word had now returned, and new people were joining a local church.

Since the early days, Arnold had generally spent more time in New Zealand than in Australia when he was in this part of the world, because that was how God had opened the doors for him. Many others with itinerant ministries often skipped New Zealand, or at best made only a short stop, going straight to Australia. Arnold never had any regrets about spending a longer period of ministry in New Zealand. On balance, he tried to come "Down Under" once every two years. However in 1999, he did not make it to New Zealand, because the door to Japan and to Austria had opened for the very first time for Ariel Ministries, plus there were other commitments to fulfill in Germany. Of course, Arnold was chided for staying away for such a long stretch, so he committed to doing his best to travel to New Zealand consistently once every two years.

Taking place amid Arnold's five weeks in Australia was a ten-day teaching tour in Japan, the third through Harvest Time Ministries. During this trip, he ate either Japanese or Chinese food. Since these were two of his favorite cuisines, his teaching tour was very rewarding in more ways than one. The Japanese people were very surprised that Arnold knew how to use chopsticks, especially since he was left-handed!

Arnold was equally heartened to see those who had been hurt by the extremist movements in Australia now hungry for the expository teaching of God's Word. Many, who had turned away from attending any meetings four years earlier, now sought the opportunity to learn. Some traveled quite a distance to get to the meetings and even took lots of notes. For the first time, two short camps, each three days in length, were conducted in two different locations in Australia. Both were well attended, reflecting an obvious interest in the study of the Scriptures from a Jewish perspective.

Except for Perth in the western part, all the meetings were arranged through a local Jewish ministry, Manna International. Arnold appreciated its like-mindedness with Ariel Ministries in its beliefs and goals. Hence, he rejoiced to see how beautifully the believers had networked together to bring about his teaching itinerary. A very special highlight in Melbourne was meeting and spending time with Rabbi Harold R. Vallins, a Messianic Jew, who had previously received training and attained credentials to be an authentic rabbi.

AFTER THREE AND A HALF MONTHS of ministry work overseas in New Zealand, Japan, and Australia, Arnold finally returned to the United States in mid-July 2001, in time for the twenty-eighth season of Camp Shoshanah. Just prior to the English-speaking camp, a three-day French-speaking camp was launched and organized by Jacques and Sharon Gabizon, who headed Ariel Canada. In his spiritual walk, Arnold had always felt the hand of God upon his life. However, there were periods when he felt this more strongly than at other times. For reasons he could not explain or pinpoint, Arnold felt a deep sense of the goodness of God in connection with the camp ministry this season in a special way that he had not experienced in a long time.

As was his practice in recent years, Arnold spent about ten days in September teaching in various cities throughout French-speaking Quebec. Only Montreal was a bi-lingual city with many English speakers. While staying in the far northern town called Chicoutimi, the horrific attacks on the twin towers of the World Trade Center in New York City occurred on the eleventh of September 2001, sending shock waves around the world. The rest of Arnold's tour was clouded by this tragedy. Most of the questions and answers following each study session focused on the significance of this attack. Arnold was quick to point out that this event was not a fulfillment of any specific Bible prophecy and certainly not that of Revelation 18. God's prophetic program (Deuteronomy 32:8-9) was based on how world events affected Israel and Jewish history, not how they affected the United States, no matter how profound or tragic the event. As he subsequently traveled to his speaking engagements, he noticed a markedly different feel to the country. These were certainly changing times, and life would never be the same again after that fateful day. He prayed that many would now seek Messiah Jesus for their salvation, solace, and comfort.

FOLLOWING A THREE-WEEK AUTUMN BREAK with Mary Ann up in the beautiful Adirondacks, Arnold resumed his schedule. Toward the end of October 2001, he headed off to Germany. Emerging from the Holocaust, who could have foreseen the number of present-day German churches so interested in Bible teachings from a Jewish perspective? In his initial ministry years, whenever he came across an older German individual, Arnold would often wonder what role that person had played toward the Jews during the Nazi regime. As the years progressed, after the older generation died and the younger generation grew up, such questions dissipated from his mind.

To save on trans-Atlantic airfares, Arnold usually tried to combine a couple of itineraries on the same trip to obtain maximum usage out of the funds spent. So after wrapping up his conferences in Germany, he took a short eight-day trip to Israel, specifically to Jerusalem. He had been invited to lecture on "Israelology" at the Israel College of the Bible and to speak at the Jerusalem Baptist Church. Since the last week of September 2000 the preceding year, when the Second *Intifada* had broken out in a few spots, the news media partook in a feeding frenzy about the dangers of the entire country.

> Although CNN would make you believe that the whole country
> is up in flames, the fact is that the trouble spots are
> quite localized, and it is very safe to visit Israel. I
> walked the streets of the city and felt very safe. When
> people ask if I plan to cancel the 2002 study tour, I tell
> them, "in no way." Even if all the trouble spots were all
> active at the same time, it would only affect two and a
> half days of this five-week tour. I am looking forward to
> it, especially since the one in 2004 will be the last one
> I am planning to do.[58]

In the interim before this trip, the Israel College of the Bible had moved its premises to a large building on the "Street of the Prophets," which was previously owned by the Christian and Missionary Alliance. This was the very same building where Arnold had lodged during his student days in Jerusalem and where he and Mary Ann had later resided when they spent two years in Israel. Being there triggered a sea of memories for Arnold. This was where all

---

[58] Excerpt: *On The Road*, January-February 2002

the neighbors had taken refuge during the Six-Day War and where he had run a mini-Bible institute during the second year of his and Mary Ann's sojourn in the country over twenty-eight years earlier. It was so good to see the edifice being used for the teaching of God's Word once again. A while later, the college moved its premises yet again to a new location in Netanya. Though the time in the Land was extremely short, Arnold still had an opportunity on this trip to fellowship with some close believers and to spend a little bit of personal time with two of his Israeli cousins.

Upon his return to the United States in late November 2001, Arnold spoke at two messianic congregations, one in San Antonio and the other in Fort Lauderdale, Florida. Both were sound and balanced in their teachings and theology. When he and Mary Ann were living in San Antonio, not one messianic congregation could be found there then.

Arnold's last engagement for 2001 was participating in a mid-December conference sponsored annually by the Pre-Trib Research Center, whose primary purpose was to defend the literal interpretation of Bible prophecy and the pre-tribulational Rapture of the Church. Arnold presented a paper entitled "The Millennial Temple Sacrifices—Literal or Allegorical?" It was so well received that a publisher expressed interest in it as part of a larger work.

As the year drew to a close, Arnold felt very grateful that he was able to stay on track with his engagements without having to reschedule. With so many thousands of lives in turmoil and adversely affected by the tragic event of September 11th, he earnestly prayed for open hearts:

(God)... *who would have all men to be saved and come to the knowledge of the truth. For there is one God, one mediator also between God and men, Himself man, Messiah Yeshua, who gave Himself a ransom for all; the testimony to be borne in its own times;* (I Timothy 2:4-6) *For there is no distinction between Jew and Greek: for the same Lord is Lord of all and is rich unto all that call upon Him: for, whosoever shall call upon the name of the Lord shall be saved.* (Romans 10:12-13)

In this time of national tragedy, especially with *Chanukah* and Christmas approaching, Arnold longed for people to know and receive the magnificent gift of God's Son to mankind and not to reject Him:

Every good gift and every perfect gift is from above, coming down from the Father of lights, with whom can be no variation, neither shadow that is cast by turning. (James 1:17) *(Yeshua)... came unto His own and they that were His own received Him not. But as many as received Him, to them gave He the right to become children of God, even to them that believe on His name: who were born not of blood, nor of the will of the flesh, nor of the will of man, but of God.* (John 1:11-13)

It cost God the life of His Son, *Yeshua,* dying as the sacrificial Lamb and shedding His precious blood on the cross, to make it possible for mankind to be saved. Only through His atoning work and His substitutionary death can those who call upon His name be saved. There is simply no other way to avoid a lost eternity except to receive Messiah Jesus into one's heart as one's personal Savior. This national tragedy underscored the importance of responding to the Gospel message upon hearing it, as one's life can be snatched away instantly without warning, and it would be too late:

Wherefore, even as the Holy Spirit says, Today if ye shall hear His voice, Harden not your hearts... (Hebrews 3:7-8a) *...behold, now is the acceptable time; behold, now is the day of salvation...* (II Corinthians 6:2b).

Afternoon Opium Cake

In 2002, an even-numbered year, Arnold traveled once again to Germany for nine weeks in January and February, including a few days of teaching in England at the start and a week in Switzerland at the end. While in Germany, Arnold planned to visit with Hanna and Manfred Künstler. Ever since Hanna had reconnected with Arnold seventeen years earlier, the Künstlers had served as volunteer representatives of Ariel Ministries in Germany, translating the radio manuscripts and quarterly *Ariel Ministries Newsletter,* which they mailed out to those on Ariel's German contact list. They also collected donations on behalf of Ariel. After many years of tireless work and dedication, it was now time for them to retire.

The visit was very special and touching. Moved by a wistful wave of nostalgia, Arnold mused in his heart about the inevitability of change.

> The problem with the passing of time is that nothing stays
> the same, and what we see is constant transitions. One
> needs to cherish the pleasant moments of the present and
> then fondly remember them as they become the past, and the
> future imposes itself on us.[59]

Thankfully, God provided another worker for Ariel Ministries in Germany just at the right juncture—Georg Hagedorn, based out of Düsseldorf, who had frequently served as Arnold's interpreter. Agreeing to take on the responsibility, Georg signed a preliminary branch agreement to represent the ministry in Germany.

Arnold's visit with another family of German believers was equally gratifying. The father, a graduate of a Swiss seminary, was an elder at a Brethren congregation in Karlsruhe in southwestern Germany. Arnold had befriended him while on a speaking engagement there in the past. Through a series of subsequent contacts, the family arranged to send their teenage daughter, Sarah, to the United States to live with the Fruchtenbaums for one year to improve her English. She was partway through her yearlong stay, when Arnold traveled to Germany. He had the joy of fellowshipping with her parents twice on the same trip. For dinner one evening, her mother prepared Arnold's favorite German dish, a delicious veal cutlet in a cream sauce, which he savored with delight.

In the spring of the preceding year, Sarah's parents had traveled to the United States for a visit. For the first time, they attended a *Shabbat* service at Arnold and Mary Ann's place of worship, *Shuvah Yisrael.* They also had an opportunity to participate in their first-ever Passover *Seder.* It meant a lot to them to see the environment where their daughter would be spending an entire year. Now, they were relieved to hear from Arnold that Sarah was so well liked. She was a tremendous help to Mary Ann around the house, as well as to the Ariel staff with her streak of German efficiency. She enthusiastically volunteered about three days a week at the office, yet accomplished the equivalent of a full-time worker.

At a Bible institute during his third week, Arnold taught a thirty-five hour seminar on the Book of Ezekiel. About fifty people enrolled, many having driven a long distance to get to the venue. Most knew some English, but did

---

[59] Excerpt: *On The Road,* March-April 2002

not always possess the right words to express an idea. A typical German custom was their traditional, daily afternoon cake-and-coffee time, with tables in the fellowship hall usually laden with a variety of sumptuous cakes. One looked very interesting. While Arnold was trying to figure out what kind it was, a German lady kindly came over to help. In her limited English, she declared, "Dat ist opium cake." Arnold was bemused.

```
I had noticed the staff was happy and joyful all the time,
but I thought it was due to being Spirit-filled! Since
Word of Life is a Christian school, I knew it could not be
an "opium cake," so I took a piece to find out what it
was. It turned out to be poppy seed cake.⁶⁰
```

In Arnold's absence, Mary Ann lived through quite an ordeal back home, dealing with two separate car accidents over a two-week period. The first occurred one evening on the crowded Los Angeles freeway. She was on her way home in her van, after having dropped off some friends at the airport, when the car in front of her stopped suddenly right in the midst of rush-hour traffic. Not having sufficient reaction time to slam on her brakes, Mary Ann rammed her van into the back of the car in front of her. The force of the impact totaled her own van, while the car in front emerged with minor damages only to the back bumper. The driver appeared to be fine and was able to drive away, after both parties took care of the insurance formalities. A tow truck brought Mary Ann home.

Needing a car to get around, she began driving Arnold's old 1987 Dodge. After her traumatic experience, Mary Ann stayed away from the freeways and drove on the smaller streets. One day while she stopped at a red light, someone suddenly crashed into her car from the back and totaled it. Unfortunately, the woman who hit the car had no insurance coverage, which was illegal in California. Shaken by her ordeal, Mary Ann called Larry Feldman, the pastor of *Shuvah Yisrael*, who kindly came to pick her up and drive her home.

They praised and thanked the Lord that Mary Ann suffered no serious injuries, and that the two recent accidents did not turn out to be a life-threatening situation for any of the parties involved. Mary Ann was only

---

⁶⁰ Excerpt: *On The Road*, January-February 2002

slightly bruised in this accident, but none the worse for the wear. However, she and Arnold now needed to replace not just one but two cars as soon as it was financially feasible. They beseeched the Lord in prayer to provide. Within a relatively short period, God supplied them with a used Toyota Camry, personally gifted by a member of the Ariel board of directors! Arnold and Mary Ann were both very grateful for this provision.

OVER THE YEARS, Arnold had kept in touch with some of the former members of the men's morning discipleship group, the *minyan*, which he had initiated and taught during the early years of Ariel Ministries in San Antonio. One of the men, Jake Hogue, and his wife, Jeannie, had a great deal of respect for Arnold. The couple and their children were all very fond of him. On occasion, the family had also socialized with the Fruchtenbaums. When it came time for their daughter's baptism, she specifically requested Arnold to baptize her. At that time, the Ariel Home Office had already relocated to California, and his itinerary was very full. Yet, he rearranged some of his flights, set aside an afternoon and made a deliberate detour to San Antonio to baptize her. The family was very moved and, years later, continued to feel grateful for Arnold's time and for what he had done for their daughter.

A special moment came up, when Arnold was invited to a reunion of the former members of the *minyan*. Among the men in that group was Charmaine's husband, Mark. Since Charmaine had played a major role as the administrative assistant in helping to get Ariel Ministries going in the initial years, she organized the get-together for old times' sake. Everyone, in particular, Arnold, appreciated and enjoyed the reunion. Although there was no "opium cake" served, the fellowship was no less euphoric! Arnold wondered if it felt so good here on earth to reconnect with people from the past, how much greater the joy would be in Heaven.

Off the Road

With all the spaces on the 2002 five-week Israel Study Tour booked by November 2001, the waiting list got longer. Preceding this tour, Arnold was also scheduled to lead a group from a German Bible college for two weeks. He planned to fly out in late April, first to Frankfurt, Germany, store most of his luggage there, take a direct flight to Tokyo for a ten-day teaching itinerary in Japan and then fly back via Frankfurt onto Israel.

Unfortunately, the day before he was due to depart for Europe, he was instructed at the last minute by the Ariel board of directors to cancel the two study tours. This decision was taken in large part based upon the board's misplaced apprehension of perceived dangers in Israel from the recent exaggerated media reporting. While initially Arnold had absolutely disagreed with the board's conclusion, he nevertheless submitted to their authority and took the painful but inevitable steps to organize the cancellations. In the long run, he regretted his own decision and wished that he had instead accepted the alternative—the board's resignation—and pressed on with the two tours. As a result of those cancellations, Arnold's reputation for being faithful to Israel in all circumstances was negatively affected long term.

By the time Arnold returned home from Japan in mid-spring 2002, over two and a half years had elapsed since he had first badly twisted his right ankle. In the interim, the scheduling of his surgery had turned into a long, drawn-out saga. Each time, either a delay was encountered, or something cropped up necessitating a date change, prolonging the pain in his ankle. Being in the habit of running three to four times per week, Arnold was caught in a bind. The slightest jogging would trigger streaks of pain after only a few steps, a reminder that running was simply not possible for the time being. He would have to be content with walking.

The original X-ray taken in Canada right after his mishap in the fall of 1999 had shown nothing broken, so the HMO[61] at the time decided that a course of physiotherapy would suffice. Arnold felt frustrated, as it seemed that clerks with barely a high school education were making these important medical

---

[61] Health Maintenance Organization

351

decisions, rather than doctors with expertise and experience. His physiotherapy continued to no avail. Whenever he walked uphill or climbed a set of stairs, his ankle would be in severe pain.

At the suggestion of an Ariel supporter in Hawaii, also a jogger, Arnold bought a pair of high-tech, top running shoes. While vacationing with Mary Ann up in the Adirondacks in the autumn of 2000, he donned on those shoes and started to walk a fixed roundtrip route of five miles, where the trails wound up and down around the mountains. Eager to jog again, Arnold tried running on the downhill paths. Surprisingly, he felt very little discomfort on those downward slopes. Not having jogged for over a year, his sore leg muscles took several days to recover. He ventured to jog downhill a second time and managed to cut his total roundtrip walking time by about fifteen minutes. His legs took only a day or so to recover. Not wanting to push too far, he did not attempt to run uphill or on level ground. Still, he was pleased with his progress.

In December 2000, fifteen months after the sprain, with no visible improvements from the physiotherapy, the HMO finally approved an MRI on Arnold's injured ankle to get a clearer indication of what might be wrong. The doctors would then ascertain whether or not surgery was necessary. Early in 2001, when Arnold's podiatrist examined the MRI reports, he verified that his ankle was indeed very badly sprained and recommended surgery. Apparently, the damage on the cartilage and tendon was much more severe than shown on the original X-ray.

A total of six weeks had to be set aside for the recovery process, including the first two weeks on crutches. Given Arnold's heavy travel schedule, it was not easy to find such a block of time. The earliest possible slot was in mid-August 2001, right after the Camp Shoshanah program. This meant that Arnold had to live with the sprain for another eight months or so. It was not a major inconvenience for him, because he could still walk around. However, he was in a constant state of discomfort or some form of pain most of the time. Meanwhile, the physiotherapy was discontinued.

Rearranging and squeezing all his Camp Shoshanah classes of the last day into the previous evening, Arnold left the day before the end of the program. When he got to the clinic, he discovered that there was a mix-up with some of his pre-operation medical tests. By the time the confusion was straightened out, the window for the surgery was closed. The main surgeon had to go out of town. Before leaving, he ordered Arnold to stop his jogging immediately, as it would exacerbate the pain, further aggravate the condition of his ankle, and likely cause more serious damage. Again, the surgery had to be rescheduled, this time to mid-December 2001, after Arnold got back from a short trip to Germany and Israel. Upon his return, Arnold ran into yet another snag. The clinic wanted to push his surgery three days forward. However, the assistant surgeon could not accommodate. When the main surgeon found out about Arnold's upcoming trip overseas in January 2002, he did not approve of any traveling so soon after the procedure. So, yet again, the surgery had to be postponed—this time to mid-August, right after the 2002 Camp Shoshanah program—another long eight-months' wait. The surgeon's secretary made it absolutely clear to the clinic that under no circumstances could Arnold's new scheduled date be changed again.

This time though, Arnold did not have to wait eight months for his surgery. Due to the forced cancellation of the Israel Study Tours, he unexpectedly ended up with a hole of two months in his itinerary. So by the time he returned to the United States from Japan, he finally had his surgery at an outpatient clinic in early May 2002. Instead of one hour, the operation took two hours. Once the surgeon probed the ankle, he saw that it had sustained more damage than what had shown up on the MRI. In addition, there was a bone chip that needed to be removed. Hence, the surgery became a bit more involved than previously anticipated. Instead of simply fixing the problem with a probe, the damage required some cutting. After a number of stitches, the foot was bandaged up, and the patient was sent home to start the recuperation process. It was a small consolation for not leading the study tours in Israel, but Arnold was grateful to the Lord for the ankle surgery and the recovery time, both of which did not interfere with his subsequent speaking schedule.

It would take up to six months before Arnold could even contemplate jogging again. In his characteristic dry sense of humor, he light-heartedly remarked that he would have to stay out of the Pope's parking lot, referring to the place where he had sprained his ankle. In fact, Arnold frequently enjoyed joking about his sprain being the result of a Catholic conspiracy against the Messianic Jews!

WHILE "OFF THE ROAD," Arnold had plenty of time to read and catch up with paperwork and correspondence. He also spent many hours doing research on his manuscripts, having full use of his extensive library. Used to being away from home, it was a major adjustment for him to be immobilized in one location for such an extended period. He missed not being able to take a study group to Israel this year. He remembered with fondness the three previous tours of the year 2000. He had led two additional, separate groups for two weeks each—one before and one after his normal five-week study tour.

The groups on the shorter tours from Memphis, Tennessee, were connected to a discipleship ministry headed by Tom Murray, an Ariel board member at that time. Having been on one of Arnold's tours in the past, Tom did a good job of preparing the participants in advance. They were all very motivated to learn, so it was both a privilege and a pleasure for Arnold to show them the Land of Israel the way it ought to be seen. They had a wonderful time and got to see a lot more than on a regular tourist-type trip.

Those on the longer five-week intensive tour knew from the outset that it would be more than a traditional sightseeing tour. The Ariel worker in St. Petersburg, Russia, was overjoyed to join the group. The tour was very plainly described as a complete overview of the entire Land from a biblical, historical and geographical perspective. Overall, it allowed the group to trace the journey of the twelve spies to ...*see the land and the people that dwell therein, whether they are strong or weak, whether they are few or many.* (Numbers 13:18) It would also help to illuminate the Old Testament and the Gospels through examining the geography of Israel and how it related to biblical events and themes, entailing studying the history of the Jews and also of the State of Israel.

Arnold designed his own itinerary, covering many biblical sites. To keep the costs down, he made all the local transportation and accommodation arrangements himself and did the guiding and teaching as well. Since study was such an integral part of the tour, the participants were asked to read the materials in advance to be well prepared. Unless couples were both totally committed to a tour of this nature, they were strongly advised to consider other options. So were those merely interested in sightseeing. Only adults aged eighteen years or older, who were healthy and fit, were accepted. The pace was rugged with plenty of walking while visiting the various sites for six days a week, with one free day off to rest or spend in whatever way the individual desired.

The optional leg to Jordan that year turned out to be an interesting experience for Arnold and the group.

I have had a variety of Jordanian guides (in Israel, I can do my own guiding, but this is not possible in Jordan, where a Jordanian-assigned guide is required)...some better than others. The guide I had this year was very easy to work with and was willing to follow my lead as to what the group got to see and do. I had to be very careful not to upstage him, and I had to warn the group not to put me in a position where this might happen, reserving any questionable comments he might make for our private evening sessions.

After he finished his presentation when we were at Pella, I pointed out some things on the Israeli side that could be seen from there, such as Mount Gilboa, the Hill of Moreh, and the Beit Shean Pass. He mentioned to me that he was totally unfamiliar with the other side and was glad for me to point those things out to the group. During a period when we were driving some distance, which did not require too much discussion, he happened to look at my book, *A Study Guide of Israel*, especially at the Jordanian supplement... As we were coming to the hotel, he asked if he could make a copy of the Jordanian section to see in advance what the group was reading so that he could keep on top of things. I not only agreed, but also told him I would be happy to send him a copy when I got back to the U.S.A. For the following three days, I noticed how he made use of my Study Guide. Because he was of Moslem background, he admitted he knew very little about the Old and New Testaments. He began using my Study Guide to fill in the blanks in areas he was not familiar. As we traveled the length of the King's Highway from Amman to Petra, he would frequently just read to the group from my Study Guide notes, apparently ignoring the fact that they each had their own copy...

During the trip, the group was able to realize the difference between my tour and a tourist-type tour. They noticed how many pictures they had to take only from a moving bus, and they also noticed how often I had to intervene to get the bus to stop in order for them to take the pictures they wanted. They began to appreciate the way I handled the Study Tour and informed me of it, for which

> I was grateful. All in all, this guide was the friendliest
> of the Jordanian guides I have had so far and I hope to be
> able to use him again for future trips, as he was so easy
> to work with.[62]

Alas, that wonderful trip took place two years prior, and the only thing Arnold could do was to reminisce about it during his recovery at home. Before the Camp Shoshanah program started in July 2002, he wore a moon boot and used crutches while traveling to engagements in several states. At Camp, he no longer needed the crutches, as he could hobble and limp around with the aid of his moon boot. He was heartened that his ankle was gradually healing and strengthening. Though confident that he would be walking normally soon, Arnold knew deep down inside that the chances of ever jogging five miles daily again were rather slim.

In the fall of 2002, because Arnold was still experiencing pain in his ankle, his doctor prescribed some medication to ease the discomfort. There was no consistency in the way the pain came and went. During his annual autumn vacation with Mary Ann up in the Adirondacks, Arnold noticed that when walking three to four miles, his ankle appeared to hold up, but later while resting, the pain would return. His doctor pointed out that this condition might last for the rest of his life. If so, Arnold felt that he could still be content the way the Apostle Paul was: *My grace is sufficient for you: for My power is made perfect in weakness.* (II Corinthians 12:9b) He would look to the Lord to strengthen and sustain him in his times of pain.

Perhaps, it was the timing of his surgery in parallel with the natural progression of the aging process that caused him to pause and review his life more often than in the past. It seemed that his health was entering a new phase in his autumnal years. Life was very fragile at times, and unexpected things could happen at any given moment, making each and every day precious. To others, Arnold seemed to have mellowed in many ways. His personal newsletters started expressing a slightly nostalgic tone, occasionally even mentioning what he was feeling. He appeared to relate to people in a more personable way than before, almost as though he wanted them to get to know his inner thoughts. Perhaps, arriving at a certain stage in life, one's perspectives matured, and life itself took on more depth of meaning. Going by

---

[62] Excerpts: *On The Road*, September 2000

the lifespan of three score and ten, that is, seventy years, Arnold would have only eleven years left. He prayed that God would grant him an additional ten years beyond seventy, so that he could continue serving the Lord in Jewish ministry.

Window of Time

For quite some time now, Mary Ann's health had become progressively worse. Unable to balance herself, she often had difficulty walking without falling over. Even when standing still, she needed to lean against a wall. For the most part, her speech was normal, but at times she struggled to get her words out. The numerous tests done locally to diagnose the cause proved to be futile. Eventually, her doctors suggested the Mayo Clinic in Rochester, Minnesota, reputed for its advanced medical systems.

When she phoned for an appointment in the spring of 2001, she discovered a long waiting list for up to one year. However, she had the option of simply showing up to be wait-listed for any cancellations on the spot. After much prayer, Mary Ann took the risk and flew to Rochester on her own, while Arnold was away in New Zealand and Australia. Once there, it was clear that the Lord's hand was upon her accommodation arrangements. The motel she stayed in was just across the street from the Mayo Clinic with a tunnel connecting the two buildings, which meant she did not even need to go outdoors. In addition, her room was right next to the elevator, shortening her walking distance.

By God's grace, within two to three days of registering, Mary Ann was accepted as a patient. For the next five weeks, she underwent test after test, meeting many of the medical staff along the way. She instantly connected with a primary doctor assigned to her, trusting her expertise. This doctor gave Mary Ann a prescription for a walker that had a seat and secure handbrakes, and she was able to purchase it while there, significantly improving her mobility. Whenever she had to stand still for any length of time, she could simply sit. She referred to it as her "pre-Harley," while asking other patients with motorized walking devices how they liked their "Harleys."

The letter that the doctors of the Mayo Clinic sent to Mary Ann's neurologist in California listed eleven specific diagnoses, none of which were neurological. The last test revealed that problems existed in various parts of her brain, though not fitting any understood pattern. However, the doctors did identify and effectively treat her neuropathic pain with a medication called Neurontin. The next year involved follow-up visits with various specialists. Most viewed her condition as MS or multiple sclerosis, but were equally reluctant to pinpoint it as a definite diagnosis.

While Arnold was home in May of that year recuperating from his ankle surgery, he had plenty of time to observe Mary Ann's condition, which was degenerating. Even after seeing three specialists, there was no unanimity in their deductive conclusions, except that there was no cure, although the symptoms could be treated with appropriate medication.

One physician ordered Mary Ann to stop her physiotherapy, as it was exacerbating the problem. For long distances, he advised her to use a motorized wheelchair instead of a walker and took the initiative to fill out all the paperwork for insurance payment of this expensive item. He believed that within a year, she would need it on an ongoing basis. How this would affect the lives of Mary Ann and Arnold was something that only time would tell. They left the situation entirely in God's hands.

In the fall of 2002, an MRI on Mary Ann's spine revealed that some of the bones in the neck area seemed to be fused. Three disks in the upper cervical spine of her neck had started to compress the spinal cord, the result sometimes of a neck surgery. Never having had such a surgery, her condition was a source of concern for the doctors. Meanwhile, she was losing feeling in her hands and could not tell how firmly she was grasping anything, constantly dropping things. Thus, all the dishware at home was changed to unbreakable plastic to accommodate her condition.

Unable to use her hands for even small tasks, it became clear that Mary Ann needed help around the house. Sarah, the student, who had been living with the Fruchtenbaums for a year, had just returned to Germany after the 2002 Camp Shoshanah summer program, where she had asked to be baptized by full immersion. She had been a great help to Mary Ann, who was very sad to see her leave. Mary Ann even jokingly threatened to hide Sarah's passport so she would have to stay. On the lookout for someone else to assist at home, a young woman from Ukraine, one of the top students at Chafer Theological Seminary, came to Arnold's mind.

It turned out she was living in a house that had just been sold. Everyone had to move out by the end of October just about the time we needed someone to move in with us. God has answered this prayer, both hers and ours and once again Mary Ann will not be alone when I travel. Mary Ann drilled Bogdana on her attitude toward cats. In fact, while we were at Camp, she had Bogdana visit the house and spend an hour with the cats to make sure there were no allergies to worry about and to make sure Bogdana can get along with the cats. When Bogdana passed the cat-scan test, she was a shoo-in. I suspect that when Mary Ann checked with the cats by phone, they had approved their new servant.[63]

Two different neurologists warned Mary Ann that the compression in her spinal cord would eventually progress to paralysis. One of them believed that surgery would be helpful to restore feeling into her hands, while the other was not so certain, believing that the results could go either way. If successful, Mary Ann would be able to do many things for herself, including driving. However, the surgery could also do nothing for her or worse, possibly even leading to permanent paralysis. It was not a decision to be made lightly, and Mary Ann was advised to go for a third opinion. Much prayer was offered on her behalf, as there was a window of only two to three months before the progressive damage became irreparable.

A last-minute surgery was scheduled on the 14th of November 2002 at the UCLA—University of California in Los Angeles—Medical Center, about forty-five miles from where the Fruchtenbaums lived, but only one mile from Adele's place. So, they spent the night there, before heading off to the hospital early the next morning. Arnold rescheduled a few of his speaking engagements, in order to accompany Mary Ann through all the preliminaries up to the moment she was wheeled into surgery.

The surgery took a full three hours, and the point of entry, to my surprise, was through the front of her neck. The surgeon came to talk to me afterwards and told me he found everything he expected to find... and told me the

---

[63] Excerpts: *On The Road*, September-October 2002

359

surgery included not only the decompressing of the disks but also the removal of "stalactite-type growths" and the insertion of a plate to make sure this does not happen again. This means she will lose approximately 15 to 20 percent of her neck's motion... (This opens the door to refer to Mary Ann as my stiff-necked wife—which I may use at more appropriate moments) Overall, the surgeon was very pleased with the way things went. He also said two more things that were a major answer to prayer.

First, Mary Ann will eventually get the feeling back in her hands. That can take six months or more, since nerve endings do not regenerate as quickly as other parts... However... to stop the road to paralysis will be immediate. The second thing... was a surprise. He thinks this surgery should also improve Mary Ann's ability to walk. He did not guarantee this. Nevertheless, in his opinion, the compression was causing her to lose the ability to walk. Up until now, the other neurologists had ascribed her loss of walking ability to the neurological disorder. Because the doctor had to pull aside her vocal cords and swallowing muscle, she would not be able to eat solids for a while and would probably not be able to talk at all for perhaps two weeks. (I suppressed the temptation to ask him if that specific phenomenon could be prolonged)...

Our HMO had only approved a one-night stay at the hospital. We felt that was inadequate for such a major surgery. God again answered our prayer, and the medical staff overruled, which resulted in a five-day hospital stay for Mary Ann. She was then released to a rehabilitation center located in Santa Monica that is also run by UCLA. The HMO approved a two-week stay. This facility is located about a mile from my mother's house, but in the opposite direction. Mary Ann regained her talking ability fairly quickly, and we have had long conversations on the phone. I had to hit the road again a few days after her surgery.

There was even further answer to prayer. Our HMO will not pay for home care. We are not able to afford to hire someone, and Mary Ann would still need help after being released from the rehabilitation center. By the grace of

God, my 79-year-old mother, not a believer, invited Mary Ann to her house to care for her. My mother is a very good cook, but she still has to puree everything, because Mary Ann has not recovered enough to swallow solid food. Under normal circumstances, my mother would plow her with lots of Jewish penicillin (chicken soup), but Mary Ann is allergic to chicken, and that will not work. This also means her recovery will take soooooooooo much longer!

And, there is yet another answer to prayer on the way. To avoid becoming a problem for my mother, Mary Ann does not want to overstay her welcome and is planning on moving back home on December 16th. She will still need someone to help her for at least two or three weeks while recuperating at home. We had no local leads, since those who are more than willing are also working and are not free to help. Through a series of Internet communications that went from California to Canada to Wales in Great Britain, a young woman prayed about the matter and on her own, without being asked, offered to fly in to help Mary Ann at home... She will be flying in on December 15th and will be ready for Mary Ann when she gets home on the 16th. She will stay until January 10th.[64]

The young woman from Wales was Jenni Lerner, a Jewish believer. She was well acquainted with Ariel Ministries, having been to Camp Shoshanah several times. Her offer of help at a time of need was an example of selfless service, a much-appreciated answer to prayer. While Mary Ann's neck surgery was successful, the problem of imbalance remained. The likelihood of using a walker for the rest of her life was very high. As the recovery process continued with more feeling returning to her hands, the scar on her neck gradually became less visible. For the next six months or so, she still needed her neck brace when going out.

Sadly, Mary Ann's ability to travel with Arnold would be severely limited in the future. Gone would be any "exotic" vacations, rare as those had been, like the time when they visited seven different islands in the Caribbean. At best, she may have a window of two to three years left to freely move around for air

---

[64] Excerpts: *On The Road*, November-December 2002

travel. Thus, Mary Ann planned on taking three trips in 2003 with Arnold to places that held special meaning for her. While they prayed consistently—without presumption—for God's divine intervention, she viewed the upcoming trips as perhaps her last to these places and looked forward to them with quiet anticipation.

IN EARLY JANUARY 2003, Arnold had a four-day teaching engagement in a town near San Antonio, Texas, and Mary Ann went with him, the first of her three trips. She stayed with her best friend, Jan, and had a lovely visit. Though not able to attend any of Arnold's meetings, she was well enough to participate in a few of the gatherings of long-time friends and supporters of the ministry. Most of their friends from their San Antonio days were still living there, so the visit was special for them.

After returning to California with Mary Ann, Arnold flew off to Alaska for a brief teaching stint before heading off to Hawaii at the end of January for five weeks until early March. Mary Ann joined him for two weeks, the second of her three trips. Arnold rented a motorized scooter for her to get around on her own during the day. Her trip turned out to be extra special, as her youngest sister, Kathy, and her husband, George, were in Hawaii to celebrate their twenty-fifth wedding anniversary. A highlight for Arnold was teaching a course on the Messianic Jewish Epistles at the International College and Graduate School. As more congregations got wind of Arnold's itinerary in Hawaii, they, too, wanted him as a guest speaker. Despite his busy schedule, he squeezed in all the new requests.

In mid-March, Arnold headed off to Israel, a few days in advance of Mary Ann. For many years, she had been asking for a private trip to Israel, with no study group and no scheduled engagements for Arnold. It would be the third and most important of her three trips, likely her last to the Land she so loved. Two of Arnold's Israeli cousins arranged for a wheelchair to be waiting for her at their hotel in Tel-Aviv. A mere two days after her arrival, the second American war in Iraq broke out on the 20th of March 2003. Within a few weeks, the American forces reached Baghdad. Many believers in the U.S., fearful of the war's effects on Israel, were frightened away from visiting.

If we are going to call ourselves Messianic Jews, then this is the time to show our loyalty by going there and not abandoning Israel in her time of need. Otherwise, we prove ourselves to be nothing but fair-weather friends.[65]

My observation while here, as usual, is different from what is reported... Throughout the whole war, life continued along normal lines. That is the nature of the Israeli spirit. If the Arabs bomb something, the Israelis quickly rebuild it and make a point of returning to it... They refuse to allow terrorists to intimidate them into staying home. Americans could use a good dose of such a spirit. There is a right way and a wrong way to respond to terrorism. The Israelis respond the correct way. Otherwise, it would prove that terrorism works and only invite more of the same. Americans need to learn that terrorism is to be confronted and not compromised with. For those reasons the streets of Israel are safe, and Mary Ann and I never felt any sense of danger while there.

And no, this war did not fulfill any prophecy either... However, some could not resist resorting to "newspaper exegesis." It is a given that Babylon, located in southern Iraq, is to play a major role in Bible prophecy. But, nothing that happened recently is directly relevant to Bible prophecy. Yes, it may be stage setting for such fulfillment, but it is too soon to tell and speculation only gives prophecy a bad name...

Besides wanting to go to those places that had special meaning for her from the days when we lived in Jerusalem, Mary Ann wanted to see two things in particular. The first was museums in different parts of the country. I am not a museum person, but this was her trip, and I had agreed she would be the one to set the itinerary. On this trip, I walked through more museums than I had ever walked through in my entire life! But since visiting museums was important for Mary Ann, it also became important for me.[66]

---

[65] Excerpt: *On The Road,* January-February 2003

[66] Excerpts: *On The Road,* March-April 2003

In reality, Arnold had a strong aversion to museums. When asked later if he might have changed his mind, his reply was an immediate and resounding "No!" He never intended to step foot in another museum ever again!

Spring was Mary Ann's favorite season in Israel, when flowers were in full bloom across the country, including the Negev Desert. The second on her particular wish list was to see these spring flowers.

> They come up for a short time each year from about mid-March to mid-April. Not every spring is a good year for flowers, since it is dependent upon the kind of winter Israel has had. This year, in the providence of God, Israel had the best winter in over ten years. There was a lot of rain and snow, making this one of the best springs to travel to Israel. Mary Ann saw myriads of flowers in a variety of colors; this was one of the highlights of the entire tour. I praise the Lord that the year He chose to break the drought was the same year Mary Ann chose to travel to the Land of Israel, maybe for the last time.[67]

Israel being a hilly country, it proved quite a challenge for Arnold to push the wheelchair around. He humorously remarked afterwards that he had built up some biceps just in the three and a half weeks! They enjoyed fellowshipping with other believers with whom they had a long association in the Land. They also got together with Arnold's Israeli family members. Except for one, all of Arnold's aunts and uncles had passed away by this time, leaving only cousins. One of them organized a cousins' get-together at her home, treating everyone to their wonderful, warm Jewish hospitality. Like typical Israelis, Arnold's cousins were all very secular in their lifestyle and outlook, with no interest in Orthodox traditions, nor any leanings toward spiritual matters. Arnold faithfully continued to pray for his relatives to come to salvation in *Yeshua*.

A Jewish believer from their messianic congregation in Irvine, also suffering from MS, had written a prayer request to be healed and asked Mary Ann to insert the piece of paper in between the large stones of the Western Wall of the Second Temple in Jerusalem. As Mary Ann drew near, torrents of tears suddenly gushed forth, inundating her with a flood of raw emotions. That this visit may well be her last touched a sensitive chord within, exposing her

---

[67] Excerpts: *On The Road*, March-April 2003

feelings of loss and grief, leaving her awash with waves of melancholy. Short of God's divine intervention, she knew that her condition would continue to degenerate day by day. In the deep recesses of her soul, she mourned the loss of her mobility, wistfully recalling how she used to walk normally. Now in a wheelchair, she was dependent upon others even for the simplest of daily tasks. Through her tears, Mary Ann silently prayed for the Lord to grant her strength and perseverance to adjust physically and emotionally to her new life, now wrought with physical limitations. She took comfort in the Lord's unfailing Word that promised: *My grace is sufficient for you: for My power is made perfect in weakness.* (II Corinthians 12:9)

Despite the sadness, Mary Ann felt profoundly moved and grateful that God had blessed her with this precious opportunity to be here in Jerusalem at this magnificent holy site of prayer. As she slipped the little folded piece of paper between the large stones, a surge of poignancy mingled with a deep abiding hope infused her with an aura of peace and acceptance—a tender moment that would stay with her a long, long time.

On their last day together in Israel, Arnold and Mary Ann went for a picnic at a park atop a hill, part of the Jerusalem Forest. The spot that Arnold had picked was idyllic. Myriads of colorful wild flowers, still in full bloom, covered the hillside like thousands of intricate paint drops showered across a brilliant emerald canvas. Wafts of fragrant scents from the flowers floated dreamily on the wings of the gentle breeze. Against a cloudless, clear blue sky overlooking the Old City, the Valley of Hinnom and the Mount of Olives, the panoramic view from every angle photographed like a vivid postcard, bringing into sharp focus all the picturesque details, a truly spectacular snapshot to remember.

The next day, Mary Ann flew back to the United States, while Arnold stayed behind for two more days to make preparations for the two back-to-back, five-week tours coming up the following year. He took care of whatever arrangements that could be made a year in advance, leaving the rest of the details to be worked on as time progressed. With the *Pesach* Feast only about a week away, Arnold purchased a Passover kit to take to the Ariel representative in Germany, which he planned to borrow for the Passover demonstrations during his five-week itinerary, beginning in two-days' time.

In the middle of his teaching tour in Germany, Arnold took a side trip to Switzerland to conduct an Easter Conference on the topic of Bible prophecy, which more than a thousand people attended. At the end of his time in Germany, he flew to England for a three-day teaching conference.

After another round of speaking engagements back in the United States in early June, the Lord provided Arnold and Mary Ann with a special two-day stay at a fancy hotel in Palm Springs, California, virtually free of charge. As their thirty-fifth wedding anniversary was approaching in a few weeks, they enjoyed their getaway as a sort of pre-anniversary celebration. Mary Ann did really well in spite of her walking limitations. While Arnold was inwardly very concerned whenever he witnessed her falling over, he simply learned to entrust her health to the Lord. The couple of days spent enjoying the beauty of the desert scenery was a lovely way for them to have time alone together before Arnold's next long teaching trip overseas.

Touch of Agony

Traveling as an itinerant Bible teacher over the years, Arnold found that his leisure suits were starting to wear out. Knowing that his flight route in mid-June 2003 from Tokyo, Japan, to New Zealand involved a stopover in Singapore, he planned a two-day layover. He wanted to have some new leisure suits tailor-made to replace the old ones he got in Asia fourteen years earlier. As it turned out, due to an outbreak of SARS[68] and the sharp decline in tourism there, Arnold got a very good price.

From Singapore, he was supposed to fly to New Zealand by catching a connecting flight that same day via Hong Kong. Upon arrival, Arnold discovered that his flight to New Zealand had been cancelled, causing an upheaval in his itinerary. Totally unplanned, he now had to stay overnight in Hong Kong. The airline did not even offer to pay for his hotel bill. Because of this unforeseen delay, he was forced to cancel his first meeting in New Zealand, something he hated to do.

Since his original return flights also included an overnight stay in Hong Kong and then in Singapore, Arnold decided to make the best use of this

---

[68] Severe Acute Respiratory Syndrome

unexpected layover to get more new leisure suits tailor-made. Hong Kong's tourism was also adversely affected by the SARS epidemic, so he got an even better price. With a deposit paid, he could collect his suits on his return leg. Having an aversion to ties, leisure suits worked well for him, even though they may have gone out of style for decades. Arnold figured that these new leisure suits would last him for the rest of his ministry years.

The Ariel New Zealand branch, officially established in Auckland since December 2002, had lined up his entire itinerary. Except for the first cancelled meeting due to his delayed arrival, the rest of Arnold's schedule around the country, including a six-day camp, took place as planned. Mottel Baleston, a longtime friend of the ministry and teacher at Camp Shoshanah, flew in to co-teach with him at the camp.

On his return trip home, Arnold prayed that no other events would force other unexpected changes in his travel plans. He enjoyed traveling and usually did not mind putting up with all the adjustments and occasional flight disruptions that an itinerant ministry often entailed. Otherwise, the long hours of flying, the inconvenience of adapting to the time zone changes, eating foreign foods, and sleeping in countless motel rooms for a large part of the year would be difficult to handle.

Back home, Mary Ann held up pretty well most of the time. On occasion, even with the assistance of her walker, she would lose her balance and take a fall. She resisted using a wheelchair in the house, simply to avoid being reminded of her lifelong irrevocable condition. Accomplishing daily tasks became a constant struggle, which slowly took its toll on her emotions. Very pained to see his beloved wife facing this ongoing trial, Arnold felt helpless in not being able to stop her neurological degeneration. He prayed for God's divine empowerment to enable Mary Ann to make the best of her situation.

In mid-2003, about a year and a half after Mary Ann's car accident on the Los Angeles freeway, the situation reared its ugly head again. At the time she hit the back of the vehicle, the other driver appeared to be fine, having no problems walking and driving away. Now, after such a long lapse of time, the man from Philadelphia, Pennsylvania, decided to sue. The papers filed against Mary Ann claimed that the driver was so badly injured he was unable to work and needed compensation for the rest of his life. Although the claim was so obviously fraudulent, the man had found a lawyer who was willing to represent him as an invalid victim. To handle the case with the courts, Mary Ann's insurance agency had to assign a lawyer, who was obliged to take a couple of trips to Philadelphia to question the plaintiff regarding his side of the story. If the man had been so badly injured, why did he not go to a doctor right away instead of waiting for over six months before seeking medical attention? The two sides found themselves at loggerheads. To break the stalemate, the parties finally agreed to arbitration instead of going directly to court.

Unfortunately, the amount of money that the arbitration decided to award the plaintiff was far more than what Mary Ann's insurance company was willing to pay. There was no other recourse but to take the matter to court. This whole situation was one more hurdle that the spiritual enemy had thrown in their path, which Arnold and Mary Ann did not need at this challenging time in their life. They simply entrusted the situation into the Lord's hands and prayed that He would overrule the final outcome. Eventually, the case was settled out of court.

AFTER ONLY A FEW DAYS at home with hardly enough time to fully recover from his jet lag, Arnold flew up to Camp Shoshanah. The 2003 summer marked the thirtieth annual discipleship program, a major milestone in the Camp's history. Sadly, between thirty to forty people had to be turned away, due to a lack of sufficient accommodations on the campgrounds. This situation emphasized the urgent need for more expansion work to be carried out as soon as the building permit could be attained. A top priority was the construction of a new kitchen and dining hall facility.

Arnold's fall schedule proceeded at a fast clip. In late August, he taught his annual course at Chafer Theological Seminary in southern California. After a few days at the Home Office, he flew to Montreal for his annual teaching tour in Quebec, Canada, followed by a quick trip to speak at a church in Lansing, Michigan, where Mary Ann's brother-in-law, George, was a pastor. It was the last engagement before Arnold and Mary Ann went to the Adirondacks for a respite from ministry work.

While there, Arnold celebrated his sixtieth birthday on the 26th of September, a special personal milestone. He had plenty of time for quiet reflection to review his life and see the gracious hand of God upon him every step along the way. In light of his ankle injury four years earlier, it had only slowly dawned on him that he was no longer a young man. Time had passed very quickly, and there was still so much to be done. Twenty-five books of the Bible still needed to be researched and taped as part of the *Ariel's Bible*

Commentary series, which he wanted to complete and leave behind, among other works, as part of his legacy.

Strolling through the back roads of the Adirondacks, Arnold marveled at the beauty of the autumnal colors. The landscape appeared so much deeper, richer and more vibrant in the fall, when the leaves reached their maturity, bringing out the full gamut of tones in their color palettes. As he contemplated the parallels of the autumn season to his current stage in life, it occurred to him that this could potentially be his most productive period, having now reached a level of spiritual maturity where God could use him in even more far-reaching ways.

In mid-December 2003, Arnold had the unique opportunity to teach in Singapore at the Mount Carmel Bible Presbyterian Church, a fairly large congregation, consisting mainly of English-speaking Chinese as well as some bi-lingual speakers. The man who arranged the meetings first came across Ariel through some tapes that he had received while studying in England. A number of years later, he was able to get his church to agree to a conference. The teachings on "Prophecy and the Jew" and "Prophetic Significance of the Feasts" were well received. What a long way the ministry had come since the early days when Arnold had to knock on doors to get a meeting! Thanks to the Lord, nowadays it was the other people requesting meetings instead, such that Arnold's schedule was constantly booked more than two years out.

Before year-end, Ruth Wardell would be turning eighty. Some, who had known her for many years, including a group from the former Messianic Youth Fellowship, planned and organized a wonderful surprise birthday party for her in Plano, Texas, where she lived. Later, Ruth recounted how appreciative she felt that Arnold and Mary Ann had taken the time to travel all the way there to be at her party, knowing how busy Arnold's schedule was. Yet, he would not have missed this opportunity for the world, to celebrate his spiritual mom's special day.

ARNOLD BEGAN THE YEAR 2004 with an extended teaching itinerary overseas in Europe. After a long flight to Germany and storing most of his luggage at the airport hotel in Frankfurt, Arnold took a short side trip to England to hold a three-day Bible conference in a small town called Normandy. When the agent at the British passport control asked Arnold where he was going, his reply, "Normandy," elicited the retort, "You mean you are on your way to France." When Arnold explained that he was heading to Normandy, England, the agent insisted there was no such place. Having traveled to the same rural town of Normandy a few times before, Arnold assured him that the place really did exist in England. After a few more rounds of friendly debate, the agent eventually gave up, stamped Arnold's passport and let him in. At least, the participants knew of its existence!

The church sponsoring the conference was a very supportive one. The attendance of a particular Jewish believer was a special joy for Arnold. She was the artist who had lodged in the same building as Arnold and Mary Ann during their time in Jerusalem. Ever since they dropped her off in England in the summer of 1973, they had not seen or heard from her. When Arnold taught at this church the last time, her sister from the nearby vicinity had attended the meetings and told her about the speaker. In turn, she made contact with Arnold via E-mail. She had become a recognized artist in her country, was married with grown children, and going strong with the Lord. It was wonderful for Arnold to see her again, and Mary Ann regretted not being able to join this happy reunion.

Back in California, before fully recovering from his jet lag, Arnold flew to San Antonio, Texas, in mid-March 2004 for a two-day speaking engagement at Wayside Chapel. Once back home, he had just enough time to pack for his trip across the Atlantic, this time to prepare for his upcoming, back-to-back Israel Study Tours. With Arnold entering the autumnal years of his life—time being a precious commodity and other areas of the ministry requiring his focus and attention—these would be the last of the lengthy tours he would be conducting. Interest was thus very high. Following the abrupt last-minute, forced cancellation of the tour in 2002, Arnold gave those participants first priority this year if they chose to go. To allow for as many people as possible to take part, he offered two such tours back-to-back and increased the number of spaces available per tour from twenty-seven to thirty-five, utilizing four mini-vans instead of three per tour. As a precautionary safety measure, Arnold rented a bulletproof bus for their two-day visit through the West Bank.

Prior to the two English-speaking tours, Arnold guided a German group for two and a half weeks through Israel from late March to early April 2004. The director of Word of Life in Germany headed up the group and also served as Arnold's interpreter.

About half way through the German tour, the leader of a terrorist group was assassinated by Israeli forces. Ahmad

```
Yassin  was  the  founder  and  spiritual  leader  of  an
organization  that  has  encouraged  Arab  children  to  blow
themselves  up  in  crowds  of  Israelis.  The  hotel  rooms  had
TV's  displaying  CNN.  Therefore,  the  Germans  got  a  good
taste  of  the  difference  between  that  which  is  reported  by
the  news  media  and  what  is  actually  happening.  One  example
will  suffice.  The  news  broadcast  stated  that  the  Israelis
in  Jerusalem  were  so  afraid  of  reprisal  that  the  streets
of  Jerusalem  were  empty,  because  everyone  stayed  home.
However,  the  only  part  of  Jerusalem  that  was  empty  was  the
Arab  side  as  they  observed  a  three-day  period  of  mourning
for  a  terrorist.  The  Jewish  side  of  Jerusalem  was  full  of
people  on  the  streets  and  on  the  buses…  We  found  it  so
difficult  to  get  around  the  streets  due  to  traffic  that  we
wished  the  news  broadcasters  were  accurate.  But  they  were
not,  and  they  are  not.  Their  anti-Israel  bias  clearly
shows,  and  it  is  a  shame  that  so  many  people  in  the  USA
believe  them!  As  the  Germans  who  were  with  me  can  testify,
Israel  is  safe. [69]
```

Upon the German group's departure, it was Passover week. Arnold had a ten-day interval of ministry work before the first English-speaking tour was due to start. His three-day conference at a congregation in Beersheba concluded with a Passover *Seder* with about two hundred people in attendance, mostly Russian Jews. Since his first contact with this congregation in 1966 during his student days in Israel, it was a joy to see its considerable growth.

In Jerusalem, Arnold spoke twice at the Messianic Assembly to which he and Mary Ann belonged while living in Israel between 1971 and 1973. He also had the privilege of speaking at a new congregation in the city of Arad. Also taking time to fellowship with other believers whom he had known for a long time in the Land, he derived so much joy in connecting with people from his past.

```
Every  now  and  then  the  past  also  presses  itself  into  the
present  with  its  own  pleasantness  that  is  sweeter  than  the
smell  of  myrrh. [70]
```

---

[69] Excerpts: *Ariel Ministries Newsletter*, Spring 2004

[70] Excerpt: *On The Road*, May-June 2002

God answered Arnold's prayers for both English-speaking groups to be eager learners, who developed camaraderie with one another. Some adversities did occur, though coming from outside the groups and not from within. The first group of thirty-four participants, mainly Americans from Hawaii, was dubbed the *Shaloha* tour, a combination of *Shalom* in Hebrew and *Aloha* in Hawaiian. The second group of thirty-five people had a distinct international flavor, representing the United States, Canada, England, Australia, New Zealand, Holland, Germany, Hungary, Japan, plus a young woman from Israel, whose mother had taken part in one of Arnold's initial tours some thirty years earlier, when Ruth Wardell brought along a group of teenagers from the M.Y.F. in New York. A good number were from previous tours, wanting to see Israel again, plus many first-timers. All zealous in their studies, they were a joy for Arnold to show around, making his time in Israel all the more worthwhile.

Rather than having a preference for certain sites, Arnold embraced them all equally in his heart with an abiding attachment. Though some places were prettier than others, he could never bring himself to pick out a favorite spot. His last day in Israel would be a difficult one for him, especially the moment when he had to board the plane to return home. Thus, his time in Israel was bittersweet, as he would truly miss leading the lengthier tours. Nonetheless, the Lord had impressed upon him that it was now time to put his energies into producing the *Ariel's Bible Commentary* series and to develop and expand the Camp Shoshanah program.

I leave Israel with sadness. It is not that I will not be back; I expect to be back in 2005 and 2006 and, Lord willing, thereafter… I would be willing to arrange, conduct, and guide this type of tour in the future—on one condition. A group of at least twenty people needs to be organized and the funds collected. I will then be happy to make the reservations and serve as guide. I am even willing to lead for… five weeks, but I know that… most groups will only be free to travel for two weeks and a few for three weeks… Thus, as I went through the whole country this time, I knew I might never see some places again in this life. I am known for not showing my emotions, but that does not mean I do not have them. I felt sadness and a touch of agony as I turned my back on places that, humanly-speaking, I will not see again, because it is only possible to see them on the five-week tour.[71]

THIS TIME, MARY ANN WAS NOT ALONE during Arnold's lengthy time away. Her niece, Rachel, flew in from Albany, New York, to spend a month with her. Later, her youngest sister, Kathy, came to visit her from Michigan. Bogdana had finished her seminary studies and moved away. Mary Ann was now looking for someone to come to the house twice a week to clean and prepare the meals. Two strong men were needed to help rearrange some furniture to make the house more accessible for her wheelchair and her walker. There were many simple things that Mary Ann could no longer do.

Even taking care of the pets became more and more difficult. Mary Ann and Arnold decided that as the cats died off, no new ones would be adopted. For the past thirty-six years of their marriage, they had always had cats in the household, occasionally even as many as seven at one time. Recently, the last of their cats had died, and Arnold and Mary Ann now became a "cat-less" family. This, too, was part of the transition and adjustment in the new phase of their life going forward.

Seeing Mary Ann slowly lose her mobility was extremely difficult for Arnold. Being a very private person, he kept his pervading dull, aching, inner pain to himself, and rarely talked about it even to his close friends. He prayed privately to God for His strength and protection over Mary Ann and continued to trust the Lord's sovereignty over their life.

Since Ariel Ministries' inception some twenty-seven years earlier, Arnold had been away from home at least twenty-five days per month within the United States. When abroad, his absence often stretched to several months. Over the years, he had attempted to curtail some of his travels, to little avail. His schedule was still as full as ever with no reprieve in sight. A paradigm shift was imperative in the way he served.

Several years earlier, the Ariel board had given Arnold a directive to start cutting back on his time away from home and to make some serious changes to his overseas itineraries. To save on transoceanic airfares, Arnold tended to

---

[71] Excerpts: *On The Road*, May-June 2004

stay abroad for two to four months in a row. To assist his wife, he needed to be at the home base for longer periods.

Part of Arnold's transition to a new travel pattern included terminating those intensive five-week tours to Israel and making cuts to his local U.S. itinerary. It was with great reluctance that he wrote letters to some of the churches where meetings had already been confirmed to ask for a postponement by a year or more. In the habit of adhering so rigorously to his schedule, it was not an easy exercise for him. Even more difficult was canceling some meetings permanently, as he did not plan on returning to those places again. Having developed a warm and close relationship with some of the churches, it was with a heavy heart that he removed them from his teaching itinerary. Given the new travel policy, he regretfully had to make some hard choices.

While most of Arnold's manuscripts, books and tapes were either written or taped during times away from the Home Office, there were certain projects, such as the *Life of Messiah* manuscript, which were of a different nature and necessitated him to be at home in his extensive library to complete the research portions on the rabbinic background. He started this project decades earlier, but had not yet seen it to completion. It now became a priority to finish the book. When the Ariel board of directors had undergone a complete change with all new members by mid-2004, it formulated a new set of guidelines, stipulating the number of days that Arnold could be away from home in any given month. While he knew full well what his priorities were, he nevertheless felt the agony of having to let go of his extensive travels.

The new board was well aware that this paring down of Arnold's travels would prove to be a difficult and challenging phase for him. Arnold was an extreme creature of habit, almost to a fault. For decades, he had been used to traveling frequently in the United States and fulfilling long teaching itineraries abroad. Going on trips was second nature to him. To a certain extent, he had quite a strong-willed and stubborn personality and needed a firm board of directors to steer him and Ariel Ministries accordingly in the 21st century. Relying on the Lord's wisdom to guide him, Arnold planned to cut his next overseas teaching trip by half the time that was originally scheduled.

At the end of Camp Shoshanah in the summer of 2004, as usual, Arnold taught for two weeks at Chafer Theological Seminary. Following two days of speaking in South Carolina, he headed up to Canada in mid-September for a one-week teaching tour around Quebec. Toward the end of September 2004,

Arnold and Mary Ann took their annual fall break in the beautiful Adirondacks. Gary Demers, the camp supervisor, did a great job in completing the extension to their cabin the day before their arrival. The much-needed new bedroom came in very handy. Arnold, being a night owl, liked to stay up late into the wee hours to research or to write, while Mary Ann needed her sleep, especially when feeling unwell. In the middle of their three-week break, she had to be hospitalized for a few days due to acute dehydration and needed to rest after being discharged. Arnold could keep on working in the living area as late as he wanted to without disturbing her rest and sleep in the adjacent bedroom. The new enclosed screen porch was also a delightful feature. Mary Ann could now sit there and enjoy the nice view across the campgrounds while getting some fresh air, without having to use her walker or leave the cabin.

Adapting to Another Move

While casting his mind over the past as he was writing up his editorial for the upcoming summer 2005 issue of the *Ariel Ministries Newsletter*, Arnold dwelt on the importance of discipleship and of making the most out of the number of days that God had given each person. Perhaps, it was because of the many changes that Ariel Ministries was undergoing at the time, or because he was experiencing the autumnal years of his life, but as of late, his communications had a wistful echo of nostalgia.

As of this writing, I'm sixty-one years old. My ministry has been primarily a teaching ministry. I have had the joy of teaching the Bible from a Jewish perspective all over the world. In Psalm 90, Moses instructs Israel to number their days and I am doing so, now that mine are passing. As of now, there are a little over 3,000 days left before my seventieth birthday. Only the Lord knows how many actual days I have left before seeing Him face-to-face. It has been my prayer since the beginning of Ariel Ministries that when my days are completed, I will have been known as a faithful Bible teacher and that because of our ministry, others will follow in the "footsteps of the Messiah." But how will I know if I have effectively completed my God-ordained life's work? Can I know whether or not I have run the race well before my passing? That is a question we should all consider.[72]

The first half of 2005 had been very hectic for Arnold. Following a speaking engagement in New Mexico in early January 2005, he flew to Hawaii for a two-month itinerary. In early March, he traveled to Japan to fulfill his annual ten-day teaching tour through Harvest Time Ministries, mainly in Tokyo and Osaka. He then continued on to New Zealand for five weeks of speaking engagements. Back in the United States, due to a number of circumstances, the 2005 French Camp was rescheduled for the year after. Likewise, the Russian Camp was also postponed until 2006. During the English-speaking camp, it was a thrill for the ministry to break ground in faith for the construction of the new kitchen and dining hall structure to accommodate the growing number of people wanting to attend. As the camp discipleship program became more widely known, it had been heartbreaking for Arnold during some years to have to turn away many applicants, due to a lack of space.

Three days prior to the end of the program, Arnold flew back to California to be with Mary Ann. She was undergoing her second spinal surgery, which thankfully proceeded well without complications. This time, he took care of her at home during her recovery period, pulping and liquefying all her food, and helping out in a myriad of other ways. They were both very grateful to the Lord that her condition steadily improved. Hence, Arnold could resume his commitments for the rest of the year.

From late August to early September 2005, he spent one week teaching in Alaska. After fulfilling his engagements in the western part of the United States, Arnold and Mary Ann took their annual fall vacation and enjoyed the splendid autumn colors of the Adirondack Mountains. In late autumn, Arnold went to Canada on two separate occasions to teach in the provinces of Alberta and Ontario. In early December, he presented his personal testimony and also led a devotional time at the fourteenth annual Pre-Tribulation

---

[72] Excerpts: *Ariel Ministries Newsletter*, Summer 2005

Conference in Dallas, Texas. His last speaking engagement of the year took place one week before Christmas Day, after which he and Mary Ann spent a short time off together.

EARLIER IN THE SPRING OF 2005, the new Ariel board concluded that it would make more sense, especially from a financial standpoint, to move the Ariel Home Office back to San Antonio. The ministry's rent and operating costs in California were skyrocketing and showed no signs of abating anytime soon. Though the area in southern California had a much larger Jewish population than in San Antonio, Arnold was away from the home base so often that he had no time for a focused ministry to the local Jews. The general cost of living in San Antonio was about one third that of southern California, more sustainable for the ministry long term. Other viable reasons favoring a move back included the purchase of a building for the ministry in San Antonio, so the board decided to forge ahead.

Arnold himself was neither for nor against the move back to San Antonio. He remained neutral just as he had with the ministry's relocation out to California some twenty years earlier and was again willing to follow the board's lead. Being a free spirit and at the same time a creature of habit, he needed support and accountability in completing some of his writing projects and in cutting back on his travels, something he struggled with. Having most of the board members living in the same city would help him greatly. It seemed, however, that Mary Ann was not so keen about the move. She felt very comfortable with her doctors in California and with her friends both inside and outside of Ariel Ministries and was reluctant to be uprooted again. It took a while for her to eventually agree to the move, but she did so with some serious reservations.

Thus, during the months of January and February 2006, Arnold and Mary Ann went through the major job of packing up their home in Irvine. Having lived in southern California for over twenty-one years, it was no small task, especially in view of Arnold's extensive library, which had grown even larger over the years. They would not have been able to complete the task without the help of friends who came and faithfully packed one box after the other. All their belongings were then loaded onto a big moving truck to be taken to San Antonio and placed in storage. Extra challenges from Mary Ann's use of a motorized wheelchair had to be taken into account. However, all things considered, the packing and moving went smoothly. Some friends of theirs drove Arnold's car all the way to Texas for him, while Arnold and Mary Ann flew directly to San Antonio during the first weekend in March.

There, they stayed temporarily in a furnished two-story house belonging to Wayside Chapel. Normally reserved for their missionaries on furlough, the house happened to be vacant for about a two-month period until late May, right around the time Arnold and Mary Ann needed lodging. While the new Ariel building was undergoing renovations, Arnold turned one of the upstairs rooms of the house into his temporary office. Since the master bedroom was located on the ground floor, it was also very convenient for Mary Ann to get around in her wheelchair.

Meanwhile, they set about actively looking for a suitable home for themselves. After a time of intensive searching, they found a one-level house that could work well for them, given some minor remodeling. It was located in a town called Helotes, just outside the greater San Antonio area, within a twenty-to-thirty minute drive from the new Ariel Home Office. Their offer was accepted, and the house purchase was closed on the 12th of April 2006, with the title transfer date set for the 25th of May. Ariel Ministries purchased the house in its name to serve as a parsonage for Arnold and Mary Ann, thus alleviating their need to pay for housing costs and associated property taxes. The ministry also paid for the renovation work to enable wheelchair accessibility. The shower in the bathroom, which was connected to the master bedroom, needed enlarging to make it user-friendly for Mary Ann. Floor-to-ceiling shelves were custom-built in two rooms to accommodate the many thousands of books in Arnold's massive library.

The renovations in the parsonage were completed just before Arnold and Mary Ann had to move out of their temporary house by the 22nd of May. Because the remodeling had spread a layer of dust everywhere inside the house, a group of volunteers from Wayside Chapel came and did a major cleaning as soon as the title transfer went through. Shortly thereafter, the moving company delivered all their belongings that had been in storage. Arnold was overseas on a speaking tour in Australia at that time, so Mary Ann moved in on her own the following day and slowly began the time-consuming task of unpacking and settling in. They were both very grateful to the people at their home church, who proved to be immensely helpful in a unique Texan style, as well as to the Ariel Home Office staff, who assisted in so many ways.

Their house in Irvine, on the market since December 2005, had not as yet been sold. They had received a few offers, but the prices were far too low to be worth considering. Praying earnestly for a sale soon, they hoped to avoid the same kind of stress from an unsold house that they had experienced in the past. In the intervening twenty-one years of living in the same house, its market value had increased dramatically. They needed the proceeds to purchase a custom-made van specifically designed for the physically challenged. Here in San Antonio, they had been renting such a van, enabling Mary Ann to drive on her own while she still had enough mobility to do so, thus not needing to depend upon others to drive her around to do her shopping or go to her appointments. Nor did she have to end up largely confined to the house, as had been the case in California. However, the high costs of renting a special van were prohibitive, and they could not sustain the ongoing rental expenses for too much longer.

It was thus a tremendous relief for Arnold and Mary Ann when their house in California was finally sold and closed on the 27th of July 2006. Due to a drop in the housing market, the sale price was considerably lower than what they had wanted. Nevertheless, they were thankful that they now had the funds to order a custom-made van from the agency, which cost $60,000. Their insurance company would not cover it, so with the capital gains from their house sale, Arnold and Mary Ann could make the purchase outright and remain debt-free. The Lord's protective hand was evident, as one thing was for certain. They had sold their house just before the big housing market crash in California, followed shortly by a severe nationwide recession.

ON THE FIRST OF FEBRUARY 2006, the new Ariel Home Office officially opened its doors in San Antonio, Texas, with a brand new staff. None of the previous workers in the Tustin office transferred with the ministry. Arnold, hence, had a new executive secretary, Denise Velarde, whom he had interviewed and hired on one of his previous trips to San Antonio. The new staff was very busy, retooling the delivery systems of the audio Bible study materials into the CD format, the written manuscripts into PDF files, and the videotapes into the DVD format. It was a huge undertaking in addition to their daily work. The results of this endeavor would enable Arnold's teachings to be launched around the world and to have a significant global impact that otherwise would have been inconceivable just a few years earlier.

Although Arnold was originally scheduled to go to Europe on a teaching tour from January to March 2006, the Ariel board of directors, for a number of pragmatic reasons, requested that the itinerary be cancelled. This change of plans worked out well, allowing the Fruchtenbaums about three months to pack up their house in California, move and look for a house in San Antonio. In April 2006, Arnold's travels were minimal with speaking engagements only in a few states.

At the beginning of May 2006, Arnold went overseas to Australia on a one-month teaching tour. From there, he flew to Japan and then to Israel, where he served as the tour guide to a group from Reno, Nevada for two weeks. It turned out to be the kind of group that he especially enjoyed taking around, and he praised God for it.

> The group included people from other states and four women who came from Perth, Australia. In spite of some typical Israeli-style hassles, including having two of the vans broken into on the first night, the group took all things well. It was during this tour that the Arab terrorists kidnapped an Israeli soldier which later, after I returned to the U.S.A., led to a similar event in the north, which in turn led to a flare-up. But the flare-up is geographically limited, and Israel is otherwise quite safe to visit...[73]

By the time Arnold returned to the United States in early July 2006, Mary Ann had already moved into their remodeled house for about six weeks while he was away for nine. In between several of his speaking engagements during the month of July before the Camp Shoshanah program began, he had a total of about ten days free to unpack his one hundred and twenty boxes of books, in addition to the boxes of household items. He managed to unpack most of his books, with twenty-seven boxes left to go. At the same time, Mary Ann also asked him to go shopping for plants and flowers, so that she could beautify the front and backyards. Having no more cats, gardening had become an important part of her life and a major factor to her happiness. With the help from others, she planned on making the yards look like a beautiful forest garden. On balance, Mary Ann appeared to be adjusting well

---

[73] Excerpt: *On The Road*, August/September 2006

to her life back in San Antonio, renewing old friendships that had begun over thirty years earlier, which was put on hold when they moved out to California.

In mid-August 2006, about a week after Camp Shoshanah, Arnold flew to Israel to serve as the tour guide and teacher to a group sponsored by Calvary Chapel in Kauai, Hawaii. Participants came from the United States, Canada, Australia, and England. The four-week tour included a visit to Jordan.

Arnold also spoke in three different Israeli Brethren congregations in Haifa, Jaffa, and Jerusalem. A conference on *Rosh Hashanah*, or Feast of Trumpets, was held just outside the city limits of Jerusalem. Two of the congregations appeared to have been well taught, which made it easier for Arnold to teach the Word in a deeper way.

When he returned home during the third week in September 2006, Arnold and Mary Ann took their annual autumn break up in the Adirondacks. While there, they saw the structure of the new kitchen and dining hall being prepared for the new roof to go up. They prayed that sufficient funds would come in for the building to be completed by the summer of 2008. The rest of the year was again filled with speaking engagements in various states as well as a trip to teach a seminar at a Bible school in British Colombia, Canada. In early December, Arnold attended the annual 2006 Pre-Tribulation Study Conference in Dallas, Texas, which he very much enjoyed. He wrapped up the year by going up to Canada for a second time before mid-December on a one-week conference tour in Quebec.

PART VII

~ *Trust* ~

Commit your way unto Jehovah;
Trust also in Him,
and He will bring it to pass.

(Psalms 37:5)

Shortly into 2007, Arnold flew to Honolulu, Oahu, one of the eight islands of Hawaii, for his two-month itinerary. Mary Ann joined him five days later. After organizing a condo, they flew to Kauai, their favorite island, for two weeks of ministry. Arnold taught almost every night plus a full day at a Bible college connected to Kauai Calvary Chapel, while Mary Ann enjoyed the company of a group of women from one of the newer churches that had recently opened wide its doors to Ariel Ministries. They had been praying that she would come to Kauai this time and thoroughly enjoyed wheeling her around to various places. Very quickly, they learned that she was not only a cat lover but also a Bob Dylan fanatic, taking every opportunity to expound on his lyrics. For the Fruchtenbaums' send-off, many church members, all wearing Bob Dylan T-Shirts, gathered at the airport and presented Mary Ann with a special T-shirt to wear when she got back to Oahu.

It was gratifying for Arnold and Mary Ann to learn that some members of this thriving new church had been discipled in the past by friends of theirs, who had lived on Kauai for many years. Arnold hoped to return many times in the future to minister and to teach at this church. In all his years of ministry in Hawaii, he had seen many changes with the passage of time. Some pastors transferred away to other states; others eventually got promoted to glory. Certain churches closed down; others, having turned to a form of Replacement Theology, no longer welcomed Arnold's teaching ministry. Yet, as one door closed, God would open up another.

In February, midway through their stay in Hawaii, Arnold and Mary Ann received an urgent phone call, which they had been dreading. Beth, Mary Ann's younger sister, was in her last days in her stiff battle with cancer. Having gone into remission for a while, the cancer had reared its ugly head again in the previous fall of 2006, this time with a vengeance. Beth had subsequently undergone a special treatment of chemotherapy with no certainty that it would work for her. Their mother had passed away several years earlier in 2003 from cancer. Hence, Mary Ann wanted to spend as much time as she could with her sister in Albany, New York, a three-hour drive south of Camp Shoshanah. So, before Arnold resumed his ministry schedule after their autumn break of 2006 in the Adirondacks, he had arranged for the two sisters to be together while he was away. Mary Ann's youngest sister, Kathy, had quit her job in Michigan to spend the last few months in Albany. Now sadly, Beth was losing her valiant fight.

As soon as Mary Ann got the phone call, she flew to Albany to be with her sister during her last week. Beth, already a believer in the Lord, phoned Arnold with some serious questions about what would happen to her upon death. He was able to comfort her, and later, Mary Ann shared that the phone call took the edge off Beth's pain. Once her soul had departed for Heaven, Arnold cancelled a conference in Hawaii and flew to Albany to join the family for the funeral. Kathy's husband, George, presided over the ceremony, while Arnold gave a short presentation of the Gospel. The next day, the Fruchtenbaums flew back to Hawaii, and Arnold resumed his itinerary.

Over the years, they had felt a sense of family in Hawaii, developing relationships not only with the pastors but also with individual lay people. Yet, like the shifting sands on a beach, even among their close "Hawaiian Circle," there were those who had moved off the islands, while others succumbed to illness and passed through the veil. Only one pastor, Tom Kalili, founder of the Berean Bible Church in Hilo, whom Arnold had met twenty-nine years earlier, had served all these years at the same church. Except for one occasion, Arnold had spoken at that church on every trip, always glad to spend time with this pastor. Another individual, Ron Yanazaki of Honolulu, was a zealous supporter and promoter of Ariel Ministries from the start. Arnold would miss these two individuals a great deal, but accepted that their work on this earth was done and the Lord had called them home, all part of life's transition.

Many people from the past were happy to see Mary Ann in Hawaii again. Arnold and Mary Ann and their "Hawaiian Circle" still enjoyed going out after the services to a restaurant or a coffee shop to continue their Bible discussions and spend time together in edifying fellowship. One couple had even named their baby after the ministry! Another lady, a new believer, who was concerned about the admonitions she had received in regard to giving her baby a Hawaiian name with pagan connotations, was delighted when Arnold suggested that she could just as easily give her baby a Hawaiian name with a biblical message.

Before they left Hawaii, Arnold and Mary Ann had a nice dinner with their "Hawaiian Circle" at their favorite seafood restaurant in Waikiki. The *aloha* spirit toward the Fruchtenbaums remained strong through the years. The core group, consisting of both native-born as well as non-native Hawaiians, habitually went out of their way to assist Arnold and Mary Ann, greeting them upon their arrival at the airport, getting them to the rental car and then to the condo. To welcome them on their first evening, the group would plan a nice Hawaiian poolside dinner. They also attended as many meetings as they could. Upon the Fruchtenbaums' departure, they would once again assist in any way needed. Arnold hoped to maintain his *chiburim*[74] with these cherished ties and, Lord willing, to continue ministering to the beautiful believers of Hawaii for many years to come.

FROM ABOUT MID-MARCH TO THE END OF APRIL 2007, Arnold and Mary Ann traveled to New Zealand for a six-week stay. It had been nineteen years since they first visited the country in 1988. They started out with three free days to get over their jet lag and to rest. Some supporters had arranged for a house to be available for their use near Queenstown, a popular tourist destination, situated by a lake at the foot of the Alps in the South Island. The house was located several kilometers away from the town center, right along the lakefront. Mary Ann enjoyed two full days of touring the area, with Arnold pushing around the rented wheelchair.

An elder of a church in Queenstown then drove them through the beautiful mountainous roads of the Southern Alps to Christchurch, Arnold's favorite city in New Zealand. For the next five days, Arnold fulfilled various speaking engagements, one of which was at an independent church where he had first spoken nineteen years earlier. The original pastor had moved away, but the new leadership had maintained contact with Ariel Ministries over the years. Mary Ann was able to meet up with the faithful supporters whom she had only heard about, but had never had an opportunity to meet until now.

Leaving the South Island, Mary Ann took a flight up to Auckland in the North Island for one week on her own, while Arnold flew to Wellington, the capital. He taught an all-day seminar on a Saturday and spoke at an Anglican church on Sunday morning. The minister was a strong believer in Israel's future, rejecting the tenets of Replacement Theology, which was a very unusual stance for an Anglican, particularly in New Zealand where most adhered to Replacement Theology with hardly any Bible teaching in the churches.

From Wellington, Arnold was taken by car to Palmerston North, another one of the four cities where he had first spoken nineteen years before. In the

---

[74] Hebrew for "connections"

intervening years, sadly, the original church had closed its doors to Ariel Ministries. However, this second church was organized by a father-and-son team who were strong believers in the Bible's teaching about Israel's future. For three days, morning and evening meetings were held, all well attended. Arnold then flew to Auckland to join Mary Ann.

Ariel New Zealand in Auckland had arranged a rental car for them. They drove two hours south to a Christian camp where a one-week Ariel Kiwi Camp, the sixth of its kind, was held. Stephen Ger, a Messianic Jew from the United States, who had also taught at Camp Shoshanah from time to time, joined to co-teach. Arnold always enjoyed camp settings, as they were a nice break from the church conferences.

Many participants were new to Arnold, while others had been attending for many seasons. For the first time, a gentleman visiting from India—who had been introduced to Ariel Ministries by a local New Zealander—attended the camp. This gentleman's attendance would later prove to have a providential impact upon Ariel's mission field. Much to Mary Ann's amazement, she had an opportunity to connect with people who remembered her from nineteen years earlier! She also enjoyed meeting many in person whom she had only heard about in the past.

By the time the camp was over, Mary Ann had already mapped out a scenic route for Arnold and her to enjoy on their way back to Auckland. Although the drive was beautiful, it ended up taking nearly five hours instead of two! In Auckland, Arnold rented a motorized scooter for Mary Ann to allow her the freedom to move around the "City of Sails," referred to as such due to the huge number of sailboats around the Auckland harbor. While Arnold and Stephen held an all-day seminar, Mary Ann took a boat ride to spend the day at an island bird sanctuary off the coast.

Intending to stay for four weeks out of the six, it was soon time for her to return home. Arnold was free on her last two nights, so they went out and enjoyed a couple of seafood restaurants in town. The same day that she left, Arnold flew to the Hawkes Bay area on the eastern coast, where he held a weeklong conference at a Brethren church, staying with a family whom he had known for many years. This couple had joined his five-week tour to Israel on two separate occasions. Arnold was then driven to the town of Cambridge to teach at a Bible school with students enrolled from various countries. Back in Auckland, he taught a full-day seminar to a South Pacific group before flying home.

After a weekend conference in San Antonio, Arnold spent about a week at the Home Office before heading off to Japan in mid-May for his annual ten-day teaching tour. For the rest of June and early July, he worked on his writing projects at the Home Office before going up to the Adirondacks for the thirty-fourth season of Camp Shoshanah. A brand new two-week program was launched with distinct topics, still based on a five-year cycle to precede the established three-week program. Over the years, many had completed the five-year cycle of the three-week curriculum and wanted further studies.

SHORTLY AFTER CAMP, Arnold flew to Hungary in late August 2007 for the eighth international gathering of the Lausanne Consultation on Jewish Evangelism. Held every four years in different locations, this six-day conference took place in Keszthely on Lake Balaton about two-hours' drive from the capital, Budapest. Arnold enjoyed fellowshipping with new participants from diverse countries as well as renewing old ties. After the conference, he drove his rented car to Budapest, where he planned to take in the sights that were relevant to Jewish history, not as a tourist, but to see what was left of a once major Jewish center.

While records have dated Jewish presence in Hungary as far back as the second and third centuries, they began settling in earnest in the eleventh century. Down through the ages, despite anti-Jewish laws and cycles of expulsion and resettlement, there were periods when the Jewish community was able to thrive and prosper. One instance was in the mid-1500s when central Hungary came under Ottoman rule. Another notable period occurred during the latter 1800s, when the Jews learned *Magyar*, the Hungarian language, and underwent a strong assimilation process. Even so, waves of discrimination frequently persisted. When Hungary aligned itself with Nazi Germany and Fascist Italy during World War II, the local Jews thought they could be spared from being deported to German-occupied Poland. This was not to be. They became easy victims, when the German Nazis occupied Hungary starting in March 1944. The Hungarian government readily supported the Nazis' anti-Semitic policies on Jewish ghettos and deportation of the Jews. This marked the beginning of the most horrific year of sufferings that the Hungarian Jewry had ever endured. Truly shocking was the cooperation extended to the Nazis by non-Jewish fellow citizens. Over half a million Jews were deported from Hungary from April 1944 onward. It was estimated that roughly one third of the 1.1 million Jewish victims at the

Auschwitz-Birkenau extermination camps were Hungarian. Tens of thousands more also perished on the death marches from Budapest to Austria.

Calculations on the number of Jews in Hungary before the Holocaust ranged from 700,000 to 750,000—up to 850,000, if including the 100,000 Jews already converted to Christianity in the annexed territories—and from 80,000 to 190,000 after the war. During the post-war communist rule, many Jews either made *Aliyah* to Israel or immigrated to other countries. Although the figures varied considerably, the generally accepted number of Jews left in Hungary was about 70,000 mostly in Budapest, which had once been a metropolis with a thriving Jewish populace of several hundred thousand.

The majority of the Jewry remaining in Hungary was very secular. Since the fall of communism in 1989, a modest spiritual revival of Jewish observance seemed to have quietly developed. At the peak of its Jewish life, Budapest boasted one hundred and twenty-five synagogues, most of which were destroyed during World War II. While there have been only rare cases of overt violence against individual Jews in Hungary in recent decades, the deep-seated anti-Semitic sentiment of hatred toward the Jews was outwardly exhibited through the destruction of tombstones in the Jewish cemeteries and the vandalism of existing synagogues. Today, there are around twenty-six synagogues along with several Jewish high schools and a seminary that later became a Jewish university.

Arnold's hotel was situated in the old Jewish quarters in the eastern part of Budapest, where most of the current-day Jewish community organizations were located. Other than the Great Synagogue within five blocks' walking distance from his hotel, Arnold did not know firsthand of any other sites to visit on his own. Yet the Lord had made a wonderful provision for him through the hospitality of Ivan and Rita Nagy, the Hungarian couple who had attended Camp Shoshanah nine years earlier during its twenty-fifth season in 1998. Over the intervening years, the distance had prevented them from attending again. However, they continued to remain interested in Ariel Ministries. Recently, while browsing through the Ariel website, they discovered from Arnold's itinerary that he was going to be in Hungary for two weeks. They quickly got in touch with him and helped to arrange a few teaching sessions in Budapest. Although Gentile believers, this couple knew all the Jewish sites in the area and gave Arnold a private tour of some of the destroyed ancient synagogues as well as the modern ones that tourists did not get to see. They also visited other Jewish places of interest and spent time at the Holocaust Memorial Center of Budapest, where Rita was employed.

During World War II, one of the borders enclosing the Jewish ghetto in Budapest was Dohány Street, where the Great Synagogue stood. Completed in 1859 with a seating capacity of about three thousand, it served as a shelter for many people during the war. The ark inside contained about twenty-five *Torah* scrolls recovered from other destroyed or looted temples during the war. In the rear courtyard, the Raoul Wallenberg Holocaust Memorial Park displayed a weeping willow tree made of granite and steel. The metal leaves bore the inscriptions of the names of the Hungarian Jewish Holocaust victims, commemorating their suffering and murder. Another memorial nearby honored those "Righteous among the Nations" who had helped to rescue tens of thousands of Hungarian Jews. In the adjacent Jewish Cemetery were mass graves containing the bodies of over two thousand Jews from the ghetto, who had died of starvation or from the freezing cold during the winter of 1944-1945.

Close by was the Jewish Museum, built between 1930 and 1931 where the two-story house of Theodor Herzl, the leader of Zionism, once stood. Three of the four rooms in the museum housed Jewish religious relics and ritual objects used for *Shabbat* and the High Holy Days. The last room displayed a very moving Holocaust exhibit. A domed-building next door, called the Heroes' Temple, served as a memorial to the more than ten thousand Jewish soldiers who died fighting for Hungary during World War I. Thousands more Hungarian Jewish soldiers had been wounded or disabled.

Not far from the Jewish quarters was the new Holocaust Memorial Center of Budapest, which opened its doors with great fanfare on the 15th of April 2004—the first of its kind in Eastern Europe to be established and run by a state. The opening date commemorated the sixtieth anniversary of the day when the Jews were first rounded up and confined in the ghetto. The complex comprised a restored synagogue originally built in 1923, a new structure with exhibition halls tracing anti-Semitism in the country, plus archives. On a memorial glass wall outside were etched the names of Hungarian Jewish Holocaust victims.

Because Rita worked at this center, the tour was even more personal. Arnold fully enjoyed visiting the various Jewish sites, all the more because a Messianic Jewish couple had joined him. This couple was from the French-speaking part of Belgium and had attended Camp Shoshanah earlier in 2006. In contact via

E-mail since, they had arranged to meet up with him in Budapest. Delighted to meet Ivan and Rita, this Belgian couple got to see all the different places with Arnold. The group had a wonderful time of fellowship, tracing the various aspects of Jewish history in Budapest. They even had lunch at a Jewish restaurant, sampling an array of Eastern European dishes as well as Israeli cuisine.

Through the Nagys' pre-arrangement, Arnold spoke on a Sunday at a Brethren church and then taught for three nights at a Bible school, founded after the collapse of the communist regime. Word had spread about his visit to Budapest, leading to a good turnout for the meetings. The week went by all too quickly, and it was time for him to leave for Germany. Arnold deeply appreciated the hospitality and assistance of Ivan and Rita Nagy, who later went on to head up Ariel Hungary in 2011. The Belgian couple accompanied Arnold to Germany on their way back home, and even attended his speaking engagement in Düsseldorf, where the representative of Ariel Ministries, Georg Hagedorn, interpreted for him. It was a joy for Arnold to have spent time with them all.

Upon his return to the United States during the second week of September 2007, Arnold's fall schedule was packed as usual, except for a few weeks of break with Mary Ann up in the Adirondacks. During the last two weeks of December, they were able to spend their entire winter vacation together with only a few interruptions. They visited Arnold's mother at her home for three days and also spent some time with several of his siblings. Sadly, they were all still non-believers. Arnold was especially concerned about his mother, who was already in her eighties, yet to encounter her Messiah. He had prayed that there would be an open door for him and Mary Ann to witness to her about their faith in *Yeshua*. However, every time there seemed to be a slight opening and Arnold broached the subject, Adele quickly shut down the conversation. It was disappointing for Arnold, but he continued to persevere in prayer for his mother and siblings to overcome these stumbling blocks and come to salvation in Jesus, their Jewish Messiah.

Bumps Along the Path

As the realization dawned on Arnold that he was approaching his mid-sixties, his personal newsletters began to take on an even more nostalgic and intimate tone. This surprised many, since he had not been one to readily express his inner feelings to those around him. Though still a very private person, Arnold's newsletters in the autumnal years of his adulthood began to reflect an underlying sense of openness to share his thoughts. Ongoing friendships seemed to occupy a more valued place in his life, and he certainly did not take his health for granted. Even in the most blessed of times, his life tended to carry a mix of trials and disappointments.

In early January 2008, Arnold and Mary Ann traveled to Albany, New York, to attend the wedding of her niece, Rachel, the daughter of Beth, who had been promoted to glory less than a year before. Although January was not the best time to visit the northeastern part of the United States with its icy cold winters, they enjoyed the touching celebration with the rest of her family. They both experienced an array of emotions—happiness for Rachel and her new life ahead, juxtaposed against waves of sadness at the remembrance of Beth whose passing was still fresh on their minds—intermingled with an acute awareness of both the fortitude and the fragility of life. After three days of the biting cold in New York, they were glad to return home to sunny Texas.

Over the last few years, Arnold became increasingly aware that he was slowly losing his hearing in his right ear. He thought that it was simply due to the aging process. However, the scans revealed that the bones in the middle ear had not fully developed and were now separating, resulting in hearing loss. The specialist attributed the cause to a poor diet in one's childhood, which in Arnold's case happened to be an accurate diagnosis. He recommended surgery, as he believed that this would restore much, if not all, of Arnold's hearing. Arnold, of course, got a second opinion by consulting Mary Ann, who agreed with the doctor. So, plans were made for the operation to take place in late January. Part of the preparations for the ear surgery required an EKG, or electrocardiogram, to check on the health of his heart. Due to some abnormalities that appeared on the EKG, Arnold's ear surgery had to be postponed until March 2008. The new date just happened to land on a day in between two speaking engagements in different states, so Arnold had to cut short a conference by one day, in order to fly back home for the surgery. Rarely did he ever have to cancel or postpone a meeting, but the date of the surgery was firm and it needed to be done.

The operation seemed to go well, but it would take two full weeks before he could know for sure if it had improved his hearing. In the meantime, his right ear was all bandaged up so that any hearing through that ear was completely blocked. During the two weeks of recovery time, Arnold was prohibited from flying. Hence ten days after the surgery, in order to get to his next meeting at one of his favorite churches in Indiana, he took a long thirty-six hour train ride plus a further three hours of driving to get there. This was Arnold's first long train journey in the United States. The food on the train was no more palatable than airline food and in some instances, even worse. However, he got a private compartment all to himself with a couch that folded out to become a bed at night. He had plenty of time to process a lot of paperwork from the office and also got some good restful sleep.

It was rather awkward to listen with only one ear, but Arnold managed to get through the meetings without any difficulties. Thankfully, by the time the conference ended, it had been exactly two weeks since his ear surgery, so he could take a return flight home to San Antonio. When he got the bandages taken off, Arnold found that although the surgery had been successful, he had not fully recovered all of his hearing.

Unfortunately, another health issue cropped up. The doctor believed that Arnold had diabetes, so he was put on a special diet right away, with a daily prescription tablet. Knowing that his life was in the Lord's hands, Arnold simply considered these things to be bumps along the path of life. He prayed that God would either heal him or grant him the grace to get through it all. His only concern was the accomplishment of the goals that God had set out for him.

Sometime earlier, Adele had asked Arnold and Mary Ann to visit her in California in April 2008, as she had some matters that she wished to discuss with them. At eighty-four years of age, she still enjoyed good health. Arnold prayed once again for an open door of opportunity to witness to his mother about the Jewish Messiah and hoped that she would not shut down the conversation yet again. Disappointingly for Arnold, when he and Mary Ann visited her for five days in early April, she would not allow even a crack in the conversation to be opened for them to share about the Messiah. Undeterred, Arnold did not give up hope as he continued to intercede for his mother and his siblings.

What a welcomed contrast Arnold experienced while on his annual ten-day teaching tour in Japan toward the latter part of April 2008. The believers were very attentive and eager to learn the Word of God. They showed a great deal of support for Israel and the Jewish people. Aware of the global economic downturn and, in particular, the economic crisis in the United States, the Japanese believers contributed a very generous monetary gift to Ariel Ministries, for which Arnold and the staff were deeply grateful.

IN EARLY MAY 2008, Arnold flew over to Israel to lead a tour. Since the spring of 2004, he had stopped leading the intensive five-week Israel Study Tours through the ministry. Privately though, he was still open to leading tours of any length for groups who could organize themselves. In the interim, he had led a few two-week and three-week tours. This time, a number of previous participants from various countries had decided to organize themselves to travel together on a "Reunion Tour" and asked Arnold to be their guide for the five-week version. Never having anticipated such a request, due to time constraints and the recent economic downturn, this came as a very pleasant surprise. Of course, he gladly agreed, as the longer length of time allowed him to show the group the entire Land the way it ought to be seen. Jackie Fierman, a missionary staff member of Ariel Canada in Montreal but working in Quebec City, felt especially blessed to be able to join this group for the entire five and a half weeks including the optional visit to Jordan.

> As is my custom, I arrived in Israel a week before the group got there so I could overcome the jet lag and get everything ready. I was shocked to discover how sharply the cost of touring Israel had risen since I had been there last year. The airlines all added a fuel surcharge of over four hundred dollars to the cost of the ticket, and that raised the cost of the tour. Furthermore, touring in four vans also raised the cost. I am thankful that several participants in the group chose to pay for most of the gas, which helped keep me from running out of funds to cover expenses. The high cost of gas was not the only problem we encountered. The incredible fall of the U.S. dollar also weakened our ability to get our normal arrangements, and so everything was higher: the hotel rooms, the meals, and the entry tickets, among other expenses.

In the past, I have always been able to project the rise in cost for each trip from year to year, but this time I greatly underestimated, since I didn't anticipate that the weaker dollar and rising fuel prices would have such a major impact. I am happy to say that the group held together really well and helped when they could, such as buying their own lunches on many occasions. I still arranged the "special lunches" that I include in all my tours so that everyone can experience the wonderful variety of Israeli cuisine. There was no cutting back on that!!!!!! …I am happy to report that we were able to see most everything we wanted and needed to see. On two occasions, I was able to rent a bulletproof bus for tours into the West Bank, and this enabled us to get to places we could not have accessed by van. At the end of five weeks, the majority of the group continued with me to Jordan for four additional days. There we traveled the whole length of the country from north to south…

It turned out there was more to do in Israel… A very vibrant and well-taught messianic congregation in Haifa invited me to do a series on the Book of Revelation over the course of three Sabbaths. I had taught there on previous trips on a one-time basis only, but I was able to accommodate this series during this trip, since the tour group had Saturdays off for free time… The congregation in Haifa was founded even before Israel's War of Independence in 1948 and is being led by a group of elders with excellent biblical knowledge. The group was studious and paid close attention, for which I was very glad. Only a minority of messianic congregations in the USA and Israel are well taught, and this was certainly one of them. I look forward to future relations with this congregation. Incidentally, one of the elders of that congregation attended Ariel's Camp Shoshanah about thirty years ago and now functions as a lawyer in Israel.[75]

---

[75] Excerpts: *On The Road*, Summer 2008

Arnold reconnected with a couple whose wedding ceremony he had conducted some years earlier in England. Theirs was a wonderful love story between a British Gentile bride and an Israeli Jewish groom. She had attended Camp Shoshanah for three summers and then studied at the Hebrew University in Jerusalem. Along the way, the two met and fell in love, got married, and had been living in Israel, looking forward to a future ministry. In the meantime, they had become parents to a beautiful baby. Arnold made sure that he took lots of photos of the baby with the parents to take home to share with Mary Ann, as she too had gotten to know the couple in the past and would appreciate the pictures.

He also took time to visit his Israeli relatives, and brought along a draft of the book on the family history that David S. Turner, a supporter of Ariel Ministries, living in Holland, had put together based on the English version of the transcribed and translated interviews that Arnold had recorded in Hebrew decades earlier with his aunts and uncles. They had all since passed away. Yaakov was the first, followed by Yehoshua, Genya, then Chumah, the youngest, leaving only Chankah, the oldest of the three aunts, and Reuben, the husband of Chumah, as the last two of the Holocaust generation to pass away. In her final years, Chankah had suffered from Alzheimer's disease and could no longer even recognize Arnold when he visited in the year 2000.

Now that only the children of the Holocaust generation were left, Arnold's cousins, who were in his age bracket, began to take a keen interest in tracing the family history. Thus, he wanted to show the draft of the book to one of his cousins to get her input. Nurit was indeed able to provide extra information and additional pictures, which were eventually added to the book.

This intensive five-week Israel Study Tour was truly a special gift from the Lord, as Arnold was also joyously able to be in the Land when Israel celebrated the sixtieth anniversary of its establishment as a nation.

Back in the United States during the last week in June, Arnold and Mary Ann spent a beautiful five-day getaway along the Texas coast to celebrate their fortieth wedding anniversary in 2008! They had a lovely, refreshing time together, taking it easy, enjoying good food and a relaxing pace and even some horseback riding. Looking back over their life, despite the many bumps along the path, they thanked and praised God for His love, care, provision, and manifold blessings upon them and the ministry.

AFTER THE FIRST-EVER, THREE-DAY CONVOCATION of all the Ariel workers gathered under one roof at the Home Office in late October 2008, Arnold and Mary Ann traveled to Kauai, their favorite island in Hawaii, on a personal vacation to mark their special year.

> Mary Ann is normally with me for at least part of my teaching tour in Hawaii. However, during our recent vacation (on Kauai) in November, a severe medical disorder developed during the last two days of the trip. Upon our return to Texas, it was obvious that she would need surgery. Since the problem was related to her MS, there is a limitation as to what can be accomplished. As an "out-patient," Mary Ann was at the hospital in the morning and at home in the evening... In the course of her recovery, they discovered that she had a tumor on her gall bladder. They could not tell if it was cancerous or not. As Mary Ann lost both parents to cancer, as well as a sister just two years ago, we were concerned about this development. We decided on additional surgery as soon as possible. Just three weeks later, her gall bladder was removed. Praise the Lord! The tumor proved to be benign, but as the doctors do not know what it is, they are conducting further tests. Mary Ann's recovery has been very slow. We would ask you to pray for a complete and speedy recovery.[76]

Echoes of Nostalgia

For nine weeks between the early part of January through the first week of March 2009, Arnold taught and ministered on five different islands of Hawaii followed by a trip to New Zealand and Japan. Because his itinerary had

---

[76] Excerpts: *On The Road*, Spring 2009

already been scheduled nearly two years in advance, it was too late to alter those commitments even with Mary Ann's recent ill health. Upon their conclusion, he would be limiting his travels overseas for the remainder of 2009 to just one more pre-arranged trip to Europe.

The thirty-sixth season of the 2009 English-speaking Camp Shoshanah program saw new attendees from three additional countries—Malaysia, Italy, and India. As Mary Ann was not able to drive her special van to the camp this year, she had originally planned on flying up there to join Arnold for most of the five weeks. However, her recovery from the two surgeries was still very slow, and she had to be in her wheelchair all the time, which would have made flying an awkward endeavor. Thus, she cancelled her trip to the camp this season to stay at home to rest. Arnold wished that she could have been there with him to witness the progress of the building work and to meet the various participants. However, she simply could not make it.

Soon after camp ended, Arnold flew over to Europe for a three-week tour to Germany and the U.K. from mid-August to early September 2009. He relished the time he had for renewing old friendships and making new ones, while teaching the Bible to those who hungered after in-depth learning of the Word. More Ariel resource materials were now available in German, resulting in a wider circle of people in Germany becoming more aware of Ariel's teaching ministry. Arnold's short, one-and-a-half week stint in the U.K. covered three churches each located in a different town plus teaching at a youth conference in yet another town. While the contents of his teachings were unparalleled, many international students, whose mother tongue was not English, sometimes found it hard to follow him, due to his peculiar mixture of accents and unusual tonality. Even native English speakers often had difficulties, especially when he spoke at a very fast pace. Some in the U.K. occasionally teased him about needing an interpreter from Arnold's English to the normal English!

Back home, a very special reunion of all the individuals, who had been saved under Ruth Wardell's ministry among the young Jewish teenagers in her New York City days, was held in her honor at the exact same Camp *Sar Shalom* site in Honey Brook, Pennsylvania. Arnold was especially heartened to reconnect with the former members of the M.Y.F., taking many nostalgic trips down memory lane, reminiscing about all the wonderful times they had together with Miss Wardell.

Toward the end of September 2009, Mary Ann had recovered enough to go with Arnold to their little cabin up in the Adirondacks for a time of rest and refreshment. It was always a delight for them to spend time in this part of God's creation, drinking in the resplendent beauty of the surroundings and letting the Holy Spirit renew their inner being.

Cutting back on his travels for the rest of 2009 was a huge adjustment for Arnold. Most of his time was spent at the Ariel Home Office, working on his writing projects and teaching a short course right there on the premises in the new conference hall that had only recently been completed.

The lady, who had assisted Mary Ann for the past two and a half years, departed in November. The Fruchtenbaums were very thankful for the help that this fellow believer had extended. After her departure, Arnold spent the rest of the year at the home base and personally looked after Mary Ann. Due to her deteriorating condition, she could no longer take care of herself and had to depend upon a wheelchair at all times to get around. They were both relieved and grateful to the Lord that in early January 2010, Tovyah Kravitz would be moving to San Antonio to help care for Mary Ann. Arnold had known Tovyah since her birth, when her parents, Ken and Ruth, had served for a period of time as caretakers of Camp Shoshanah. Having finished high school, she was looking for new opportunities and accepted the position for at least one year. This was God's provision for Mary Ann in answer to prayer.

With the caretaking situation all arranged at home, Arnold later flew to Australia, where he taught from the last week of February to the end of March 2010. The wonderful people at Manna International had put together his itinerary from start to finish. While traveling as a passenger in a car in Perth, Arnold's favorite city in Western Australia, a violent hailstorm erupted, a very unique experience for him. The huge hailstones pounding down resembled the size of bricks! Thanks to the Lord's protection, their windshields held strong, while they witnessed those of other cars being shattered.

One of the highlights of his trip was a four-day camp held in Wyee outside of Sydney. There, Arnold was delighted to meet a Polish couple, residing about forty-five minutes away from the venue.

> They had immigrated to Australia about 12 years ago and became believers. As they grew, they realized that they were not getting any solid Bible teaching in the church they were attending. They went on the Internet and discovered the Bible lessons of Ariel Ministries and began

```
taking them on their own. Taking a look at my itinerary,
they were surprised that I was scheduled to teach at the
camp (one that was close to their home). They tried to
apply, but all spaces were full, and there was no room.
But being determined to get as much Bible as they could,
they commuted each day from their home. My Polish is very
limited, but I got to use it with them a bit. The wife on
two occasions fixed pirogi, a form of Polish ravioli or
kreplach. She learned that I liked it, although she hated
fixing it. It was a joy meeting them, and I look forward
to a long-term relationship… They have now connected with
other Arielniks and will be able to share that way.⁷⁷
```

Back home, Arnold noted that Mary Ann seemed to be doing better on some days and worse on others. However, she was very happy with Tovyah, her new helper living in their home. She really liked this young woman as a person, who was faithful, responsible, and easy to get along with. Tovyah often went above and beyond her job description to help care for Mary Ann's needs, and the two got along famously.

Soon it was time for Arnold to be on his way overseas again, this time to Japan. Compared to previous years when he usually taught for ten days, this teaching tour was somewhat shorter, lasting only five days. From Japan, he flew to Israel to prepare for the intensive three-week tour he was leading through the Land as well as Jordan. It had been two years since he was last in *Eretz Yisrael*, when he led the "Reunion Tour" in the spring of 2008—for Arnold, too long of an interval to be away. The new group consisted mainly of Chinese participants from Perth, Australia, and Arnold was grateful that things went very smoothly.

Since late 1990, when there was no longer an official Ariel representation in Israel, Arnold had longed to have another Ariel couple on the ground, but his hope never seemed to materialize. With most of the nation not knowing their own Jewish Messiah, he was keenly aware that Israel was a big spiritual harvest field for Ariel Ministries, just waiting to be reached. However, God had His own timing, and usually that meant waiting upon Him. Jesus once said to his disciples: *The harvest is plenteous, but the laborers are few. Pray ye*

---

⁷⁷ Excerpts: *On The Road*, Summer 2010

therefore the Lord of the harvest, that He send forth laborers into His harvest. (Matthew 9: 37b-38) That was exactly what Arnold did. He prayed.

At long last, in late November 2009 the preceding year, God raised up a Messianic Jewish couple, originally from Kazakhstan, to head up Ariel Israel. In addition to their native Russian, Sasha and Lilian Granovsky were also fluent in Hebrew and English. It was a pleasure for Arnold to catch up with them on this trip. The tour group from Australia also got to meet them. After nineteen years, in His perfect timing and in His own way, God had finally answered Arnold's prayers for Ariel Ministries to have an active presence in *Eretz Yisrael.*

Coming Full Circle

In June 2010, en route home from Israel, Arnold had the unique privilege of teaching at various churches in Poland. Twice before, he had visited the country on personal trips, but this was his first ministry opportunity. At the time the teaching request initially reached him, Arnold was totally unaware that other life circumstances were unfolding in parallel and converging at just the right time to bring about for him a profound and deeply moving personal experience. Looking back, he could only marvel at God's impeccable timing in sequencing the many events to bring the Fruchtenbaum family history full circle for him.

Three years earlier, Jan Marek Kopytek, who had first heard about Ariel Ministries through reading some of Arnold's books, contacted him about a teaching tour in Poland. Over several summers, he had attended the Camp Shoshanah program and at one point also participated in one of the tours to Israel. With Arnold's schedule fully booked for more than two years out, it took close to three years for this itinerary to finally materialize. Raised in Poland, residing in Germany, fluent in Polish, German, and English, Jan Marek would pre-arrange all the meetings and serve as Arnold's interpreter at the different venues throughout the tour.

Landing in Warsaw, which was to serve as their base, Arnold met up with Jan Marek who flew in from Germany. They rented a car to drive to the diverse meetings in Warsaw, Palowice to the south, and Olsztyn and Ostroda to the north. Though the churches were small in size, the sessions were well attended and the people were very zealous in studying the Scriptures within a Jewish frame of reference.

Before heading to Palowice in southern Poland, Arnold had a free day in Warsaw. He eagerly anticipated spending time at the Warsaw Jewish Cemetery, which he had first visited thirty years earlier in 1980. On that particular occasion, he simply did not have enough time to undertake a thorough search of the massive, neglected grounds to locate his great-grandfather's gravesite, and thus abandoned the endeavor for another trip. On his second visit in 1999, the cemetery was closed for Passover week, so the search had to be postponed yet again. This time, however, Arnold came armed with more pertinent information.

A few months prior to this trip, Arnold had received a message from the author of his biography, with some interesting and exciting news regarding his great-grandfather's gravesite at the Warsaw Jewish Cemetery. She had been doing some research and happened to come across a virtual cemetery site on the Internet, containing a database of all the tombstones at the cemetery. Knowing that Arnold's great-grandfather was buried there, she did a further search and not only discovered the exact location of Baruch Simchah's grave, but also unearthed information that identified seven other gravesites, all belonging to members of the Fruchtenbaum family at large. Three of them were gravesites of Baruch Simchah's parents and sister. Each headstone had been assigned a five-digit identity number, providing a systematic way of locating the gravesites. Alongside the transcription and translation of the Hebrew that was carved on each headstone, the database on the Internet also included a picture of each individual grave marker.

Apparently since 1996, a small society called the Friends of the Warsaw Jewish Cemetery had endeavored to raise money toward the upkeep of the grounds and to compile an index of all the tombstones of those buried there. However, funds were slow to come in. Ten years later at the end of July 2006—thanks to the sponsorship of one generous Jewish man from the United States—the actual inventory project finally commenced in earnest. A small team of dedicated workers undertook the mammoth task of recording the written information from all the tombstones, totaling between 100,000 to 250,000. The team subsequently embarked on the long and arduous task of transcribing the Hebrew and translating it into Polish and English to be entered into a newly created database on the Internet in the form of a virtual cemetery. At its completion on the 18th of November 2009, the team began to enter further information onto the database and to correct errors. The entire project was targeted for completion by July 2010, shortly after Arnold's visit.

The only entrance to the massive cemetery on the outskirts of the city was through a small gateway on Okopowa Street. As a show of respect, all men entering were required to cover their heads, generally with a *kippah*— "skullcap" in Hebrew. As Arnold and Jan Marek approached on foot after parking the rented car, Arnold wondered whether the dilapidated state of the grounds had improved since the last time he saw it. For quite some time now, it had been under the management of an organization called the Warsaw Jewish Community, with a rabbi in charge of the administration of the entire cemetery, which had continued to be in use even during World War II up to the present day. Much to Arnold's relief, it had been greatly cleaned up and repaired and thus much easier to walk around.

With the printout of the numbering system in hand and with Jan Marek's help with the language, Arnold was finally able to locate the gravesite of his great-grandfather, Baruch Simchah Fruchtenbaum. What a special blessing this momentous occasion meant for Arnold! His long-awaited wish had finally come true, and he was standing in person at his great-grandfather's gravesite, seeing it with his very own eyes! All his life, Arnold had heard so much about this ultra-Orthodox Jewish *rebbe* of Pultusk from different surviving members of his family. Embellished over time, some of the stories became almost legendary. Now, nearly seventy-nine years after his great-grandfather's death on the 21st of September 1931, Arnold was at last physically present at the very spot where Baruch Simchah had been laid to rest. It seemed surreal.

Time stood still as Arnold remained transfixed in his thoughts for about half an hour in front of the grave. Fragments of his family's history drifted through his mind like a kaleidoscope in slow motion, while torrents of deeply mixed emotions swelled up inside him. No words seemed adequate to describe how he felt—from the sheer joy and excitement of finding the gravesite to the deep sense of grief and loss of what was and could have been yet thankful that his great-grandfather had been spared the pain and anguish of witnessing the senseless murder of so many members of his family in the ravaging destruction of the *Shoah*. How inconceivable it would have been for Baruch Simchah to ever imagine that his own generation would be the last to flourish in the town of Pultusk, much less that his surviving children would be uprooted and expelled from their home and country, never to live there again.

After taking numerous photos, Arnold and Jan Marek set off to search for the other seven gravesites of the Fruchtenbaum family. With the aid of the numbering system, they initially located six out of the other seven gravesites. Some were situated about fifteen to twenty minutes' walking distance apart. At each spot, Arnold took many photos and spent about ten to fifteen minutes in contemplation. Again, he felt overwhelmed with mixed emotions. It was gratifying for him to stand in front of the gravesites of Baruch Simchah's parents—Schmuel Asher Fruchtenbaum and his wife, Frumet— Arnold's great-great-grandparents. Because the father's name of the deceased was also inscribed in Hebrew on the headstone, Arnold could read on it the name of Schmuel Asher's father, Zeev Tzvi Fruchtenbaum. He also saw the gravesite of Baruch Simchah's sister, Gitel. Arnold was amazed at how many of his family members were buried in this cemetery, including a male ancestor who had died back in 1866! Indeed, the Fruchtenbaum family had forged deep roots in the town of Pultusk.

Established in 1806, the Warsaw Jewish Cemetery was one of the largest in Europe in its day and one of the fortunate few that had averted the fate of wholesale destruction by the German Nazis during World War II. When the ghetto in Warsaw was sealed in mid-November 1940, with well over 400,000 Jews crammed into a habitable area of less than three and a half square kilometers or about one and a half square miles, the cemetery within the ghetto wall boundaries remained in use with only one entrance open, where Nazis were posted on guard. To gain access, mourners were required to obtain special passes. Initially, the residents who died in the ghetto were buried in individual graves. Soon, the number of deaths got so large due to disease, starvation, and freezing cold winters, that the dead were buried in mass graves dug right there.

Arnold had known all along that some members of the extended Fruchtenbaum family had been forced into this ghetto and later lost their lives. The date of death inscribed on the headstone of one of the graves revealed an interesting clue. The wife of one of the Fruchtenbaum men died in mid-September 1941 and was buried in her own individual grave. This meant that some of the other family members were still alive within the ghetto at that time. Unfortunately, it was not known whether they were later deported to an extermination camp such as Treblinka or Sobibor or whether they perished as a result of the crushed uprising in the spring of 1943, hence buried in one of those mass graves in the cemetery. Sadly for those other family members, there would be no individual graves or headstones to honor their memory.

As much as they tried on that day, Arnold and Jan Marek failed to find the seventh gravesite and ran out of time. They were obliged to leave, as they needed to drive to Arnold's next meeting at a Brethren church in Palowice in southern Poland. Two days later, on their way to Olsztyn in the north, they stopped in Pultusk and spent time walking around the neighborhood where the Fruchtenbaum family once lived. Having just located the gravesite of Arnold's great-grandfather, this visit made the family's life and history become more real. With the help of Jan Marek's Polish language skills, Arnold found out many new things about his heritage.

After a few days of ministry in northern Poland, Arnold and Jan Marek drove back to Warsaw, where they once again stopped at the Warsaw Jewish Cemetery. This time, they asked the rabbi in charge for his help in locating the last Fruchtenbaum gravesite that they had previously failed to find. The rabbi was rather reluctant at first, but Jan Marek spoke to him in Polish and finally persuaded him to at least point them to the general vicinity where that gravesite might be. The rabbi ended up taking them directly to the spot that Arnold had hoped to find.

On his long trans-Atlantic flight back home a couple of days later, Arnold's thoughts lingered upon his touching experience at the cemetery. Having seen the gravesites, his connection with his family roots in Poland now took on a deeper meaning. In a very intimate, yet inexplicable way, he felt more complete, as though another crucial piece of the puzzle had been restored to its rightful place in his family's history.

As the first-born son, his great-grandfather had carried on the family's longstanding dynastic tradition, fulfilling the role of *rebbe* of a sub-division of the *Ger Chasidim* in Pultusk. He had taught the *Tanakh* and the traditional rabbinic writings at the local synagogue just as his forefathers had done for generations past. Arnold wondered what it would have been like to engage in a serious but lively discussion of the Scriptures with Baruch Simchah. Were it not for the Holocaust, Arnold's father would have also been slated to follow in his great-grandfather's footsteps. However, their tradition had come to an abrupt end with World War II, and life for the Fruchtenbaum family was forever altered.

Since his great-grandfather's death, no first-born son of the Fruchtenbaum family had ever formally taught the *Tanakh* in their homeland of Poland. By God's providence, Arnold's life had taken a different turn, and he encountered Jesus, the Jewish Messiah. Yet like his great-grandfather who had been a scholar of the *Tanakh*, the Old Testament, Arnold, too, had immersed himself in the in-depth study of God's Holy Word including the *Tanakh* as well as the *B'rit Chadashah*, or the "New Covenant" Scriptures, the New Testament. While standing at the gravesite, it dawned on Arnold that in a unique sort of way, he had indeed carried on the family tradition through his ministry as a Bible teacher, not as a *rebbe* in the way that Baruch Simchah would have expected, but as a messianic itinerant teacher in the way that God had ordained. It was significant and befitting that on his first Bible teaching tour in Poland, Arnold was blessed to have finally located the gravesite of his great-grandfather, the respected *rebbe* and teacher of Pultusk.

As much as the German Nazis had wreaked havoc in their lives, expelling the Jews from their hometown of Pultusk, they did not succeed in completely wiping out the Fruchtenbaum family. Some family members may have been brutally murdered and the lives of the surviving members severely disrupted, yet the family line was not broken and had ultimately remained intact. The Fruchtenbaum name continued to be perpetuated in the United States to the present day. On this trip to Poland, Arnold felt that he was picking up the thread and continuing the family tradition right from where his great-grandfather had left off in terms of teaching the *Tanakh*, but with the additional truth of the promised Jewish Messiah, *Yeshua*. On so many levels, the Fruchtenbaum family history had come full circle for Arnold. What a special blessing from the Lord!

Arnold planned to go back to Poland again in September 2012. A number of churches where he had ministered this time had asked him to return, and new churches also extended invitations. The next time, Arnold intended to spend three to four days in Pultusk to learn more about the daily life of his family. He wanted to walk the same streets and frequent the same places that they did, before the Nazis drove them out. While not a single Jew was left living in Pultusk, there still remained signs of a once vibrant Jewish world that echoed through the corridors of time. Now, the next Fruchtenbaum generation including Arnold and his cousins, Batya, daughter of Genya, and Nurit, daughter of Chankah, planned to continue returning to Pultusk to keep alive the remembrances of a once large and cohesive ultra-Orthodox Jewish family, whose daily lives had been intricately woven into the very fabric of their thriving Jewish community that tragically was no more.

THE THIRTY-SEVENTH SEASON OF CAMP SHOSHANAH ushered in a few important changes. A decision was made to rename the program, "The Shoshanah Program of Messianic Jewish Studies," since it actually operated more like a Bible school program than a summer camp. The recently instituted two-week curriculum was already in its fourth year, and this season, each week was designed as a separate stand-alone. For the first time, a new one-week program, the full, uncondensed Life of Messiah course, was added as the sixth week:

> Mary Ann was also with us for four of those weeks. She drove up with her caretaker, Tovyah, and due to her physical limitations (because of MS) we planned the trip very carefully and precisely. I am thankful that they arrived safe and sound. Mary Ann spent a good part of each day in bed, but people came in almost daily to visit her, including those she had never met before. This gave her a great deal of satisfaction. More than one person told me how much happier she seemed this year than the previous years, and I think that was very true. A large part of Mary Ann's contentment is due to her caretaker Tovyah and how well she takes care of Mary Ann both at home and on location. Mary Ann had to leave Camp Shoshanah two days early and head for Michigan, so that she could attend her nephew's wedding.[78]

Toward the end of September 2010, Arnold's longtime ministry co-worker, Dan Rigney, suffered a massive heart attack and was promoted home to glory, five weeks short of his seventy-fourth birthday. It was a bittersweet time for the Ariel family as the staff reminisced about how this faithful servant of God had impacted all their lives. In the quarterly newsletter, Arnold wrote a touching, personal tribute to honor Dan's remarkable service to the Lord through Ariel Ministries. It seemed befitting that the first Ariel mission

---

[78] Excerpt: *On The Road*, Fall 2010

worker also became the first to be called home into the glorious presence of the Lord forever, completing a full circle.

With the first decade of the twenty-first century behind him and a new year shortly dawning, Arnold looked back in awe at all the wonderful things that God had done in the thirty-three years of Ariel Ministries' existence. Many Jewish people had come to know their Messiah through Ariel, and numerous believers had grown in their knowledge of the Word. Arnold prayed that God would continue to grant much spiritual fruit to the ministry in the years to come. Having seen his great-grandfather's gravesite with his very own eyes and feeling a deep connection to his roots in Poland, his heartfelt prayer was for God to close the loop in the circle by bringing all his family members to faith in *Yeshua*. What a joyous day that would be!

Over the years, God had shown Himself steadfast and faithful to Ariel Ministries despite the many ups and downs, challenges, and hardships that frequently cropped up and assailed the ministry. As the work grew and expanded, God's blessing was evident at every turn. At times when doors of certain churches were closed to Arnold's expository teaching, other doors would open up elsewhere. With the technological advances of the Internet, more people around the world were able to gain access to the resources and teachings of Ariel Ministries, which otherwise would not have been possible in the past. Each year brought about new changes that were both exciting and humbling, as Ariel Ministries continued its mission to evangelize the Jewish people and disciple both the Jewish and Gentile believers to grow to spiritual maturity in the Word. As far as Arnold could see, Ariel Ministries was well on its course of further growth and expansion, and he looked forward to the Lord's abundant blessings upon the ministry in the future.

Epilogue

God's Faithfulness

Having been expelled from his home upon his high school graduation, Arnold had indeed paid a high price for his belief in *Yeshua Ha'Mashiach*. Coming from a long line of first-born sons in a traditional ultra-Orthodox Jewish family with origins in Poland, he was the first—and thus far the only one—in his family to encounter and embrace Jesus as the Jewish Messiah. From that point onward, his life was assailed with many challenges and trials, yet filled with great joy and hope in the Lord with His immeasurable blessings. God in his bountiful mercy had provided Arnold with a true family in the Body of Messiah and blessed him with the gift of teaching God's Holy Word in its Jewish context.

When Arnold departed from his parents' home in California with a heavy heart awash with sadness on that Saturday morning in June 1962, with nothing more than a suitcase and $120 in his pocket, his only recourse was to trust the Lord for his future and depend entirely upon His love, care, and provision. How marvelously God had supplied all his needs throughout the subsequent years, bringing wonderful believers to encourage and come alongside him. Little could Arnold have imagined then what God, in His grace, would do in and through his life! Fifty-two years later at the age of seventy, having dedicated himself to reaching the Jewish people with the message of *Yeshua Ha'Mashiach*, he could only look back with awe at God's faithfulness.

Arnold never ceased to be amazed at the far-reaching impact of Ariel Ministries and all that God had brought about, bearing witness to the truth that "God's work done in God's time will never lack God's support." Countless people in various parts of the world had been blessed through the literal interpretation of biblical truth taught from a Jewish perspective. How graciously God had blessed his obedience to start a new and distinctive Jewish ministry!

Arnold's dream of returning to Israel to lead another long, intensive five-week Israel Study Tour was about to come true for him once more. In the spring of 2014, the entire program would be filmed for the first time and produced as a study resource on DVD. In doing so, more people around the world would get to see the many holy sites around *Eretz Yisrael* through the DVD. Praising the Lord and rejoicing at the gift of this unique opportunity to be in his beloved Land once again on this lengthier tour, Arnold's heart overflowed with gratitude to be doing what he so loved. How manifold were God's blessings to him!

Seeing the tremendous progress at Camp Shoshanah over the recent years brought deep encouragement to his heart. Having set foot on the campsite in the Adirondacks for the first time in 1959 as a youngster at the Memory Camp, Arnold could never have contemplated that one day, he would be teaching a summer discipleship program there year after year, now for forty years. It was profoundly gratifying to see the new kitchen and dining hall finally operational for the very first time in the summer of 2013.

In those early days, neither could Arnold have ever conceived that one day, a year-round school would be launched for those who wished to study the Scriptures in-depth from a Jewish perspective at a college or seminary level. Targeted to start in September 2015, this burning vision that had inspired Arnold so long ago would soon become a reality with Ariel's School of Messianic Jewish Studies opening its doors. How marvelous was the Lord!

From the time that Arnold and Mary Ann had crossed paths near a birch tree on the way to the lake at Trout Pond, God had led them on a special life journey. Theirs was a beautiful love story, lived out in gracious submission before God. As they continued to serve God through their individual spiritual gifts that God had bestowed upon each, their yearning to reach the Jewish people grew stronger and their love for each other deeper with each passing day. Arnold's heartfelt wish was for each of his earthly days to count in the service of the Lord.

Yearning over the years for the salvation of the Jewish people and in particular, for that of his own family members, it was Arnold's prayer that they may one day also come to know the saving grace of *Yeshua Ha'Mashiach*, Lord and Savior of the world. Sadly, his sister, Margaret, had already passed away in January 2013 without any certainty that she had received the Messiah before she breathed her last. Arnold's fervent hope was for the scales over his family members' spiritual eyes to be lifted and their hearts to be opened to receive the Gospel message.

In submitting to God's call in 1977 to start a new, distinctive Jewish ministry balancing evangelism and discipleship, Arnold was amazed at God's faithfulness—humbled anew at the multitude of spiritual fruit borne from that one seed of obedience to God's call. He was God's chosen fruit called into the ministry of itinerant Bible teaching to bear spiritual fruit among God's Chosen People in these "latter days." For Arnold, God's call rang true back then, even as it did now:

...and that repentance and remission of sins should be preached in His name unto all the nations, beginning from Jerusalem. (Luke 24:46b-47)

Arnold's life and his trust in Messiah *Yeshua* could testify to the truth:

He is faithful that promised... (Hebrews 10:23a)

What a God we serve!

Editor's Note: On the 16th of May, 2014, Arnold's spiritual mom and beloved mentor, Ruth Wardell, passed on to glory. The following text is the eulogy he presented during a memorial service held in her honor. It once again reveals the impact this most excellent daughter of the Living God had on his life.

In Memoriam of Ruth Wardell

By Dr. Arnold G. Fruchtenbaum

The background that led to my first contact with Ruth Wardell occurred in Germany in the city of Ulm in 1949. We had recently escaped from Poland, walked through Czechoslovakia, and crossed into Austria where we came under the jurisdiction of the American military authorities. They brought us into West Germany and settled us in the first of six different Displaced Persons' Camps. These camps mostly housed Jews who came from different regions of Europe and were now stateless, searching for settlement in different parts of the western world.

Theo Burgstahler was a Lutheran pastor who was also representing what was then the American Board of Missions to the Jews (ABMJ, now renamed as Chosen People Ministries). His responsibility at the time was to hand out clothing to Jewish refugees, and that is how first contact was made. He and his daughter, Hanna, made several visits to the D.P. camp my family stayed at, but I was not involved in the conversations that took place and so do not know all that was being discussed. What I do know is that he happened to have a copy of a *Chosen People* magazine. After having learned that we had applied for immigration status to the USA, he presented it to my mother. He did not give her the whole magazine, and so she never got to see the exact nature of the ministry. He simply tore off the front cover with the New York City address on it and encouraged her to visit the organization when we arrived. All she understood was that this was a Jewish organization that would help immigrant Jews upon arrival. It was that, but it was a bit more than that, and by the time my mother learned the whole story, it was too late in my case.

Two years after receiving the cover, we left West Germany and arrived in New York where we settled into a Jewish community in Brooklyn. One day, my mother took the subway to Manhattan where the ABMJ headquarters was located. There she had contact with Daniel Fuchs, but she was unable to communicate with him since she did not speak English yet and he did not speak Yiddish, Russian, Polish, or German, all of which my mother spoke. So all that got done that day was that our name was taken down on a 3x5 card, and it was conveyed to her that we would be contacted some time later.

"Some time later" turned out to be five years later when the ABMJ opened up its new East New York Branch in Brooklyn, not far from where we were living at the time. Apparently, the 3x5 card was still on file, and it was given to Ruth Wardell. She visited us and invited us to attend what was then called a Hebrew-Christian meeting. Out of curiosity, I decided to go. I remember sitting in a rather small meeting hall in the back, listening to what was being said. Ruth was not the speaker, but she was there observing my reaction. What disturbed me was that the speakers used the Hebrew Bible to talk about Jesus. Ruth could see it would not be a good time to share "the four laws" with me. Instead, she challenged me to accept a New Testament and see if Jesus did not do all that the Messiah was supposed to do. I accepted the challenge and took a prophecy edition of the New Testament home with me. I did read it and was surprised as to the Jewishness of the book.

As Ruth recorded in her own biography, she was rather surprised as to how much I knew of the Hebrew Bible at my age. It was the result of my father's training of me at the D.P. camps of Germany. So she decided she needed to be better prepared in dealing with me next time. She also realized that using the King James Version would not be wise. So she got a hold of what's commonly known as *The Leeser Bible*, a translation of the Hebrew Scriptures by an Orthodox Jewish rabbi that she knew would be more acceptable to me. When I returned to the meeting center, she sat down with me and went from one messianic prophecy to another, showing me the fulfillment in the New Testament that was given to me, and thus I became a believer.

The East New York Branch only lasted one year, and I was the only Jew who came to faith at that center. During that year, I was being discipled, and Ruth was the primary one discipling me. I was living in a very large Jewish community, and there were no other believers anywhere near me with whom I could fellowship. But I found fellowship in the weekly meetings, and three times during that year, Ruth organized retreats. Young messianic believers from different parts of NYC would gather for these retreats at the Liebenzell Mission in New Jersey, and these were the highlights of my spiritual life at that time. We also began the Messianic Youth Fellowship under Ruth's sponsorship and published a mimeographed newsletter. That is where I did my first writings. In many ways, they were childish, and Ruth always enjoyed letting people know of those articles for the rest of her life!

About a year after my salvation, we left Brooklyn, "immigrated" to America, and settled in California. That pretty well put me out of the loop, and I missed the New York fellowship immensely. My father's opposition to my faith grew more intensive. However, I was able to attend the ABMJ meetings in Los Angeles under Martin Meyer Rosen (who later became Moishe Rosen of Jews for Jesus), but there were no other believers my age. I attribute the fact that I was able to maintain the faith to the frequent correspondence with Ruth over the four years I lived in Los Angeles. On two occasions, I was able to go the Camp *Sar Shalom* where Ruth taught, and then to the ABMJ Memory Camp run by Burl Haynie. But summer would end, and I returned home and had to face my father's frequent attacks.

The day after I graduated high school, I was expelled from home and returned to New York City. I once again attended Camp *Sar Shalom* and once again had extended contact with Ruth. For two years, while at Shelton College in northern New Jersey, I frequently spent the weekends at Ruth's home in Levittown, Long Island. Ruth would often arrange for about five or six young Messianic Jews to give their testimonies in churches in the different parts of the Northeast, and I was able to take part in all of those weekend excursions. I would sometimes have to hitchhike to the churches, but she would then drop me off at the town near Shelton College. By that time of night, all bus services would cease, and I would have to walk three miles, sometimes with heavy snow on the ground, to get back to campus and arrive in the wee hours of Monday morning. With morning classes only about four or five hours away, I would sleep in my clothes so that I could make it to class on time!

During my third year of studies, Shelton College moved to the southernmost tip of New Jersey, to Cape May. I was now too far away to participate in the Messianic Youth Fellowship, and my contact with Ruth was minimal. However, near the college was the coastal town of Wildwood where the Cattell family had befriended me. One weekend, they invited the fellowship to their house. They even arranged for us to speak at the nearby church! That weekend was very rewarding for me and allowed me to renew my fellowship with Ruth and the others of my age.

For my senior year, I transferred to Cedarville College in Cedarville, Ohio, and my contact with Ruth was only by correspondence. After graduation, I went to Israel to study at the Hebrew University in Jerusalem, and Ruth and I continued our correspondence.

After finishing my studies in Jerusalem, I moved to Dallas, Texas, to begin my four years of training at Dallas Theological Seminary. I was still single but got engaged during my first year to Mary Ann, and we decided to get married that summer. She was attending school near Boston, and I was now living in Dallas, but we were getting married in New York City at the ABMJ headquarters in Manhattan, and Daniel Fuchs performed the wedding.

So how were we going to arrange all this? Ruth came to the rescue. For a week before the wedding, Mary Ann stayed at her house, and I stayed in Brooklyn at the ABMJ center, which was no longer being used that much for ministry since the Jewish people had moved out of the area. Ruth aided with all the preparations, and when it was obvious that we would run short on the food items during the reception, she made sure that it got re-supplied so that no one went hungry. Ruth was a real lifesaver for a very successful wedding.

After graduating from seminary, Mary Ann and I moved to Israel for two years of ministry. During our first year there, the ABMJ paid for Ruth and her co-worker, Eleanor Bullock, to visit Israel, and I was asked to take them around the country. I was happy to do so. While they stayed at some good five-star hotels, Mary Ann and I slept in our VW camper, and somehow we survived. Ruth was so happy with the tour that she returned a year later with about twelve to fifteen young people. Again, I became the tour guide. I had to rent a second VW van, and Lloyd Carsen, who later became Tuvya Zaretsky, was my other driver. On this second trip, which took about a month, even Ruth tented, and she did well.

There were many subsequent contacts with Ruth. She later moved to Los Angeles while Ariel Ministries moved to Orange County, and so there was once again frequent contact between us. Later, she moved to Plano, Texas, while Ariel moved back to San Antonio. I would see her at least once a year in Dallas and always took her out to dinner, thankful for her role in my salvation and spiritual life. It was also rewarding to see her come to our Camp Shoshanah program, first as a youth worker, then at least three times as a student. Her former student now became her teacher! She was always sure to bring others with her.

Ruth has now moved one more time, this time to her home in Heaven, and Mary Ann and I already miss her. She will not come back to us, but we shall be going to her for a heavenly reunion. I would like to dedicate the following Scriptures to her:

¹⁹ For I know that this shall turn out to my salvation, through your supplication and the supply of the Spirit of Messiah Yeshua, ²⁰ according to my earnest expectation and hope, that in nothing shall I be put to shame, but that with all boldness, as always, so now also Messiah shall be magnified in my body, whether by life, or by death. ²¹ For to me to live is Messiah, and to die is gain. ²² But if to live in the flesh, –if this shall bring fruit from my work, then what I shall choose I know not. ²³ But I am in a strait betwixt the two, having the desire to depart and be with Messiah; for it is very far better: ²⁴ yet to abide in the flesh is more needful for your sake. (Philippians 1:19-24)

⁶ For I am already being offered, and the time of my departure is come. ⁷ I have fought the good fight, I have finished the course, I have kept the faith: ⁸ henceforth there is laid up for me the crown of righteousness, which the Lord, the righteous judge, shall give to me at that day; and not to me only, but also to all them that have loved his appearing. (II Timothy 4:6-8)

⁴ For indeed we that are in this tabernacle do groan, being burdened; not for that we would be unclothed, but that we would be clothed upon, that what is mortal may be swallowed up of life. ⁵ Now he that wrought us for this very thing is God, who gave unto us the earnest of the Spirit. ⁶ Being therefore always of good courage, and knowing that, while we are at home in the body, we are absent from the Lord ⁷ (for we walk by faith, not by sight); ⁸ we are of good courage, I say, and are willing rather to be absent from the body, and to be at home with the Lord. ⁹ Wherefore also we make it our aim, whether at home or absent, to be well-pleasing unto him. ¹⁰ For we must all be made manifest before the judgment-seat of Messiah; that each one may receive the things done in the body, according to what he has done, whether it be good or bad. (II Corinthians 5:4-10)

⁵⁰ Now this I say, brethren, that flesh and blood cannot inherit the kingdom of God; neither does corruption inherit incorruption. ⁵¹ Behold, I tell you a mystery: We all shall not sleep, but we shall all be changed, ⁵² in a moment, in the twinkling of an eye, at the last trump: for the trumpet shall sound, and the dead shall be raised incorruptible, and we shall be changed. ⁵³ For this corruptible must put on incorruption, and this mortal must put on immortality. ⁵⁴ But when this corruptible shall have put on incorruption, and this mortal shall have put on immortality, then shall come to pass the saying that is written, Death is swallowed up in victory. ⁵⁵ O death, where is your victory? O death, where is your sting? ⁵⁶ The sting of death is sin; and the power of sin is the law: ⁵⁷ but thanks be to God, who gives us the victory through our Lord Messiah Yeshua. ⁵⁸ Wherefore, my beloved brethren, be ye stedfast, unmoveable, always abounding in the work of the Lord, forasmuch as ye know that your labor is not vain in the Lord. (I Corinthians 15:50-58)

¹³ But we would not have you ignorant, brethren, concerning them that fall asleep; that ye sorrow not, even as the rest, who have no hope. ¹⁴ For if we believe that Yeshua died and rose again, even so them also that are fallen asleep in Yeshua will God bring with him. ¹⁵ For this we say unto you by the word of the Lord, that we that are alive, that are left unto the coming of the Lord, shall in no wise precede them that are fallen asleep. ¹⁶ For the Lord himself shall descend from heaven, with a shout, with the voice of the archangel, and with the trump of God: and the dead in Messiah shall rise first; ¹⁷ then we that are alive, that are left, shall together with them be caught up in the clouds, to meet the Lord in the air: and so shall we ever be with the Lord. ¹⁸ Wherefore comfort one another with these words. (I Thessalonians 4:13-18)

Author's Acknowledgments

A lthough I wrote this book in relative isolation, spending long hours late into the night over a period of years, including most weekends and holidays, no book of this nature comes to fruition on its own. There are a number of people whom I wish to thank for their contribution in taking trips down memory lane. The stories that they remembered from the past have helped to enrich this biography. In particular, I wish to express my gratefulness to all those who cordially extended their hospitality to me during the initial research and interviewing phase of this writing journey.

To Miss Ruth Wardell, for the invaluable support and for having kept the Messianic Youth Fellowship newsletters from so many decades past, which gave an inside look at Arnold as a teenager. To Miss Wardell's former neighbors, my grateful thanks go to Janet Ludgar for those delicious meals cooked in advance.

To Jake and Jeanne Hogue, for the many long hours spent in talking openly and for the encouragement received during the initial stage of this project. To Charmaine and Mark O'Neill, for recounting the many anecdotes of the early years of the ministry. To Bob Futoran, for the clear recollection of the many summers spent at the Memory Camp.

To Dr. Barry Leventhal, for according a meeting despite a very busy schedule and for the moving accounts of the visit to the death camps in Poland. To Miriam and Sam Nadler, for digging out old photos and for taking candid trips back to the early days. To Natalia Fomin and family, for the gracious hospitality extended during my brief stay in town.

To the former staff at the previous Ariel Home Office in Tustin, California, for assisting with various requests, and to Donna Wixson for coordinating the meetings. To Denise Velarde at the current Ariel Home Office in San Antonio, for much-appreciated words of encouragement and support, an ever-readiness to answer queries and for liaising the drafts with Dr. Fruchtenbaum—for all that and much, much more.

To Mary Ann Fruchtenbaum, for the many hours of conversation covering the various facets of Arnold's early life plus your own personal story. Last but not least and most importantly, to Dr. Arnold G. Fruchtenbaum, for extending to me this unique opportunity to write your life story and for time spent in recalling past events. It has been an honor to work on this project as a first-time writer. I can only hope that in some small measure the final result lives up to your expectations.

To Christiane Jurik, for assembling the Editorial Note entitled "A Most Excellent Bible Exegete," which gave the book the balance that it needed, and to the contributors of that segment, for their perspectives on Dr. Fruchtenbaum's ministry. Also to Christiane Jurik, for collecting the photos and for the layout of the section, "Life in Pictures."

To all those who have prayed this project to completion, words seem inadequate to express my thanks and appreciation. I have felt your prayers throughout this writing journey and have been buoyed up by the comfort of God's Holy Spirit during the difficult and arduous times. If it were not for God's grace and the Holy Spirit's inspiration, this book may not have come about. Although I do not know you personally, the Lord most assuredly does. Thank you again for all your faithful prayers.

My eternal gratitude, praise, and love belong to God Almighty for my life as a "wild olive branch," which has been grafted into the olive tree through the Holy Spirit to be an eternal partaker of the glorious richness and love that is *Yeshua*. For this, I count myself most richly blessed in Messiah Jesus. To Him be the glory forever. Amen.

L. Jesse Grace
April 2014

Illustration and Photography Credits

The publisher would like to thank the following for their kind permission to reproduce their photographs and illustrations:

Book Cover: Dr. Arnold G. Fruchtenbaum

First Steps: Dr. Arnold G. Fruchtenbaum

First Vehicles: Dr. Arnold G. Fruchtenbaum

The Family Grows: (top left and bottom) Dr. Arnold G. Fruchtenbaum; (top right) Susanne Martin.

Finding Messiah: Dr. Arnold G. Fruchtenbaum

Early Life as a Believer: Dr. Arnold G. Fruchtenbaum

Influential Men: (top left and bottom) Dr. Arnold G. Fruchtenbaum; (top right) Mundo Cristao (http://www.mundocristao.com.br/autordet.asp?cod_ autor=5).

Arnold and Mary Ann: Dr. Arnold G. Fruchtenbaum

Camp Heathcote becomes Camp Shoshanah: Mottel Baleston

Attire: Dr. Arnold G. Fruchtenbaum

Israel Study Tours:
First page: (illustration of shirt) Bob Morris; (top right) Matthew Lipsey; (bottom) Dr. Arnold G. Fruchtenbaum.
Second page: (top) Dr. Arnold G. Fruchtenbaum; (middle left and bottom) Jacques Isaac Gabizon; (middle right) Dr. Arnold G. Fruchtenbaum.

Connections: (top) Mottel Baleston; (bottom) Dr. Arnold G. Fruchtenbaum.

Conference Speaker: (top) Mottel Baleston; (bottom) Dr. Randall Price.

To the Uttermost Ends of the Earth:
First page: (bottom right) Mottel Baleston; (all other pictures) Dr. Arnold G. Fruchtenbaum; (passport illustration) Jesse and Josh Gonzales.
Second page: (top left) Dr. Arnold G. Fruchtenbaum; (top right) Jan Marek Kopytek; (bottom) Mottel Baleston; (illustration) Jesse and Josh Gonzales.
Third page: (top) Beth Fearnley; (middle left) Lilian Granovsky; (middle right) Dr. Rita Nagy; (bottom) Paul Cohen.

Where It All Began:
First page: (top right) Mottel Baleston; (all other pictures) Christiane Jurik.
Second page: (top) Christiane Jurik; (bottom) Mottel Baleston.

Ariel Ministries in Texas:
First page: (middle left) Dr. Arnold G. Fruchtenbaum; (all other pictures) Jesse Gonzales.
Second page: Jesse Gonzales
Third Page: (top) Jesse Gonzales; (bottom) Roxanne Tretheway.

Ariel's School of Messianic Jewish Studies: Dr. Arnold G. Fruchtenbaum; (illustration) Jesse Gonzales.